From the
Polish Underground

From the Polish Underground

Selections from *Krytyka*, 1978–1993

Edited by
Michael Bernhard and Henryk Szlajfer
Translated by
Maria Chmielewska-Szlajfer

The Pennsylvania State University Press
University Park, Pennsylvania

This translation has been made possible in part by a grant from the Wheatland Foundation, New York, and the Central and East European Publishing Project, Oxford.

Library of Congress Cataloging-in-Publication Data

From the Polish underground : selections from Krytyka, 1978–1993 /
    edited by Michael Bernhard and Henryk Szlajfer ; translated by Maria
    Chmielewska-Szlajfer.

    p.   cm.
    Includes bibliographical references and index.
    ISBN 0-271-01400-8 (cloth : alk. paper)
    ISBN 0-271-01401-6 (pbk. : alk. paper)
    1. Poland—Politics and government—1945– 2. Poland—Social
conditions—1945– 3. Poland—Economic conditions—1945–
I. Bernhard, Michael H. II. Szlajfer, Henryk. III. Krytyka.
DK4436.F75   1995
943.805′6—dc20   94-18841
                                           CIP

Published by The Pennsylvania State University Press,
University Park, PA 16802-1003

Contents

SECTION V: HISTORY

List of Tables

Preface

I owe several words of introduction to the reader of this book. I do not want to write here about *Krytyka* as such. In his introduction Michael Bernhard, a student of the history of the democratic opposition in Poland, presents the journal's history, its ideological and political evolution, and its social milieu, that is, its editors and authors, and to some extent its audience as well.

I want to add only one thing. *Krytyka* was and is nonpartisan. It is not a party publication; it has never represented any political group and has never had its own political line. The editorial board wants the quarterly to provide a forum for an exchange of views, and thus (remember its relatively elitist nature) to influence intellectuals and people from the world of politics. This does not mean that the personnel associated with *Krytyka* have not played or do not play any political role. For instance, one of our editors, Adam Michnik, the *spiritus movens* of the journal in its heroic period (1978–81), is a former member of parliament and cofounder and editor of Poland's best-selling newspaper, *Gazeta wyborcza* (Electoral gazette). Jacek Kuroń, the quarterly's cofounder and minister of labor in the first postcommunist government and more recently in the cabinet of Hanna Suchocka, is another conspicuous example. Today, some members of our board continue to serve as high state officials. Yet in keeping with our rules, in their editorial work for *Krytyka* they do not advocate their opinions on current questions of policy.

It is impossible to overemphasize the importance of the change of regimes in Poland and the psychological and "methodological" consequences of this change for the journal. Since the revolution of 1989, when the democratic opposition began peacefully to remove the communists from power, Poland has embarked on a massive systemic experiment, a transformation from communism to capitalism and democracy.

To describe and analyze these changes accurately—be they social, economic, cultural, or psychological—we need a cognitive apparatus suitable to the task. To describe our present reality, to diagnose social and political dangers, to articulate the challenges faced by all Poles, intellectuals and the political class in particular, requires, first and foremost, a new language. We need to reevaluate and refine the political concepts we have used in the past. If we do not, we will fail to understand what is transpiring in Poland and the other former communist countries. It seems obvious that the conceptual "tools" one needs to analyze the functioning of repressive systems and to describe their characteristic social and individual behaviors differ from those one needs to seize the changing, complicated, fluctuating reality of a period of building democracy and a market economy. If we were to hold to notions and linguistic formulations that were more or less adequate to describe our totalitarian past, that of so-called really existing socialism, it would be easy to misconstrue the current political, economic, and ideological realities.

For instance, I do not believe that an understanding of the politics or the ideological struggle in present-day Poland is possible using conventional understandings of "Left" and "Right." Poland is in a period of transition. A society and the legal and political institutions characteristic of market economy are only now being formed. It is possible that this dichotomy—as it is understood in Western Europe—may one day reflect the Polish reality if there is further development in the direction of democracy and the market.

Like everyone else, *Krytyka* must cope with the new, unfamiliar, rapidly changing situation. Starting from our unique political and ideological premises, we have been trying to find our own place in this new reality. Much is at stake in this struggle—whether Poland will have an open, individualistic, pluralist, liberal, market-oriented society, and whether it will become part of a united Europe, open to the outside world and the free circulation of ideas and people.

I want to thank the editors of the present book, Michael Bernhard and Henryk Szlajfer. Without their dedication, *From the Polish Underground* would have never seen the light of day. I also want to thank Maria Chmielewska-Szlajfer, who translated sixteen of the nineteen chapters. She had to struggle with the range of diverse and often very difficult texts. Last but not least, I want to thank The Pennsylvania State University Press and our editor there, Peter Potter, for the publication of this book, which I hope will bring the reader nearer to this fragment of Poland's most recent political and intellectual history.

Jan Kofman
Editor-in-chief, *Krytyka*

Warsaw, January 1994

Introduction

Michael Bernhard

The first issue of *Krytyka* appeared in the autumn of 1978. The journal was envisioned as a quarterly of high intellectual quality, publishing work drawn from the social sciences and the humanities. The journal's purpose, however, as its subtitle—*Kwartalnik Polityczny* (a political quarterly)—made clear, was not academic. *Krytyka* was intended as a forum for open discussion about Polish public affairs, history, and culture, in order to preserve and defend the independence of critical thought in Poland. By the 1980s it had become a fixture of the Polish intellectual and political scene. It became required reading even for those who did not agree with its underlying premises.

Krytyka appeared in what can be described as the early stages of the reemergence of "civil society" under communism in Poland. In Poland, more so than any other country of the former Soviet bloc, large numbers of citizens built underground political organizations, an alternative public sphere, and a competing political culture that constituted a potent threat to the power of the ruling authorities. Political organizations were formed not only in traditional bastions of intellectual dissent but in worker and peasant communities as well (Bernhard 1993, 146–47 and chap. 7). All this organizing activity culminated in the summer of 1980 with the birth of the trade union Solidarity.

Throughout the 1970s and 1980s Poland maintained a system of preventive censorship, which included the screening and approval of the content of all print and broadcast media prior to their publication or airing, as well as official state monopolies in broadcasting and the distribution of printed material.[1] For this reason *Krytyka* was not published through official channels but "beyond censorship" (*poza cenzurą*). It was printed and distributed illegally but, despite the efforts of the police, with some regularity, although not always four times a year.[2]

The author wishes to thank Paula Golombek, Krzysztof Jasiewicz, Peter Potter, Scott Spendlove, and Henryk Szlajfer for their comments on earlier drafts of this introduction.

The Poles circumvented censorship by means of "underground" publications written, edited, printed, and distributed outside the official system of mass communication. Although most English-speaking readers associate such publications with the Russian term *samizdat* (self-publishing), the Polish underground press was more developed than its Soviet counterpart. In Poland the history of the underground press reaches back to the country's nineteenth-century struggle for independence. It also played a critical role in national life in the struggle against Nazi occupation during World War II. In Poland such publications are not called *samizdat* but *bibuła* (tissue paper).

The modern Polish "underground" press became an important element in the resistance to the communist regime in the late 1970s. In 1976, with the foundation of the Workers' Defense Committee (KOR), the largest, most successful, and most significant of the pre-Solidarity opposition movements, the Poles began to develop an effective alternative to the constrained forms of official public communication open to them. The development of this underground press was an essential step in the development of mass opposition movements like Solidarity. *Krytyka* is one of a select few underground publications that predated Solidarity and survived to see its eventual triumph at the polls in 1989.

By the time *Krytyka* began to appear, underground publishing in Poland had already begun in earnest. Both the Workers' Defense Committee and other underground movements such as the Movement for Human and Civil Rights (ROPCiO), a more conservative and explicitly nationalist competitor to KOR, had well-established bulletins in circulation.[3] At this time too, an extensive system of distribution (*kolportaż*) for underground publications had been organized in most major cities and many smaller communities, and a number of underground publishing houses had begun to function.[4] These publishing houses had established covert printing facilities and had begun to publish banned and censored books as well as newspapers and journals.[5]

Krytyka was one of a small number of Polish underground publications that resembled the "thick journals" (*tolstye zhurnaly*) popular with the Russian intelligentsia. It was not the first Polish underground journal of this sort. The first was *Zapis* (The record), which first appeared in January 1977 and was devoted to the publication of literature and poetry rejected by the censors (Barańczak 1977, 11). In October 1977 two other "thick" publications also made their debut. One was *Spot-*

kania (Encounters), which originated in the politically and socially engaged milieu at the Catholic University in Lublin (A.B. 1978). The
second was *Puls* (Pulse), which originated in the city of Łódź (Dym
1978). Later in the 1970s, a neoliberal "thick" journal, *Res Publica*, also
appeared, followed by other titles in the 1980s. In addition, a range of
publications focused primarily on day-to-day political concerns also
began to devote a part of their space to more analytical and polemical
articles. This was done, for instance, by ROPCiO's *Opinia* (Opinion)
and by two journals that emerged from the KOR milieu, *Głos* (The
voice) and *Biuletyn informacyjny* (Information bulletin).

Krytyka began as part of the larger oppositional milieu that grew up
around the Workers' Defense Committee (KOR) and its successor, the
Social Self-Defense Committee "KOR" (KSS "KOR"). In the early
period of its existence, *Krytyka*'s editors were all linked with KOR in
some way, as were many of its contributors, and the journal received
financial support from the committee (Lipski 1985, 416–17; and KSS
"KOR," *Komunikat* 23[1978]: 12–13).[6] However, *Krytyka* was never an
official committee journal; it never claimed to speak for KOR as a
whole, and the committee never tried to control its content.

Throughout its existence *Krytyka* was printed by the Independent
Publishing House (NOW-a), the earliest of underground printing concerns, which was also closely linked with KOR.[7] In its earliest period
Krytyka came out in a print run of between one and two thousand
copies (interview with Jan Walc; Cecuda 1989, 170). In the 1980s this
rose to between two and three thousand, with some issues reaching as
high as four thousand.[8] Today, now that the journal comes out legally,
its circulation stands at more than two thousand copies, a very respectable number for a serious publication under contemporary Polish conditions.

As a special sort of publication devoted to the preservation and development of an independent and critical intellectual culture, *Krytyka*
did not cover day-to-day political events in Poland in detail. Nor was
it consciously used as a organizing tool, like many other *bibuła* publications, to attract new followers. Its political commitment was more
long-term. Much of its political writing was strategic and programmatic in nature or sought to interpret contemporary events in their
larger context. The journal also sought to uncover and educate the
public about the "black areas" in Polish history and culture obscured
by censorship. This latter aspect of *Krytyka*'s mission worked to coun-

teract the enfeebling "forgetting" of the past that Milan Kundera (1991, 151–55) has so strongly decried. This filling-in of historical blank spots was seen not only as a process of recovering a politically "usable past" but also as valuable in itself.

Krytyka's founders came from the wing of the Workers' Defense Committee that was inspired by the Polish Socialist Party (*Polska Partia Socjalistyczna*, or PPS). The PPS had been established in the late nineteenth century and was affiliated with the Second International, the branch of the socialist movement that evolved into the social-democratic and labor parties of Western Europe.[9] One of its earliest and most influential members was Józef Piłsudski, the most important military commander and politician of the Polish drive for independence that came to fruition in the final stages of World War I. Piłsudski, of course, went on to reject the PPS soon after independence and later became the dictator of the interwar Polish Republic (1926–35).

The editorial board of *Krytyka* discussed its intellectual connection to the PPS in an editorial in an early issue: "The ideals of the PPS are near to us, which is why in seeking our predecessors in national history we fully identify with the socialist movement" (Kuroń & Starczewski 1980, 86).[10] However, they did not completely identify with the entire legacy of the PPS. In particular, the editorial spoke of how the anti-Catholic aspects of past PPS ideology were warranted only when they expressed opposition to "intolerance, chauvinism, xenophobia" disguised in clerical garb, and not when Christian values expressed "the highest values of European culture" (86–87). The editors also disapproved of the postwar activists who had led the PPS first into close collaboration and then merger with the communists, resulting in the moral compromise and ultimate destruction of the party (88–90). The editorial most strongly identified *Krytyka* with the decentralized, anti-étatist tendency of the PPS associated with the political thought of Edward Abramowski (87–88).

As with many of the publications that were started by KOR members and activists, the title of *Krytyka* was significant in that it harkened back to a famous publication from the Polish past.[11] In the case of *Krytyka*, its name was taken from a periodical published in Kraków by Wilhelm Feldman at the turn of the century (Cecuda 1989, 180; Lipski 1985, 202–3). Feldman, born into a poor Orthodox Jewish family from provincial Poland, managed to attend gymnasium and university in Lwów (present-day Lviv), Kraków, and Berlin. He became an independent socialist, was sympathetic to assimilationist currents in Jewish thought, and stongly favored Polish independence. During the time he edited the first *Krytyka* (1901–14) it carried a mix of socialist-inspired articles on political, economic, and social topics and artistic and literary works, as well as criticism and reviews. A large part of the journal's cultural offerings were inspired by the cultural avant-garde of the day—*Młoda Polska* (Young Poland) (Janusz 1985, 88–91). This movement was akin to developments in art and literature in fin de siècle Europe, incorporating elements of modernism, symbolism, decadence, and neoromanticism.

Unlike Feldman's *Krytyka*, today's does not carry literary or artistic works. Its focus has always been political. It has sought to propound a modern and critical view of contemporary developments in Poland. *Krytyka* did so when its editors and contributors saw themselves as engaged in a struggle for freedom of thought against the communist system before 1989. It continues to try to advance this view today. In the first issue, the editors published a statement of purpose that indicates how they saw their role in updating the traditions that inspired them:

> Educating people to take part in public deception, teaching them to be blind to public cruelty, destroying people's feelings of responsibility toward public affairs—these are methods never mentioned in official "development programs"; these are the methods always used in the system of totalitarian domination.
>
> One of the many effects of the functioning of the system is the destruction of all manifestations of publicly expressed, independent, critical thought about public affairs.
>
> Thought whose fundamental characteristic is the search for truth about socially significant facts, processes, and phenomena free of doctrinal limitations and institutional pressures, thought that reveals the sphere of the sovereign rights of the human individual in society, as well as the sphere of powers of society to decide its own fate, thought standing against apathy and social passivity, xenophobia, as well as attitudes of resignation from national sovereignty—political thought conceived in this way is for us valuable in itself and something we want to defend by engaging in it. This means through contention, polemical exchange, and controversy, through the airing of various points of view.

These are the premises and motives for the foundation of the journal *Krytyka*.

However, these are not the only ones. Above all, the journal was created as an expression of the conviction that the anti-totalitarian opposition needs a new type of political consciousness. Such consciousness will not be only an emotional expression of disagreement with the present social reality or a direct response to the existing situation, but will search for a new vision of the world.

Krytyka thus will not present a simple negation of the officially propagated system of values, but must surmount them, which means that it must surmount the sort of thought which—defining itself in direct opposition to that system—has become incurably subordinated to it. (*Krytyka* Editorial Group 1978, 5)

After the declaration of martial law in 1981 the political orientation of *Krytyka* ceased to be explicitly social-democratic. Although it had always been an eclectic journal, airing a wide range of viewpoints, it became increasingly open to a variety of democratic perspectives. Jan Kofman described this change in the following fashion: "The State of Emergency also significantly widened both the pluralism of authors and the thought which they presented. On one hand, authors who had recently been party members like Michał Jagiełło and Wojtek Lamentowicz came to us . . . , and on the other hand, we also began to publish work from the pens of Father Tischner and Father Życiński" (Kofman & Surdykowski 1989, 7). In the late 1980s *Krytyka* began to take on a political tone that was on balance somewhat more liberal-democratic than social-democratic. Today it still continues to air a wide variety of viewpoints.[12]

The original editors of *Krytyka* were Stanisław Barańczak, Konrad Bieliński, Jacek Kuroń, Jan Lityński, Adam Michnik, Stefan Starczewski, Jan Walc, and Roman Wojciechowski. Starczewski served as the first editor-in-chief. The crucial role in bringing this group together was played by Michnik, whose home served as the center of contact for the journal in this early period (Kofman & Romanowski 1992, 8; Kofman & Surdykowski 1989, 7). Miklós Haraszti and Václav Havel, important resistance leaders in Hungary and Czechoslovakia, were also listed on the masthead as editors. Jacek Kuroń explained

their presence on the editorial board in the following terms: "We realized how very important all these small things are for overcoming Polish xenophobia" (1991, 84).

The editorial board remained unchanged for *Krytyka*'s first five issues. The masthead of the fifth issue (1979) listed a new editor,
Włodzimierz Mart, who had been involved with the initial efforts to
organize the journal and had contributed to the first issue. Mart was in
fact a pseudonym for Jan Kofman (Kofman & Surdykowski 1989, 7).[13]
In the ninth issue, the last published before the declaration of martial
law in 1981, Marek Beylin, who had been involved in editorial decisions since 1978, also was added to the editorial board. Then, until late
1987, the editorial board went underground. Instead of listing its editors on the masthead, *Krytyka* announced that it was edited by a group
(*Redaguje zespół*). With the internment of Stefan Starczewski during martial law, Jan Kofman assumed the responsibilities of editor-in-chief (Kofman & Surdykowski, 1989, 8). With *Krytyka* no. 26 (1987) the editors
were again listed on the masthead, with Kofman as editor-in-chief.
The only other members remaining from the old board were Adam
Michnik[14] and Marek Beylin. Several new people, who had stepped
into important editorial roles since the declaration of martial law in
1981, were acknowledged publicly for the first time—Mirosława Grabowska, Piotr Łukaszewicz, Robert Mroziewicz, and Rafał Zakrzewski. Since then several new members have joined the editorial staff.[15]

The first issue of *Krytyka* was just over two hundred pages long.
The lion's share of this issue was devoted to responses to a free-form
questionnaire sent to more than twenty prominent Poles living in Poland and abroad titled "Ten Years after the March Events." For many
of the people associated with *Krytyka* the events of March 1968—the
eruption of student strikes and riots and their suppression by the authorities, the repression of critical Marxism within the party, and the
anti-Semitic campaign that led to the emigration of a large part of Poland's remaining Jewish community—was a formative event. The issue also included an article by Andrzej Szczypiorski titled "Dissidents
and Reality" (*Dysydenci i rzeczywistość*), Václav Havel's famous "Open
Letter to Gustav Husak,"[16] Alexander Solzhenitsyn's essay "The Smatterers" (*Obrazovanshchina*),[17] and two book reviews.

Krytyka's contents are quite eclectic. The articles selected come from
a number of diverse fields and include pieces by many of Poland's
leading intellectuals and writers, as well as contributions from the Po-

lish exile community.[18] Over time, the editors developed sections that serve to organize the journal's contents. Perhaps the greatest amount of space in *Krytyka* has been devoted to Polish politics and twentieth-century history. Much of this material has appeared in the section "Contemporary History" (*Historia najnowsza*), which has appeared in almost every issue of the journal. In many issues from the 1980s there were also special subsections devoted to articles on the Solidarity experience.

Early in its history, *Krytyka* included published sections on two democratic political alternatives to communism and right-wing dictatorship in twentieth-century Polish history. A large part of the sixth issue (1980) was devoted to the PPS, and a similar section appeared on the Polish Peasant Party (*Polskie Stronnictwo Ludowe*, or PSL) in number 10/11 (1982).[19] In the latter issue an ongoing section devoted to biographical "Portraits" (*Sylwetki*) profiled Stanisław Mikołajczyk, the wartime prime minister of the Polish government-in-exile and leader of the PSL's unsuccessful attempt to contest the establishment of communist power after the war.

Political issues were also taken up in a series of articles on martial law that appeared in three consecutive issues (no. 12 [1981], no. 13/14 [1983], and no. 15 [1983]), a special section on political "normalization" ("Wokół 'normalizacji,'" no. 17 [1984]), and a second special section on the events of March 1968 (no. 28/29 [1988]). (Henryk Szlajfer's piece in this book originally appeared in one of these special sections on martial law.) The "Contemporary History" section also examined the sensitive topic of Polish-Jewish relations when the issue was still somewhat taboo in Poland (no. 15 [1983]). That special section published a number of articles that were pathbreaking in their dispassionate tone and willingness to confront difficult issues directly. The piece by Stanisław Krajewski [Abel Kainer, pseud.] in this book was published in that issue.

Political articles that were geared toward the more immediate issues of the day or that had a more polemical bent appeared under such headings as "Evaluations and Analyses" (*Oceny i analizy*) and "Positions" (*Stanowiska*) or simply appeared at the beginning of individual issues as feature articles under no special heading. *Krytyka* also published documents of historical interest and extensive interviews with figures of contemporary political and historical importance. The interview with Jacek Kuroń in this book is an example of the latter.[20]

The journal also devoted a part of almost every issue to cultural questions under such headings as "Culture" (*Kultura*), "Politics and Culture" (*Polityka i kultura*), "Literature and People" (*Literatura i ludzie*), "Literature and Politics" (*Literatura i polityka*), and "Pictures from an Exhibition" (*Obrazki z wystawy*). A section of "Banned Sociology" (*Socjologia bez debitu*) also appeared on a fairly regular basis, as did one on spiritual and religious life—"Testimony" (*Świadectwa*).[21]

Economics received less intensive coverage in *Krytyka*, but special sections on economic topics began to appear in the mid-1980s (for example, "Gospodarka—oceny i analizy" [The Economy—Evaluations and Analyses], in no. 21 [1986]). *Krytyka* also had contributors who wrote regular columns (more on them below) and an active book review section—"About Books" (*Nad książkami*). Beginning in the mid-1980s, it also regularly published a list of "Publications Submitted" (*Publikacje nadesłane*) to the journal, which kept Poles informed about what had been published underground and in other countries in Polish and other languages.

Although the vast majority of the articles in *Krytyka* were written about Polish subjects for a Polish audience, the journal was by no means parochial in its coverage of contemporary events and culture. It kept its readers in close contact with intellectual developments in the West by translating shorter works by a number of important writers and intellectuals.[22] It also published a large number of articles on the other countries of Eastern and Central Europe, thus introducing Poles to the unofficial culture of neighboring states. It translated a large number of pieces by prominent dissidents, as well as by writers and intellectuals in exile, from the Soviet Union, Yugoslavia, Hungary, Czechoslovakia, and East Germany.[23] Several issues of *Krytyka* contained special sections devoted in whole to the problems of these countries. The first special section of this type appeared in the second issue (1978) and discussed developments in Czechoslovakia. It included pieces by Václav Havel, Pavel Kohout, and Jan Patočka, as well as documents from Charter 1977.

A second special section on Soviet bloc countries appeared in *Krytyka*'s fifth issue (1980). It was introduced by a piece written by Marek Beylin, Konrad Bieliński, and Adam Michnik titled "Poland Is Located in Europe" (*Polska leży w Europie*). It included two of the more important essays that emerged from the Charter 77 group in Czechoslovakia—Vaclav Havel's "Power of the Powerless"[24] and Vaclav

Benda's piece "The Parallel Polis." It also included an interview with Hungarian dissidents György Bence and János Kis, as well as other articles about Czechoslovakia and the German Democratic Republic.

Krytyka no. 9, published in 1981, was devoted in its entirety to articles from the Hungarian underground press, including selections from Miklós Haraszti, György Bence and János Kis, Iván Szelenyi, András Hegedüs, János Kenedi, György Dalos, Lászlo Rajk, and Tamás Bauer. Other issues were devoted in part to Yugoslavia (no. 10/11 [1982] and no. 30 [1988]), to Russia (no. 28/29 [1988]), to Russia and Ukraine ("Na Wschodzie," no. 30 [1988]), to the Germans (no. 23/24 [1987] and no. 30 [1988]), and to what the Germans thought about Poland ("Niemcy o Polsce," no. 8 [1981]). With time, pieces of this nature began to appear under their own special headings, such as "The Neighbors" (*Sąsiedzi*), "By the Neighbors" (*U sąsiadów*), and in recent issues, "A Europe of Nations" (*Europa narodów*). On one occasion (no. 16 [1983]) the "Contemporary History" section was devoted to the subject of "Stalinism" in the bloc and included articles on the manmade famine in Ukraine, the Berlin Uprising of 1953, and the persecution of Czechoslovak communist leader Rudolf Slansky.

The articles for *From the Polish Underground: Selections from Krytyka, 1978–1993* were selected by Henryk Szlajfer, myself, and Jan Kofman, the present editor-in-chief of *Krytyka*. We consciously decided to select a large number of pieces by authors who are not well known to an English-speaking audience, in addition to works by a number of *Krytyka*'s better-known writers. We have divided the book into five sections—Politics, Sociology, Culture, Economics, and History, reflecting the diversity of the subject matter treated by *Krytyka* over the years. We have also tried to pick articles that represent a wide range of political views in Poland. The sympathies of the authors run from social-democratic to moderately conservative. Thus in a number of cases readers will not be able to detect much in common with the PPS tradition that inspired *Krytyka*'s founders. Although the political orientations represented herein reflect the journal's diversity, the collection does not contain an article that represents the nationalist or Christian-national right, or the postcommunist left. In contemporary Poland such authors tend to write for journals other than *Krytyka* (Kofman & Romanowski 1992, 8).

In compiling the Politics and Sociology sections, one of our concerns was to give English-language readers an overview of Polish politics from the declaration of martial law in December 1981 to the present. Since there is a great deal written on Solidarity's origins and its activities in 1980–81 in English, we have chosen not to concentrate on *Krytyka*'s earliest issues. We felt it was important to include a number of pieces on the period following martial law specifically because there has been less written on and translated from this period.

The Politics section begins with Henryk Szlajfer's "Under the Military Dictatorship," which appeared in one of the journal's special sections on "Martial Law" (penned under the dual pseudonym of Jan Kowalski and Andrzej Malinowski). This piece offers a detailed overview of the situation facing Poland after Jaruzelski's coup d'état in December 1981. Comparing Poland to the Czechoslovakia (after 1968) and Hungary (after 1956), Szlajfer develops a framework for understanding the problem of restoring order (normalization) in communist regimes racked by general unrest. He then turns to a discussion of the specific characteristics of the military regime, including its dubious legal status, its propaganda, its use of repression, and its economic strategy. Szlajfer leaves little hope for an easy normalization of the country, fearing that the junta's policies may lead to a new era of barbarism in Poland.

The next two articles in the Politics section discuss the narrowing of political options during Jaruzelski's dictatorship and the problems this development posed for a democratic solution of the Polish crisis. They not only criticize the regime but also debate the merits of Solidarity's strategy for resistance. The first piece, "About the Future," was written by Krzysztof Wolicki (under the pseudonym "Zey"). This article is a sample of the political commentary and analysis he provided in his regular column for *Krytyka*—"Seen Differently" (*Widziane inaczej*). Wolicki dissects two different views of Poland's future. One view, the "papal," in its pure religious form hopes for long-term national renewal on the basis of a purer faith in God. He characterizes the strategy of Solidarity and the mainstream political opposition as a secular version of this view. The second view of Poland's future, the one advocated by the regime's ideologues and propagandists, sees the nation as recalcitrant and largely incompetent and treats national values as symbols to be manipulated in the service of power. Wolicki points out how the confrontation of these two views has separated the nation from the state, which may well weaken the nation's ability to establish authentic authority in the future.

The second piece on the dilemmas of Polish politics in this period is

Marek Beylin's "Language and Pluralism" (written under the pseudonym of Gustaw Lin). Beylin analyzes the language of the Solidarity
underground as the key to understanding the self-definition and values
of Polish society. His impression is that the underground press is
highly undifferentiated and that it presents a black-and-white, Manichaean view of the world that although facilitating mobilization against
the state is nevertheless politically dysfunctional because it suppresses
careful consideration of strategy, tactics, and political goals.

The last two pieces in the Politics section discuss aspects of the collapse of communism in Eastern Europe. The first is provided by Jan
Kofman, Krytyka's editor-in-chief, who in recent issues has begun to
provide a regular series of seasonal commentaries on politics. This earlier effort, "Driving with the Brakes On," discusses the reaction of the
West to the events of 1989 in a critical review of a report drawn up for
the trilateral commission by Henry Kissinger, Yasuhiro Nakasone
(former prime minister of Japan), and Valéry Giscard d'Estaing (former president of France). In "Stealing Away in the Dead of the Night"
Marcin Kula tries to understand why "existing socialist" systems collapsed with such relative ease in 1989. He shows how the elite had no
stake in the perpetuation of "the old regime," but closes with several
observations that warn us against thinking that a transition to democracy will be as easy as the collapse of communism was.

The Sociology section's four articles continue this analysis of recent
developments in Poland. In "The Transition from Authoritarianism to
Democracy" Włodzimierz Wesołowski presents a broad overview of
developments in Poland in the late 1980s. He discusses why the system
collapsed and the communist regime's unsuccessful attempt to save itself by negotiating a power-sharing arrangement with Solidarity. Wesołowski then turns his attention to some of the problems that may
obstruct a transition from authoritarianism to democracy. He presents
the situation in late 1989 as one where a transition is under way, primarily within the parliament and government, but where there are still
remnants of the old system in place. He outlines some of these remnants and the potential problems they might pose, including the economic crisis, an underdeveloped party structure and system of intermediary organizations, and the role of the old communist nomenklatura
in the state.

Krzysztof Jasiewicz's article "The Polish Voter—Ten Years after

August 1980" is representative of the Polish school of empirical sociology, whose work sometimes found its only possible popular outlet through the "Banned Sociology" (*Socjologia bez debitu*) section of *Krytyka*. Jasiewicz, who hid his association with the journal under the pseudonym of Jan Powiórski, was one of a group of sociologists who did restricted empirical work on the values and attitudes of Polish society throughout the 1980s (see Adamski et al. 1981, 1982, 1986, 1989). He uses the results of this and other studies to explain Polish voting behavior through 1990, including the rise of surprise presidential candidate Stan Tymiński.

The last two articles in the Sociology section are typical of the humanist-interpretive school in Polish sociology and address very recent issues. Joanna Kurczewska's article, "The Polish Intelligentsia: Departure from the Scene," discusses how the transformation of politics and economic circumstances is eroding the critical role of the intelligentsia in defining and structuring Polish national life. In "The Social Boundaries of Economic Reform in Eastern Europe," Edmund Mokrzycki discusses the constraints that society's response to economic shock therapy will have on the course of economic reform.

The Culture section concerns itself with issues larger than pure aesthetics. Even where the articles are concerned with specific artists and their works, they are cast in the light of their social context and meaning. The first two pieces examine the works of specific authors. In "According to Mackiewicz" Jerzy Surdykowski attempts to comprehend the significance of the renewed popularity of this uncompromising ultra-right-wing author while trying to let the author's words speak for themselves. The author of the second piece, Andrzej Werner, has written a number of columns for *Krytyka* under the heading "Passion and Boredom" (*Pasja i nuda*). In one installment—"At an Unbearable Crossroads"—he tries to come to grips with the aesthetic detachment of the exiled Czech writer Milan Kundera, American neoconservatism, and the relationship between politics and art by reviewing the Polish translation of Norman Podhoretz's *The Bloody Crossroads* (not surprisingly, he finds that art is usually the loser).

The last two pieces are more general commentaries on the state of Polish consciousness after the events of 1989. In "The Autumn of the Ideologues" Józef Życinski, a Catholic bishop, decries historicism that subordinates the understanding of history to a predetermined teleological end. He also expresses concern both about the lack of a conscious understanding of the past in Polish society and the lack of attempts to overcome the legacies of the distorted ideological picture of the past painted by the old regime. In "Three Fundamentalisms" Adam Michnik discusses the development of exclusive belief systems based on nationalism, religion, and ethical purity. He points out how, in concert with a populist language of revolt, such fundamentalism constitutes a new authoritarian threat.

As mentioned earlier, specialized coverage of economics was something to which *Krytyka* did not devote much space until recently. The pieces selected are not technical in nature and thus should be easily understood by general readers. In Western academic terms, these pieces would be seen as political economy. The first piece, Jerzy Osiatyński's "Sources of Opposition to Market Reforms in Centrally Planned Economies," begins with a discussion of the major types of economic reforms of planned economies. He then pinpoints the bureaucratic and social interests that will suffer as the result of each type of reform. This discussion not only helps us to understand why economic reform has failed in the past but also identifies the kinds of resistance to the market and to property reform which are emerging in Poland today.

"Civil Society and the Market in Real Socialism," by Piotr Ogrodziński, is a wide-ranging philosophical essay that discusses and compares the differences between capitalist and socialist models of economy, society, and politics and the difficulties in moving from one to the other. Drawing on a wide range of philosophical, political, and economic sources, including Braudel, Hayek, Kornai, and Staniszkis, he attempts to understand the development trajectory of "real socialism" from its genesis to its collapse. The final selection in this section is an exchange of opinions on the possible paths "Toward a Market Economy" in Poland. Jan Winiecki advocates a free-market liberal position, whereas Ryszard Bugaj defends a social-democratic option.

The collection closes with a History section. Although we have not stressed the first period of Solidarity's legal existence (1980–81), this collection would not be complete without some reflection on that time. For this reason we have chosen Janka Jankowska's interview with Jacek Kuroń, "In Every Situation, I Look for a Way Out." Kuroń, one of the most important intellectual figures of the Polish opposition, gave this interview in June 1986. He talks at length about his personal history and his experience as a Solidarity activist and adviser. Kuroń sheds new light on his formative experiences, as well as on important conflicts within the union and the problems it faced in negotiating with the party.

The last two pieces attempt to come to terms with issues of extremism, ethnic chauvinism, and intolerance in Poland's past in an open and critical fashion. In "About Niewiadomski" Anna Bojarska discusses the assassination of the first president of the interwar Polish Republic, Gabriel Narutowicz, by a protofascist, Eligiusz Niewiadomski, in 1922. She discusses the effect this had on destroying the fledgling democratic institutions of interwar Poland, including Józef Piłsudski's decision to stage a coup d'état in 1926. Bojarska shows how Niewiadomski's action led in some sense to Piłsudski's disavowal and betrayal of the principles of democracy and tolerance he had earlier espoused.

Finally, in "Jews and Communism" Stanisław Krajewski (writing under the pseudonym Abel Kainer) examines a stereotype held by many in Poland—that "Jews were the major support for communist power in Poland (and elsewhere), or readily offered their services to that power and received certain privileges in exchange." This belief is supported by the number of prominent communists in the immediate postwar era who came from Jewish backgrounds. Krajewski approaches this difficult subject by posing three fundamental questions: Did the Jews create communism? Was communism attractive for Jews? Did the Jews rule the Polish People's Republic? In answering them he shows that the stereotype is unjustified.

We hope that this selection of articles will leave readers with a richer understanding of the revolutionary changes that engulfed Eastern and Central Europe in our time. Developments in Poland present a unique perspective because the rebirth of civil society and the latest round in the struggle for democracy and national sovereignty there began earlier than in any other country in the bloc, even before the foundation of Solidarity in 1980. *Krytyka* was founded in the earliest stages of this process. Over the course of its fifteen-year history it has left us a detailed analytical record of how the communist system in Poland slowly rotted away from the inside. Today *Krytyka* continues the work of analyzing the critical issues facing Poland and East-Central Europe, even as the societies of the region try to remake themselves.

Notes

1. For details on this system of censorship, see Curry 1984.

2. There were several sparse periods in *Krytyka*'s publishing record. The period directly after the declaration of martial law was particularly difficult. The publication of no. 10/11, scheduled for late 1981, was delayed until 1982. From late 1981 until 1983 only two issues (nos. 10/11 and 12) were published. In the three-year period from 1984 to 1986 only four issues (nos. 17, 18, 19/20, and 21) appeared. In 1989 and 1990 only three issues appeared (nos. 31, 32, and 33). *Krytyka* managed to keep up a quarterly production schedule only in 1980, 1983, 1987 (when three issues and one double issue came out), and 1988. On average over its whole lifetime, *Krytyka* has managed to publish close to three issues per year.

3. KOR published *Komunikat* (Communiqué) on a monthly basis, and its members also produced two other journals closely related to the movement's activity: *Głos* (The voice) and *Biuletyn informacyjny* (Information bulletin). Before the publication of *Krytyka*, KOR circles also began to publish a biweekly for workers called *Robotnik* (The worker). ROPCiO's most important publication in this period was *Opinia* (Opinion). Splits in the movement led to a proliferation of competing organizations, many with their own publications, such as *Gazeta Polska* (Polish gazette), *Aspekt* (Aspect), and *Rzeczpospolita* (Commonwealth). During this period, student movements also arose in a half-dozen major Polish cities, and each published information sheets and bulletins on a regular basis. For a representative sample of these organizations and their publications, see Bernhard 1993, chap. 6 and pp. 257–58. For the most comprehensive summary of the organizations and publications of the Polish opposition of the 1970s and 1980s, see Cecuda 1989.

4. For an enlightening and highly humorous account of the intricacies of the technical aspects of underground publishing, see Walc 1980, 1–11. On the lengths to which underground publishers went to procure the equipment necessary for their work, see Stewart Steven's discussion of the misadventures that Mirosław Chojecki, the head of the earliest independent publishing house, NOW-a (*Niezależna Oficyna Wydawnicza* [Independent publishing house]), had with the police (1982, 249–54).

5. The journal itself played an important role in bringing out banned books through its own "Library of the Political Quarterly *Krytyka*" (edited by Jan Kofman). It published more than thirty volumes, including both translations of classics not readily available in Polish and original works. The series includes major works by Popper, Arendt, Weber, and Havel. Many of these editions are still in print today, and the series continues to publish important contemporary works.

A recent attempt to catalog the range of alternative unofficial organizations in the period 1976–89 uncovered 280 political groups, 76 underground publishing houses, and 435 different underground magazines, journals, and newspapers (Cecuda 1989).

6. Later *Krytyka* financed itself through various sources, including its own revenues, contributions from friends, the underground Social Committee for Science (*Społeczny Komitet Nauki*), and sales of reprints overseas by *Aneks* and *Index on Censorship*.

7. Certain issues of *Krytyka* were also printed by another underground publisher that emerged out of the KOR milieu—*Krąg* (Circle), and until no. 17 (1983) it was also reprinted in London for its Western audience by *Aneks* and *Index on Censorship* (Cecuda 1989, 24, 170; Karpiński 1985, 116, 159).

8. This was the highest circulation for a periodical of this type in the 1970s and 1980s. The largest share of issues was distributed in Warsaw, so its influence was strongest there (Kofman & Romanowski 1992, 8).

9. The ethos of the PPS is succinctly summed up in the name of its resistance organiza-

tion during World War II—*Wolność, Równość, Niepodległość* (Freedom, Equality, Independence; or WRN). Unlike the communists, the PPS stood strongly and forcefully for Polish independence as being in the interest of the Polish working class. Also unlike the communists and other political currents in Poland, the PPS was committed to parliamentary democracy. Although there were other political parties that supported independence and parliamentary democracy, the PPS was unique in its commitments to social equality and to achieving socialism by democratic means and in its working-class, trade-unionist base.

Its notion of equality not only was socioeconomic but also explicitly included a tolerant attitude toward Poland's numerous ethnic and religious minorities. In the context of late-nineteenth-century imperial Eastern Europe, this meant that the PPS was radical in at least four dimensions: the political, the social, the economic, and the national. (I do not mean to imply that the PPS was radically nationalist. Its stand, combining support for national independence and ethnic/religious tolerance, marked it as distinct from nationalist currents in Polish politics.)

The PPS was one of the largest parties in Poland before Piłsudski's coup d'état of 1926 and played a major role in forging the interwar labor movement. During World War II it was one of the coalition members of the Polish government-in-exile, first in Paris and then in London, and its activists participated heavily in the underground struggle against German occupation. In the latter stages of the war, the PPS split into pro-Moscow and WRN factions. The former, with the help of the Soviet secret police, took control of the party apparatus after the war and led the PPS on a course that ended in the party's demise through a merger with the communist Polish Workers' Party (*Polska Partia Robotnicza*) in 1948.

10. Although this editorial was written by Kuroń and Starczewski, a note at its end stated: "This text was discussed by the editorial board of *Krytyka*, and it expresses the opinion of the group" (90).

11. For instance, *Robotnik* (The worker) was named after the late-nineteenth- and early-twentieth-century bibuła publication of that name edited by Józef Piłsudski. Similarly, *Biuletyn informacyjny* (Information bulletin) was named after the main bulletin of the wartime Home Army, the armed noncommunist resistance to German occupation.

12. For instance, see the recent exchange between Adam Michnik and Bishop Życiński in *Krytyka*, no. 41/42 (1993): 25–48.

13. Although many people wrote for *Krytyka* under pseudonyms, Kofman was the only editor in the early period to keep his identity masked.

14. For several long periods in the 1980s, Michnik was interned or arrested and thus was unable to play as central an editorial role as he had previously.

15. For instance, *Krytyka*, no. 40 (1993): 2, lists the following editorial personnel:
Editors: Marek Beylin (managing editor), Jan Kofman (editor-in-chief), Piotr Łukaszewicz (deputy editor-in-chief), Adam Michnik, Rafał Zakrzewski
Editorial Staff: Jan Cywiński, Mirosława Grabowska, Jan Tomasz Gross, Janusz Jankowiak, Krzysztof Jasiewicz, Andrzej Kopacki, Sergiusz Kowalski, Jarosław Krawczyk, Robert Mroziewicz, Andrzej Osęka, Jerzy Surdykowski, Henryk Szlajfer

16. Havel's letter is available in English translation in many different collections, including Havel 1992, 50–83.

17. Solzhenitsyn's essay discusses the philistinism of the new Soviet intelligentsia. For the English translation, see Solzhenitsyn 1974.

18. A representative but by no means exhaustive list of Polish intellectuals and writers who are well known in the West includes Leszek Kolakowski, Stanisław Barańczak, Jan Józef Lipski, Edward Lipiński, Stefan Kisielewski, Jacek Kuroń, Władysław Bieńkowski, Adam Michnik, Czesław Miłosz, Zbigniew Herbert, Józef Tischner, Bronisław Geremek, Andrzej Wajda, Włodzimierz Brus, and Jadwiga Staniszkis.

19. This issue was ready for publication just before the declaration of martial law in 1981. Its actual publication was delayed until 1982.

20. Other important Solidarity figures were extensively interviewed in this series, including Andrzej Gwiazda, Karol Modzelewski, Janusz Onyszkiewicz, and Jan Rulewski.

21. In more recent issues the sections on sociology and spiritual matters have new titles, for example, "Society and Change" (*Społeczeństwo i zmiana*, in no. 36 [1991]) and "The Church and the Faithful" (*Kościoł i wierni*, in no. 38 [1992])

22. *Krytyka* published French-speaking authors Eugène Ionesco, Jean-Marie Domenach, Jacques Julliard, Albert Camus, Jean-François Revel, Julien Benda, Marc Bloch, and Pierre Hassner. It also published a number of German authors—Golo Mann, Jürgen Habermas, Peter Handke, and Heinrich Böll. Prominent English and American authors included Norman Davies, Hugh Trevor-Roper, Fritz Stern, Irving Howe, George Orwell, Arnold Toynbee, and Zbigniew Brzezinski. It also published other prominent Western intellectuals such as Shlomo Avinieri and Benedetto Croce.

23. Individual pieces were published by Miklós Haraszti, Ferenc Fehér, and György Konrad from Hungary; Nico Hübner and Wolf Bierman from the former German Democratic Republic; Alexander Zinoviev, Alexander Bukovski, Vladimir Nabokov, Varlam Shalamov, Tomas Venclova, Viacheslav Chornovil, Viktor Nekrasov, Lev Kopelev, and Joseph Brodsky from the nations of the former Soviet Union; Milovan Djilas and Edvard Kardelj from Yugoslavia; and Jiří Lederer, Jiří Pelikan, Zdeněk Mlynář, and Milan Kundera from then Czechoslovakia

24. Havel's essay was very influential in some circles in Poland. Zbigniew Janas, one of the founders of Solidarity in the Ursus Tractor Factory and later the head of Solidarity in Mazowsze, mentioned how he and Zbigniew Bujak, the deputy chairman of Solidarity in 1981, were strongly affected by reading Havel in *Krytyka* ("Interview with Zbigniew Janas," 49). For the English translation of "The Power of the Powerless," see Havel 1985.

References

A.B. 1978. "Pierwszy numer *Pulsu*" (The first issue of *Pulse*). *Zapis* 5 (January).

Adamski, Władysław, et al. 1981. *Polacy '80. Wyniki badań ankietowych* (Poles '80. Results of survey research). Warsaw: Instytut Filozofii i Socjologii, Polska Akademia Nauk.

———. 1982. *Polacy '81. Postrzeganie kryzysu i konfliktu* (Poles '81. Perception of crisis and conflict). Warsaw: Instytut Filozofii i Socjologii, Polska Akademia Nauk.

———. 1986. *Polacy '84. Dynamika konfliktu i konsensusu* (Poles '84. The dynamics of conflict and consensus). Warsaw: Uniwersytet Warszawski.

———. 1989. *Polacy '88. Dynamika konfliktu a szanse reform* (Poles '88. The dynamics of conflict and the chances for reform). Warsaw: Centralny Program Badań Podstawowych.

Barańczak, Stanisław. 1978. "Dlaczego *Zapis*?" (Why *The Record*?). *Zapis* 1 (January).

Bernhard, Michael. 1993. *The Origins of Democratization in Poland: Workers, Intellectuals, and Oppositional Politics, 1976–1980*. New York: Columbia University Press.

Cecuda, Dariusz. 1989. *Leksykon opozycji politycznej, 1976–1989* (Lexicon of the political opposition). Warsaw: BIS ZSP.

Curry, Jane, ed. 1984. *The Black Book of Polish Censorship*. New York: Vintage.

Dym, L. 1978. "*Spotkania*" (Encounters). *Zapis* 5 (January).

Havel, Vaclav. 1985. "The Power of the Powerless." In *The Power of the Powerless*, ed. John Keane. New York: M. E. Sharpe.

———. 1992 [1975]. "Dear Dr. Husak." In *Open Letters, Selected Writings, 1965–1990*. New York: Vintage.

"Interview with Zbigniew Janas." 1985. *East European Reporter* 1, no. 3 (autumn).

Janusz, Michał. 1985. "*Krytyka* Feldmanowska" (Feldman's *Krytyka*). *Krytyka*, no. 19/20.

Karpiński, Jakub. 1985. *Polska, Komunizm, Opozycja: Słownik* (Poland, communism, opposition: A dictionary). London: Polonia.

Kofman, Jan, and Andrzej Romanowski. 1992. "Pismo myśli politycznej. Z profesorem Janem Kofmanem, redaktorem naczelnym Kwartalnika Politycznego *Krytyka*, rozmawia Andrzej Romanowski" (A journal of political thought. Andrzej Romanowski interviews Professor Jan Kofman, editor-in-chief of the political quarterly *Krytyka*). *Tygodnik Powszechny* 12 (22 March).

Kofman, Jan, and Jerzy Surdykowski. 1989. " Będzie inaczej. Rozmowa z Dr. Janem Kofmanem, redaktorem naczelnym Kwartalnika Politycznego *Krytyka*" (It will be otherwise. A conversation with Dr. Jan Kofman, editor-in-chief of the political quarterly *Krytyka*). *Literatura* 84 (September).

Krytyka Editorial Group. 1978. ' Od redakcji" (From the editors). *Krytyka*, no. 1.

Kundera, Milan. 1991 [1967]. "A Nation Which Cannot Take Itself for Granted." In *From Stalinism to Pluralism*, ed. Gail Stokes. New York: Oxford University Press.

Kuroń, Jacek. 1991. *Gwiezdny Czas* (The starry time). London: Aneks.

Kuroń, Jacek, and Stefan Starczewski. 1980. "Od redakcji" (From the editors). *Krytyka*, no. 4.

Lipski, Jan Józef. 1985. *KOR: A History of the Workers' Defense Committee in Poland, 1976–1981*. Berkeley and Los Angeles: University of California Press.

Michnik, Adam. 1993. "Belka i źdźbło" (The beam and the blade). *Krytyka*, no. 41/42 (fall).

Solzhenitsyn, Alexander. 1974. "The Smatterers." In *From under the Rubble*. Boston: Little, Brown.

Steven, Stewart. 1982. *The Poles*. New York: Macmillan.

Walc, Jan. 1980. "My wolna wałkowa" (We of the free roller). *Biuletyn informacyjny* 38 (June).

———. Interview by Michael Bernhard. Cambridge, Mass., November 1986.

Życiński, Józef. 1993. "Nowe perspektywy dialogu" (New perspectives on dialogue). *Krytyka*, no. 41/42.

Note

This book contains a glossary of names and terms from Polish history and culture. It is arranged alphabetically and appears at the back of the book. Names, terms, and important phrases that may be unfamiliar to some readers have been marked with an asterisk (*) the first time they appear in any contribution.

Editorial interpolations, corrections, explanations, translations, and comments appear enclosed in brackets in the text. For pseudonymous articles, the author's real name is given in brackets.

Section I

Politics

1

Under the Military Dictatorship: Between "Freeze Frame" and "Restoration"

Krytyka, no. 12 (1982)

Jan Kowalski and Andrzej Malinowski
[Henryk Szlajfer]

It is necessary for the people to either be free, which would be the best thing, or to at least feel free because such a belief is followed by valuable consequences.
                                        —Diderot to Catherine II

As a philosopher you work on paper which will bear everything, whereas I, a poor empress, work on human skin which is much more sensitive.
                                        —Catherine II to Diderot

Introduction: The Short Breath of Theories and of Politicians

A military coup in a "people's democracy"? No social theory foresaw such an occurrence, at least not in Eastern Europe. To be sure, military dictatorship did loom in the Soviet Union during the struggle to succeed Stalin (Marshal Zhukov, for example, was accused of having a

We dedicate this text to our friends from Lublin and Łódź, from the "Manifest Lipcowy," "Jastrzębie," "Rymer," "Katowice," "Dębieńsko," and "Szczygłowice" mines, from the "Bail-don" and "Katowice" steel mills, from the FSO car factory, and from the "Warski" shipyard. (The text published here is a fragment of a larger whole—the editors of *Krytyka*.)

"Bonapartist disposition"), but that threat was recognized by both the East and the West as an unmistakable deviation from a model in which the army was unconditionally subordinated to the party (as its mailed fist).

Thus, in keeping with this generally accepted model, in "people's democracies" the struggle for power is waged *through the party,* not alongside it or over its head. This model seemed unshakable even in Stalin's time. During the Great Purges of the 1930s, the Soviet secret police, despite its extensive autonomy and impunity, was still under formal as well as actual control of the party elite. The army, after Stalin and the secret police decimated its elite, gave up any political ambitions of its own. Obviously, the police and the army were politically and economically powerful (recall the NKVD's★ "economic empire" based on forced labor), yet they were not the only ones who wielded power. The defeat of the secret police boss, Beria, in the race for unlimited power in 1953 is irrefutable testimony to this. The history of the Polish Ministry of Public Security (MBP) and military intelligence in the early 1950s, or the mechanisms of the power struggle in the years 1967 and 1968, provide the same lesson.

Both theory and practice seemed to support the belief that there was no room for any military dictatorship *over and above the party* in socialist states. In his book *The Sociology of Political Relations* (which is an archetypical work of Polish political science), Jerzy Wiatr claims that military dictatorship appeared only in "slave" and "bourgeois" states.[1] To describe our own political system, Wiatr resorted to the following tautology: "Socialist state = socialist republic." The only exception to this tautology, recalling Voltaire's story about killing sheep by casting spells, was distant China. In the case of China, Wiatr tried to be as objective as possible. He wrote, "The military-bureaucratic dictatorship, the result of the Cultural Revolution in China in the mid-1960s, is a deformation of the political system." Next, in keeping with that model, Wiatr went on to conclude that China had "abandoned the Leninist principle of integrating the army and the rest of the state apparatus, and of subordinating it to the civilian authorities—in favor of some form of military domination."[2]

Yet one cannot strongly fault political scientists for not having foreseen the possibility of military dictatorship in Poland. In March and even in December 1981, the threat of a state of emergency was discussed in terms of a classical political and police operation in which the

army would take part but in which it would be controlled by the traditional centers of power. If any warnings were issued at all, they were
in very general terms, as theoretical variants of possible scenarios
rather than on the basis of the analysis of actual trends. In practice, the
telling remark made by Jadwiga Staniszkis in June 1981, "In conditions
of a prolonged implosion of the state, every organized group recognized as a command center can become one," was ignored.[3] At the
time it was taken for granted that there could be only one decision-
making center, the one selected by the reform movement. At the end
of November 1981, Władysław Bieńkowski actually avoided taking
any definitive position by saying, "In a situation like ours, the most
common result is a new dictatorship resulting either from the suppression of revolutionary or reform movements, or also from their victory. In Poland, where strong antidictatorial attitudes prevail, such a
turn of events is not very likely, but everyone knows that history does
not give much consideration to people's preferences."[4]

Keeping in mind the course of the Polish October* of 1956 and the
"December events"* of 1970, the Solidarity leadership, representing
the "average" consciousness of the entire society, did not take into
account that the founders of the Military Council for National Salvation* [WRON] would come to the conclusion that *all* the traditional
institutions of power were completely worn out. A junta columnist
depicts the putschists' thinking very precisely by stressing that
WRON's founders felt they could no longer rely on anyone: not on
the party ("which was being brutally expelled from workplaces"), not
on the Sejm [parliament] (its "desperate attempts at mediation were
being simply ridiculed"), and not on the Council of State (which "had
long ago relinquished its constitutional prerogative of regulating public
life by means of decrees").[5] Academia was not alone in its lack of sociological and political insight. Both analysts trying to explain what
had happened, and the reform movement's activists, found themselves
in the situation that [Stanisław] Ossowski, in considering the events of
1956, described as "the short breath of reflective thought" necessitated
by the pace of change.[6] (This applies not only to the period right before
13 December 1981 [the date of Jaruzelski's coup], but also to the way
the situation of the country was generally perceived and analyzed in
the second half of the year.)

The discussion below is not meant to correct the theory. Our goal is
a practice-oriented analysis of events, a particular "prognosis of future

conditions." This is what the current situation requires. We therefore present a tentative sketch of the military dictatorship. This sketch is our first step toward an analysis of the directions of our further struggle, its goals, and its forms.

It is also necessary to evaluate Solidarity's practical activities critically. This task, as painful to the authors as it is to every active member of the reform movement, is nevertheless essential, not to find relief by confessing our sins but to understand why we lost this battle. In this difficult self-reflection, we will be guided by Michał Bobrzyński's* rule, which, though written in the nineteenth century, has lost none of its applicability: "Today, when no one is able to appreciate the vital significance of the external conditions, we can use them as an excuse to avoid responsibility; however, keeping science and the public good in mind, it is exactly this responsibility on which we should lay the greatest emphasis."[7]

Dictatorship Does Not Mean Stagnation

One should discuss the course of the military coup d'état and its direct military consequences (its impact on the respective abilities of the parties to the conflict to take action) in terms of particular "capabilities." The coup imposes a specific set of rules of action, a set of standardized activities based on military discipline and established in a definite order. Hence as a "capability" the coup is nothing but a real "war game" whose tactical goals are first to paralyze and disrupt the enemy's organizational and information networks, then to call into question the traditional form of solving conflicts, and finally to deprive the enemy of the possibility of undertaking coordinated action.

The "war game" of a coup d'état is always a *military episode* in a wider social process. It is not our intention to make light of attacks by the army and police on Solidarity and other independent civic organizations, nor do we wish to diminish the plight of the victims of these attacks. By describing the coup d'état as a mere military episode, we only want to point out that the actions by the army and the police have a definite place in a larger range of measures aimed at the elimination of long-term threats. The physical and mental terror of putting the army on the streets is not an aim in itself.

A coup d'état seen from the perspective of its direct effects primarily takes the form of a "freeze frame"; it stops all old conflicts. The coup does not eliminate the sources of these conflicts; it only prevents their consequences from being expressed in a wider area than for which there is room. In this sense the Polish coup in its character and slogans resembled a standard preventive counterrevolution. *However, the "freeze frame" is not the strategic goal of the "war game." Its goal is the construction of the axis leading from the "freeze frame" to "restoration."* We are currently observing the first attempts to construct such an axis. In principle the junta has achieved its direct military goals, and thus the basic condition of the "freeze frame" has been accomplished.

However, when it comes to "restoration" the problem becomes more complicated. What this "restoration" should be remains unclear both to the public and to the coup-plotters. Yet we should not overestimate the significance of this fact. The present state of uncertainty is but transitional, but not in the sense that we should expect society to resist immediately and vehemently. To expect this would be excessive optimism. All the same, one can argue that *what this "restoration" will be like does not depend on the dictatorship alone,* for the junta does not exercise total control either over the economy (foreign trade and agriculture in particular) or over the majority of Solidarity's social base. The junta's present control of the working class is nothing but police control.

It is important to recognize that the junta has some chance of success. Despite the shock we lived through on the night of 12–13 December 1981, despite the ongoing outright terror, and despite the blind hatred, we must not delude ourselves that now we can expect only disaster, that the dictatorship imposed on society will mean a complete standstill, an end of the world, then a happy and merry renaissance. Such a prospect, prompted by despair, stands no chance of fulfillment. *The challenge we are facing is instead a long and toilsome march toward a renaissance.* It will be a march, not a standstill. In our opinion, just as the coup d'état has its internal logic, so does the system of military dictatorship. However, it is not the internal logic alone that matters.

Under specific conditions military dictatorship is able to produce its own *developmental dynamic,* and the desire for "restoration" is nothing else but the expression of a practical effort to begin this dynamic. *Dictatorship does not necessarily mean stagnation in the economic sphere, in the disposition of social forces, or in politics.*

Inasmuch as the "freeze frame" means neutralizing the means of taking practical action in its old form, without doing away as yet with the social forces participating in "historical" conflicts, the transition from "freeze frame" to "restoration" will already be an expression of measures aimed at the creation of a new disposition of social forces. This will mean the destruction or considerable weakening of certain groups and the establishment or strengthening of others. The "freeze frame" halts the exchange of blows for a moment. Measures meant to promote a "restoration" may not only sharpen old conflicts to a limited extent, but also open up *new areas of conflict* and permit *new forces* to take part in these conflicts.

All the same, it would be a misunderstanding to believe that there is a clear dividing line between the "freeze frame" and "restoration." There can be no such demarcation as long as we remain under military dictatorship with all its consequences (martial law, the suspension of habeas corpus and other civic rights and freedoms). For a "restoration," it is necessary, already in the "freeze frame" period, to start the process of dividing the old social forces that supported the reform movement. Military dictatorship creates particularly favorable conditions for this. It even accelerates it by the simultaneous use of physical, mental, and economic terror; demagoguery ("black propaganda"); and political corruption. Also, the dictatorship will create "new actors" (primarily from its own ranks) whose role is to polarize and create conflict among existing social forces. These "new actors" are supposed to accomplish a particularly important mission, to create *the social and political conditions* for the implementation of the "restoration" program. These conditions will complement the existing *military conditions*.

It is obvious that the military dictatorship left to itself, lacking social support ("new actors"), would hardly be in a position to do nothing. Its primary dynamic would be one of destruction and terror. Unlike military dictatorships in capitalist countries (for example, in Chile), the Polish junta has no "natural" allies on which to rely, particularly in the economy. Under Polish conditions, the symbiosis between "politics" and "economy" is too strong to allow the putschists to rely right now on any significant social forces who could insulate them from direct everyday contact (and conflict) with the working class.

The junta's "intellectuals" are aware of the dangers that excessively long social isolation could pose. This is why the junta must immediately create civilian forces by fracturing civic resistance and resuscitating organizations that are already as good as clinically dead. In other words, it must create at least an imaginary "public opinion" and "civil society." In a system with no tradition of military dictatorship, where that is a shocking form of rule, the junta's illegitimate origin may soon become a source of serious "concern" to traditional power centers. Therefore, it is vital to the coup plotters that a limited number of civilian forces be "mobilized" and that they show—with the junta's blessing—their social utility.

During the "freeze frame" stage, with its unique "total sovereignty" of the military rulers, politics and traditional bargaining are replaced by the intrigues of cliques and personal alliances. This is a special kind of court politics, the basic rules of which can be found in descriptions of any randomly selected despotic system. Such court politics will prevail until the emergence of the social forces selected by "civil society." Experience teaches us not to treat personnel shifts among the generals, sharp personal conflicts, rash resignations, and new appointments as [signs of] the imminent end of dictatorship. Even if the next general, with Jaruzelski's scalp in his hand, announces "the end to errors and deviations," this does not have to be, and certainly will not be, "the real end of the Great War."

During the "freeze frame" stage, personnel changes will, as a rule, indicate a conflict between individual options and opinions. The phase leading to "restoration" will raise the problem of basic social and economic choice and will most probably re-create the pre-August personification of group interest (for example, X as the spokesman for "technocrats," Y as an ally of "liberals and intellectuals," Z as the leader of the hard-liners, and so on). Needless to say, one should not lose sight of these personal configurations and of their ever-changing social character. However, one should perpetually keep in mind that *the socio-economic context of these personal configurations will ultimately decide the future of military rule as a whole.* This context, created by the interplay of measures taken by the junta and the public's resistance, will determine whether Poles will be given one more chance for structural reform. There will be no "miracle of rebirth" or a sudden deus-ex-machina-like growth of peasant and worker resistance without the creation of a socioeconomic context and without the practical experience that the military dictatorship is nothing but psychological and economic terror and destruction. In this context the end of dictatorship could coincide with a conflict between generals or with any other "minor event" we cannot foresee today, just as no one could predict the immediate cause of the Peasant War in sixteenth-century Germany, the Russian Revolution of 1905, or the strikes of August 1980 in Poland.[8]

"Restoration" as a "Lay Counterreformation"

"Restoration" as we employ it here is a term whose conceptual limits have yet to be determined. One can at best point to certain underlying tendencies already discernible both in political propaganda (manipulation) and in the economy. One can also cite historical analogies in order to sketch out a map of variations in policy aimed at "restoration."

"Restoration" literally means a return to an original state of affairs. At first glance, our use of this term implies that we anticipate a return to the situation before August [1980]. Such a turn of events cannot be ruled out, although it does not seem very likely at the moment. This is why in our analysis the term does not mean a "simple" restoration of the old system. On the contrary, we maintain that such a recurrence, although desirable from the point of view of the military dictatorship (obviously without the frantic crises politics of the Gierek★ team), is not possible yet.

Presently (that is, in the next few months) "restoration" can be only a counterreformation. It seems that the most interesting and, from our viewpoint, useful definition of this term is the one given by Leszek Kołakowski years ago:

> A church reform movement if it is rooted in the authentic tendencies of the organized church collectivity, more often than not, cannot be overcome any other way but by a counterreform that adopts some of the slogans and aspirations of its opponents, but in such a way that these slogans are given interpretations that keep them within the limits of canonical discipline. In other words, an effective counterreformation must as a rule feed on certain ideas of the reformation it is trying to strangle; it must assimilate the mental substance that threatens to become a factor in its disintegration; it must . . . take over certain ideological elements of the reformatory movement to destroy their reform-

ist structure and through that paralyze the seeds of organizational separatism inherent therein.[9]

Continuing our reflections on the "restoration" as a lay analogue to a
religious counterreformation, we also want to point out that its potential strategic aim is undoubtedly the restoration of the status quo ante,
but in a particular form. This "particularity" is derivative of the course
of the process of the lay counterreformation. If we say that after the
cycle of Reformation and Counterreformation, the church became a
qualitatively different institution, we can presuppose that postrestora-
tion society will not be the same as it was before. Nevertheless, certain
basic characteristics of society will remain unchanged, and even if not,
the potential change will be uncommonly subtle. Despite the Reformation and Counterreformation, the church is still the church.

The reform and counterreform movements that reemerged, although not as sharply in subsequent centuries, inspired the "productive
forces" of the church. According to the declared intentions of the military rulers, the "restoration" should be a lay equivalent of an enervat-
ing movement that will extend the life of the "basic framework" of the
sociopolitical structure. In other words, the "restoration" should become equivalent to and play the role of a "crucial reform" about which
Michał Kalecki wrote the following:

> Let us assume that, in spite of the ruling class, strong public
> pressure brings about such a radical reform of the system that—
> short of destroying the existing relations of production—this
> reform provides a new opening for a further development of
> productive forces. A paradoxical situation emerges: a "crucial
> reform" that has been forced upon the ruling class can lead, at
> least temporarily, to the stabilization of the system.[10]

A "restoration" of this kind *is, from the point of view of the junta "liberals," the optimal solution.* Although having all the virtues of a revolution controlled from above, it allows the remnants of the reform
movement to be institutionalized, "new actors" to be created, and the
conspicuous forms of dictatorial power to be abandoned. This type of
"restoration" makes it possible not only to maintain the "basic framework" of the old structures but also to limit their own negative impact

on the mechanisms that would make it possible for these structures to survive.

It was no accident or expression of intellectual inertia that one of the first coded signals sent by the dictatorship was the catchword "Hungary" (in the context of economic reform and the future liberalization of the one-party system). By analogy one could justifiably conclude that the junta's diehards will give the countersign "Czechoslovakia" (and the "normalization" Husák★ declared in April 1969) to the catchword "Hungary." The diehards hope for a "restoration" understood literally, that is, the total destruction of all reform-movement organizations and the obliteration of all traces of them from social consciousness. The diehards are ready to repeat the words of the comte d'Antraigues, that diehard of the French counterrevolution, "I shall be the counterrevolution's Marat, cutting off thousands of heads, starting with my own."[11] (As our diehards are interested primarily in saving their own heads, they are merely a poor copy of that French romantic of counterrevolution.)

Thus the military dictatorship will have to decide on which side of the ship they should drop the gangplank that will lead them from the "freeze frame" to "restoration." From the point of view of the post-August reform movement, this is a choice between a "liberal" fist in a glove and the unconcealed punch of a diehard. Whether a third possibility will appear depends on the strength of the protest movement and its program and its ability to carry out a relatively independent policy in the face of a considerably stronger and at present triumphant enemy.

The "Moment of Transition" Will Be Decisive: Historical Parallels

Above, we mentioned Hungary and Czechoslovakia as two different variants of "restoration." Risking further oversimplification, we believe that it was *the moment of transition* from the "freeze frame" to long-term socioeconomic stabilization that was decisive in the two countries' adopting different variants of "restoration." The situations we describe today as "different models" were anticipated neither by static understandings of the initial conditions at the moment of transition nor by the a priori programs for "restoration" (declared intentions). How the respective initial conditions were overcome, namely, *the practical move* from "freeze frame" toward "restoration," turned out to be the decisive factor.

From a historical perspective, the different paths of evolution in Hungary and in Czechoslovakia are difficult to explain. In turn, to treat the initial conditions from where these countries started in 1956 and 1968 as absolutes or to interpret them statically makes the prospect of a sensible explanation even more remote. There is no doubt that in October 1956, after the second Soviet military intervention and after the suppression of the general strike in Budapest, Kádár and his group were closer to normalization of the Husák type than to the "restoration" they were to launch in 1961–62 by gradual liberalization and economic reforms. Their stigmatization as traitors, total social isolation, the thousands they had put to death, and the economic crisis were not the sort of achievements that promote dialogue and mutual compromise. It should be stressed that until 1960–61 liberalization of any sort had been out of the question and that Kádár settled accounts with his enemies within the party in a ruthless manner (remember the fate of Imre Nagy* or the less tragic fortunes of Lukács,* Déry,* and the others). It was only at the beginning of the 1960s that the Kádár regime abandoned the logic of destruction, terror, and the forceful creation of the prerequisites for economic and political "restoration." It was at that time too that the conciliatory slogan "He who's not against us is with us" began to mean something concrete.

In Czechoslovakia, following the intervention of the Warsaw Pact forces in August 1968, the situation was the diametric opposite. At the beginning, nothing seemed to indicate that there would be a return to the Novotný* era. Despite the intervention, a strong reform-oriented faction continued to exist, and a strong workers' council movement that grew up after the intervention seemed to be an optimistic sign that everything was not yet lost. Nevertheless, in a short time (within several months) the Czechoslovaks lost everything; both political liberalization and economic reform came to an end. Today Czechoslovakia not only has political prisoners, a gagged culture, and social apathy, but is also, as Premier Štrougal put it, a perfect candidate for a "museum of technology." Husák, who only reluctantly mentioned the intervention at a meeting of communist parties in Moscow in 1969, is now a perfect symbol of that intervention.

How can these differences be explained? Of course, one can suggest that the decisive factor leading to one and not another path of development was simply the quality of the new power elite, the talents of its particular members and their political imagination. There is no doubt that Husák's team was and remains bland, desperately "gray and bureaucratic" compared to the members of the Kádár group, who in comparison are vigorous and who have wide intellectual horizons.

One can also point out the different political climate that prevailed in the Soviet bloc in 1956. This factor, although difficult to measure, played, we believe, a major role in János Kádár's policies. His unconstrained fury after Khrushchev's removal from power indicated that the Soviet leader was some sort of "silent partner" in Hungary's policy of "restoration." Husák had to contend with a different kind of leader and with a different policy within the bloc. A flirtation with polycentrism and internal reform was quickly replaced by a policy of "unity" in response to the strategic balance of forces on a world scale. The reformist experiments were gradually supplanted by a peculiar "Prussian path of development," best exemplified by the German Democratic Republic. We should also add that the policies of Nixon and Kissinger, based on an updated version of the political thought of the Congress of Vienna and the Yalta agreements as they understood them, only froze the situation in Eastern Europe in its own way (namely, the Sonnenfeldt doctrine).

The explanations offered above, although correct, represent only small parts of the "restoration" process in the two countries. If we were to consider mental and external circumstances alone, we would inevitably arrive at some variation of "conspiracy" or "political pathology" theory. Although such theories are very popular, none of them explains the differences in these two paths of development satisfactorily.

We think one should reach somewhat deeper, into the area of macrosocial processes. One can plausibly argue that the shock in Hungary was profound enough (involving a total collapse of the old political and state structures) to make a "simple" return to the Rákosi* period (without its murderous "eccentricities" though) tantamount to the murder, imprisonment, or emigration of a considerable part of the population. *Hungary went through a civil war*, and this was decisive in all further decisions made by its power elite. The policy of "goulash socialism" could not be carried out without a reduction of terror and economic reform. The appropriateness (at least until the late 1970s) of the Kádár group's economic policy allowed them, after the "freeze frame," to break out of an impasse and to initiate a new developmental dynamic. But as we said before, the years from 1956 to 1961–62 played out in Hungary as a silent drama in which the "revolt syndrome" was brutally dismantled.

That events in Czechoslovakia were comparatively less dramatic and that the structures of the pre-1968 regime still existed despite the Prague Spring combined to create conditions that allowed for an easy return to traditional rule. The authorities managed to overcome economic stagnation without lowering the living standards of working people too much. The need for reform, although raised universally, proved to be, at least in the short term, replaceable by a policy of increased centralization of planning and management. The stimuli for a Hungarian-style "restoration," born at the time of the Prague Spring, were too weak, and the disintegration of the reform-minded groups was speeded up by external pressure. The Czechoslovak diehards made skillful use of this pressure and the possibility of implementing their choice of economic program ("reform" versus "turning inward") in support of a conservatively understood "restoration."

At first glance, the conclusion that one can draw from this type of interpretation is not optimistic. One can maintain that such an interpretation implies a dramatic perspective—that a "restoration" that is not a simple return to the old system and its methods of rule is a function of the intensity of the shock suffered by the power structures and the public, with the measure of that intensity being the type of resistance offered by society (armed struggle, general strike).

Yet we do not think that this is the inevitable conclusion. In our short digression on the history of various types of "restoration," the bloodiness of events is not the key factor. *"The intensity of the shock" is based not on the form public resistance takes (for example, war) but on the extent to which the reform movement actually encroaches on traditional power centers and deprives them of their old certainty about taking action and of their social backing. The presence (or absence) of alternatives in the economic policy (with respect to the economy as a whole and its particular sectors) is another factor. Yet another factor is the degree to which the aims of the reform movement have been internalized by the public and by the centers of power, even if this internalization is selective in character.* To be sure, the "intensity of the shock" caused by civil war or foreign intervention sharpens and makes the need for stabilization and reform extremely dramatic. Yet without the accompaniment of other conditions, even this socially most costly form of shock is itself not sufficient to ensure an innovative "restoration."

At the beginning of this section, we said that the conditions prevailing at the onset of the "moment of transition," even those most favorable to the reform movement, cannot mechanically preordain the choice of a specific variant of "restoration" if they are understood statically. It is worth adding here that they also do not predetermine the possibilities for the realization of a "third road" connected to the demands of the whole reform movement and not just some of its elements. The choice will be decided by the "moment of transition," which is a complex *process* combining measures taken by power centers and the public's reaction to them into an organic whole. This is because the starting conditions of the transition process are not constant. They can be withstood or transformed. On the contrary, the uniqueness of the "moment of transition" lies exactly in overcoming the conditions that at the beginning of the process appeared as constraints on action. We shall discuss these general theses using the example of measures to increase consumer prices substantially.

A Change in the Initial Conditions: The Logic of the "Price Operation"

In a stable and developing economy, price changes are usually a natural element in the economic landscape. That workers struggle for a greater share of national income is also a natural element of this landscape. It is extremely rare that price increases (in combination with other conflicts) become the major arena of the struggle for social and political reforms. This, though, is the case in Poland.

The problem already existed before the coup. Although it was not always clear to the majority of the union's members and activists, the price issue played a fundamental role in determining Solidarity's and the authorities' lines of action in the open conflict that preceded martial law. The intensity of the conflict quickly robbed the problem of prices (just like any other economic issue) of its independent character and made it a part of a larger strategy of promoting fundamental structural reform. The problem of prices, however, was not just part of the economic struggle, because it could not be solved in "pure" economic terms.[12]

Whether before or after 13 December 1981, the "price operation" has lost nothing of its urgency because the real needs of the economy as a whole depend on it. Therefore, it cannot be ignored or postponed until some time in the future. The problem lies elsewhere. As a major starting point of the transition from "freeze frame" to "restoration," price increases continue to be a political bomb with a delayed fuse. They constitute a danger in the sense that their shock effect can go beyond the junta's aim of "depoliticizing" socioeconomic life. Instead of solving the problem, they may actually provoke a series of dictatorial measures in both management and government.

For a while, the coup d'état has warded off the dangers of organized grassroots pressure on the shape of the economic policy and of unified economic, social, and political demands. This, however, does not mean that by the same token the military dictatorship has gained public acceptance for the idea of drastic price increases or that once the whole "operation" has been completed it will be possible to return to the normal economic mechanisms and keep economic conflict under control. The absence of public approval and lack of certainty of economic success can give rise to a cumulative process of *self-consolidation* and *particularization* of the military dictatorship.

We begin the analysis of this process, which is only in its embryonic stages, with a quote from Georg Lukács. His observation was made from the perspective of a "sociotechnician" of revolution. This does not diminish the cognitive value of his observation, but under current circumstances even enhances it. Lukács wrote:

> The most oppressive phenomena associated with proletarian power—namely, high prices and the scarcity of goods, . . . are the direct consequence of the slackening of labor-discipline and the decline in production. These [problems] . . . can only be solved when the causes of these phenomena have been removed.[13]

This can be done in two ways:

> Either the individuals who constitute the proletariat *realize* that they can help themselves only by bringing about a voluntary strengthening of labor-discipline, and consequently a rise in

production; or, if they are incapable of this, *they must create institutions that are capable of bringing about this necessary effect*. In the latter case, they create a legal system through which the proletariat *compels* its own individual members . . . to act in a way that corresponds to their class interests: *the proletariat turns its dictatorship against itself*. . . . But one must not hide from the fact that this method contains within itself *great dangers for the future*.[14]

The remarks above, written in 1919 and influenced by War Communism in Russia, have acquired a special importance in our present situation. One can, of course, read in them a cynical manipulation of ideas and an attempt to justify "naked force." This kind of cynicism, though, is not the result of an absence of moral principles, but only a summary observation of practical life. One can also rebel against the use of dictatorial methods "in the name of a class, the people, mankind, and so on," but this kind of political blindness is not characteristic of groups who have the means of coercion at their disposal. This is why it might be worthwhile to look carefully at the implications of Lukács's remarks and to apply them to the Polish context.

"Dictatorship over the proletariat," currently exercised in the form of military dictatorship, must fulfill a specific economic role. The direct police control established over the working class ("formal control" as the director of the "Kasprzak" Radio Factory in Warsaw euphemistically called it)[15] after 13 December 1981 *primarily* had political functions (destruction and prevention). From now on, its *first and foremost* function will be overtly economic. It will affect the conditions of reproduction of the labor force and the direction and method of the implementation of the economic policy. The curfew, a ten- to twelve-hour shift in militarized enterprises, the omnipotence of military commissars, and the complete subordination of the state and economic administration are not merely police harassment but a conscious policy of *economic terror* with long-term consequences. The junta's economists from the Military Political Academy (WAP) are brutally frank on this matter. We shall return to it below.

The planned "price operation" is the first measure aimed at fundamentally changing the conditions of the reproduction of labor. It embraces all classes, strata, and walks of life. The extent of this "operation" is unprecedented, and the magnitude of the shock it will send will be much greater than the shock Poles suffered as a result of the increase in consumer prices in 1953. Without going into details, one can argue that *the current operation is aimed at reducing the purchasing power of the average wage to the level of the mid-1950s. This is expressly clear in the relation* between the estimated future average nominal wage (taking partial compensation into account) and the planned prices for food, services, and durable goods. This means that a leap backward of more than a quarter-century awaits us, and that is not all. Such a radical decline in the population's living standard and purchasing power will involve a "shock to civilization" as well. This will be caused by a sharp decline in family spending on items other than food, tea, coffee, cigarettes, rent, energy bills, and so on. In 1979 these expenditures made up nearly 60 percent of the working family's expenses.[16] One can expect that after the implementation of the "price operation" these expenses will consume about 85–90 percent of average family income. Spending on culture, vacations, durable goods, and clothing will be reduced radically. In 1953 this kind of "shock to civilization" was not that great because of the different structure (and level) of family expenditures at that time. In this way the planned "price operation" will take Poles back to when the worker "earned so little that the problem of choice did not exist at all."[17]

The depth and character of the economic crisis do not give the military rulers a chance to "consume" the political and social threats related to such a radical lowering of the population's living standard. The dictatorship cannot hope for a quick recovery of the country's economy or expect a boom in the near future. This is why they will in this phase concentrate their activities first and foremost on neutralizing threats. This is because the direct short-term and medium-term goal of the "price operation" is not so much to play certain social groups against others, but to stifle total effective consumer demand. Only token gestures of marginal economic importance (cafeterias in places of work, fiscal preferences for certain small groups, and so on) will be possible. In certain industries the policy of curtailing effective demand will help create *an artificial surplus on the supply side.* To make a travesty of a well-known dictum by Michał Kalecki, we can say that the increase in the number of paupers will not endanger the creation of that surplus.[18] This maneuver, although perhaps necessary to quickly create *a surplus for export,* deprives the military rulers of the ability to give preferential treatment to wider social groups and to bribe the public on the eve of any electoral campaign (the junta will, however, have enough to satisfy the army, the police, and a part of the central party and state apparatuses).[19] This will deny the military government the chance to construct a "community of economic interests" that will support it.

The military also feel insecure because they do not know when Poland's Western creditors will soften their hard position. Therefore, they must at all costs create an exportable surplus (even if only in the quarterly balance of trade) to ensure that enterprises can obtain expensive commercial and short-term credits to maintain their supply of imports. The "price operation," by introducing a new exchange rate (via new supply prices) and by restraining internal demand, creates a quasi-automatic expansion in exports. However, this "export orientation," which has been a goal for many years, will materialize only in a bastardized form under military rule: as a wasteful exploitation of natural resources, as exports at dumping prices, and as an artificial glut on the domestic market.

The "price operation" as described above was a threshold that Solidarity could cross only by radically violating the balance of forces achieved by the "Warsaw Agreement of March 1981."* *As a trade union*, Solidarity could not accept such a drastic lowering of the living standards of its members. This threatened the total disintegration of the union. The violent reaction by the delegates to the second round of the Solidarity Congress to news of an increase in prices for cigarettes and alcohol showed clearly that Solidarity activists should have been as concerned about the measures taken by the authorities as about the reaction of their social base. In the subsequent weeks the activists' panic grew even worse when they realized that the authorities had managed effectively to paralyze their halfhearted "excursion" into the sphere of production (namely, the August appeal of the National Coordinating Commission* [KKP] for eight working Saturdays in mining). Starting in October, despite the initial boycott of Resolution 199 of the Council of Ministers, mining output on Saturdays designated as free began to grow in accordance with the rules laid down by the government. By the end of November, the shifts on Saturday had already produced more than 200,000 tons of coal, showing a sharp rise in production (against 130,000 tons in September).

In a way it was in the order of things that the union next tried to convert economic problems into ad hoc policy propositions aimed at breaking the deadlock through a direct attack on the institutions of public life. "Pure politics" was a form of escape from the insoluble economic problems of the "price operation" and thus guaranteed that unpopular economic measures would have to be taken in the future. In a word, the expectation was that it would be possible to secure the "voluntary consent of the proletariat" to increased economic difficulties by giving Solidarity a share in political power.[20] The possibility of a different variant, that of military dictatorship, was simply disregarded.

It seems very likely that the military rulers intend, at present, to use the planned "price operation," among other things, to create the mechanisms that will set in motion the process of its *self-consolidation*. It will still be possible to overcome the "bottleneck" of a drastic cut in the effective demand if the *basic* provisions of martial law stand and, moreover, are complemented by additional measures in the area of *labor relations*. To be sure, the "price operation" alone will promote a certain automatic response based on employees' self-exploitation, but this could prove too weak. For this reason the spokesmen of the dictatorship call for new supplemental measures.

These new measures in the area of labor relations are to compensate for the "enthusiasm" and "voluntary discipline" that are missing today. They consist, most broadly speaking, in the abolition of the old system of *employment security* and *the social safety net*. (Although the old system left very much to be desired, all the same it provided a certain limited protection against forced pauperization.) Under a capitalist system, we would metaphorically refer to these sorts of measures as the "predatory laws of the market"; in reference to Poland a less literary description— *economic terror*—will do.

No workers, engineers, or clerks can be sure that they will keep their job or find another. Even in industries that suffer from manpower shortages (such as mining), the threat of dismissal, of being blacklisted, or of being deprived of special financial privileges (like the "Miners' Charter"*) can be and is used quite effectively. (For instance, every miner who took part in the strikes following 13 December 1981 had to go through the humiliating process of reapplying for his job and for maintaining his privileges under the "Miners' Charter.") Next, drastic cuts in their purchasing power will force workers to look for additional sources of income, to work harder, and to work for longer hours.[21] Also, the selective changes in technical norms planned by the military dictatorship are aimed at increasing the self-exploitation of labor. Moreover, one can expect steps to impose exceptionally harsh work discipline. The attention paid by the diehards to the new, draconian decree on stricter work discipline in Romania should be seen as very indicative of and in line with the junta's philosophy.[22]

The list of supporting measures does by no means end with those we have mentioned. In order to ensure self-exploitation institutionally, the economists from the Military Political Academy (WAP) propose to suspend the workers' right to free Saturdays no matter what, even in enterprises that have not been militarized. The commander of WAP's Economic Department, Colonel Tadeusz Grabowski, is critical of last year's agreement on free Saturdays. He says: "Martial law lets us rectify this anomaly. It should be kept in mind that the martial law decree reads: 'The worker is obliged to work six days a week.' This rule should be extended not just to militarized enterprises alone."[23] Although WRON instructed the government to recognize the validity of the "February agreement"* (which the government did in an executive order dated 18 December 1981), one should remember that the diehards see the problem in a different light. Colonel Grabowski's statement was made after publication of the government order concerning free Saturdays.[24]

If we add to the picture presented above the numerous dismissals from the state apparatus and from industry, political purges, and so on, we can detect the outlines of "labor peace" based on police control and economic terror. It takes dictatorship to maintain this kind of "peace." The diehards, who demand the consolidation of dictatorial rule, can take as their justification not only political dangers but also "objective economic need." The logic of their argument is very simple: "Otherwise we cannot vouch for the further course of events" [!]. In this situation, the liberals can do nothing but try to weaken or lift the most primitive forms of police control, at the price of giving consent to political and economic terror. In both cases, however, consolidation of military dictatorship is the conditio sine qua non. In his public statements, Deputy Prime Minister Rakowski treats this thesis just as banally. He told foreign reporters: "The State of Emergency introduced on 13 December opened up a promising stage for Poland from which the national economy can return to normal. We should consolidate the foundations of this normal situation. For this reason, we cannot today give a concrete date for the end to martial law."[25]

The process of the dictatorship's self-consolidation will inevitably be accompanied by that of its particularization. This means the abandon-

ment of the "universal" principle of creating only the conditions necessary for "normal" economic activity and embracing the "need" to
extend centralized control and intervention to particular areas of economic and public life. A reconstructed organization of military commissars will get involved in the complex system of civilian "interest
groups," in setting priorities and the pull of pressures and counter-
pressures, and so on. By attacking one chosen problem, the junta will
create chaos and stagnation in other areas. When one observes majors
and colonels telling plumbers how to repair a broken pipe (no joke),
one remembers the Cuban "sugar crop of 10 million tons"* and the
long-standing economic mess it created. The junta and its executive
apparatus will be forced to give up the comfortable and desirable role
of the system's "guardian" and to become a "party" to divisive conflicts.

Independent of the economic impact this kind of change will have,
the authority of the army as a "national force" that stands above the
"dirt" of civilian life will also be at stake in this process of particularization. If the sense of this authority is best expressed by the term "order," then the particularization process will inevitably lead to the erosion of this traditional image of the army and of its tasks. The military
dictators will have to soil their hands. It must be stressed, however,
that inasmuch as the role of the "guardian" fits in perfectly with the
army's concept of its own "mission," the imminent process of getting
entangled in the "normal" process of making economic decisions
causes instinctive misgivings in the officer corps. A telling statement
was made by Colonel J. Dwornik. He had been the commander of a
Regional Operational Group since the end of November and on 13
December 1981 was appointed commissar of several large factories,
among them the "Fablok" locomotive factory in Chrzanów and the
"Paris Commune" mine in Jaworzno. The colonel said, "Looking
ahead, we must think of reform. Yet to introduce it is not our task,
and I do not think it would be good if army officers oversaw this. *The
only thing we want is to bring discipline and order into the work of enterprises.*
In other words, we want to make preparations for reform."[26]

It is doubtful that the officers' dreams will come true. Everything
seems to indicate that the army is disposed to intervene ever more
deeply into the thicket of problems of civilian life. The junta is not the
executive apparatus of the traditional power centers; *it is a new power
center.* In this role it is visible on the level of the state as a whole, as

well as in the smallest enterprise or scientific institute. As the new power center, the junta cannot maintain social peace on its own. It must also fight an unceasing and quiet struggle with traditional power centers trying to regain their old influence and seize the initiative. On at least two fundamental matters the junta failed to achieve full victory. In the so-called social commissions, which had originally been conceived as "purely technical" apparatuses for the economic administration of enterprises, the party has been carrying out a campaign of "self-rehabilitation" and has been incrementally gaining control over companies.[27] A similar process can be observed in the so-called Civic Committees for National Salvation. The "committees" quickly rose from the status of the junta's "voluntary police" to the position of the primary instrument for "building (national) reconciliation under new conditions."[28] It is obvious that the junta does not exercise exclusive control over the committees as they are at present structured. "Triangular struggle" between military commissars and the executive bodies of the basic party organization and the district [or voivodship]* party apparatus occurs often. The junta cannot ignore it. It is based on popular hostility, terror, or passivity. The interests of the economic administration (another "side" to contend with) complicate it. On the contrary, the junta's members have fought strenuously because their own survival and future depend on its outcome. And as we said earlier, the junta's questionable "ideological and doctrinal" origins prevent it from withdrawing, at least neither today nor tomorrow. The junta has no guarantee whatsoever that once it relaxes the pressure or returns to the barracks either the workers or the party and state bureaucracies will not jump down its throat.

From the reflections presented above it follows that any attempt by the military to change even one of the basic starting conditions of the "moment of transition" will put it in a dilemma similar to the one the Hungarian rulers faced. We mean preparations for a future liberal "restoration" (as a declaration of intentions) by dictatorial methods. On the other hand, any restoration in the short and medium term will entail the continuation of dictatorship, its consolidation, and at the same time the destruction of all reform movement organizations. The next probable dilemma will exclusively be concerned with which methods should be used.

This scenario, however, does not take into account the actions of institutions resisting the dictatorship (the church) or the social forces the junta has been destroying (first and foremost Solidarity). This scenario also does not include the "new actors" the junta created (or resuscitated, for example, the Polish United Workers' Party* [PZPR]). Furthermore, the scenario does not pay enough attention to the country's changing external environment (the question of Poland's debt and credits), which may open up other options. For these reasons we treat the conclusions presented to this point as a first attempt to prepare the reader for our full hypothesis about the process of transition from the "freeze frame" to restoration.

To formulate a fully developed hypothesis requires us to abandon analysis based on analogies and deductions. This requires concrete analysis of particular parts of the post-coup reality and emerging tendencies. This task is hellishly difficult; it resembles a desperate "race with history." We hope, nevertheless, that we will not so much create a "simulation of reality" as catch the basic logic of events and their direction. This is why we will not present a full characterization of the junta, but a preliminary sketch of it.

Dubious Legalism

The Military Council for National Salvation (WRON), the symbol of the coup d'état and military rule, has had problems finding a place in the country's constitutional order. From the point of view of *the real disposition of forces,* the issue of the formal and legal basis for the creation and activities of WRON is not very important, yet it cannot be disregarded completely. The idea that "might makes right," although confirmed on a daily basis, does not diminish the significance of the socially accepted opposite that "right makes might." Therefore, WRON cannot (and does not want to) depict itself as "naked force." On the contrary, its propaganda makes every effort to mask its lack of a legal foundation and to gloss over the image of military dictatorship and coup d'état. Therefore, in his address the junta leader, General Jaruzelski, assured the nation that "there will be no military dictatorship in socialist Poland,"[29] and the speaker of the Sejm [Stanisław] Gucwa, whom the coup saved from political death, obediently repeats that WRON "is a political structure that acts through the constitutional bodies of the state and administrative power."[30] Last but not least, a

junta columnist uses Stalinist dialectics ("A socialist forest is qualitatively different from a capitalist one") to say: "Political enemies are
now trying to persuade the people that the army wants to establish
dictatorship. They use foreign patterns to prove that every use of force
by the military is associated with dictatorship. Our answer can, of
course, be brief—not every one. Ours is a socialist army."[31]

It might be fruitful to begin to describe the military dictatorship by
discussing this particular problem. It is especially important for Poland's foreign relations. By violating the established legal order and
international agreements, military dictatorship has ceased to be, in
light of "international law" and post-Nuremberg legal doctrine, the internal affair of the captive society. Dictatorship and the breach of law,
no matter whether in Chile, Israel, South Africa, or Poland, is a legitimate concern of world opinion and international institutions. *The principle of noninterference does not apply to dictatorial governments;* therefore,
they cannot refer to "international law" to protest special interest in
their domestic policy. *Diktat* in relations with dictatorial regimes is legitimate. One should only regret that, under the pressure of *Real-
politik*, it is adopted too selectively.

The formal and legal aspect of WRON's foundation and of the imposition of martial law can be reduced to three questions. The first
concerns how WRON was established and its place in the country's
constitutional order; the second concerns the violation of the internal
and international legal order; and the third has to do with the relation
between the legislative procedures of martial law and the idea of the
"state of emergency" (we raise the latter issue because the junta repeatedly declares that martial law in Poland "can be compared to a state of
emergency in other countries").[32]

How the Military Council for National Salvation was set up remains
unclear. We know only that WRON was not created by the Sejm or
the Council of State, and that the constitution of the Polish People's
Republic does not provide for a supragovernmental institution to control the state administration, including the Council of Ministers. From
the statements of its spokesmen, we know that the junta was created
even before the Council of State decided to impose martial law. Colonel Tadeusz Malicki, deputy chairman of the Committee for National
Defense (KOK), acknowledged this without any doubt: "In December
1981, WRON recognized the mortal danger threatening our country
. . . and *approached the Council of State* about invoking its power to

impose martial law over the entire territory of the Polish People's Republic."[33]

One can thus state with justification that the manner in which WRON was established was a glaring violation of the established legal order. The Council of State found itself face-to-face with a demand from a junta of generals.[34] Our argument that the Polish military have carried out a successful coup is based on how WRON came into existence and on the fact that WRON actually forced the Council of State to impose martial law.

We should return to the counterargument quoted above that WRON acts *through* the constitutional organs of power and does not replace them. This counterargument is unsupportable. To begin with, one can cite a number of historical examples of how a successful junta legitimated itself by means of the old organs of power. For instance, in 1964 the Brazilian generals did not arbitrarily appoint a new president, but made a terrorized parliament elect the candidate nominated in the "generals' primaries." Neither did they replace the former organs of administrative power; they "merely" subjected them to rigid control, reserving for themselves the right to interfere in administrative activities in the form and to the extent that they thought fit.[35] Generally speaking, how a dictatorship controls the constitutional authorities, especially its executive bodies, is a "technical aspect" of the exercise of the dictatorial power. The situation in Brazil, Chile, or Greece (under the rule of the "black colonels") is, from this point of view, only a variant of *the modern model of dictatorship* originally worked out by the Nazis.

This model demonstrates the possibility of a functional combination of routine and "arbitrariness," and thus the possibility of working out a specific balance between the constitutional authorities and the dictatorial apparatus. This functional linkage allows the dictatorship to achieve its goals independently and through the offices of the constitutional authorities it controls. In the literature on the subject, we find the following description of this functioning dictatorial system:

> Centralization on the highest level (in the form of the Ministerial Council for the Defense of the Reich) corresponded to the union of the organs of both civil and political administration and the territorial authorities of the military administration, as well as the establishment of special commissariats for the de-

fense of the Reich. . . . The new offices were to direct or literally to "control" . . . the centralized civilian authorities within
the area of each military district. . . . The "Reichskommissar"
had no formal authority over the civilian administration; his
"control" depended upon arbitrary encroachments into areas for
which other organs were responsible by issuing one-time instructions, when *warranted in an emergency*.[36]

Without resorting to analogies as easy as they are superficial, it
should be stressed that the "technical aspect" of the coup d'état and
dictatorial rule is in principle *the same* under all dictatorships, even
those as different as the Nazi dictatorship and the one established by
WRON. Behind sham legality lies either the transformation of law
into an instrument of crime or a disregard for law. In Poland, we must
contend with an attempt to maintain a theatrical legal facade ("observance of the law"), while in practice dictatorial "control" is put into
effect. The declarations issued since 13 December 1981, beginning with
phrases like "WRON has consented to . . . ," "WRON shall carefully
consider . . . ," "WRON has instructed the government . . . ," demonstrate this beyond any doubt. The actual domination of military commissars manifests itself in their control over the activities of industrial
and administrative establishments, housing estates, the foreign trips of
academics, or the publications of the Polish Academy of Sciences. It
would be truly difficult to describe WRON's position within the constitutional system better than General Jaruzelski himself did when, in a
speech to the Sejm on 25 January 1982, he defined it as the "administrator of martial law."[37] One thing should be added: WRON is like the
"administrator" of an estate whose owner is not present. We conclude
this discussion of this aspect of military dictatorship, with two questions: To whom is the junta subordinate, and to whom is it responsible? The answer is simple: *To God and to history*. In this lies the essence
of dictatorship.

The junta violated both national and international law by two actions. The first was the Council of State's usurpation, on WRON's
recommendation, of the lawmaking prerogatives of the Sejm while it
was in session. The second was the violation of the International Covenant on Civil and Political Rights of 1966, which Poland ratified.

Although the constitution of the Polish People's Republic grants the
Council of State the exclusive right to impose martial law, the consti-

tution also reserves lawmaking prerogatives for the Sejm, and in particular it does not allow the Council of State to issue decrees when parliament is in session. The four decrees (and the legislative actions taken by other organs of state and administrative powers on this basis) issued by the Council of State on 12 December 1981 are, from a constitutional point of view, illegal and thus constitute a glaring case of abuse of the prerogatives vested in that institution. It should also be forcefully stressed that this was not a simple violation of procedure but an explicit *violation of the constitution.* This lawlessness means that the junta cannot morally require citizens to demonstrate their support in action. Only the threat of force can compel the citizenry to take such actions. One should recognize, moreover, that acts committed after 12 December 1981 defined as crimes in the martial law decrees (for example, striking) are not crimes under normal Polish law.[38] In this sense, *those Solidarity and party members, students and peasants who were arrested because of the participation in strikes or other protest actions organized after 12 December 1981, are not prisoners but captives of the junta,* victims of an "internal war" waged on the people.

The unlawful character of the Council of State's decrees was also exposed in the statements of lawyers who continue to serve as Sejm deputies at the junta's behest.[39] During a joint session of the Sejm Commission on Internal Affairs, Administration, and Justice with the Commission on Legislation on 13 January, Deputy Łopatka, director of the Institute of State and Law of the Polish Academy of Sciences, said: "The decrees were issued when the Sejm was in session. However, when one considers the entirety of constitutional requirements, one must conclude that [those decrees] *were necessitated by the situation.*" Deputy Czeszejko-Sochacki, chairman of the Polish Bar Association, grasped the problem in a much simpler way: "The Council of State was under the stress of necessity to issue the decrees discussed. In the light of *the higher political rationale,* the dispute over whether the situation required decrees or anything else is pointless." These two arguments, typical of the "might makes right" philosophy in its purest form, led to objections from only two of the deputies present at that session. During the plenary meeting of the Sejm on 25 January 1982, several independent deputies (including those from the caucus of the Polish Catholic Social Union* [PZKS]) voiced objections. Under the present conditions ("a parliament of fools"), dissenting voices should be seen as virtually depriving the junta of even the appearances of legality (in 1968 the objection of the "Znak"* deputies played a similar role) despite the majority's approval of the junta's actions.

The International Covenant on Civil and Political Rights[40] was violated in two ways. First, although Article 4 of the covenant is explicit about the duty to advise the United Nations Secretary General about the expiration date for martial law and of the suspension of rights, the junta stubbornly refuses to give even an approximate date of the end to its rule. In his address to the Sejm, Jaruzelski told the deputies outright not to look "at the calendar." With regard to the economy, he announced a "long period" of dictatorship.

Second, Article 4 allows for a suspension of civil and political rights "when exceptional public danger threatens the nation's existence and the danger has been officially proclaimed." This clause, however, does not apply to a number of the covenant's provisions that cannot be suspended even under martial law. In particular, it does not apply to Article 18, which reads:

> 1. Every person has the right to freedom of thought, conscience, and religion, or conviction according to one's own choice, as well as of practicing one's own religion or beliefs individually or in common with others, in public or in private, by worship, participation in rites, practicing, and teaching.
>
> 2. No one may be subjected to pressures that constitute a violation of freedom of conscience or conviction according to one's own choice.

Within less than two months of the imposition of martial law, the junta has managed to provide ample evidence of its violation of this article, particularly in the area of repressing people for their "beliefs" as well as for their attempts to "express" them. We discuss this issue in greater detail later in our analysis.

The third problem is the relationship between "martial law" and the "state of emergency." In the junta's propaganda there is a tendency to identify the installation of the dictatorial regime with a "state of emergency." This is aimed at presenting as "normal" a situation in which all fundamental civic and political rights have been suspended by treating exceptionally harsh and merely strict regimes as equals.

We begin here with the contention that the martial law provisions of the constitution of the Polish People's Republic raises associations that its promulgators might not find very flattering. This is because it is reminiscent of the "Defense Act" passed by the Nazis in 1938. That law "introduced the concept of a state of national defense . . . , but without accurately defining when it was to be proclaimed and on what precisely it depended." What is more, "the onset of armed conflict was not needed to declare 'a defense alert' [*Verteidigungszustand*]."[41] A similar provision can be found in Article 33 of the Polish constitution. In order to avoid weak analogies, however, we want at this point to express our belief that the absence of an "ordinary" state-of-emergency provision in the constitution is the result of the promulgators' philosophy ("Under socialism a situation necessitating the imposition of the state of emergency is out of the question") rather than of a conscious intention to dramatize the reaction of the authorities to the threat of internal conflict. We can therefore suppose that what was behind the promulgation of a martial-law provision was the threat of a foreign attack. At the present moment this is, however, an insignificant detail.

But the practical consequences of martial law and of the state of emergency are not trivial at all. At this point, we believe it is worthwhile to refer to the coup in Chile in 1973, which came to be of particular interest to, among others, the Ad Hoc Working Group appointed by the U.N. General Assembly, which examined the state of civil and political rights after the Pinochet junta came to power.

Chilean law allows for a "state of siege" to be proclaimed. This is equivalent to a "state of emergency" in cases of foreign aggression or "internal unrest." "Martial law" can be imposed only in the face of the threat or outbreak of war. Should a "state of siege" be proclaimed because of internal unrest, the authorities may not suspend most civil and political rights and, in particular, habeas corpus. The observance of martial law and the extension of the jurisdiction of military courts is unlawful.

Pinochet's junta pulled a fast one by interpreting "internal unrest' as "internal war" and treating an internal rival as though it constituted a foreign attack. The extensive outline of the Ad Hoc Working Group's findings reads:

> Military courts will have jurisdiction only in cases when a state of siege has been proclaimed in response to foreign attack . . . , but not in case of "internal unrest." The junta could thus mobilize the legal system by using the criminal subterfuge of a phony

war. As a result, normal judicial procedure was replaced by military courts: habeas corpus was ignored, and arrest and imprisonment became possible without any formal procedure.[42]

In Poland such tricks were unnecessary because, thanks to Article 33 and the violation of law, it was possible to impose martial law without war. In a de facto way, war was declared on Solidarity and the majority of Poles. In this sense, then, a legal analogy between the Polish situation and the Latin American doctrine of "internal war" is relevant. We are not referring to the wider powers granted to military courts, the militarization of the economy, or the suspension of habeas corpus (for example, by the institution of internment★) alone. *The problem lies in the eradication of the civic organizations created after August 1980* (in the language of the junta this is called a "temporary suspension of activities"). On 25 January 1982 Karol Małcużyński, one of the few deputies who refused to support the junta, asked the Sejm: "With whom does one consult on important matters such as price increases if trade unions and civic organizations are not functioning?"[43] The point is that, as in Brazil or Chile, the activities of "our" junta are not aimed at limiting the spread and effects of internal unrest or at the restoration of the constitutional order. Their primary aim is *to destroy the "enemy,"* to smash its forces and organizational structure. Hence, comparisons with a state of emergency are worthless and can be treated as propaganda because they obscure the dramatic realities. There is a fundamental difference between a limited police operation and a war waged by a regular army. It is a war aimed at extermination.

"Black Propaganda"

The formal and legal aspects of the coup d'état and the establishment of WRON provide only a framework for understanding the social reality after 13 December. The portrait of the junta was created by its own actions, primarily its propaganda. Its propaganda, even while it distorts reality, reflects the junta's style, mentality, and anxieties. Although it resorts to lies and conscious manipulation, it still contains a paradoxical truth. By repetition, the junta's propaganda tries to transform these incantations into a fictitious reality that social groups will come to internalize. Several years ago Michał Głowiński wrote that a characteristic trait of "newspeak"* is the use of a kind of magic: "Words do not exactly refer to reality, they do not exactly describe it, they rather create it. What has been authoritatively said becomes a reality."[44]

However, this description only fits an "ideal type" of propaganda; it emphasizes its ultimate goal. What we have today seems to strive for this "ideal" by dismantling "bad stereotypes," "purging" consciousness, "verifying" attitudes, revealing the "truth," and so on. Simply put, before the junta tries to realize its ultimate goal, it must carry out some destructive tasks. This cannot be done by subtle methods or in a nuanced fashion. A butcher's job requires an axe. This is why the junta's propaganda is "black propaganda": a mixture of lies and intimidation, absurdities that violate the existing consciousness of society but that are augmented by force and practical measures.

The junta's propaganda is based on *a theory of the enemy*. Without embarking on a discussion on the varieties and particulars of such theories, we shall only say here that the dichotomous vision of the world and of social conflicts ("good guys against bad guys") is its constitutive trait. This trait alone, however, is not enough. It must also offer *a procedure for demonizing* this dichotomy. [Max] Horkheimer and [Theodor] Adorno describe the end result:

> Obscurantist systems allow us today to achieve something which, in the Middle Ages, was made possible by the official myth of the devil: to arbitrarily assign the world outside a sense just like the one an individual paranoiac gives it according to his/her own peculiar pattern. Because nobody else sees this is exactly why this seems so mad.[45]

Notwithstanding the citation above, its fundamental element remains unchanged: the desire to create a delusional reality and a belief in the real power of incantations as observed by Głowiński. One practical step in operationalizing this procedure is the creation of *an image of the enemy*.

The image of the enemy is uncommonly lively, revealing several of the "black propaganda's" substantive levels. This is a result of both the richness and the complexity of the empirical material, as well as of the size of the audience to which the propaganda is addressed. This propaganda is addressed to both the "losers" and the "winners." In the "losers," it is designed to raise doubts and strike terror. For the "winners," it confirms their belief that the coup was "necessary and beneficial." The image of the enemy is created by *attributing specific purposes, methods, motives, and characteristics* to them.

Each level of propaganda supposedly "unmasks" and shows the "true" face of the enemy. Thanks to these measures, everything that occurred between August [1980] and December [1981] has begun to come into question. People begin to have doubts about the past seventeen months because the concrete events discussed in the "black propaganda" are always depicted as evidence of hostile activity. Workers' protest is depicted as having a "healthy core," always constructive and never radical. Yet it remains a murky and imprecise abstraction. This is understandable because to create an "enemy" by attributing certain characteristics to them one must start by obscuring their social base, and its mass and relatively autonomous activities.

However, this procedure brings incredible results at first. The public consciousness begins to reflect not only the memory of the events prior to the coup d'état, but the effects of the "black propaganda" as well. Certain characteristic cracks and paradoxical rationalizations of events begin to appear, yet remain at odds with the fictitious reality presented in the propaganda. It is enough to cite just one example of how some weeks after the coup a blue-collar worker from the "Świerczewski" Metal Factory in Warsaw saw the history of the last several months: "The fact is that the feelings of Solidarity members had radicalized considerably. This was, in my opinion, used by extremists for their own political ends, and this in particular, not just the workers' honestly motivated radicalism, was the cause of Solidarity's abandonment of its statutory provisions."[46]

Re: purposes. As a rule, the long-term aims of "black propaganda" are very vague. The Confederation for an Independent Poland★ [KPN] is an exception to this rule. Its aims are explicitly defined as subversive. Also, "black propaganda" readily uses the method of "unwarranted inference."

The former minister of culture and the arts, Zygmunt Najdowski, gives perhaps the shortest description of the enemy's aims: "The struggle revolved not so much about power as about socialism. The question of power was a secondary derivative of the general issue."[47] Such a description, although not saying much, has the virtue of going beyond "black propaganda," ideologizing the conflict of aims, and thus ennobling the enemy. The same can be said about the descriptions formulated in the language of specialists in the "techniques of power." As they formulate the issue, the problem of power (of the state) is stressed as a goal in itself, pushing the question of ideological choices into the shadows. Nevertheless, they do observe the principle of a certain minimum respect for the enemy.

"Black propagandists" present the enemy's aims in a different fashion. In their depiction there is, for instance, no difference between the Solidarity leadership and the Gierek team. The "extremists" also want to "get their share of the proverbial spoils, but by destroying the socialist state and seizing power."[48] These shoddy morals are, in turn, attributed to spiritual nihilism. The enemy is somehow associated with secret international centers who harbor sinister designs. Thus we can read that "the leaders of KOR [Workers' Defense Committee]* are really jackals of ultraleft international revolution. They are widely known for their firm ideological and organizational connections with the Fourth [Trotskyist] International and are a nest of sworn enemies to all the spiritual values that underlie the nation's well-being."[49] In "black propaganda" that refers to ideology, the charge of Trotskyism is made often. The authors of "black propaganda" are very well aware that what this means is lost on 99.9 percent of Poles, and they try to capitalize on this.

The attempts to concretize the enemy's aims in so general a fashion boils down either to a partial description of some aims or to the postulation of some aim on the basis of an "unwarranted inference." With regard to partial aims, attention should be paid to the problem of economic power. This is a particularly interesting case in view of the public discussion on economic reform, workers' self-management, and so on, held in the summer and autumn of 1981. Here is the post-coup version of this discussion, presented by Lieutenant Colonel [Emil] Bil:

> The economic reform as worked out by Solidarity's economic experts was the key to a seizure of power by that union. The basis of this conception was a change in the forms of socialist property, among other things for the transformation of social into group property. Workers were thus to take over the state-owned enterprises and to divide them among themselves. This whole scheme, whose aim was reprivatization of the means of

production of a particular sort, was to be supported by capitalist banks, the future shareholders.[50]

The meaning of this text is contained in its last two sentences. They allow for the specification of the enemy's long-term goal by means of "unwarranted inference."

"Unwarranted inference" makes it possible to attribute to the enemy a purpose that, although it is meant to be kept secret from "the masses," can be deduced from the enemy's presumed desire to destroy the state and "really existing socialism." As much as Lieutenant Colonel Bil restricts himself to writing about "reprivatization of a particular sort," R. Karpiński explicitly writes that the enemy's main goal was "to gradually restore capitalist relations in the economic structure of society."[51] A staff reporter for the official army newspaper makes it perfectly clear by revealing that what the enemy was actually up to was the introduction of fascism in Poland [!]: "Surely, capitalism would be restored by force, but then it would adopt its most degenerate forms. I will not state its name, but we know it all too well."[52]

In short, these are the aims of the enemy as presented in the "black propaganda." In our analysis, we say nothing of a number of details related to, for example, the Independent Student Union, Rural Solidarity, factory self-management, and other independent organizations. After all, our point is not to capture every nuance of the propaganda, but to recognize its basic line.

Re: methods. To reconstruct the enemy's methods, "black propaganda" uses induction. Because there was a coup d'état and military rule was established ("the lesser evil"), it assumes that the Solidarity leadership was planning a counterrevolutionary coup ("the greater evil").

In this case, there is a close connection between the main theses of the "black propaganda" and those propounded by the junta. This is understandable because without such theses the junta would have no justification for its existence. In fact, these theses are directed toward the very plotters and executors of the coup. The theses enlighten them about the dangers they have happily avoided.

The only serious problem the junta faces in this regard is that the military blow somehow missed its target. The only opposition the armored vehicles and ZOMO* shock troops met in the industrial enterprises of Silesia and Gdańsk was that put up by defenseless workers. The defenders did not have arsenals or underground broadcasting stations. The only things the junta apparatus managed to find were a handful of guns and hand-grenades in private apartments. The weapons used by the "Wujek"* miners against ZOMO were their working tools—picks, chains, and axes. Today the "black propaganda" must make up for this flaw in the scenario—by its intensity and the use of every possible medium of communication (including forgeries) and forum (such as the Sejm).

We start with a statement from WRON. According to the generals, the enemy was planning "a counterrevolutionary coup. . . . Proof abounds that in recent weeks they took specific steps in this direction."[53]

Almost two months later, the junta's propaganda had not made much progress in developing and supporting the thesis that Solidarity had planned an "armed coup." They had to quickly disavow some of their "evidence." Here are two relevant examples. Grzegorz Palka's* proposal to establish a workers' guard during the Radom meeting of Solidarity leadership turned out to be a half-baked idea that was not seriously pursued. Also, the intent of the "active strikes"* that had been planned for several enterprises in Łódź at the end of December 1981 was to give the economy a boost by making use of idle production capacity and subjecting enterprises to the control of *legal* self-management bodies, not at "paralyzing the economy." (That active strikes would have been a form of action that could have posed greater dangers to those in power is another matter. Furthermore, the initial preparatory stage for active strikes had already revealed that the authorities were sabotaging production and that the self-management bodies directly supervising selected enterprises were incapable of action.) In sum, to make their claims, the junta and its propaganda apparatus were forced to resort to provocation and "unwarranted inference."

This provocation was quite similar to "Plan Z," which played a significant role in the Pinochet coup of September 1973 "because unfortunately the majority of the armed forces believed it existed."[54] It has to be remembered that Pinochet charged that President Allende and the Popular Unity government had, according to this plan, attempted to murder almost the entire officer corps. The army thus had to defend itself as well as the constitution. In the Polish coup d'état, alleged lists of people to be "eliminated" (including communist party members, Sejm deputies, policemen, army officers and their families, and so on) played a role similar to that of Plan Z in Chile.

Instead of those who drew up these "enemies lists," it is those who were "saved from death" who maintain that these lists exist. Politburo member Albin Siwak, in the autumn of 1981 at a public meeting in Bytom, warned of the need to arm "dedicated comrades" with pistols. He now claims: "Documents found in the building of Solidarity's Mazowsze★ chapter include papers indicating that there were plans to kill me. . . . The list of people to be killed individually or together with their entire families is fearfully long."[55] A Marxist philosopher from the Military Political Academy, K. Ochocki, wrings his hands: "Terrifying and thrilling is the face of the counterrevolution in light of the published (?!) instructions and plans of Solidarity leaders who were preparing to slaughter their political opponents in cold blood."[56]

Even before the coup, however, the junta had explicit knowledge of the existence of "enemies lists," of plans to attack housing estates, and so on. Officers from the army and the Ministry of Internal Affairs were advised about these through their own special channels (such as "secret information" and meetings of Circles of Military Families). For example, the wives of higher army officers living in Warsaw's Stegny district were fully convinced that they would be murdered along with their children. This panic, orchestrated from above, was intensified by specific organizational measures that were undertaken with the help of such organizations as the Association of Retired Career Officers. Members of this association "were aware of the imminent danger long before the imposition of martial law. . . . Someone had to safeguard the security of their houses and housing estates in the face of the danger of an attack by Solidarity fighting squads."[57] This is why the "Rembertów" Battalion, composed of retired career officers, was formed and quartered in barracks *long before 13 December 1981* (only to be dissolved at the beginning of January 1982).

The main purpose of this "psychological war," which included "warnings," "secret information," the "Rembertów" Battalion, and also the "marking of the apartment doors of militia and Security officers,"★ was to consolidate all elements of the apparatus of repression around the junta. *That aim was achieved.* However, the influence of "black propaganda" on the majority of the public has not been exceptionally strong. For this reason as well as others, Colonel Przymanowski made a theatrical speech to the Sejm, using it as a forum to spread lies about a Solidarity-prepared "night of long knives." It is typical that the head of the junta made no comment on this subject, restricting himself to the standard charge that Solidarity had sought confrontation.[58]

"Unwarranted inference" is supplemented by testimony from these "saved from death." All events that preceded or occurred as a result of the coup d'état are rationalized as preparations for a "massacre." Take, for example, the reforms needed in the penitentiary system. The lawyers' community and Solidarity raised this problem before 13 December 1981. Now "black propaganda" not only blames Solidarity for the infamous disturbances at Otwock,*[59] but also infers that the struggle for a humane penitentiary system was mere pretense: "What Solidarity really meant . . . was preparation for additional prison breakouts. Those who managed to escape punishment for their crimes could reinforce the ranks of the counterrevolution."[60]

The strike in the "Piast" coal mine in Tychy, which lasted from 14 to 28 December 1981, is presented in a similar light. The "black propaganda" portrays the one thousand miners who endured until the last day of the strike (initially the whole shift, about 1,800 men, walked out) as helpless victims of Solidarity's terror. Therefore, we must not forget that the strike of the "Piast" miners (they spent two weeks *underground*) was the most desperate and heroic struggle waged by Polish workers to date. Only people who know the conditions in mines can understand just how great the determination of the striking miners must have been, and the menace their protest must have represented to the junta. The "black propaganda" had to belittle its significance at any price. Thus to the provocation of an "enemies list" it has added attacks against union "terrorists" who kept one thousand miners underground. In truth the article by Z. Skuza should be recognized as moderate in tone. Skuza wrote that "the terror spread by Solidarity among the striking miners was just a small indication of what could have happened to the whole of society." Having said that, he comes to the point: "Public opinion was thrilled by the announcement of a 'night of long knives.' . . . Those were not mere empty words."[61]

Re: motives and characteristics. The enemy's morals are always depicted as base and their attributes as repulsive. In this way the "black propaganda" gives us a picture of *people corrupted by money, cowards, provocateurs, and the nationally alien.* Such attributes are not new; they were used in "black propaganda" in previous years and other political crises. One can safely say that it recycles stereotypes deeply embedded in the subconscious of its creators. They have just touched up these stereotypes a bit for a new occasion. There is no sense in dwelling on this familiar problem. It is enough to give a handful of examples that reveal the style of the military dictatorship.

The main theme of a report from Szczecin by Lieutenant Colonel Piecuch could be summarized as: *the cowards from Solidarity do not hurl themselves under tanks but run away to large industrial enterprises.* He writes:

> The "Adolf Warski" shipyard is Western Pomerania's largest industrial enterprise. The peace of the entire region depends on the situation in the yard. Solidarity extremists were well aware of this when they built a nest for their hostile activities there. They did this behind the backs of the shipyard workers, in case anyone wanted to tan the extremists' hide. The declaration of martial law by WRON was their signal—like rats from a sinking ship they rushed to the shipyard.[62]

They organized the union in order to live at the expense of the workers is the leading theme in texts like the following: "Established facts indicate that certain gentlemen who were directing the work of Solidarity chapters, particular sections, and regional branches quickly realized how they could profit from union dues."[63]

Yet these attacks on "corruption" often go awry, as in the attempt to present the withdrawal of 80 million złoty from Wrocław Solidarity's account as a "crime." The affair was promptly hushed up. Sensational news from Łódź was described in an equally naive fashion: "*Workers' Voice* recently advised its readers about the earnings of Solidarity's top leadership. . . . Eight out of the nine of them received more than 20,000 złoty each in November."[64] However, the photocopy of the ledger showed that no member of the chapter presidium had a salary that exceeded 12,000 złoty. The higher payments in that particular month were due to back pay. Anyone who has had even incidental contact with the work of the Solidarity executive boards (especially in Łódź, Warsaw, Gdańsk, and Lublin) could have noticed the doggedness with which audit commissions pursued any financial irregularity. By doing so, they more than once frustrated attempts to improve the security of Solidarity's activities. Today we are paying a stiff price for that.

They were trying to poison the miners—this is how the "black propaganda" describes the incident in the "Sosnowiec" mine. Colonel Zieliński writes: "The District Court in Katowice was to hear the case against W. Figiel on 27 October. Yet the case was not heard because somehow on that day some unknown persons dropped ampules full of a stinking liquid at the gate of the mine, poisoning several people. . . . What a curious coincidence!"[65]

Accidentally, one of the authors of this article was in Katowice on that day. The case against Figiel was not heard, on the pretext that "the district court judge was sick," whereas the poison was spilled when Figiel was still in Katowice. Needless to say, the persons who spilled the poison have not been found to this day.

They are nationally alien and they fight against the church—this has been another theme of "black propaganda" newspaper columns since 13 December. Attacks against Janusz Onyszkiewicz (until October 1981 the press spokesman for the Solidarity National Coordinating Committee), who maintained a rather moderate position, have been particularly fierce. An anonymous author writes: "It is rumored that [Onyszkiewicz] is descended from the same Ukrainian family as Mirosław Onyszkiewicz, the bloody commandant of the Ukrainian Insurrection Army★ . . . who used pseudonyms such as 'Bilyi,' 'Orest,' and others." Having said that, the writer is quick to assure the reader that "these or other relatives of Onyszkiewicz, or those of any other person, should be of no consequence whatsoever."[66] Other union activists are charged with contacts "with émigré circles and Zionist, Trotskyist, and Western subversive centers as well."[67] Colonel Wisłocki, a representative of counterintelligence, said bluntly: "Solidarity's recent actions were largely an effect of the activities of the Western intelligence services."[68]

In turn, the "black propaganda" makes use of the authority of the church to demonstrate that the Solidarity extremists fought this supremely national and Polish institution because they were fighting the PZPR and the government! Hence, Antoni Macierewicz, a nationalist and Catholic from the Mazowsze chapter, was transformed overnight into an enemy of Cardinal Wyszyński★ and of the church. Next, Jacek Kuroń, a former PZPR member, "openly approved of the internment of Cardinal Wyszyński" in 1954 (of course, contrary to the policies and statutes of the party!).[69] Last but not least, Professor Bronisław Geremek★ tried to exclude from the KKP the advisers who were associated with the church.[70] Being nationally alien, he tried to neutralize the influence of true patriots and Poles on the course of events. In terms of characterizing Solidarity activists, the author who makes things most clear is the Marxist philosopher from the Military Political Academy cited above. He writes that "many of the Solidarity ringleaders [were] in point of fact common thugs and psychopaths."[71]

The examples given above convey the military dictatorship's style of national "renewal." Actually, one could endlessly quote their blatant lies, beginning with how the Security Service stages provocations and blames them on Solidarity, and ending with economic fraud. The "black propaganda" is engaged in an all-out war, not against the masterminds of the "armed coup" that might have been, but against society. They have waged war on reason, not on the "enemies of socialism." Colonel Kwiatkowski coldly and cynically observed that he and his colleagues had entered the stage of "defeat of propaganda" (as if in total disregard of the fact that this remark was published in the "black propaganda's" leading organ, *Soldier of Freedom*).

Nothing, however, indicates that the junta will change its favored style of propaganda. On the contrary, one should expect mounting aggression against Solidarity that will emphasize the union's espionage and sabotage activities. With the reappearance of "previously suspended magazines and journals,"* propaganda addressed to the intelligentsia is sure to intensify. Our two-month experience with martial law clearly indicates that there is a relatively large group of intellectuals ready to serve the junta as a "liberal chorus," even at the price of "the destruction of reason."* *Whatever form a "restoration" imposed over the wreckage of a crushed Solidarity assumes, it will require intensive propaganda, which will partially liquidate and transform the "historical memory" of society.*

The Extent and Forms of Repression

The military dictatorship justifies its existence by repressing individuals and institutions. It rationalizes the junta's existence in terms of the effectiveness of its actions to ensure "public security." In the absence of real threats, the repressive apparatus will no doubt create them. The implementation of these plans for *a police state,* however, are a matter for the future. Today the junta faces society's stubborn resistance and is exposed to real dangers.

The almost total blackout of information makes it difficult to assess the full extent of repression. All figures given by junta spokesmen should be treated with caution until they are either confirmed or corrected by independent sources. However, figures are not what matters most. Even the official data concerning the numbers of interned and detained demonstrate the mass character of repression and the junta's ambition to repress all reform movement structures, as well as all social groups and classes in general. Solidarity is the primary, although not the only, target of the junta's attacks. Organizations independent of Solidarity, such as peasant unions, workers' self-management bodies, artistic and scientific associations, and even certain PZPR branches have been subjected to various forms of repression. In qualitative terms, the junta's repressive measures appear to be aimed at *total, not just selective, destruction.* They affect society as a whole.

In comparison with quantifying the extent of repression, it is easier to identify its major methods. Thus, alongside the most brutal forms of repression, such as murder, shooting, and beating, the repressive apparatus also relies on internment, imprisonment, fines, dismissals from work, mandatory loyalty oaths, blackmail, and so on. We must emphasize, however, that our reflections, which are meant to draw attention to the problem, cover a relatively short, six-week period. This is important in compiling *a typology of the forms of repression.* The "freeze frame" period is governed by its own rules, which differ from those of the "moment of transition." An exhaustive "Report on the Repression and Condition of the Working Class under Martial Law" (that is presumably how one would update the title of Engels's famous brochure) is a matter for the future. Perhaps this sounds brutal, but in view of the tragic aspects of repression it is subject to such an unambiguous moral and political evaluation that it ceases to have the character of a "problem." Actually, *the problem to be solved is how to fight the various forms of repression most effectively; there is no sense in discussing the "meaning" of repression as such.* How can one defend oneself from repression? How is it possible to protect people against blackmail that can destroy their character? Where is the line between "normal life" and more or less conscious collaboration with the junta? All these questions require practical answers and actions, so they can be answered only from everyday experience, not through theoretical discourse.

By applying a "quantitative" criterion, we can distinguish two basic forms of repression: *internment* on the basis of administrative decisions, and *prison sentences* by civil and military courts. During the coup d'état and in the first weeks of martial law, these two forms of repression were used on a mass scale. At present (the end of January 1982) the junta seems to prefer summary proceedings to internment.

Particularly drastic forms of repression included killing and shooting at people in breaking strikes directly after 13 December 1981. By the junta's order, firearms were used against strikers in the "Wujek" mine where ten miners died (including three who died in the hospital as a result of gunshot wounds) and also in the "Manifest Lipcowy" and "Moszczenica" mines (in Jastrzębie), where ricocheting bullets wounded several miners. At least three people died in Gdańsk during street demonstrations on 17 December 1981. The number of people beaten by ZOMO is hard to pinpoint because beating was and is the most common form of repression.

According to the official data, 5,906 people were interned during the first days of martial law. By 5 January 1982, some 839 of them had been released.[72] As of 29 January, as many as 4,129 remained interned.[73] With the exception of peculiar "showcases," internees have been kept in jails, often in close confinement (at Sieradz and Włodawa). In January 1982 the rules of internment were made stricter. On the basis of information provided by the justice minister, it turns out that they are analogous in principle to the rules of temporary arrest that were in force until the end of the 1960s.[74] There is abundant evidence that internment orders were carried out with notable brutality. Cases of sadism, such as advising the families of internees that their loved one had been "shot" during an "attempt to escape," have also been reported.

According to the official figures, 1,274 people had been arrested by 5 January 1982. In this same period 170 people were sentenced to prison (including 35 by military courts).[75] By 15 January 1982, some 299 people had been tried summarily for participating in or organizing a strike.[76] On 30 January, there were 205 street demonstration participants arrested in Gdańsk.[77] Since mid-January, the share of criminal cases related to the distribution of union leaflets and bulletins and to the organization of a Solidarity underground has risen steadily.

In terms of the number of arrests, Upper Silesia and Gdańsk are without a doubt the most "privileged." Upper Silesia "leads" in terms of the severity of prison sentences. In this region the longest prison sentences handed down so far have been seven years for members of the strike committees in the "Huta Katowice" steel mill (Wojciech Narusiński), in the "Piast" mine (Zbigniew Bogacz), and in the "Ziemowit" mine (Mirosław Stroczyński).[78] On the other hand,

Mazowsze has so far been treated relatively leniently. The heaviest prison sentence in Warsaw was given to a defendant in a trial of "Ursus" tractor factory workers—three and a half years.

It is difficult now to explain the extreme differences in how Solidarity members in Warsaw and in Upper Silesia are treated. We believe, however, that a number of factors have been significant, including the much greater radicalization of the masses in Silesia, the strategic economic importance of this region (and hence the need to use the "shock therapy" to overcome workers' resistance), the history of greater brutality in relations between the workers and the authorities, the "retaliatory" character of the repressive measures, the region's isolation in terms of communication and information, and the summary nature of court trials. On the other hand, in Warsaw the relative openness of court sessions and pressure from various "interest groups" has exerted an effect on the sentences. In certain cases the junta has preferred to take no notice of strikes and strike committees. It has acted with restraint by trying cases in the misdemeanor courts and imposing fines (as in the cases of the strike of the administrative officers and junior researchers of the Polish Academy of Sciences on 15 December 1981, the strikes in the FSO car factory, in the "Polkolor" television factory, and other enterprises). We think that *one should keep these facts in mind when working out union tactics.*

The severe repression directed against the union's organizations and membership are complemented by less-dramatic measures. Those victimized by such measures form something we might call the "circle of the wronged." Here we mean primarily measures like fines and other penalties imposed by misdemeanor courts for the violation of martial-law regulations (first and foremost: curfew violation). Even if we leave aside the criminals affected by the regulations, there is still a sizable number of citizens who have felt the effects of the junta's rule. It should be added here that among those fined or briefly confined are many participants in strikes. By 5 January 1982, under the terms of the martial-law decree, the misdemeanor courts had punished 30,939 people, including about 17,000 people sentenced to confinement (the latter penalty usually involved the loss of work).[79]

The assortment of repressive measures also includes attempts to break people's character. On one hand, the junta extorts a "loyalty oath" from Solidarity members employed in state-run institutions and on the other hand, it blackmails union activists (either a "loyalty oath" or internment!). Like the forms of repression discussed earlier, these too are directed from above on the junta's initiative and with its approval. They are an important element in the strategy to destroy the movement for reform.

As early as 17 December 1981, *at Jaruzelski's behest,* General Janiszewski, a member of WRON and chef de cabinet of the Council of Ministers, issued the following order:

> Keeping in mind the full and proper execution of the tasks of the state institutions, by the order of the Chairman of the Council of Ministers I request that within the next three days you conduct special talks with those employees of ministerial-, central-, voivodship-, and local-level offices who belong to Solidarity. In the course of these talks they must be informed that further affiliation with this, currently suspended, trade union cannot be reconciled with civil service. If the employees concerned want to continue to work in the civil service, they should withdraw from the union. In case of refusal, their respective work contracts should be immediately terminated in accord with the labor law regulations.[80]

As a result of this order, purges in state-run institutions, schools, and universities have continued, and Solidarity factory committees have been dissolved. For example, under threat of losing their jobs, nearly all members of the Solidarity committee in the Communications Ministry have given up their union membership. In turn, on 9 January 1982 the Ministry of Science, Higher Education, and Technology sent special "Guidelines" to college rectors directing them to ensure that their "staff would properly implement the instructional and educational process."[81] In the mass media, character assassination and purges continue to this day.

On 6 January 1982 in a homily at the Warsaw Cathedral, Józef Glemp, the primate of Poland, decried this sort of repression, especially "loyalty oaths" and forced resignations from Solidarity. "To elicit such declarations from people is unethical," he said.[82] The junta responded to this challenge duplicitously. The communiqué that followed the Joint Government-Episcopate meeting of 18 January 1982 read: "Representatives of the Episcopate voiced their concern about reprisals against citizens and cases of injury to their self-esteem. Rep-

resentatives of the government replied that this was not their intention."[83] This was, however, only a seeming abandonment of such
forms of repression. The junta has not desisted from purges or from
forced "loyalty oaths," although it has tried to keep this quiet. A week
later, however, Jerzy Urban,* the government press spokesman, this
time speaking up as a columnist, left no doubt about what "the authorities' intention" was. In his opinion, purges and forced "loyalty oaths"
were nothing other than the highest form of freedom and manifestation of human dignity.[84]

The most serious form of repression to affect institutions committed
to reform has been the abolition of union freedoms through the suspension of Solidarity and of other trade unions. In post-coup Poland,
as in nineteenth-century Western Europe, modern Third World dictatorships, or normal neo-Stalinist systems, "the workers' cause" is
primarily a subject of interest to the police. Today what constitutes a
crime is not so much an antisocialist or counterrevolutionary activity,
but *trade-union activity*. The list of people detained and sentenced to
prison by civil and military courts after 13 December 1981 is composed
primarily of Solidarity activists and members who continued their statutory activities after the coup. Yet as we have already said, Solidarity
is not the only institution to have been repressed by the military junta.
One of the first decisions of the military rulers suspended the majority
of the legal organizations and associations. The Independent Student
Association [NZS] has been officially "disbanded." According to data
from the Ministry of Internal Affairs, "governors in forty voivodships
have suspended the activities of 380 associations, including forty-eight
nationwide ones."[85] Among the associations suspended have been the
Polish Writers' Association, the Polish Journalists' Association, the cultural societies of national minorities, organizations of lay Catholics—
including PAX,* the Clubs of the Catholic Intelligentsia* [KIK], the
Polish Catholic Union* [PZK], and the Polish Catholic Social Union
[PZKS], the Union of Democratic Youth,* and regional cultural associations. To these one should add all scientific societies subsidized by
the Polish Academy of Sciences, starting from the Polish Historical
Society and ending with the Polish Society for Latin American Studies.
which were suspended by the decision of Professor Gertych, the Academy's first deputy secretary general. In some of the associations and
organizations not suspended on 13 December 1981—for example, the
Polish Economic Society—military commissars in cooperation with

docile board members have been purging "disloyal" activists. Similar purges preceded the reactivation of organizations suspended earlier (for example, PAX). Repression has also affected the self-management movement. Despite the detention of a number of self-management activists, the junta has suspended all previously elected workers' councils and founding committees. At the same time, one of the Sejm commissions urgently created just after the coup was the Commission for Workers' Self-Management. Its only task has been to pass "death sentences" on regional councils for the cooperation of self-management bodies formed after July 1981 and on the Founding Committee of the National Self-Management Federation (KFS), established in October 1981.[86] Relying on "unwarranted inference," Sejm deputies themselves have observed that "these organizations would attempt to replace the abolished "associations of enterprises"* and to seize the prerogatives of ministries."[87] Adam Łopatka, the Sejm commission chairman, who as recently as November 1981 was unable to explain to a meeting of the Polish Journalists' Association why regional councils and the KFS were "at odds with the relevant laws," decided after the coup that the KFS "was a manifestation of civil disobedience to the law just passed by the Sejm." It is worth adding here that the junta has been extremely reticent about self-management bodies, restricting itself to promises to let them resume their activities at some unspecified future time. At the same time, however, the junta has been ruthlessly dismissing all dissident factory directors. Directors who were elected by workers' councils or who delayed in carrying out WRON's instructions have simply been fired.[88]

The forms of repression discussed above are supplemented by administrative intervention in culture, the arts, and education. Publications are censored, theater repertories have been limited, and so on.[89] Teachers have been subjected to indoctrination from above. In both these cases the junta has met with relatively strong passive resistance that has been difficult to break. Take, for example, the "educational campaign" organized by the commissars of the Pomeranian Military District. Until 25 January 1982 the military commissars were instructing teachers in 2,438 elementary, secondary, and vocational schools in northern Poland. From the junta's point of view, the results of this campaign were not too promising: "A considerable number of teachers do not take any part in the processes of socialist education of the young. They do not see, do not understand, or do not want to understand their role in school in the country's present situation."[90]

The types of repression, characteristic of the "freeze frame" period, are at present undergoing a step-by-step transformation. Overt mass repression, based on sheer force, is being replaced by routine police and court procedures. In this particular regard, the junta clearly aspires to individualize repression, to cleanse its repressive measures of the stigma of "arbitrariness" and transform them into "penalties" on disobedient individuals. Undoubtedly, "restoration" based on mass terror cannot be realized. The junta's intentions can be categorized as a transition from *a state of mass terror* to *a state of individual terror,* respectively relying on "offensive" and "defensive weapons."[91]

At least two factors, however, inhibit the path from mass terror ("offensive weapons") to individual terror ("defensive weapons"). First, the junta's policy makes mass protests by workers and other social groups inevitable and thus makes the abandonment of mass terror impossible. Second, the junta is by no means satisfied with the present personnel in many institutions; therefore, further purges are quite likely. A third factor will probably become important in the coming months—the rebuilding of Solidarity's structures and some of their organizational and decision-making abilities. If this process is not stopped abruptly, the junta will soon face dangerous enemies, because every *organized section of society* is opposed to dictatorial rule (however, the belief that Solidarity has influence throughout *the whole of society* is excessively optimistic at this moment). As soon as this third factor emerges on a wider scale, the potential for a return to the most drastic forms of mass terror will increase too.

In "everyday life" certain restrictions limiting personal mobility and allowing the police to keep track of people's private lives will be gradually abandoned. Such restrictions, which are easily avoided by organized structures, are only an element in the "psychological war" between the junta and the public ("defensive weapons"). Restrictions of this sort (such as military checkpoints on the outskirts of towns or the searching of buses and cars) leave the public with the feeling of a sui generis occupation. In its day-to-day activities the repressive apparatus clearly does not take the long-term psychological and political impact of these kinds of restrictions into consideration. Short-term rationality has prevailed over long-term considerations. This all acts to fix the junta in the public consciousness as an isolated clique. It opens the eyes of the workers and other social groups and lets them see that they have been dealing with a system that "secures civil conformity and obedience not on the strength of laws stemming from the national spirit and sanctified by its customs, but rather through fear and the enslavement of minds by the force of bloodthirsty severity and lawlessness."[92]

Economy: From Crisis
to the "Bottom" of the Crisis

The United States Air Force pilot who razed Ben Tre, a town of thirty-five thousand in the Mekong Delta, explained: "We had to destroy the town in order to save it."[93] One can detect elements of the same "philosophy" in the junta's economic measures. Like the pilot who destroyed the town in the name of a "supreme goal," the military dictatorship—also in the name of a "supreme goal"—accelerates the onset of the low point of the economic crisis. This fact, at first ignored after 13 December 1981, is becoming more and more obvious. *The first six months of 1982 will no doubt be a period of deepening crisis, not of low-level stabilization.* The "economic miracle" the junta secretly expected will not take place. Though a number of factors that the junta believed had magnified the crisis in 1981 have been overcome,[94] this has just exposed *the real causes* of the decline. These were in part inherited by the junta and in part created by their own action. Therefore, we will treat opinions like those of an economist from the Military Political Academy, who said that "in 1981 our crisis reached its 'bottom,'" as sheer propaganda.[95] However, it is worth stressing here that "civilian" economists make much more realistic prognoses. Some have even written that "despite the exceptional depth of last year's economic crisis, the downward trend in the economy may continue."[96]

By seizing power, the junta abruptly changed the field on which the problem of crisis has been played out to this point. The elements of "political game," which were taken into account in the anti-crisis policies formulated by the government and Solidarity prior to 13 December 1981, were transformed into the factor deciding the directions for and methods of extricating the country from the crisis. Thus the junta faced the need to reformulate the basic conditions and premises of the anti-crisis policy. Although it may sound paradoxical to those who subscribe to the theory of a "strong state," this task is considerably more difficult today than before the coup. Through terror, the junta has achieved short-term economic equilibrium and political security. At the same time, however, it has increased the sphere of economic insecurity beyond measure. The fact is that *the Polish economic crisis, which manifests itself in numerous technical and supply bottlenecks, is due to the absence of the power centers' autonomous control over the basic conditions of simple and extended reproduction.* The coup d'état has not changed the situation; on the contrary, it has intensified it in the short and medium terms. In the long run, how the current crisis will be overcome depends not only on the junta's fate, but also on the structure of the Polish economy, as well as on its status in the world economy (autonomous or "neocolonial").

In the above discussion of the logic of the "price operation" we argued that the extent and depth of the price operation would inaugurate successive phases of dictatorship leading to the self-perpetuation and particularization of the military dictatorship. Now we move on to consider the other economic premises for this hypothesis, concentrating on short-term processes. We maintain that the economic decisions made at present will have a decisive impact on the basic economic outline of the "restoration" and on future political solutions (see section on historical parallels, above). At present the political consequences of economic decisions are direct and immediate—there has been none of the time lag between economic decisions and their political consequences characteristic of times of economic expansion, and no separation or autonomy of politics from the economy.

Dependence on foreign sources of finance, capital goods, and raw materials makes the junta feel insecure. Certainly, the coup d'état did not create this dependence, but the establishment of military rule heightened the negative impact of this dependence on the economic situation of the country. The "debt noose," somewhat loosened by the "Paris and Vienna Agreements of 1981,"* is becoming tight again. It is a gloomy paradox that the next stage of debt relief will come at the expense of Polish workers and of their living standard. The coup has freed Western commercial banks from "noncommercial" obligations and political restrictions, which until 13 December 1981 made it impossible for them to apply the traditional criteria and practices of international business. Dealing with the junta, it is much easier for the American banks concerned to adopt a rigid position. In the summer of 1981 one of their representatives described it as more businesslike than propping up [the debtor].[97] Next, under the slogan "the defense of national sovereignty," the junta out of necessity undertook an economic maneuver based on an extremely orthodox interpretation of deflationary policy and of the defense of the country's balance of payments. In this way the junta has to some extent met in advance the standard requirements the International Monetary Fund (IMF) sets for governments applying for significant financial help:[98] "The typical Fund program—freezing wages and limiting government spending," writes Wendy Cooper, "is designed to strengthen the balance of payments of countries that are in debt."[99] The standard IMF prescription *always* includes three basic treatments: anti-inflationary policies (including a freeze on wages and curtailment of nonproductive expenditures), devaluation of the national currency, and guarantees for the security of foreign investments.[100] It will be difficult for banks and the IMF to question the opinion of Zbigniew Karcz, director of the Finance Ministry's Foreign Department, who said: "Within the short time since the imposition of martial law, measures have been taken like those suggested to us by international economic centers as conditions to ensure stabilization. Foreign reports emphasized the need to increase coal output and to reform food prices. We have started doing both."[101]

The Jaruzelski government began these measures earlier in 1981. Until 13 December 1981, however, its extent was naturally limited because of Solidarity's opposition to price increases. On the other hand, in the area of foreign trade where the union's "populist" actions (for example, regarding meat) were less effective and often taken in a haphazard way, the government managed to introduce drastic import cuts and this way to accumulate, for the first time in many years, a modest surplus in its trade with the West, to the tune of about $66 million.[102]

The coup d'état made it possible to carry out the "price operation" immediately and to create a "labor reserve." This had already been put in motion in May 1981 after experts from Western banks studied the Jaruzelski government's economic plan and deemed it a mixture of pure propaganda and completely groundless economic forecasts.[103] On the other hand, to defend the country's balance of payments today has become a much more difficult task, and its effects will be felt for a long time. We should remember that after the Western commercial banks had prepared a draft agreement with the Polish government (signed in Vienna in October 1981), other credit decisions were also considered. The authoritative opinion at the time read: "It is estimated that by 1985

[Poland] will need $12–15 billion. There are reasons to believe that bankers would be ready to grant new loans, perhaps in form of financing specific exports, but one can hardly imagine that they would grant a loan simply to finance Poland's balance-of-payments equilibrium.[104]

The coup brought about a radical change in the situation almost overnight. The indeterminate duration of Western trade and financial restrictions, the unresolved problem of refinancing the major part of Poland's debt (about $25 billion, short-term credits included), and the denial of access to the Eurodollar market and to transaction credits diminishes (or even destroys) the pre-coup readiness of Western bankers and industrialists to participate in the reconstruction of Poland's economy. It goes without saying that even today the banks are ready to do anything to recover at least some of the money invested in the Polish crisis. Crazy ideas to invest billions in construction of a highway that is supposed to facilitate the transport of the recovered capital, however, are out of the question. Probably the Poles will have to construct this highway themselves. Therefore, it is worthwhile to study the relevant short-term goals of the junta, starting from foreign-trade forecasts.

The "quantitative" forecast (see Table 1.1) of the Planning Commission can be summarized in four points:

1. The export and import growth indices for the first two quarters of 1982 (columns 5 and 6) indicate that the junta is seeking relative improvement in the overall foreign-trade balance. This is to be achieved through a substantial reduction of the foreign-trade deficit with the West. The forecast for this year's second quarter predicts that Poland will achieve a foreign-trade surplus of 230 million transferable Polish złoty (about $76 million).

2. Compared with 1981, the total foreign-trade volume will markedly decline. Sharp changes in this regard are also planned in the level of imports from both the Soviet bloc and the West. In 1981 the ratio of imports from the bloc to those from the West stood at 1.84 : 1, whereas the plan for the first and second quarters of 1982 provides for ratios of 2.05 : 1 and 1.75 : 1, and 1.80 : 1 for all six months.

3. Foreign-trade policy in the first and second quarters will treat the dollar and the ruble trade zones differently. In the first quarter, the foreign-trade deficit with the "bloc" should grow, whereas in trade with the West a relatively large surplus (compared with 1981) should be accumulated. In the second quarter, the foreign-trade deficit with

Table 1.1. Short-term foreign-trade prognosis (in millions of transferable Polish złoty).

	Quarterly Average (1)	First Quarter 1982 (2)	(2) : (1) % (3)	Second Quarter 1982* (4)	(4) : (2) % (5)	(4) : (1) % (6)
			Soviet Bloc Countries			
Exports	6,525	5,100	78.1	6,330	124.1	97.0
Imports	8,300	7,200	86.7	7,000	97.2	84.4
Balance	−1,775	−2,100		−670		
			Capitalist Countries			
Exports	4,550	4,400	96.7	4,900	111.3	107.6
Imports	4,500	3,500	77.7	4,000	114.2	88.8
Balance	50	900		900		
			Total			
Exports	11,075	9,500	85.7	11,230	118.2	101.4
Imports	12,800	10,700	83.5	11,000	102.8	85.9
Balance	−1,725	−1,200		230		

SOURCES: "Komunikat GUS o sytuacji społeczno-gospodarczej kraju w 1981 r.," *Rzeczpospolita*, 29 January 1982; "Główne założenie projektu planu na I kwartał 1982 r. opracowane przez Komisje Planowania," *Życie Gospodarcze*, 24 January 1982.

*Estimate.

the "bloc" is to be reduced, and at the same time the considerable surplus with the West maintained.

4. If the same trend in foreign trade with the West continues in the second half of the year, this would ultimately produce a yearly foreign trade surplus of 3.6 billion transferable złoty (about $1.2 billion). Such a surplus, combined with grants and long-term financial credits from various sources,[105] would make it possible for Poland to continue paying back *a part of the interest*[106] on the accumulated debt. In trade with the "bloc," however, one can hope, in line with projections, that in the second half of the year imports and exports will balance. All the same, it is highly unlikely that Poland will have an export surplus with the ruble-trade countries in the current year.[107]

We will begin our "qualitative" evaluation of the Planning Commission's forecast with the statement that *it predicts a continued sharp decline in industrial production and in national income* in the first six and probably all twelve months of the year. This decline will result from a negative shift in the income multiplier by a reduction in supply imports from both East and West, but primarily from the West.[108]

The policy of defending the balance of payments through the accumulation of an export surplus *at any price* will make new pressures on real wages and on consumption inescapable. The rate of decline in the GNP is bound to exceed the rate of decline in the GDP.

The junta's "civilian" economists no longer question the thesis that supply imports, particularly those from the West, are the main factor limiting industrial production and national income in the short and medium terms. For example, notwithstanding his grossly exaggerated assessment of the effect of the excessive material reserves and of the coal shortage (because of free Saturdays in mining) on the decline in national income in 1981, Albinowski does not dispute the contention that dependence on imported capital goods and of raw materials was responsible for more than half of the 13 percent contraction in national income.[109] Madej, chairman of the Government Planning Commission, emphasizes that at the present moment "external supplies" are the factor limiting growth in Poland.[110]

The fundamental significance of imports in the Polish crisis is not so much a consequence of the scarcity of specific raw materials as an outcome of the "investment boom" from 1971 to 1975 and the resulting industrial structure. It is estimated that the share of imported machinery and equipment (transport excluded) in the total investments grew from 32.0 percent in 1971 to 57.5 percent in 1975.[111] Those imports were concentrated in several "leading" industries that determine the growth of industrial production as a whole. As a consequence, in many of them the "renovation index"[112] approximated or exceeded 100 percent, meaning that these industries are equipped almost entirely with new machines, usually imported ones. Even more important is that the share of Western imports in the total expenditure on machinery and equipment rose from 12 percent in 1971 to 31 percent in 1975, while the share of similar imports from the "bloc" countries fell from 20 percent to 14 percent. It is worth adding here that the production effect of those imports in terms of labor productivity was imposing. The relation between the index of productivity of the machinery imported from the "bloc" and that manufactured locally was 1.43 : 1, and in the case of the machinery imported from the West it was 2.38 : 1. Last but not least, as a rule investment imports overlooked the intermediary stages of production. Because Poland imported peculiar final production "modules," bottlenecks arose not so much in the industry concerned or in the technological process itself, but because of the country's balance of payments[113] and in the respective balances between industries.[114]

The consequence of these processes is the uncommonly strong dynamic of the Polish economic crisis. One can argue with reason that negative multipliers related to each of the factors mentioned above are usually larger than one and contribute to the "explosive" nature of the crisis. Comparisons with Kalecki's theory of economic cycles suggest that we have a peculiar variant of the crisis of overaccumulation. In this kind of crisis, characteristic of the monopolistic economy, "fluctuations in output mainly reflect changes in utilization of equipment."[115]

In the case of the Polish crisis, changes in the degree of utilization of equipment, especially in the manufacturing industry, are decided, both in the short term and in the medium term, by the volume of import supplies. This means that the cumulative decline in production is not limited by the depreciation level or by self-regulating "brakes" or "stabilizers" built into the system of local production. In theory there is no minimum consumption level of manufactures that could also act as a limiting factor. To some extent these crisis-conducive tendencies find their reflection in the "explosive" nature of the crisis. Therefore, with the present industrial structure inherited from the 1970s, one cannot determine the "ultimate" level of production at which the crisis would "bottom out" or whether it will be above a level where a considerable part of the productive capacity would be depreciated.[116] Neither can one argue that in the short or medium term industrial production and national income will automatically fluctuate near the zero-growth rate, because the forces that maintain simple reproduction are largely dependent on the same factors that govern and boost growth (extended reproduction). Therefore, our conclusion regarding the short and medium terms is as follows: *It is the volume of import supplies that directly determines the "bottom" of the crisis as well as the level around which industrial production and national income fluctuate.* In the long term, as the structure of industry frees itself from limitations resulting from its dependence on imported capital goods and raw materials, the situation can change. This, however, will be a lengthy process. As early as in December 1980, Czesław Bobrowski observed that any significant change in the structure of the economy "will become feasible only when we will be free to choose our investments. . . . We will be free to choose our investments in four to five years, hopefully."[117]

From the figures quoted by Madej it seems that at present only 60 percent of production capacity is utilized on average.[118] This percentage also differs from industry to industry.[119] According to Madej, "the drop in industrial production in the first quarter of the year could be as high as 8 to 10 percent compared with what was produced at the same time a year ago. *In manufacturing this drop will be more serious.*"[120] Several days later, the Planning Commission lowered its estimate of industrial production, expecting a drop of 10 to 11 percent.[121]

Having no practical means at the moment to slow this trend on a wide scale, the junta acknowledged that it was useless to maintain the fiction of planning, and so on 23 December 1981 it withdrew the provisional budget from the Sejm. At the same time, the junta moved toward a hypercentralized system of sectoral management of the economy. Bobrowski made the following comment on those decisions: "I am afraid that enterprises will be managed not by directors but by efficient procurement agents. This threat is becoming increasingly real."[122] On 5 February 1982 the junta forced the Planning Commission to change the provisions of the "Government Program for Overcoming the Crisis and for the Stabilization of the Country's Economy" of July 1981.[123] The junta no longer makes recommendations on such targets as "stemming the downward trend in living standards" or "setting factors in motion to increase national income and product." Maintaining living standards would be at odds with the tactics of the new economic policy, and increasing national income is not feasible within the confines of the new policy in the short or medium term. "Regaining the country's economic sovereignty, reducing industry's excessive dependence on imports, and reorienting industry toward a wider use of local raw materials and intermediary goods" have become the junta's first aim (in its hierarchy of priorities).[124]

This fundamental change of priorities is fully reflected in the draft of the Planning Commission action program for the first half of 1982. Without deluding themselves about the possibility of quickly switching to production using local substitutes or materials and components imported from the Soviet bloc, the Planning Commission adopted a very clear criterion in constructing their program: "The levels of the domestic supplies of fuel, raw, and intermediate materials have been adjusted to the volume of imports. The resulting surplus has been allocated for exports, which should alleviate difficulties in foreign trade."[125]

To clarify this picture, we shall divide industry into three groups:

1. Manufacturers of products for export, weapons, basic consumer goods (medicines and goods to maintain personal hygiene), and agricultural inputs, using import-intensive technologies.
2. Manufacturers of other goods, using import-intensive technologies.
3. Manufacturers of products using technologies that are not particularly or not at all import intensive.

The Planning Commission intends to maintain production, above all, in the first and third group. In the "optimistic" variant (complete satisfaction of the first group's demand for imported inputs), enterprises primarily from the second group will face the threat of having their production interrupted. If, however, the first group's demand for imported inputs exceeds the available supply (the "pessimistic" and likely variant), "special priorities" will be established (these will no doubt include the export and the defense industries). Ensuring that the first group's priorities are met could involve interrupting production even in the third group's enterprises in order to export fuel and raw materials and in this way to acquire the necessary imports. It also must be kept in mind that the volume of imports will be the product of two conflicting aims—to satisfy the import demands of the priority enterprises and to accumulate the largest possible export surplus with the Western countries. In the short run these are competing, not complementary, aims. This, however, makes the Planning Commission only more positive about their conclusion that to achieve their goals it will be necessary "to temporarily halt the production of certain factory departments, and even of entire industrial plants."

It is necessary in this context to mention aid from the "bloc" countries. In light of the economic proposals for the next six months, it seems that the trade agreements currently in force will not fundamentally change the tendencies described above. The increase in supplies promised by the "bloc" countries for the first six months of 1982 will not stem the downward trend because of their general low level. The table above indicates that the value of the *already increased* level of im-

ports in the first quarter of the year was lower than the average quarterly level in 1981. Furthermore, the real value of imports in 1982 will
be even lower in view of the worsening terms of trade, primarily in
trade with the Soviet Union. In 1981 it was 97.2 percent and, as the
Central Statistical Office [GUS] points out, "the sharp rise in prices for
fuel and raw materials in capitalist markets in previous years has now
emerged in trade with socialist countries as well."[126] In this situation, if
the considerable import surplus in the first quarter of the year is made
up in the ensuing months, with Poland's foreign-trade relations with
the West not improving, the conclusion must be that in the second half
of 1982 production will inevitably decline further.[127]

The junta's change in priorities ultimately leads to indiscriminate
cuts in demand (with respect to both production and consumption)
and to the maximization of the current export surplus without setting
any growth mechanisms in motion. *Public endurance* is the only limit to
this scenario, which will make the domestic market totally destitute.
The public's endurance is why the junta has not introduced a new
"price shock" on manufactures. [Prices for manufactures did jump in
February and March 1982.] The "economic technician," quoted above,
declared bluntly the junta's intentions when he criticized its compensation for the higher prices for staple food, fuel, gas, and electricity.[128]

Still, the program the junta has adopted, designed to make the economy less vulnerable by reducing its dependence on foreign supplies of
capital, technology, and raw materials, is in the short and medium
term primarily a demonstration of the country's problems, rather than
a solution to them. *Poland's dependence is too great to be overcome by several "leaps" without fulfilling particular political conditions.* Even the military cannot perform such a miracle (unless they declare the country
bankrupt). This thesis is illustrated by the conclusions of Tomorowicz's forecast after the signing of the Vienna agreement with private commercial banks in October 1981.[129] It discussed the possibility
of solving Poland's debt problem, assuming the goodwill of Western
creditors.

Presuming that the $25 billion due in 1982 and 1983 will be re-
scheduled as it was in 1981, Poland's "yearly liabilities will amount to
about $4 billion both in 1982 and in 1983." The Planning Commission
anticipates $3.1 billion in export revenues in the first half of 1982 and
$6.2 billion for the whole year. At the same time, they expect imports

of about $5 billion. This means that even in the most favorable circumstances Poland will have to borrow an additional $3 billion in 1982. This optimistic variant means, however, that by 1985 debt payments will grow and that it is necessary today to create conditions that will enable the economy to shoulder this burden. Even if we take into consideration Poland's own effort and the creditors' willingness to carry on with their policy of easy access to new credits and terms of repayment, Poland will pay them off no sooner than 1990. By that time, Polish debt plus the interest will amount to $34 billion. This is how Tomorowicz describes the consequences of this optimistic variant:

> My studies reveal that servicing the debt will, in point of fact, absorb almost all growth in GDP until the end of the 1980s. . . . The level of consumption in 1980 will be regained in 1985 and will remain the same until the end of the decade. If one considers population increase, one cannot rule out the possibility that in this decade Poles will not raise their standard of living to the 1980 level.

The number of restrictive provisions included in this forecast[130] means that it should be treated as a first step toward serious consideration of the country's indebtedness rather than as an "operational program" for solving the problem of the $25 billion debt. Needless to say, our reservations on the short- and medium-term aspects of Tomorowicz's forecast are less serious. All the same, Poland will not be able to pay off its debt within the next few years, and "something" has to be done about it, particularly because the current suspension of payments cannot last forever.

All things considered, we believe that during the next two or three months the junta will have to make definitive political decisions on how to solve the country's debt problem. Compared with the profoundness and all-encompassing nature of the debt's effect, all the steps taken so far, including establishing priorities in industry, are only temporary measures. They improve the quarterly balance of trade, to be sure, but at the price of the deepening crisis. Their long-term consequences, especially in terms of creating conditions favorable to solving the debt problem as a whole, are, to put it mildly, difficult to assess as yet.

We also believe that the junta's intention to pursue these policies in the near future, without finding any political solution (both external and internal), is utopian. The three powerful forces that drive Polish politics—the West, the USSR, and internal forces—will not allow the junta the luxury of political idleness and perpetuating the "freeze frame" forever. Meanwhile, options are limited:

- To continue to rule by terror at the price of a sudden (forced or voluntary) break with the West; full subordination to the USSR and a quick, Husák-type "normalization"; and a semi-autarkic economy, which in the next few years will be able to produce only an extremely low standard of living
- To seek a political compromise with the reform movement within the limits marked by the external and internal understanding of the Yalta agreements and negotiate the terms for mass economic aid
- To institutionalize dictatorship, which would reduce trade with the West to a minimum; to negotiate debt repayment and to allow direct investments in several industries if necessary; and to gradually implement a semi-autarkic economy open to the "bloc" and the Third World (the latter constituting a potential source of foreign-trade surplus)[131]

It seems that the last option suits the "spirit" of the junta's emergency economic program and the general "philosophy" of the majority group in the present power elite. The second option, which from the economic point of view is the most favorable one and which preserves some of the reformers' achievements, depends largely on the *political realism* of the program of the reform movement, whether it can be publicly articulated and defended and whether negotiation of its implementation is possible. Certainly this option is not favored by the junta as a whole. On the other hand, we see no real economic or political reason that the junta should choose the first option *today*. It may be "ideologically attractive," and a part of the elite is openly in favor of it, yet a decision to break economic ties with the West, which is very significant to the whole "bloc," does not rest with the junta alone. Such decisions can be taken only by the Soviet Union, and it will do so only if it expressly wants a return to the "cold war." Considering all the pros and cons, the Soviet Union seems to prefer a gradual approach, because the current global balance of power is disadvantageous to the USSR and because of the threat of economic collapse in Hungary and East Germany, which are particularly dependent on trade with the West.[132] Furthermore, the junta, which has not been inclined to take a unilateral decision to halt payment of Poland's debt and to declare the country insolvent, also seems to want to avoid a situation where other governments and private banks take such a decision.

It has to be stressed, however, that the "third option" (or a symbiosis of the first and the third options) depends largely on the junta's ability to play the United States off against certain Western European countries (primarily West Germany, France, and Italy)[133] and to play governments off against private banks. If, in view of the global situation, the junta's endeavors fail and the "Polish problem" is "traded" for compromise in another part of the world, or transformed into one of the many aspects of the open confrontation between the superpowers, Poles can expect nothing else but *a variant of ruthless military and police dictatorship*. In this last case, the defense of economic "sovereignty" will mean an immediate, swift, and fully conscious destruction of the economy on an unprecedented scale. Private farms, a structural "heresy" of the Polish economy, will be the first to fall victim to this destructive process. The program of "self-sufficiency in food" will be carried out with the help of bayonets and confiscations and, if met with resistance, by means of collectivization. If the peasants at present hold the junta in check, forcing it to resort on one occasion to the stick and on another to the carrot—that is, to negotiate with them—this last variant will mean an end to this "historic compromise à la polonaise."[134] On the other hand, terror-enforced sacrifices on the working class's part lead to the construction of a backward economy on the ruins of today's industrial structure. It will be able to satisfy only minimal basic needs and to finance modern enclaves in the defense industry and for the luxury consumption of the power elite. Under such a dictatorship, the short- and medium-term aims and consequences of the junta's current economic program will be monstrously aggravated and barbarized.

"We had to destroy the town in order to save it." What should we do to prevent the destruction of our town? What line should we adopt and how should we act in this dramatic "moment of transition" to prevent the transformation of this drift toward barbarism from becoming reality?

Warsaw, December 1981–February 1982

Notes

1. Jerzy Wiatr, *Socjologia stosunków politycznych* (Warsaw, 1977).
2. On 6 January 1982 all these "Leninist principles" did not prevent Professors Wiatr, Franciszek Ryszka, and Władysław Markiewicz from giving their blessing to military dictatorship in front of television cameras.
3. Jadwiga Staniszkis, "Rewolucji się nie robi, ona przychodzi sama," *Wektory*, August 1981; see also Henryk Szlajfer, "Od protestu do przewrotu społecznego," *NTO*, May 1981.
4. Władysław Bieńkowski, "Czy narodziny nowego ustroju?" *Kryteria*, 10 December 1981.
5. J. Michalczak, "Czas na rehabilitację," *Żołnierz Wolności* [henceforth cited as *ŻW*], 5 January 1982.
6. Stanisław Ossowski, "Struktura klasowa w społecznej świadomości," in *Dzieła*, vol. 5 (Warsaw, 1968).
7. Quoted from Wojciech Karpiński and Marcin Król, *Sylwetki polityczne XIX wieku* (Kraków, 1974).
8. "The 1905 revolution," wrote Camus, "started with a strike in a Moscow printing house where the workers demanded that periods and commas be counted like letters in calculating their output." Albert Camus, *Eseje* (Warsaw, 1971).
9. Leszek Kołakowski, *Świadomość religijna i więź kościelna* (Warsaw, 1965).
10. Michał Kalecki, "Uwagi o reformie przełomowej," in *Dzieła*, vol. 2 (Warsaw, 1980).
11. Cited in Jerzy Szacki, *Kontrrewolucyjne paradoksy* (Warsaw, 1965).
12. Directly related to this problem is the origin of the concept for a Social Council for the National Economy. A discussion on a "Social Agreement on Behalf of Reform," held in summer 1981 by representatives of the leadership of Solidarity, the "Network of Solidarity Works Committees in Leading Enterprises," the "Group on Behalf of Interregional Cooperation of Self-Management Bodies," and the "Civic Committee for Economic Reform," which preceded that idea, clearly indicated the lack of a material basis for continued demands for increased wages.
13. Georg Lukács, *Political Writings, 1919–1929* (London, 1968). Cited in Istvan Meszaros, "Political Power and Dissent in Postrevolutionary Societies," *New Left Review* 108 (1978).
14. Ibid.
15. *Rzeczpospolita*, 14 January 1982.
16. *Mały Rocznik Statystyczny* (Warsaw, 1981), 81.
17. Edward Lipiński, "Kształtowanie potrzeb w systemie wartości społeczeństwa socjalistycznego," in *Problemy-pytania-uątpliwości. Z warsztatu ekonomisty* (Warsaw, 1981).
18. Michał Kalecki, *Theory of Economic Dynamics* (London, 1965), 161.
19. A few days before the imposition of martial law, the military and at least parts of the police and security apparatus were given pay increases.
20. See "Program NSZZ 'Solidarność' uchwalony przez I Krajowy Zjazd delegatów" (Thesis 5 and Annex 2), *Tygodnik Solidarność*, 16 October 1981.
21. The reader can find a precise description of this procedure in Marx's *Capital* (volume 1) in the chapter on absolute surplus value. One can also find his discussion of competition among workers there.
22. The decree provides, among other things, for imprisonment from three months to two years for "leaving one's work station without the permission of the foreman or the head of the working group." The penalty ranges from five months to five years, if as a result of

the "crime," "work is disrupted or damage caused." In cases of disruption or damages, the penalty can be as high as twenty years. See *ŻW*, 7 January 1982.

23. Tadeusz Grabowski, "Gospodarka w warunkach stanu wojennego," *ŻW*, 14 January 1982.

24. It should be stressed here that the order of the Council of Ministers of 18 December 1981 gives some satisfaction to the diehards. It gives plant managers authorization "under martial law to depart from shortened working time and to order work on days off if this is necessary to implement tasks resulting from martial law." See *Rzeczpospolita*, 18 January 1982.

25. *Trybuna Ludu* (hereafter cited as *TL*), 19 January 1982. Jaruzelski said similar things to the Sejm.

26. *TL*, 5 January 1982.

27. The idea of "social commissions" was a joint initiative of WRON and the government. However, in the provinces things look different. For example, in Białystok voivodship, "the idea to establish social commissions by Party workplace organizations and committees has proved very successful." *ŻW*, 6 January 1982.

28. This was the response given to Central Committee instructors by Kazimierz Barcikowski and Walery Namiotkiewicz (the head of the Central Committee's Ideological Department). See *TL*, 8 January 1982.

29. "Posłanie przewodniczącego WRON, gen. armii W. Jaruzelskiego," *ŻW*, 28 December 1981.

30. *Rzeczpospolita*, 23–24 January 1982.

31. Col. Z. Rozbicki, "W imię ocalenia narodowego," *Rzeczpospolita*, 28 December 1981.

32. Declaration made by WRON member, Lt. Gen. Tadeusz Szaciło during his meeting with foreign reporters on 29 December 1981, *TL*, 30 December 1981.

33. *TL*, 7 January 1982.

34. Ryszard Reiff, chairman of the PAX Association, was the only member of the Council of State to vote against the imposition of martial law. In January 1982 he was removed from his position as PAX chairman.

35. In autumn 1980, Wiesław Górnicki, at present one of the junta's closest collaborators, went into public ecstasy over the Brazilian combination of dictatorship and economic development.

36. Franciszek Ryszka, *Państwo stanu wyjątkowego. Rzecz o systemie państwa i prawa III Rzeszy* (Wrocław, 1974).

37. *TL*, 25 January 1982.

38. As long as they are not qualified as crimes by other legal acts that respect the constitutional order, for example, the Penal Code. However, the draconian measures introduced by the junta do not apply to these cases.

39. The statements by A. Łopatka and Z. Czeszejko-Sochacki come from *ŻW*, 14 January 1982.

40. Its text was published in *Dziennik Ustaw* 38 (1977).

41. Ryszka, *Państwo stanu wyjątkowego*.

42. *Czarna księga: Chile* (Kraków, 1976).

43. *Rzeczpospolita*, 26 January 1982.

44. *Język propagandy* (Warsaw, 1979).

45. Cited in K. Horn, "Przyczynek do psychologii politycznej faszyzmu," in *Faszyzmy europejskie, 1922–1945* (Warsaw, 1979).

46. Col. Stanisław Kwiatkowski, "Z myślą o własnych błędach," *ŻW*, 21 January 1981. We shall return to the theses of his article in later sections.

47. Z. Najdowski, "Na jakim torze . . . ," *TL*, 26 January 1982.

48. Z. Ciećkowski, "Ludzie podobnego pokroju," *ŻW*, 21 January 1982.

49. "Niepolskie ich płody i praktyki działań," *ŻW*, 14 January 1982.

50. Emil Bil, "Potrzebny był figurant . . . ," *ŻW*, 6 January 1982.

51. R. Karpiński, "Scenariusz kontrrewolucji," *Monitor Dolnośląski*, 2 January 1982.

52. Jan Lew, "Pozór i rzeczywistość," *ŻW*, 21 December 1981.

53. "Oświadczenie WRON z dnia 16 grudnia 1981," *TL*, 17 December 1981.

54. C. Prats, *Dziennik chilijskiego żołnierza, czyli prawo ponad życie* (Warsaw, 1979). Until 23 August 1973, Prats was the commander-in-chief of the Chilean army.

55. *TL*, 8 January 1982.

56. Kazimierz Ochocki, "Teoria marksistowska wobec sytuacji społeczno-polityczne w naszym kraju," *ŻW*, 5 January 1982.

57. Z. Godziński, "Batalion kadrowy 'Rembertów,'" *ŻW*, 14 January 1982.

58. *TL*, 26 January 1982.

59. It is worth remembering here that the militia officer in charge of the operation in Otwock thanked Solidarity for its help in ending the disturbances.

60. M. Nowiński, "Od komedii do tragedii," *ŻW*, 20 January 1982.

61. Z. Skuza, "Bezwzględne metody," *TL*, 30 December 1981.

62. Henryk Piecuch, "Szczecin, decydujące godziny," *Dziennik Ludowy*, 6 January 1982.

63. M. Zdziech, "Fajne zabawy za robotnicze pieniądze," *ŻW*, 12 January 1982.

64. "Finansowe matactwa b. działaczy Solidarności," *ŻW*, 8 January 1982.

65. W. Zieliński, "Z tobą, Jasiu, nie chciałbym pracować . . . ," *ŻW*, 18 December 1981. W. Figiel, at present in an internment camp, was the chairman of Solidarity Works Committee in the Sosnowiec mine.

66. "Z zimnym wyrachowaniem." *ŻW*, 8 January 1982.

67. "Kto naprawdę ukrył się za robotniczymi plecami," *TL*, 17 December 1981.

68. *Rzeczpospolita*, 29 January 1982.

69. *TL*, 17 December 1981.

70. "Programowanie dr. G," *ŻW*, 4 January 1982.

71. Ochocki, "Teoria marksistowska."

72. Information provided by General Stachura, first deputy minister of internal affairs. *ŻW*, 8 January 1982.

73. Information provided by Justice Minister Sylwester Zawadzki. *Rzeczpospolita*, 2 February 1982. The unreliability of the official statistics on internment is demonstrated by the discrepancy between Stachura's figure of 5,906 internees and Zawadzki's of 5,429.

74. In the 1970s the regulations on temporary arrest were made considerably harsher. For this reason the justice minister can maintain today that the status of an internee differs "significantly from the rules of temporary internment." Ibid.

75. Stachura, in *ŻW*, 8 January 1982.

76. *Rzeczpospolita*, 20 January 1982.

77. "Sobotnie zajścia na ulicach Gdańska," *Dziennik Bałtycki*, 1 February 1982.

78. The "vengeance" of the repressive apparatus somehow does not apply to former dignitaries. For example, the former director of the Polish Baltic Steamship Company, J. Szymański, who was found guilty of embezzling hundreds of thousands of złoty, was only sentenced to five years' imprisonment. See *TL*, 3 February 1982.

79. Stachura, in *ŻW*, 8 January 1982.

80. Cited in *Wiadomości. Biuletyn Informacyjny NSZZ "Solidarność" Regionu Mazowsze*, 11 January 1982. No representative of the junta has ever questioned the veracity of this text.

81. *TL*, 11 January 1982. By 31 January 1982 among those dismissed as "disloyal" were the rector and pro-rector of the Merchant Marine College in Gdynia and the pro-rector of the

College of Science and Technology in Wrocław. Earlier, on 15 December 1981, WRON "disbanded" the Rectors' Conference, charging it with an attempt "to take over certain prerogatives of the state." The minister of science, Professor Jerzy Nawrocki, resigned in protest against these decisions. See *TL*, 16 December 1981.

82. Cited from a text distributed by the primate's Chancellery.

83. *Rzeczpospolita*, 19 January 1982.

84. He said, "There are cases . . . when free choice can be costly and can involve resignation from one's job and career. However, people should pay a sufficient, but moderate, price for their beliefs." Anticipating the likely objection that this "sufficient price" is unemployment and a life of distress, Urban assured readers that "the present is, after all, an extraordinary and transitory situation." It goes without saying that Urban did not mention any "unintentional" measures or the authorities' readiness to cease repression. J. Urban, "Trzeba wybrać," *Rzeczpospolita*, 25 January 1982.

85. Stachura, in *ŻW*, 8 January 1982.

86. These same *Sejm* deputies, who would not meet with representatives of workers' councils, who had a pretty foggy idea of the practical activities of self-management bodies and of regional councils, declared unanimously after the coup that "both the regional councils for the cooperation of workers' self-management bodies, as well as the founding committee of the National Self-Management Federation . . . are illegal organizations." Cited in R. Kazimierska, "Kiedy nie ma trzeciego 'S,'" *Życie Warszawy*, 20 January 1982. At the end of October 1981 one of the present authors visited a meeting in the "Baildon" steel mill attended by eight hundred representatives of self-management bodies and two Sejm deputies (who attended only after several admonitory letters). After the meeting the two deputies admitted that they "had the wrong idea about the activities of the Council for Cooperation of Workers' Self-Management Bodies (RWSP) in the Silesia-Dąbrowa Region" and offered their "help and cooperation" in the achievement of the RWSP goals. All the same, three of the members of the Silesia-Dąbrowa RWSP Presidium are at present interned, one is in hiding, and one (a pit miner) is out of work.

87. Kazimierska, "Kiedy nie ma trzeciego 'S,'" explains that "after all [these organizations] had the right to make decisions and to exercise control." Yet neither the RWSP nor the KFS enjoyed the rights Kazimierska maintains they did.

88. Particularly severe purges have been carried out in the metallurgical and machine building industries under Minister Szałajda; altogether twenty-four directors of large industrial enterprises have been dismissed (the number does not include directors removed on account of economic crimes). See *TL*, 20 January 1982.

89. See the interview with Director Bieniewski of the Department of Theater and Concert Halls, Ministry of Culture and the Arts, *ŻW*, 23–24 January 1982. In this interview Bieniewski announced increased centralization pertaining, among other things, to appointments.

90. Z. Pazdowski, "Po akcji lektorskiej w szkołach," *ŻW*, 26 January 1982.

91. The Brazilian Moreira Alves shows that the state of terror "rests its power on the permanent insecurity of all social classes. Using terror as an instrument of its policy, it places even the bureaucracy, the administrative elite, and the repressive apparatus within the circle of terror. . . . Censorship, suspicion, propaganda, manipulation, and isolation are its defensive weapons, with tortures, confiscations, unlawful imprisonment, execution, and murder being its offensive weapons." M. Moreira Alves, "Brasil: état terroriste et guerillo urbaine," *Politique Aujourd'hui* 4 (1971).

92. S. Orgelbrand, "Terror," *Encyklopedia powszechna*, vol. 14 (Warsaw, 1903).

93. R. Taber, *The War of the Flea: A Study of Guerilla Warfare Theory and Practice* (Frogmore, U.K., 1977).

94. General Stachura attributed the decline in national income exclusively to factors like "strikes, the torpedoing of coal mining, and the economic blockade." See *ZW*, 8 January 1982. It is worth observing here that, for example, the miners' strikes in 1981 caused a mere 600,000-ton decline in coal output, equivalent to one day's output. See *ZW*, 5 January 1982. Even more, as Stanisław Albinowski wrote, "Last year's decline should be no surprise to anyone. It was forecast as early as April; meanwhile the reality turned out to be even slightly better than anticipated." S. Albinowski, "Diagnoza określa terapię," *TL*, 4 February 1982. The real decrease in GDP was only 13 percent; whereas in July 1981 the government estimated it would be 15 percent. See *Rządowy program przezwyciężenia kryzysu oraz stabilizowania gospodarki kraju* (Warsaw, 1981).

95. Colonel Tadeusz Grabowski, "Gdzie leżą przyczyny kryzysowego 'dna,'" *Rzeczpospolita*, 2 February 1982.

96. (Ch.W.), "Gospodarka w 1981 r.," *Życie Gospodarcze* [henceforth cited as *ZG*], 7 February 1982.

97. S. Martin, "The Secrets of the Polish Memorandum," *Euromoney*, August 1981.

98. On 25 January 1982, Jaruzelski told the *Sejm* that the junta would pursue Poland's application for IMF membership.

99. W. Cooper, "Poland: Will the Soviets Send in the IMF?" *Multinational Monitor* 2, no. 4 (1981).

100. See Ch. Payer, "The Perpetuation of Dependence," *Monthly Review* 23, no. 4 (1971). Solidarity, however, had a very optimistic, nearly idyllic, view of the IMF. See J. Ciechanowicz, "Międzynarodowy Fundusz Walutowy," *Tygodnik Solidarność*, 2 October 1981.

101. Interview with Director Zbigniew Karcz, *ZW*, 11 February 1982

102. Data from "Komunikat GUS o sytuacji społeczno-gospodarczej kraju w 1981 r.," *Rzeczpospolita*, 29 January 1982.

103. S. Martin, "Secrets of the Polish Memorandum."

104. Ibid. From September to November 1981 Western financial circles also cautiously sought Solidarity's opinion on the matter.

105. For instance, several weeks ago the junta received about $600 million from Libya and Iraq.

106. In 1981, the interest on Poland's debt amounted to $2.5 billion. Assuming theoretically that no new loans are taken after 1981, the interest Poland should pay will be $2.5–$3 billion a year in 1982 and 1983. See J. Tomorowicz, "Jak wyrwać się z 'pułapki zadłużenia,'" *ZG*, 11 October 1981. The interest rate for transactions with Poland stands at 21 percent. See "Rozmowy kredytowe," *ZG*, 11 October 1981.

107. The trade protocol signed with the Soviet Union on 6 January 1982 provides for an import surplus of 1.2 billion rubles (about 5.3 billion transferable złoty). See *TL*, 10 February 1982.

108. According to the forecast the drop in Western imports will amount to 16 percent in the first half of the year and over 10 percent for "bloc" imports.

109. Stanisław Albinowski, "Gdy nadmiar powoduje straty," *TL*, 12 February 1982. Although Albinowski shows (though he ignores this fact in his calculations) that the structure of reserves does not reflect industry's demands, he does not mention the problem of the difference in the performance of the local and imported machinery (which again allows him to exaggerate the possible effect of import substitution and the productive use of the reserves already accumulated).

110. "W nowej sytuacji" (interview with Deputy Prime Minister Z. Madej), *ZG*, 24 January 1982. Similarly, Józef Pajestka: "The debt issue is . . . of fundamental significance and not only with regard to 1981, but the coming years as well. This issue determines our policy and chances to overcome our difficulties." [*Polski kryzys lat 1980–1981. Jak do niego doszło i co rokuje* (Warsaw, 1981).]

111. These and other data concerning Poland's imports from 1971 to 1975 come from W. Brzost, *Importowany postęp techniczny a rozwój gospodarczy Polski* (Warsaw, 1973), and S. Gomułka, "Growth and the Import of Technology: Poland 1971–1980," *Cambridge Journal of Economics* 2, no. 1 (1978).

112. This index, as defined by Brzost, is "the ratio between the gross value of fixed assets acquired from investments and the total value of fixed assets at the beginning of the year."

113. For instance, from 1971 to 1974, the value of the licensed products exported to capitalist countries amounted to 1,540.7 million transferable złoty, whereas the hard-currency expenditure involved in the purchase of all those licenses (royalties, imports of machinery, materials, and so on) amounted to 2,184.6 million transferable złoty.

114. This means that Brzost was wrong when he claimed that modernization by "technological cycles" rule out "in advance any bottlenecks in production, because the productive capacities of the entire cycle were adjusted not to the weakest, but to the strongest links in production."

115. Kalecki, *Theory of Economic Dynamics*, 130.

116. The drop in production automatically restrains only that segment of the industrial structure which does not depend on imported technology and raw materials.

117. *Z Czesławem Bobrowskim o gospodarce rozmawia Maciej Wierzyński* (Warsaw, 1980).

118. *TL*, 10 February 1982.

119. The utilization of production capacities in the tire industry is 60 percent; in the textile industry, 70–80 percent; in the footwear industry, 30–40 percent; and in the fur and leather industries, 50 percent. See *ŻG*, 24 January 1982, and *Rzeczpospolita*, 24 January 1982. It is worth adding here that already in 1980 the degree to which equipment was utilized in key manufacturing industries varied, according to optimistic estimates, between 55 and 82 percent. Considering the drop of more than 12 percent in industrial production in 1981, the figures quoted by Madej seem untrustworthy, or even deliberately falsified. In the first quarter of 1982, the utilization of equipment in the manufacturing and construction industries could not have exceeded 45–50 percent. See B. Wyźnikiewicz and L. Zienkowski, "Jakie są rozmiary nie wykorzystanych mocy produkcyjnych w przemyśle?" *Wiadomości Statystyczne* (GUS) 1 (1982).

120. *ŻG*, 24 January 1982. In the first quarter of 1981 strikes were particularly widespread (the struggle for Saturdays off, strikes in Rzeszów and Ustrzyki Dolne, and last but not least the Bydgoszcz provocation and the general strike warning that ensued).

121. "Zmiany w planie," *ŻG*, 7 February 1982. In 1981, industrial production dropped 16 percent, whereas agricultural output grew 4.3 percent. These together led to a 12.1 percent decline in the national income produced.

122. "Od wczoraj do jutra" (an interview with Professor Czesław Bobrowski), *ŻG*, 24 January 1982.

123. "Kalendarz zadań Rady Ministrów," *TL*, 8 February 1982.

124. Ibid. WRON member General Szaciło announced this goal/criterion directly after the coup. He said: "In the future, these restrictions [U.S. sanctions] will help create new means to develop Poland economically." *TL*, 30 December 1981.

125. The main outlines of the plan for the first quarter appeared in *ŻG*, 24 January 1982.

126. "Komunikat GUS o sytuacji społeczno-gospodarczej kraju w 1981 roku," *Rzeczpospolita*, 29 January 1982.

127. There are projects to manufacture specific goods specially for the "bloc" countries. Their production is doomed, however, to compete with priorities of a rank lower than that given to exports or to the defense industry—for local raw materials and energy. In view of the intergovernmental character of the relevant agreements, the production of the contracted goods will itself become the top priority. In the extreme case this can mean a choice, for

example, between a color television set for Czechoslovakia and soft soap for workers in Poland.

128. In his opinion, "only increased prices for manufactures can be used as a new weapon in the struggle against inflation in the next three months to come . . . ; as an economist I am very worried that in the short run a major price operation produces so little effect . . . therefore we must look for other methods to restore market equilibrium, both as regards supplies . . . as well as for incomes, even if we have to resort to taxes, or raise the rate of savings." See Czesław Bobrowski, "Drugi etap reformy," *Życie Warszawy*, 23–24 January 1982.

129. J. Tomorowicz, "Jak wyrwać się z 'pułapki zadłużenia.'"

130. Tomorowicz's scenario for the respective rates of export and import growth is very restrictive. He assumes that from 1981 to 1984 it will be possible to maintain a 10 percentage points difference between exports (an increase of 15 percent a year) and imports (an increase of 5 percent a year), which seems feasible only after two or three years.

131. It is worth stressing here that the entire foreign-trade surplus in 1981 was created by sales to Third World countries. See "Komunikat GUS o sytuacji społeczno-gospodarczej kraju w 1981 roku," *Rzeczpospolita*, 29 January 1982. One cannot rule out a variant of the "triangular trade" common in the fifteenth through seventeenth centuries.

132. In 1979, Hungary's debt was 2.23 times greater than the value of its exports. In the case of East Germany external debt was double that of its exports. In that same year Poland's debt was 3.16 times its exports. Current payments (principal plus interest) made up 86 percent of Hungarian exports and 55 percent of East German exports. See W. Maciejewski, "Ostro pod górę," *Wektory*, August 1981.

133. France, West Germany, and Italy have not joined the economic boycott of Poland.

134. Current agricultural policy has all the same elements of economic and police terror as those aimed against the workers in industry, although in the countryside these elements occur to a lesser degree and in a different form. For example, the extent and depth of the "price operation" in the countryside were relatively limited: prices for agricultural inputs rose by an average of 119 percent, whereas the price for grain increased by about 50 percent, and for farm produce in general—by 20 percent. See *Życie Warszawy*, 16 and 17 February 1982. According to preliminary estimates, peasant real incomes declined about 20 percent. The forms of oppression differ because the farmer is not just a producer; the farm is the center of all basic production and investment decisions despite the more stringent rules and coercion applied by the junta (contracts for the supply of agricultural products which are actually compulsory, increased and arbitrarily calculated taxes, selective confiscations of slaughter animals and cattle in local markets, and so on). So far, attempts to drastically change this situation have been prevented by a fear of food-production disaster. Therefore one should not expect any "frontal attack" against the peasants. The threat of mass-scale confiscations today can only apply to grain.

2

About the Future

Krytyka, no. 16 (1983)

"Zey" [Krzysztof Wolicki]

There are only two more or less coherent concepts of Poland's future. Although the majority of Poles, and certainly the majority of Polish intellectuals, daydream in order to escape the grim present, they are incapable of imagining the country's future. In Poland, thinking about the future, like many other things, seems to be in a state of suspension. At times, thinking about the future is used to justify an attitude of resignation. Poland finds itself in a situation whose resolution is unforeseeable. Attempts to predict the future become ridiculous and impossible when all probabilities disappear so quickly that it is impossible to predict anything even a year in advance. It is possible to spin out any number of fanciful scenarios, but none of them is probable. Despite all this uncertainty, if there are two images of the collective future, one is free to say—there are two of them!

The first of them could be labeled "papal." John Paul II has enriched the social teachings of the church with a certain philosophy of history that reflects both the messianism of the Polish romantics and Heidegger's "Night of the World" at the hour when twilight approaches. Thanks to this philosophy of history, the church and its social doctrine no longer have to oppose the course of history, as they did under Pius XII, or catch up to history—as many people interpreted the Second Vatican Council. This history has caught up with the church and its earlier opposition, and attempts to catch up are now accepted as preparations for the return of those who left its fold. This repetition of history might also be labeled a return to God. Instead of merely despairing over the poverty of the age (secularization, creeping atheism, materialism, and hedonism), the church now sees an opportunity, reasoning that even if humankind is weak and sinful the similarity of human nature to God's nature cannot be erased. Thus, paradoxically, at the end of the twentieth century, when the Enlightenment's offspring on the Left have lost hope in man's natural goodness and in the progressive course of history, it is the church that continues to be optimistic—but guardedly so.

In this philosophy of history, Poles occupy a special place. Out of all the peoples of Europe they have most strongly maintained their faith in God in its traditional sense and responded with the greatest intensity to this philosophical revival after Vatican II. The Polish faith is both the most parochial and the most universalistic, the most naive and the most enlightened, the most private and the most public, and it is oriented toward the salvation of both the individual and the world at large. This does not mean, of course, that this has been accomplished without conflict or effort, or that it will survive without the individual involvement of the faithful and their church in the earthly affairs—including martyrdom, if need be. Poles are special witnesses to the truth that the path to God is an earthly path that passes through a humanity that is fully conscious of its dignity.

Certain Vatican dignitaries, reportedly annoyed at the "overly Polish" policy of the pope, do not seem to understand that the universal church and the Polish cause serve each other. It is well known how much the church means to the Polish cause. However, not enough seems to have been said about *Poland's religious revival and its role in the defense of society's subjectivity. To date it has provided the strongest evidence for the effectiveness of the church's post-council path and confirmation of its boldest hopes for a change of epochs.* In a way, the hope of the Poles is the hope that the world is returning to God. This is why if the setbacks of the Poles were to turn into defeat it would be a defeat for the entire universal church, even if some cardinals think otherwise. This is why, this time, the church cannot ignore the cause of the Poles, its most significant ally on earth—not because the pope is a Pole faithful to his Polishness, but because the post-council church cannot treat earthly history in a merely instrumental fashion.

Thirty or twenty years ago it might have seemed that the church in Poland, led by Cardinal Wyszyński,★ was primarily engaged in a struggle for survival. Even affirmation of the right of religious freedom was interpreted as the church's right to teach rather than as religious freedom. Lay opinion, even that part of it which was otherwise hostile to sovietization, did not consider the presence of the church and the vitality of the Catholic faith to be absolutely necessary parts of Polish national character. The social program of the church, even if it went beyond its limited prewar conceptions, was then, out of necessity, reduced and fragmented by the radical change of situation. The general public knew little about the program; and, considering the conditions of parish life at that time, it could not be properly implemented. The pulse of religious life was strong, but disconnected from the main currents of public, not just official, life.

Now in the early 1980s, the situation is completely different. The church finds itself at the very center of Polish life. It is the mainstay of all forms of public life (even for nonbelievers), both in direct contacts among people and organizationally. What is more, the experience of Solidarity has proved the church's new ability to participate in the formation of a mass labor movement. Martial law has greatly increased the number of friends it has among the most creative groups of the intelligentsia, despite the controversial character and maladroitness of Primate Glemp★ and the part of the hierarchy represented by Archbishop Stroba★ of Poznań. Strengthened by this experience but also fascinated by it, the church in Poland, especially its most "papist" post-council wing, is inclined to view the situation in the categories of "society against the authorities" or even "the nation against the authorities" and to treat society (the nation) as God's people. On the basis of this identity, society is seen as invincible. The kinship, if one can call it that, between the strategies underlying the social activism of the church, of Solidarity, and of the political opposition that took part in the union, irrespective of communal worldviews and morals, stemmed from sharing one fundamental characteristic: an unwillingness to take political power. There were many reasons for this lack of interest in power. The post-council church definitively rejected all forms of theocracy. Solidarity wanted to organize a society free of the totalitarian interference of the state. The political opposition took account of geopolitical realities. Despite their different motives, this common indifference to power meant that the imposition of martial law and the related change in the policies of the authorities did not cause any major revision of the movement's strategic goals. Martial law disappointed people and left them embittered and despondent as it revealed their incurable enmity toward the authorities. However, there was no disillusionment or deep self-criticism of the type that usually accompanies revolutions that do not attain their goals, do not take power, or do not preserve their own power.

This thesis about indifference to power is obviously debatable. I have disregarded the arguments of the ruling camp, which consistently tried to instill an image of their adversary as political (and even military), because this was the only way they could understand the situation and create a proper mood in their own ranks. It seems that even the list of enemies allegedly drawn up by Solidarity was cooked up not to discredit the trade union but to appeal to the authorities' own ranks. However, in society there were attitudes present in 1981 that may have obscured society's fundamental reluctance to struggle for power. Toward the end of the summer of 1981, when the authorities were incapable of taking action to reform the economy, it seemed to many trade unionists that "whether they wanted to or not" they would just have to take over certain managerial functions. Second, there was a general confusion in the movement about its time horizon, because the ethos of Solidarity placed them in some way at a historical turning-point. If something were to happen at that turning-point, they reasoned, it did not matter whether it happened this month or in a decade. As a result, people began to dream about a time when the Russians, seeing the advantages of the new arrangement, ceased to care about the Polish United Workers' Party's* monopoly on power, or even about a time when the empire would be carried away by the winds of history. . . . The rhetoric of the Confederation for an Independent Poland* [KPN] was full of daydreaming about the "next epoch." The Workers' Defense Committee* [KOR] too dreamed about Finlandization as if it were already close at hand. . . . Although all this provided ammunition for clever propagandists on the other side, the popular movement was not engaged in a struggle to take power. Its actions were limited to demanding that the role and rights society had lost, because of the totalitarian policy of interfering in every aspect of life, be restored.

As I have already mentioned, the experience of martial law and the growing totalitarian ambitions of the authorities did not lead the movement to abandon its basic strategy of refusing to struggle for power. Nevertheless, these experiences have enriched Solidarity's political thinking at least in three areas.

Above all, they have taught us about time. Earlier, the supreme political values to which all popular groups adhered—namely, democracy, freedom, independence—remained unattainable because there had been no specific program worked out to achieve them. From a practical political viewpoint, the idea prevailed that the movement had to enter into a "social contract with the authorities." The authorities did not have a unanimous position toward society's ideals, but for geopolitical reasons they were indispensable. Although Solidarity hoped for coexistence, nobody expected a true osmosis, let alone the conversion of the authorities. This coexistence was to be based on the self-restraint of both parties. Thus the "Program for a Self-Managing Republic"* adopted by Solidarity's first congress was a list (sometimes a synthesis) of the most popular ideas of the movement. This list did not provide for a change of the system of government, but for limiting its scope and influence. For a certain unspecified time, Polish statehood would be a union of two kinds of subsystems—communist ones and self-managed ones. Theoretically, this was not impossible, but it demanded, above all, a well-worked-out interface. This meant a precise legal framework that would be strictly obeyed, based on the social contract signed in August [1980]. Only a lawful government could maintain such a heterogeneous form of statehood. That, however, raised a second question—the legitimacy of the authorities. There is no way one can expect rule of law by a government that lacks legitimacy and therefore relies on faits accomplis and overt violence.

The circumstances that accompanied the negotiation of the August 1980 agreements and the first months of their implementation caused the public to stop believing in the legitimacy of the authorities altogether. They had given the authorities a chance, but only a chance, to become authentically legitimate. Readers should keep this duality in mind. People had questioned the legitimacy of the authorities on many counts. This began with the revolution of 1944–45 (which was imported), included the economic development of the country (which had been squandered), and the "constitutional amendments of 1975"* (which marked the beginning of opposition in Poland). However, the August agreements represented a new start. They opened up new opportunities to establish legitimacy. This would have been possible if the authorities who had just signed the agreements had been composed of, despite the system and its history, Poles just like everyone else. Wałęsa's statement that "a Pole will always come to terms with another Pole" and the assurance he made in Gdańsk that "there are no losers" are the most famous expressions of this chance. In particular, it was obvious that, despite the limited scope of the systemic changes provided for by the August agreements, and even despite the acceptance by those agreements of the constitutional principles of the Polish state, *the actual implementation of those agreements would have inevitably caused the authorities to side with society in a common defense of the national interest against the pressure from the Soviet Union and the rest of the bloc.* In this way, had the communist authorities been faithful to the August agreements, they would have secured that which, except for a brief time after Władysław Gomułka* regained power in 1956, had been the most difficult for them to attain—national legitimacy.

This chance to secure legitimacy was wasted. The communist leadership in Poland has gone into a profound structural decline, a collapse in the literal meaning of the word. If on the eve of the imposition of martial law anyone had tried to draw a sociological portrait of the party's leadership, they would have been absolutely astonished by the lack of any distinct pattern. As a social group, the rulers were reduced to a pack of wolves who growled at anyone who tried to encroach on their hunting grounds. As a set of working institutions, communist rule was reduced to the police and the army, the two establishments most divorced from society, whose only explicit purpose was repression. Thus, in both these aspects, alienation from society prevailed, to a degree even more profound than at the end of Edward Gierek's* rule. In point of fact, this was not only alienation from social reality but also a detachment from the widely held vision of Poland's past and hopes for the future. It was thus an alienation from the nation. Authority that is alienated in this way is not capable of any sort of authentic coherence, of any distinct and meaningful shape, which all authority, even the most draconian and unpopular, must draw from their deep relationship with the people they rule. Such alienated authority is treated like the advanced detachment of conquerors. Their rationale and fundamental reason for being was external—"in the defense of real socialism," "in the eyes of the allies," in the Soviet Union.

Such are the paradoxes of dialectics. Authority that is so alienated, janissary, and servile to its foreign master has only one authentic argument for its legitimacy. It spared the master the trouble of intervention, so inconvenient from the point of view of foreign relations. Owing to Moscow's trust in them, the authorities could present themselves as the lesser evil. The legitimacy of the lesser evil constitutes the third aspect of the new political thinking. It is generally believed that this strange legitimacy boils down to the otherwise correct observation that we would have been worse off if the Muscovites had intervened, and that for Poland, being the Polish People's Republic (PRL) is, after all, better than being a republic of the Soviet Union. The authorities' spokesmen repeat this incessantly, and it is unquestionably their strongest argument. Those who reject this argument and its intrinsic moral blackmail in a fury that is equally justified and helpless unfortunately condemn their resistance to social isolation, and this only enhances the power of this abominable argument.

This is, however, only a part of the legitimacy of the lesser evil. As the rulers again sit in comfort and attempt to stabilize their power, the legitimacy of the lesser evil is no longer sufficient, especially as their power becomes overgrown with the falsehoods and fictitious organizations characteristic of communism. It becomes increasingly inconvenient and embarrassing. In the workshops of regime ideologists, columnists, and ghostwriters, and in forges of "socialist thought" such as the "Advanced School for Social Sciences,"★ feverish work to find some other form of legitimacy is under way. Generals and editors newly promoted to power look for it, but above all, those who seek a better legitimacy summon the ranks of the Patriotic Movement for National Revival★ who thirst for an alibi like a camel for water. For the umpteenth time in history, the raison d'état, "the superior interest of the state," is to provide this alibi. The most zealous of the zealots, Kazimierz Koźniewski,★ cries out, contrary to Słowacki,★ that it is no time to ask about what sort of Poland we want to have, but that any Poland will do. (As a matter of fact, it was directly after the imposition of martial law when Koźniewski cried out. Later he knew better what sort of Poland suited him—a gagged one.) The arguments of the loyalists fail because they are nothing but talk of the lesser evil. The Poland of Kazimierz Koźniewski, all clad in army caps, is to be that lesser evil. All the same, the lesser evil remains an evil. *Evil cannot be valuable. Even those paralyzed by the argument of the lesser evil cannot force themselves to adore it.* The legitimacy of the lesser evil automatically rules out any other legitimacy. In this way the authorities have driven down a blind alley. Their most powerful argument turns out also to be an enduring wall between themselves and society. The wall protects them, but it isolates them as well.

Now I turn to certain features of the papal vision of Poland's collective future. It is first and foremost a vision of continuity. It is not a vision of mere survival, in the sense of enduring, of somehow managing to get by. It is a vision of a tower of strength. Thirty years ago the church feared that the Stalinist terror would break the national spirit. Twenty years ago it anxiously observed the illusory character of Gomułka's "little stabilization."* Only ten years ago it was uneasy with the euphoria that accompanied the prospects for the economic miracle that Gierek hoped to achieve on credit. Now, that same church can rest easy about the spirit of the nation, as everything that could threaten it remains outside, on the other side of the wall. To be sure, one can always find the fainthearted and intimidated, but such people are hardly the building blocks of bureaucratic construction. All real social activity—that is, real national culture—is impossible on that side of the wall. The pathetic disintegration of the Patriotic Movement for National Revival—that cheap imitation of the Potemkin villages erected for the benefit of the czarina as she rode by in her carriage— seems to bear out this certainty. *This means that now the only threat to the identity of the society/nation is the society/nation itself. The other side can damage it but cannot break it. The enemy is external to the Polish world, outside the Polish fortress.*

How long can things remain this way? Should the church fear at least the inertia ostensibly implied by the stalemate described above? Will this situation frighten away the most active—for example, by driving them into exile? First, it is important to remember that continuity means inertia only in the sense of not expecting rapid victories, expansion, and satisfaction. On the other hand, the society/nation, which must persist, will *not only be one with itself but will increasingly become itself,* so that Poland becomes increasingly Polish. Otherwise, Poland will not endure. This, so to say, growing intensity of Polishness will amount to the implementation of Solidarity's model of national coexistence, with the development of all forms of cooperation, self-help, and mutual aid.

Second, leaving the enemy on the other side of the wall may seem to be at odds with the stress put on the need for dialogue and reconciliation by the spokesmen of the church and the pope himself. However, only if dialogue is viewed simply as diplomatic negotiation is it possible to think this way. A dialogue of reconciliation, however, will mean crossing over the wall, returning to the heart of the community. Obviously, reconciliatory dialogue is a negation of totalitarian attitudes. The church's perception of the dichotomous relationship of the society and the authorities is by no means taken erroneously from some socio-political theory. This is an accurate description of the historical situa-tion of the authorities vis-à-vis the society/nation. In general, the au-thorities could and should be on the same side as society. After all, both the rulers and the ruled come from the same flock.

Third, in John Paul II's vision of history, the persistence of the Poles holds a special place in God's plans. Neither the people's actions nor their acts of resistance can bring about a change of epochs. Such change depends on the great rhythms of time, which are controlled only by God. Despite this, only people can effect these changes. It is their moral struggle that shapes the course of history, in the sense that history is the product of human actions and not just another natural cycle in the inanimate world of stars and stones. This differentiation of history and nature is not simply rhetoric. It provides for a real differ-ence between human accomplishment, even if painful, and senselessly suffered catastrophes. Polish persistence is preparation, without which the change of epochs, in both its historic and human dimensions, can-not be carried out. This is the idea of "vigil" the pope raised in a ser-mon during his June pilgrimage.

So much for the first vision.

The second vision of the Polish future is that of the Polish United Workers' Party (PZPR). This view may not be shared by all members of the PZPR, but let us pay homage to Vice-Premier [Mieczysław F.] Rakowski* by attributing it to him. This is first and foremost the vi-sion of ideologists and propagandists like him, who now have a chance to test their ideas in the direct exercise of power. To the man in the street, "real socialism" is an ironic notion. It has sublime connotations, but in reality it means a poor substitute. It is as if someone called Rus-sian moonshine "potato nectar." Therefore, we do not realize that the people in the power apparatus associate this term with quite different things. First and foremost, they associate it with a sense of relief and comfort. Real socialism is connected with their stature. They have made it, and they hold it in their hands. They do not have to compare it with anything else. What are the old books and the dead dreams of the past compared with the harshest of all harsh realities? They do not have to justify real socialism. It really exists; and besides, since when does anything that exists here and now require justification? Before now there was a lot of talk about legitimacy, but real socialism sneers at legitimacy. Furthermore, really existing socialism means that people are what they are and that the authorities see them as they are: rather weak-minded, pretty lazy, fairly cowardly, and very greedy. They do not deserve better than really existing socialism; it is impossible to make anything better with people like them. Our party visionaries have always seemed to find pleasure in texts about Polish national faults and about how a stupid and greedy society pushed its leaders, who were only too kindhearted, to rebuild Poland on credit. Gierek was too soft for them, but the General [Jaruzelski] and "pig jowls" (as blue-collar workers call Foreign Minister Olszowski) will keep a tight rein on them.

Inasmuch as utopian socialism was a product of the Enlightenment's belief in humanity's natural goodness, really existing socialism is based on a belief that human beings are naturally evil. Solidarity, which caused the third great crisis of the system in a quarter of a century, supposedly demonstrated that Poles and socialism were mutually incompatible.

Is this really the case? But why can we not look at history as a paddock for breaking wild horses? Sometimes the horse throws the rider. The rider does not mind though, because the corral is enclosed and the horse cannot run away. A rider who knows how to fall will get up, dust off his clothes, and mount the horse again. In such a vision of the future, the only foreseeable dispute is whether one should first loosen the saddle or thrash the horse on the rump.

The metaphor of breaking horses is apt for really existing socialism because of its notions of humankind and national culture. The understanding of national culture is especially important here. All cultural values are relative in this understanding because of their inevitable "class" heterogeneity. Totalitarian thinking is unable to recognize the coexistence within one culture of values that are not connected by relations that result from and are subordinate to that culture, that stem from different sources, and thus in concrete situations do not work in harmony, but nevertheless do not question one another's existence and do not challenge one another's absolute significance as values in themselves. However, as much as the Leninist theory of culture once justified various forms of sectarianism, under really existing socialism [this totalitarian understanding of national culture] degenerates into total nihilism. All national cultural values become objects for the authorities to manipulate. This is justified in terms of that narrowly defined model

of humanity which is oriented toward the future of really existing socialism.

Under martial law, an American observer with a good command of
Polish told a story about his being invited to a family party at a typical
home of "the new intelligentsia with working-class roots." The guests
included blue-collar workers and intellectuals, but also a cousin who
was a policeman and another who was an enterprise director. There
was talk about politics. The American observer was surprised to see
the policeman and the enterprise director take part in the conversation
without any reservations. On every topic, including politics, "they
were on the same wavelength"; they were indistinguishable from the
others. "They were one with their family circle," the astounded American said. "What does this mean? Is such a policeman good for the
government? Whose side is the director on?"

But assuredly this policeman and this director are quite good for the
government. They do not have to be two-faced and deceitful if they
are so well grounded in their family circle. In their case it is not even a
case of mimicry. They are not even chameleons. These are people who
when they interact in all the milieus in their lives do not put on masks
but adopt the spirit characteristic of the circle in which they find themselves at the time. The essence of the phenomenon is that everything
they say outside of their professional jargon is said in quotation marks.
Speaking in quotation marks puts them under no obligation. Thus the
spiritual life of these people, at least in its discursive part, is absolutely
nonbinding. It is just small talk; thus it does not prevent them from
following orders in any way whatsoever, although it does not inspire
them with enthusiasm either. The images, symbols, and signs present
in their psyches below the discursive level have disintegrated and provide them with no support. The origin of these deadly quotation
marks or, if you prefer, of the gap between the language and the
speaker is explained on a general level by socialization in the culture of
manipulation. The decade of the 1970s was particularly ominous in this
regard. Of course, the movement back and forth between different
social circles is a necessary condition for people to develop the sort of
speech in quotation marks described here. The American caught the
policeman and the director in such an oscillation. Without such mobility, without confrontation with other groups in society, those who
speak in inherent quotation marks remain trapped in the cultural habits
of the circle to which they belong in the most important fragment of

their lives, the habits of their power circle. Even if they remain personally indifferent to the language of power, in time this language is their
only option; without it, they are doomed to be inarticulate. This is
how people sometimes forget their native tongue, although they never
really master their second language. There are many such individuals
among the older members of the power apparatus. (This other circle,
namely, one's own family, inevitably even when there is no movement
back and forth, cannot on its own counterbalance the influence of the
power circle because, in the prevailing model of the family life, it tends
to insulate itself from public life. Furthermore, the privileges that ac-
crue to power within the system seem to be even more irresistible for
women than for their husbands. As a result, the family of a prominent
person becomes even more elitist than he himself is, or it lives as if it
were ignorant of his public position and views, and does not even
want to know about them.)

However, for the social mobility of the people who speak in quotation marks to be desirable and fruitful in the eyes of the authorities, the
silent acceptance or at least toleration of their duality by the social circles they visit is necessary. Therefore, those circles must treat this du-
plicity as something normal. Fundamentally, it is precisely this tolerance that is probably the most important attribute of normalization.
Once speaking in quotation marks is recognized as something normal,
the authorities create the one and somehow indispensable link with the
public that they need—the possibility for cultural corruption.

From the perspective of the view outlined here, the most dangerous
result of the last three years, including the organization and imposition
of martial law, was the undermining of two conditions that allow people who speak in quotation marks to get by. During those three years,
party membership shrank by nearly half. Toward the end of 1983 (according to a confidential government bulletin distributed in three hundred numbered copies), there were 1.8 million members, of whom
one-quarter were pensioners and only 14 percent were blue-collar
workers. This decline in membership has continued. Because of the
age-structure and almost complete failure to recruit young people,
party ranks have been dwindling. People in the thirty-five-to-forty
age-bracket have reportedly joined the party only when this was a condition of promotion to their first managerial position. The substantial
reduction in PZPR membership is of course a sign of the declining
public tolerance for those who speak in quotation marks in their social
circles.

Under martial law, an intensified social boycott, together with the leadership's fear that their subordinates might become infected by public moods, greatly reduced the mobility of these people. Needless to say, both the drop in party membership and the social boycott were conducive to a closing of the party's albeit depleted ranks, but at the price of expanding the herd, so crucial to the system's future. Last but not least, inasmuch as anything of the ruling ideology remained (other than a few scraps hardly worth mentioning), the influence of the authorities on society was explicitly based on the absence of any coherent ideological vision, because powerful and open and ideologically colored attitudes rapidly dispersed throughout society. It became very difficult for those who spoke in quotation marks to feel comfortable with the commitment to change and reform in Solidarity social circles.

Aware of all this, the authorities hope that time will have an effect, especially in "corrupting hope." In order for time to corrupt hope, the authorities must with utmost severity convince society that it is absolutely subordinated and will permanently remain in captivity, but that it can count on certain material rewards. This does not mean the corruption of individuals in its ordinary sense—the simple buying of their services and compliance—which still exists today. On the contrary, this is a substitution of values—entire social groups and the nation as a whole must be encouraged or forced to channel their aspirations and expectations so that they are not at odds with the monopoly of power and the reconstruction of a party republic. If this substitution of values succeeds, cultural corruption will become a real possibility. A captivated people who see their captivity as inevitable will eventually come up with false justifications for it. And before long, they will find virtues in such a posture. Nothing will strengthen the ties between the authorities and society better than bad conscience.

The near collapse of the economy and the drop in the average standard of living will in no way frustrate this policy. On the contrary, the loss of almost a third of the population's real income brings about the kind of concentration on material issues that may make it easier for the authorities to realize their intentions. However, this is predicated on the ability of the authorities to define specific and dependable ways for people to improve their material circumstances. Here, though, things get more complicated. Given the severe shortage of means of production, it is practically impossible to pursue a strategy of extensive growth. Extensive methods will only lead to inflation and shatter the monetary illusion; people will more correctly assess the decline in the value of their real incomes, despite their nominal growth. *This is why the authorities cannot retreat from economic reform.* Thus every corrective measure must rely on *the intensification of the economic initiative of citizens; and beyond that, the majority of measures, on the intensification of their solidarity and functional coordination.* It may well be that neither can be reconciled with the planned total suppression of society's nonmaterial aspirations and hopes. Thus reformers in the power apparatus may feel trapped between the Scylla of economic doubt and the Charybdis of political concessions.

Similar dilemmas emerge when the question of the reconstruction of the system of administration—its degree of centralization and of its political character—is considered.

On the basis of materials that have escaped from the archives and the indiscretions of certain leaders (for example, admissions by comrades Skrzypczak,★ Łabędzki,★ Kołodziejski,★ et al.), it is possible to ascertain the extent to which the authorities pursued a two-track policy in 1981. The piles of idiotic instructions from the central committee to the voivodship★ party committees, from ministers to industrial plants, and so on—expressions of impatience and impotence—were evidence of one track: the collapse of the old central system. Under the surface, established by a set of military orders, a new centralism—martial law—was being prepared. In the first months of Poland's new era, propagandists happily suggested that certain operations that were to reduce the danger of erroneous military orders—for example, expert reports, military brain trusts, opinion polls, and developed reconnaissance—were "actually" comparable to the positive aspects of democracy, with a democracy that prevents anarchy. The managerially minded intelligentsia even believed it. But the truth (which after all was not very deeply hidden) that the military was not the best model for economic and social action soon emerged. When all is said and done, the army is suited to war, and during war you fight an enemy, not reality. If in one's own country one fights its economic and social subjects as if they were an enemy in battle for a bit too long, then one cannot help but conclude that reality is itself the enemy of really existing socialism. Thus with a heavy heart one must restrict the validity of the military model to the sphere of education where wars are merely planned. For this reason the military model is at present such a threat to culture and education, including that of enterprise directors. Meanwhile, the role of the military model in management has been declining, gradually withdrawing to the higher levels. Unfortunately, this means that the direction of the economy is highly centralized. The general's team has taken not only the military commissars and instruments for issuing direct orders with them to the center but also the essence of centralism—the license to dictate the rules of the managerial game at every level. This explains the mad pace of legislative work, if one can call it that, especially the never-ending decrees about the rules of the economic game, which is officially played on a board called the market according to the provisions for reform. In other words, the old command-and-quota system has been replaced—in the name of the "progress of reform" (!)—by discretion to set the rules of the economic game. In a way, this economic intervention by the power center has had a more adverse effect on the economy—instead of issuing more individual marching orders, barbed wire, which will be more costly to remove later, has gone up.

Of course, the overwhelming majority among the rulers who favor stabilization oppose this new military-inspired centralism. When all is said and done, one should avoid using excessively naive categorizations in this situation, for example, that the old *apparat* is naturally opposed to reform. At present, a considerable part of the local and factory-level *apparat* are inclined to "defend reform" against frantic busybodies from Warsaw. Generally speaking, the local authorities would like to reach the bottom and the peace that would come with it, because they believe that the basic conditions of stabilization have already been fulfilled. The strategists in Warsaw know better how questionable these achievements are and how much farther it is still possible to fall, especially if one has been satisfied by crawling along a bottom that one thinks is smooth for too long. To the strategists, it seems that their power center is the only possible source of initiative, whereas the lower ranks are increasingly inclined to see the center as a source of disruption of the hard-won peace. This seems all the more true when too many central initiatives can lead to all sorts of local disturbances. After all, various promises of local self-government were made to avert these sorts of events.

Finally, there is the dilemma of politicization, which although relatively well understood is blown out of proportion. On one hand, there is obviously no sense in aimlessly antagonizing people, and thus the authorities present technical and general justifications—such as the necessity of order, social peace, better management, and greater exports.

In these justifications the authorities inevitably pay homage to socialism and to the neighboring states, but as if this were a purely formal
magical practice, rather like casting a magical spell to get rid of a cow-
lick. On the other hand, the regime has increased its ideological output
in an unprecedented fashion and directly advertises its political credo.
As if aware of its illegitimacy, it has tried to malign and eliminate
every potential rival, even every slightly different concept of rule in
Poland. It is as if it wants to face no alternative.

These two tendencies are so incompatible that one cannot avoid the
suspicion that there are two different policies at work here. But this is
exactly the illusion. There are no factions, different apparatuses, or
groups behind the authorities' inconsistent line. It stems from the pressure of the same hopeless situation on the same ruling group and
power configuration. It is similar to the oscillation in output that accompanies economic crisis.

One of the important legends is the story of the supposed ideological
and political distinctness of the army, namely, the officer corps. The
story begins with the correct observation that in the entire Soviet bloc
the officer corps has lived in the spirit of authentically national uni-
forms and is sincerely contemptuous of the poverty of the political
trash produced by the party and the incompetence of civilian adminis-
trators. It is also quite probable that they feel the same contempt for a
considerable part of the Polish army's own propaganda and didactic
activities. All this, however, does not negate another truth about
which little is said, particularly in Poland: after the cautious purges of
Polish generals in the 1960s—in two waves, at the beginning of the
decade against the generals who supported the Polish October of 1956
(among others, Frey-Bielecki, Hibner, Komar, Zarzycki) and at the
end of the decade against the so-called technicians (for example, the air
force command)—*the officer corps of the Polish army under the command of
Minister of Defense Wojciech Jaruzelski became, without a doubt, the most
loyal ally of the USSR in the ruling apparatus in the Polish People's Republic, except, perhaps, for the Ministry of Internal Affairs.* The organizational
and indoctrination efforts of the command of the Warsaw Pact were
successful because, contrary to all other spheres of endeavor, the Soviet
Union to this day has never disappointed its younger brothers on one
score: its military preparedness and its willingness to use it. In the ideological sphere, the situation is dismal, and it takes an absolute cynic or
a complete idiot to preach the glory of socialist achievements in this

field. Not only apparatchiks but even security men cannot altogether trust their masters after Beria's death and the "Twentieth Congress of the Communist Party of the Soviet Union,"* although perhaps Comrade Andropov will heal these wounds to the heart. It would be hard to find an economic activist who does not believe that socialist economy has continued to fall behind capitalism. Tradespeople know, along with the whole nation, that the greenback is real money, and scientists recognize that discoveries are made and Nobel prizes are won in the United States of America. Even the wives of dignitaries prefer to do their shopping in Paris, not Moscow. . . . All the same, the picture is the direct opposite when we ask about the balance of power and the will to use it, when we talk about the Soviet army. The Soviet army has not disappointed anyone. Polish army officers have every reason to believe that history and their superiors have placed them on the side that unquestionably has the stronger battalions.

The Polish opposition was never known for its psychological acuity, particularly when it came to understanding the mind and motives of its party-state opponent. The reason for this probably was that their enemy's cultural alienation led us to discount them as traitors whose psyche could in no sensible way be of interest. However, when the number of "renegades" becomes sizable, one must admit the possibility that the national culture includes weak points and sick spots that cause desertions and alienation. This is only a seeming digression In the case of the opposition, the sick spots are deeply rooted in our national culture—the myth of martyrdom and the cult of heroic defeat. When Poles hear talk of the fatherland, they know they are in for a thrashing. Sienkiewicz's* *Trilogy* was successful because he wrote against the current (he was supposedly a traditionalist!)—to raise Poles' spirits, he gave two parts a happy ending. Only in *Pan Michal* did he bow to tradition. To the career soldier, this myth and this cult are indeed unbearable. It is not easy to continue the tradition of an army that began World War II with defeat in September 1939 and ended it with the defeat of the Warsaw Uprising [in 1944]. I believe it was a desire to side for once with the winners that caused the people in uniform to be particularly susceptible to General Jaruzelski's arguments.

The situation obviously resembles Stalin's philosophy of history. However, this time the historical destiny of the proletariat is embodied in the mission of a great power whose most, and perhaps only, efficient tool is the armed forces and the forces supporting them, namely, the political commissars of the military—the only satisfied consumers under really existing socialism.

This leads to a final bit of wisdom on the party's vision. Really existing socialism has lost every competition. It does not lead to happiness, freedom, or well-being. It cannot make shoes or write books. But it is and shall remain. Time is on its side. Nothing will defeat it. This corral, where horses are broken, is actually doubly locked. The new-style Marxist-Leninists have bet on the rock-solid permanence of the Soviet Union, under whose cover they will finally be able to comfortably furnish their own hut. Their only true aspiration is the comfort of power.

A philosopher might add at this point that although Vice-Premier Rakowski has the arrogance and vigor of a stable boy, authorities that thirst so strongly for comfort are already very old, ripe for death.

Comments

I have probably abused the reader's good faith; having promised to present two visions of Poland's future, I presented something that was at best an attempt to describe attitudes and tendencies that come to the fore when one tries to depict this future. Perhaps it was not without its use, provided the reader noticed what those two visions had in common despite the extreme differences between them. Like the angel and the devil, they have one trait in common—they both belong to the world of metaphysics. Both these visions belong to the philosophy of history—and to the philosophy of history that smacks of metaphysics—not to politics. In their respective worlds, they both enjoy ultimate approval and external guarantee—whether holy or Soviet. They are both beyond time inasmuch as the passage of time does not change their basic assumptions. This has its reasons. Neither of the institutions behind these visions, the Polish church and the party, is currently engaged in politics. Probably they simply do not have any. With its great talent for timing, the institutional church probably thinks that for now there is simply a break in the game, a political recess, and this suits the church very well. The church is praying. But the party is ruling. Can one rule without engaging in politics? Of course, one can, as long as nothing occurs that requires a political reaction—that is, as long as neither one's allies, nor one's adversaries or enemies, nor the relations between them, change. To rule a country is a routine job. This is what complete stabilization would look like. If, moreover, everyone found such a state of affairs normal, it would mean that normalization had been achieved.

Nobody needs to be convinced that stabilization in Poland has gone badly. Still, the rulers seem to be convinced that the processes they have started will inevitably lead to stabilization. This indicates that although we have not yet achieved a state of rest our direction has nevertheless already been plotted. This means that government routine is somewhat more complex than it seems, but as a matter of fact its monotony is obvious: the rulers make various appeals and cast various spells, make various threats and various assurances, even embellished in the same old way, with an artfulness that is not even worth mentioning. It is as if nitwits were playing an idiotic card game—but maybe that is an unfair characterization. The monotony and the coarseness of this sort of "political life" reflect the conviction that everything has already been invented. "Keep the course." The advisers to the present government seem to be getting paid for doing nothing.

Despite the appearance of outward stability and the congealing of the stuff of society, however, a political process has been going on in Poland in all walks of life. The rulers do not realize the significance and extent of this process. I do not believe the majority in the opposition have yet grasped it either. *It is the process of the separation of the nation from the state.*

Society's opposition to the authorities, which has shaped general political thinking and attitudes in Poland since at least the mid-1970s, assumes, if not takes for granted, that certain common values exist. Polish statehood or, in the official language, "Polish reason of state" was one such primary value. Despite the abstract discussions of whether the communist regime ("the system") is reformable or not, the social movement has undertaken several initiatives aimed at reforming the state in the Polish People's Republic (for example, the "Program for a Self-Managing Republic"), thus indicating that it acknowledges common values and that it sees in the PRL a certain common national good, even if imperfect and corrupted.

Directly after its imposition, when people still equated martial law with occupation, they hoped that this comparison was unjustified. The vivid memory of the August agreements [1980], of the peaceful course

of events, of the universal hope for reform, and finally the teachings of
the church and the myth of the national character of the army, all led
people to differentiate the harsh reality of the moment (as a product of
the ill-will of the authorities and of Soviet pressures) from the possibilities inherent in the statehood of the PRL, which had been within a
step's reach. In May 1982, in my article "Under Our Own Occupation" ("Pod swoją okupacją," *Krytyka*, no. 12), I proposed that the
social movement should "prepare itself to take over the state." Although I still support this proposition, I admit that the misgivings I
had then—about how difficult this task might prove and about how
the authorities were efficient enough to block a seizure of power—
have proved to be absolutely justified. To begin with, the opposition
made no such attempt. The opposition's main current—which focused
on building an underground society—consciously avoided political
tasks, which was probably connected to a then still-powerful hope that
the authorities, compelled by the force of realities (economic ones in
particular) would finally agree to some sort of a "reconciliatory dialogue." Because of its trade-union roots, the Polish opposition follows
its own form of economism. It believes that only the economy talks to
everyone in the same language, making misunderstanding impossible.
But to the Polish authorities, who are not supported by any economic
class but only by the bureaucracy, economic facts are telling only when
they become political facts as well, namely, when they can either consolidate or threaten their power.

When the opposition's main current, represented by Solidarity's
"Provisional Coordinating Commission"* [TKK], made preparations
to "remain steadfast in opposition," on the edges of the movement
evidence of obliviousness to the facts and of a peculiar sort of time-
traveling began to appear. The underground press began to publish
texts that called for the formation of clandestine political parties whose
only palpable task would be to formulate programs for a future Poland
(sometimes for her neighbors as well). There was no sense of timing in
plans like these, which provided for direct relations between Poles and
Russians or painted the PRL as a new *General-Gouvernement** rejected
by "the whole nation" whose frame of mind corresponded to the situation one hundred years ago, when, after the defeat of the "January
Insurrection,"* modern independence movements emerged.

However, compared with the efforts of the country's rulers, the failures and illusions of the opposition played an insignificant role in the

process of the separation of the state from the nation. Having always identified their authority with the state, *their own* power with the *Polish* state, the authorities have done everything to speed up and complete that separation process. The process was both useful and convenient to them because it deprived society of unhealthy hopes. Marx treated the state as the tool and property of the ruling class. As everybody knows, *this theory is absolutely indefensible. But as of the autumn of 1983 this is precisely the sort of state the PRL is.* Under the pretext of "rebuilding the authority of the state," the military-party leadership has grabbed ahold of the state even more firmly than before. In particular, the leadership's complete autonomy in making laws, the assertion of its authority over all parts of the administrative apparatus, the shameful willingness of the justice apparatus—beginning with the Ministry of Justice and the Supreme Court—to follow its orders, the unlimited power of the re-pressive apparatus, all point to the conclusion that the state is run by the ruling caste alone. The term "rule of law" no longer has any meaning because law is so subject to the whims and autonomy of the junta. Even further, this "cancer," in its never-ending struggle with forces in society, has tried to bring under its control even the areas thought to have enjoyed a certain autonomy: culture, higher education, and the postreform economy. If some observers still hesitate to call all this the re-Stalinization of the PRL, it is primarily because the more repressive measures are not on a mass scale (this is why those who speak publicly on the authorities' behalf emphasize their masters' magnanimity—after all, those in power are obviously free to imprison everybody), and perhaps also because the rulers do not have an ideology. The "pure pragmatism" of Minister [Jerzy] Urban's* lies are a good indicator of the prevailing atmosphere.

The separation of the nation from the state is the logical result of the line adopted by the authorities. The greater the hope for reconciliation grows, the sooner the separation will be accomplished. This separa-tion, even if convenient for the ruling team now, will ultimately mean its painful death. People like the sociologist Szczepański* or the jour-nalist Osmańczyk* understand this and even try to warn their own side, but their voices are cries in the wilderness. However, we should not show too much concern for the fate of General Jaruzelski's team.

The separation of the nation from the state could be harmful to the nation. Here I am not primarily concerned with the long-term effects of such separation, about which the advocates of iron-handed rule in Poland have always written with great glee. I do not agree with the thesis that the Poles lack an "instinct for the state," although they certainly lack a number of civic customs. To refute this thesis it is enough to mention the efficiency with which Poles rebuilt the country after World War II, and in point of fact rebuilt, after World War I, the independent statehood they had so long desired, and the self-sacrifice with which they preserved its structures during World War II. Slavery intensifies the longing for independence, although it does not prepare one for it. Yet there is no reason to be apprehensive about the Poles' love for their own, independent state. With regard to civic customs, they are mastered quickly in times of prosperity. Nevertheless, this separation can be harmful right now, because it makes Poles unlearn all things political, and we need politics badly. It must come to a situation where the public believes that politics is the only alternative to separation from the state or to capitulation before it. Poles must struggle for a Polish state whether or not the Russians change their policy or the Soviet empire collapses.

To formulate the strategy for this struggle, a specific plan is necessary. Despite this, I make note of the following here:

1. The opposition should not treat the building of an independent society as a task contradictory to an interest in matters of state.
2. Although the overwhelming majority of Poles have been expropriated of their state, on each concrete issue and in every situation, better and worse outcomes are possible, and, faced with this, people must speak their minds. It is also possible that alternatives may be fictitious, and in such cases people must be made aware of that. It is not enough to point to the prevailing situation and then throw up one's hands.
3. The state apparatus is never unified. It is necessary to deepen and take advantage of the antagonism between those who are in command and those who implement those commands.

A situation where a small minority has so completely expropriated the Poles of their state opens up new possibilities for the social movement. *Under such conditions, the Program for a Self-Governing Republic becomes a political program for the organization of the state. On this foundation it should be possible to work out a program to recover the state that would*

*be acceptable to all independence-minded schools of political thought. It is es-
sential for Poles in exile to take part in this in consultation with Poles in
Poland on an equal footing.* Compared with the other Soviet bloc countries, Poland has three distinctive features: private farming, the significance of the church, and an extensive population in exile. Despite recent changes for the better, Poles in exile currently play an insignificant
role in national affairs. The activization of the Polish exile community
is particularly important because since 13 December 1981 the Polish
question has become an international issue. Under the pretext that Soviet intervention was not direct, General Jaruzelski has done everything to make the international dimension of the Polish question insignificant. At the same time, however, he wants to justify his own
actions in terms of defense of the post-Yalta order in Europe ("the
European peace") as understood by the Soviet Union, that is, in line
with Brezhnev's doctrine that the internal affairs of the Soviet Union's
allies are international matters. The exile community's task is to act on
behalf of a "balanced internationalization" of the Polish question in
opposition to this one-sided interpretation.

The concentration of effort in the struggle for a state of the nation as
a whole and for the whole nation will by no means disrupt the building of an independent society. On the contrary, it is this independent
society, with its own independent institutions, that can articulate such
praiseworthy initiatives. *The point is that society should make greater efforts
on the level of political struggle, and in a manner that will maximally unite all
currents of opposition.* In the face of a goal defined in this way, all partic-
ularistic concepts of turning the social movement into a political party
will recede into the background and become unimportant.

I reject the recently popular appeals for a Program (spelled with a
capital P), and especially the complaints directed against the TKK for
not providing one. I also fully support the arguments of the anonymous underground organizer who in *Tygodnik Mazousze*★ [Mazovia
weekly] caustically and pertinently responded to those programmatic
jeremiads that workers at the Lenin Steel Mill [in Kraków] are not
directly fighting for the independence of Poland but for their concerns
as workers. *However, to make the everyday struggle of workers intelligible to
others, and for it to serve as encouragement and an example for others, the
deeper sense of this struggle should be explicitly and publicly conveyed by an
institution of great authority.* It can be called a Declaration of Rights, a

Proclamation, or even a Program. However, it is important that this document express *something that is already there,* not decree something that does not yet exist. Finally, I will take the liberty of guaranteeing that the struggle for the state about which I have written is already under way.

July–October 1983

3

Language and Pluralism

Krytyka, no. 16 (1983)

Gustaw Lin [Marek Beylin]

During this year's street demonstrations in Warsaw, police easily singled out people in the crowds and arrested them. Because the demonstrators resisted the police in an organized fashion, the small number of such incidents may make them seem trifling. Even if the police preyed on the crowd at will in only a very few instances, I still think that this merits careful consideration.

Solidarity mobilized citizens with social imagination, people conscious of the ideological sense of their protest. Were the protestors who filled city squares members of an already subjective collectivity, or were they merely crowds who had been deprived of feelings of their common participation in a world of values different from the existing one? Are mass demonstrations a lasting element of a program for resistance and the building of a better world, or do they merely offer an opportunity to vent accumulated aggression? Perhaps they have become like the "hate sessions" Orwell described in *1984*? Although the enemy is real, the participants became mere objects united by the immediate strength of their feelings, by the presentation of the enemy— not by their lasting sense of their common fate, future, and ideals.

These are questions of whether and to what extent a society that resists totalitarianism is a civil society, and about the sort of ties that create today's forms of collective resistance. The nature of these ties tells us about the language by which members of a collectivity recognize one another, about the goals they recognize as their own, and ultimately has a definitive influence on the effectiveness and durability of forms of resistance to overwhelming pressure.

I am not talking about the less important question of the positive effects of the demonstrations. This question is less important inasmuch as, unless they go beyond a certain critical point, street demonstrations are only contests of the readiness and strength of society and the authorities. Street demonstrations will not decide who will win; they only demonstrate society's capacity for self-organization. The passivity of the crowd in the face of the police who tear people out from its midst with total impunity can be seen as a symptom of a certain more general attitude. When all is said and done, this is the behavior of a crowd of people who, first and foremost, recognize their enemy and shower their hatred upon it, but not of people bound by ties deeper than a sudden outpouring of shared emotion. Such a crowd gives up its members to the police with indifference.

Therefore, it is worth considering here to what extent Poles remain a society of citizens deprived of their rights and freedoms, and to what extent we have become a collectivity incapable of deciding our own actions, and even one that no longer remembers how precious the right of individual self-determination is. I am absolutely convinced that this danger looms large. To be sure, history is irreversible, but only at the level of global change. One should keep in mind the history of the Czechoslovak "restoration of order"* that Milan Simecka describes so exquisitely.

In considering the grim prospect of "restoration of order" in Poland, I am not going to deliberate on the authorities' policies. They have been and continue to be discussed in detail. The strengths and the weaknesses of the authorities have been analyzed many times, but those of society have not. In discussing the latter, we should start by examining the language used to describe political realities, the language commonly used in the underground press, in political journalism, and in the documents of resistance organizations—the language we inherited from August 1980. The language used by the independent social movement seems to be particularly significant to me. It carries contents whose internalization enables one to identify with the resistance and its goals. It is in language that I perceive the basic means of society's self-identification. At this particular juncture, when independent life has gone underground, I think that the movement's documents and independent publications—which formulate goals, explain motives, and disseminate all that belongs to the sphere of values—determine society's ability to communicate on political issues.

Political commentators rarely mention society—and then only as a given, unchanging element of Polish politics. This disregard of society is not premeditated; it is not a result of the writers' insensitivity to the obvious crisis of values. Society is permanently absent as an object of political analysis because the language we use is incapable of saying anything more than that society is there, and nothing less than that once it is there it should close ranks and be "Strong and ready"* to rally against communism. The language of these two principles (of society's presence in the political arena and its shared anticommunism) is a legacy of the strikes of August 1980. At that time the public at large recognized its common enemy. That was probably the first time in the history of the Polish People's Republic that society defined itself politically. A common language of certain basic distinctions was created on the basis of diametrically opposed pairs of terms, such as the authorities/society and communism/democracy.

The popularization of these truths proved to be very useful. The simplicity of those contrasts had a much greater effect on society than all Solidarity's official statements, which were expressed in indirect language. It was thus a language imposed by our basic human community, and therefore it was very useful at the initial stage of the formation of the popular movement.

The film Man of Iron by Andrzej Wajda most fully depicts society's general political consciousness at that moment. The history of events preceding August 1980 was told in this post-August language and thus revealed these very elementary truths. The film is a fascinating record of the public imagination of the time and of the formulations that constituted the canon of socially understandable content, which allowed people to tell friends from enemies.

This demonstration of one's background was subordinated to the same principles that would rule the perception of reality after August. In practical activities, this sort of language and this kind of imagination made it impossible to rise above the formulas used in Man of Iron. On a general level, we have not risen above these formulas even today. This language of universal community, still employed today, has provided the mass power and motivation for resistance but has made it impossible to differentiate those to whom it is addressed—namely, society.

At this level of understanding, it is impossible to differentiate the particular aims of protest or to deepen the motivation for participating in the social movement. The language of opposites (the authorities versus society, democracy versus communism) has at the same time popularized a conflict-free vision of such notions as "society" and "democracy." However, where there are no more conflicts, there are no more choices. In this language there is no way to declare oneself in favor of any of the noncommunist currents, or to oppose one such current to others. There is also no way to compare different systems of values. This language blends everything into one whole: national, leftist, and church traditions, the Polish-Soviet War of 1919–20,★ the Polish October★ of 1956, the Silesian Uprisings★ and Grottger,★ pluralism and populism, freedom and egalitarianism, the vision of the recovery of Wilno,★ and a vision of the independence for the Soviet western republics [Ukraine, Belarus, Moldova, Latvia, Lithuania, and Estonia].

In this case, the democratic character of the organization is at odds with a pluralistic vision of the world. I believe, however, that it is exactly cultural pluralism—by making choices necessary—that makes possible a deeper and more value-conscious identification of the general goals for which the movement acts. Yet we were not capable of rising above the clichés of unified culture and tradition. The language of collective rebellion and community still governs our political thinking.

Politically, this language is dysfunctional. A political description of reality establishes a hierarchy of goals, formulates strategy, and outlines tactics. In our language of the collective explosion, it is impossible to rank goals according to their importance. There is, after all, no such need, because the vision of the mass rebellion is one of total victory. Why then should anyone bother to establish a hierarchy of goals if the time of triumph is near? What purpose do strategy or tactics serve? This language, first and foremost, relies on notions of spontaneity, openness, and public action. In this situation, a general mistrust of strategy and tactics begins to grow, because they are associated with misleading actions and hidden designs. This way, the full openness of our own plans becomes the opposite of political trickery. Everyone knows that such shenanigans are the domain of the enemy whose goals are base. We, for our part, have nothing to hide and nothing of which to be ashamed.

Our situation has thus been paradoxical from the very beginning. On the one hand, political decisions were being made and actions were being taken (which means that there was a broad sphere of pure politics), and on the other hand, there was a sphere of words (explanations, comments, discussions, and documents) where all was reduced to the impractical political formulas of a language of all-embracing community. At the same time, the categories of national rebellion and imminent victory made it difficult to detect the weak motivation to take part in the antigovernment community. There were indications that activism was on the wane, but as long as a vast organization existed the sense of belonging to the winning side compensated for the lack of motivation.

With a looming crisis in social attitudes, we entered the period of martial law. The crisis of the resistance movement came to light as soon as the myth of a swift victory (under martial law it was transformed into the expectation of a general strike) proved to be false. Also, the shortcomings and the dangers of the language we had inherited became evident. The social bond of resistance came to be situated on the level of a fundamental community that opposed the government in the name of its own past. However, this bond lacked one important element—expectation of imminent triumph. A crisis ensued in the three-year-old community. The factors that had allowed us to identify with the community and to recognize our own people in a dangerous situation turned out to be too weak to overcome uncertainty about the future and fear in the present. Thus a vacuum has emerged between what is and what we can say about it. This vacuum is often filled with dangerous political concepts that, instead of providing ideological rationales for resistance, propound purely organizational motivations.

One of the effects of the sustained communization of society has been the indoctrination of the public with the belief that politics has nothing to do with culture. Engagement in politics was not part of the tradition of the independence struggle. The public viewed political activity—understood as the domain of people on the margins, of redundant people (and, needless to say, of the authorities)—as something remaining outside history and the sphere of values, that is, outside the sphere of culture. Our revolution—which was self-limiting not only with regard to action but also to political thought—did not reshape the sphere of culture to include political activities as well. Therefore, more often than not politics is regarded merely as a capability, as a technique to overpower the enemy. This strictly pragmatic understanding of politics often produces concepts that could be described as purely organizational. I do not intend to discuss all the current ideas on how to resist the system. I just want to give a few examples of reasoning where

resistance free of ideological motives has been placed outside the sphere
of values. In these examples, the notion of resistance has been abso-
lutized and made into an aim in itself, so that the value system provides no reasons for resistance. These reasons lie somewhere outside
the sphere of culture and have become secondary to resistance for resistance's sake.

The first concept presupposes the existence of two leviathans. Its line
goes something like this: now that democratic Solidarity has suffered
defeat at the hands of the totalitarian regime, next time the struggle
must be a contest of force between two equal organizations. We must
beat the enemy at its own game. First, however, we must adopt certain principles of the enemy's organization. This version calls for two
totalitarian organizations—one representing the state, the other representing society. In this way the resistance in the name of values is
replaced by resistance in the name of an organization and the struggle
with the enemy.

Another concept stems from the conviction that since society's resistance fell short of expectations oppositional activity should now concentrate on infiltrating state institutions and even taking them over.
This is a classical concept of the conspiratorial practice of politics. It
can be attractive to a narrow group of activists, but not to the public at
large. This concept too loses sight of values and of any sense of political practice. Such proposals are the result of the resistance's crisis and
its inability to formulate sensible programs. Programs as substitutes
for social activism arise when we cannot propose actions that will continue to erode the system through the creation of spheres of independent social activity.

I want to mention one more dangerous type of thinking. The underground press has for some time debated whether a program or organization was more important. I want to caution the reader in advance
that I disagree with all concepts that limit society's activism to survival—that is, to the preservation of symbols, values, and elites until a
better day—and that reject organized resistance. I think, however, that
the concept of an "organization without a program" is even more dangerous. What exactly does this mean? First, it means that the world of
words, the articulation of thoughts, is less important to the adherents
of this view than organizational ties based on discipline. Second, in this
case it also means motivation to act has been reduced to the community of oppositionists. In other words, what we are struggling for does

not matter, only against whom. I think that we have to ensure that the system is perceived from the point of view of moral, cultural, and traditional values. This orientation toward reality will diminish our tendency to replace state totalitarianism with societal totalitarianism. It is obvious, though, that if we become content with such a view of the system we will not stop the disintegration of the resistance movement.

Nevertheless, it is precisely the adoption of such a "cultural" approach that could allow us to avoid using homogenizing, inconsistent formulas to describe political reality. To give our resistance a dimension other than anticommunism can make the pluralization of society's politics easier.

By finally beginning to differ with one another, we have a chance to strengthen the motivation for participating in the independence movement. Today's resistance is organized according to a solidaristic model of both society and culture. It is based on a formula of organizational differentiation and cultural and political unity. As I stated earlier, this formula, although indispensable and useful at the initial stage of Solidarity's existence, has nevertheless contributed to its organizational crisis.

We lack political pluralism. Pluralism is not based on a number of different democratic and mutually independent organizations with similar programs, but in the plurality of political programs. Political reflection and actions able to influence the public can start when the belief in cultural diversity replaces the dogma of cultural unity. We err in thinking that everything that is not communist is and should be ours. Of course, this could be replaced by some sort of democratic consensus, but individual and group identifications with different traditions and values should be more narrowly drawn. In a situation where everything is in harmony with everything else, there is no room for political thought or for independent centers that create public opinion.

4

Driving with the Brakes On

Krytyka, no. 32/33 (1990)

Jan Kofman

1

The strategic forecast discussed here was prepared at the beginning of the nineties for the influential Trilateral Commission.[1] Although considered noteworthy when it was issued a few months ago, it already seems somewhat anachronistic. Today, in the aftermath of the "autumn of nations," its datedness seems obvious. It is striking inasmuch as this report was written if not at the beginning of the summer then in the spring of 1989, at a time when the direction of change in East-West relations should not have been a puzzle to careful observers of world events, even though hardly anyone anticipated the quick pace of events, especially in Eastern Europe and the Soviet Union. The failure of the analysis attempted by Giscard d'Estaing, Nakasone, and Kissinger is the result, I believe, of both the West's fixed picture of Soviet policy and the West's memory of its mistakes of the past forty-five years.

The strategy the three propose in their report is based on two initial assumptions and on additional theses, which go into further detail. Their argument is weak because their initial assumptions are functionally and logically inconsistent, even though they are in accord with past experience. And thus, inasmuch as the first assumption (in point of fact a strategic aim), indicating the need for the West to pursue a joint policy (based on mutual cooperation and development of a positive program), is correct, then the second assumption (forecast)—"Relations with the Soviet Union and its allies will remain a mixture of containment and dialogue" (17)—has proved to be wrong already.

Were the West to accept this assumption (which fortunately does not seem likely), then considering the course of current events this position would leave it lagging behind the pace of history, formulating incorrect diagnoses or belated answers to the challenges presented, in particular, by this part of the world.

Acceptance of this second forecast-recommendation of the report would have two very serious consequences. First, despite their verbal reservations, the authors of the report treat the "East," the Soviet Union and "its allies," en bloc. In effect, the political solutions they propose barely take into account the distinctiveness of individual "Eastern" countries. Already by the spring of 1989 this approach was wrong. Today, in view of the events of the autumn of 1989 and the winter of 1990, when it is increasingly obvious that the countries of the region are the Soviet Union's "allies" formally rather than actually, this argument has become the fundamental weakness of their proposed strategy.

Second, also mistakenly, under the influence of historical experience, they incorrectly assess the actual balance of forces between the West and the Soviet Union. Because of the internal changes the Soviet Union is undergoing and the difficulties associated with this process, it is no longer in a position to expand either politically or militarily, let alone economically and ideologically. There is a great deal of irrefutable evidence that the USSR is turning inward.

In the light of this, it is highly unlikely that the West as a whole, or a part of it (such as the European Community), will find itself in a political confrontation with the states of the "East."

2

The initial assumptions of the Giscard d'Estaing–Nakasone–Kissinger analysis and its conclusions result from a static conception of international relations as an unchanging product of the relations between the super-mighty of this world. The Soviet Union, as I discuss below, can hardly be seen in this light any longer. Furthermore, for at least a year the Kremlin has not taken the lead in East-West relations. Soviet policy has ceased to be offensive (in the last several years it only pretended to be so), but in fact, has become defensive. It is another matter that

Gorbachev's initiative and flexibility, his penchant for throwing the West off balance with his new ideas on disarmament or the implementation of the Helsinki Accords, had until recently struck a responsive chord with Western public opinion and governments. However, the authors of the report exaggerate when they hint in the report about a sort of Western helplessness in the face of the dynamism of the "new thinking" in the Soviet foreign policy. In the mid-1980s, when the world was still clearly divided into two military-political and economic blocs, the relentless position of the Reagan administration, which neither yielded to excessive sentiments nor was ready to make hasty concessions, brought tangible results, the latter no doubt facilitating internal changes in East-Central Europe, and not only there.

The report by the three well-known politicians leaves the reader unsatisfied, particularly as it concerns East-Central Europe as a region and the USSR. Meanwhile, the changes taking place in the Soviet Union (such as, for example, the urgent demands for autonomy or even independence by Lithuania, Estonia, and Latvia and the similarly strong aspirations of Georgia, Armenia, and Azerbaijan, which constitute a challenge to the Soviet Union's internal order) and the countries this report refers to as its "satellites" have rapidly created a totally new situation, also internationally. Although Giscard d'Estaing, Nakasone, and Kissinger do take note of aspects of change, they nevertheless do not actually discuss their possible consequences. As a result, from its inception, the proposed strategy hardly responded to internal transformations in the "East," and thus can hardly be considered as having practical weight.

3

If we accept the authors' definition of perestroika as a policy of a radical transformation of the Soviet system in the direction of the Western concepts of market economy and democratic institutions (2), then it must be said that it is seriously imperiled by the decline in living standards, the failure of the halfhearted economic reform, and the slackening pace of democratic change in Russia. Contrasted with the faster pace of change (including economic) in, for example, the Baltic republics, this creates dangerous internal imbalances. Although the report does take note of new developments, it is surprising how relatively little weight the three politicians attach to them in recommending a strategy for the West.

The incongruity between the analysis and description, on the one hand, and the inadequacy of the conclusions the three authors draw, on the other hand, is apparent even when they encourage the Soviet reforms that move the Soviet economy closer to Western practices of market economics as one of the West's strategic goals (9). It does not seem to be an accident that they formulate the goal in this way. Had they recommended the radical goal of introducing the rules of the market into the economy, they would have had to have drawn up more effective and precise measures. Their strategic goals also would have had to have been different had they considered the long-term effect of the decentralizing tendencies mentioned above, including the weakening of the stability of not just the Soviet Union alone. A more thorough analysis of the internal situation in the Soviet Union would lead to strong Western support for Gorbachev. To be slow in supporting him, and to limit this support to very cautious moves (as Giscard d'Estaing, Nakasone, and Kissinger recommend), could, in the Soviet Union's present plight, precipitate a conservative and dogmatic reaction, partially supported possibly by Russian nationalism, which would have a definite adverse effect on East-West relations.

4

Western distrust of the Soviet Union, discernible in the report, is a product of past experience. It is absolutely true that for decades successive Soviet leaderships have hardly deviated from the cold war path. At the beginning of his career as the general secretary of the Communist Party of the Soviet Union (CPSU), Gorbachev too saw the foundation and aims of Soviet policy in the traditional categories of ideological struggle and the superpower contest. Since then, however, Moscow has clearly been abandoning its old position. This new approach and the motives related to it play only a secondary role in political practices. Today Gorbachev's men already realize that the Soviet Union is not a superpower, not so much because it lacks military might as, first and foremost, because it lacks the political will and might to respond everywhere it desires to respond. Only two or three years ago the aim of Soviet strategy indeed seemed to be to drive the United States back into the Western Hemisphere and to weaken the European Community's defenses (preferably by politically neutralizing either the whole of Western Europe or its most important part, West Germany). Yet in the present situation, to suggest anything of the sort seems to be going too far (7). Even more important, Gorbachev's men seem to be aware that really existing socialism has suffered final defeat as an ideology and as a political system, and that the way to save the USSR's position in the world in the future, to preserve its relative internal integrity and significance as a world power, is to release it from its economic backwardness and to democratize its political regime, although such a restructuring process could last years.

Gorbachev has staked an enormous amount in this game. Everything depends on the success of the program of internal reforms (economic and systemic), with the USSR's status as a twenty-first-century superpower as probably their least urgent consideration. Thus current Soviet policy is primarily oriented toward creating conditions that will enable the Soviet state to survive a period of upheaval and transformations (the *Foreign Affairs* text seems to share this opinion). A great deal depends on the survival of the Gorbachev team, who have no choice but to continue perestroika, despite the forecast challenged here. It is not at all certain that a new secretary general of the CPSU will follow in his footsteps, only at a slower pace. Such a pessimistic scenario, even if only transitory, is also possible.

In this situation, whether he wants to or not, Gorbachev must abandon the imperial ambitions of Soviet foreign policy, as the country can no longer combine its long-standing expansionism with the requirements of internal reform. Soviet willingness to accept larger reductions in its conventional forces (confirmed by the news from the Vienna conference of January 1990), the withdrawal of military support for the pro-Vietnamese and pro-Soviet government in Cambodia, or greater Soviet restraint in Central America are illuminating manifestations of the turnabout in their foreign policy. The latter decisions seem to indicate that Moscow is prepared to let Cambodia drop out of the sphere of its direct influence and that it desires to put an end to regional conflicts. Soviet troops have already withdrawn from Afghanistan.

In light of this, the West's adoption of the strategy suggested in the report would produce far-reaching consequences. That there were no consequences of that sort, that Western governments understand the difficulties of the reform team, particularly Gorbachev's group, is demonstrated by, for example, the approval expressed by Washington and other Western governments for the questionable use of military force by the central government in Azerbaijan (January 1990).

Yet for Giscard d'Estaing, Nakasone, and Kissinger there can never be too much caution. In the event the present ruling group in the Soviet Union is defeated, they are concerned with leaving the West some room for maneuver, at least militarily. Carefully considered and cautious disarmament policy is recognized as the main (and one gets the impression, a sufficient) tool to effect a relationship with the East to the benefit of the West. Although from a purely pragmatic point of view such a stand is tenable, all the same, as a foundation for Western strategy, it would to some extent limit from the outset the West's ability to influence the course of change in East-Central Europe and in the USSR itself.

5

This would be a serious mistake, especially in the light of facts that question the rationality of the relative minimalism of the proposed strategy's goals. The Soviet retreat from its current hegemonic relationship with the satellite states (which the report did not foresee) is a significant case of a retreat from general principles of policy that had been mandatory to this point. Here I mean the Gorbachev team's actual acquiescence to the complete political, systemic, ideological, and economic break with communism in the majority of Eastern European countries.

The agreement to withdraw Soviet troops from Hungary and Czechoslovakia is thus an important signal sent by Moscow to the inhabitants of those countries as well as to the West. It is obvious that other countries where Soviet troops are stationed will also request their withdrawal. These and other signals seem to indicate that the Soviet Union has abandoned the Brezhnev Doctrine. The decisions of the summit of the leaders of the Council for Mutual Economic Assistance (CMEA) in January 1990 had a similar character. The Soviet Union is no longer interested in the old forms of cooperation with the bloc countries, in the old forms of trade, and in the settling of trade balances in transferable rubles. The European members of CMEA, the USSR included, emphasize the need to redefine the aims and principles of the institution to facilitate their individual integration into the world economy. If this process fell short of their expectations, member countries would be inclined to resign from the CMEA rather than agree to the preservation of this costly fiction.

To sum up the preceding, contrary to the opinion that the Soviet Union is not yet prepared to "apply to Eastern Europe the principles of nonintervention in domestic affairs put forward by Gorbachev before the U.N. General Assembly" (7), the political and economic changes that have already occurred in this region refute this belief and go far beyond the alleged limit of the Kremlin's toleration. At present, the Soviets seem ready to tolerate the independence of the countries of the region as long as they remain in the Warsaw Pact. Nevertheless, it is quite possible that soon even this condition will be lifted. Moscow is redefining its strategic political interests, which compels it to redefine its military strategy as well. Moscow must reckon with the likelihood of the Warsaw Pact's disintegration. It is curious that in preparing their strategic forecast Giscard d'Estaing, Nakasone, and Kissinger did not take this possibility into account. Thus they did not take into consideration something that today, just a few months later, is the openly declared intention of some Eastern European governments. It is quite probable that at the price of peace with its western neighbors, and assurances that they will not install hostile governments, the Soviet Union will consent with relief to their actual Finlandization.

Here I should add a few words about a new and increasingly significant factor in the international situation—the reunification of East and West Germany. It has become the question of the day sooner than expected (not only in Poland but also for the authors of the report). In the context of the redefined relations between the USSR and the West, this problem, as well as the Japanese card (the Kurile Islands), could to some limited extent become Moscow's trump. In exchange for concessions, Soviet politicians would like to obtain from West Germany and Japan, at the minimum, substantial financial aid and investment, if not political concessions. The German question has already emerged as the gauge of Western unity and the communality of its aims. Undoubtedly, it will also affect mutual relations on the territory east of the Elbe or, perhaps, only east of the Oder and Neisse rivers.

Under these conditions, it would be frivolous to rule out the possibility that the Kremlin could be considering new ways to maintain East-Central Europe's dependence on Moscow. The fundamental evolution taking place in the region (including the USSR) is a factor the report did not foresee and one that renders the economic incentives it proposes (such as selective and limited economic aid supervised by COCOM*) inadequate and insufficient vis-à-vis the requirements of the new situation. The Giscard d'Estaing–Nakasone–Kissinger proposals seem particularly deficient when we consider that the majority of former socialist countries have opted for a quick shift to a market economy. However, the point is that the authors of the report treat Western support as a reward for good behavior, not as a change in the continued long-term and costly policy of imbuing the East with Western ideals and market economic mechanisms. When all is said and done, Western governments have already more swiftly and flexibly reacted to the new Eastern European reality. For example, they have relaxed the restrictions contained in the COCOM rules. Yet to help consolidate the changes now under way in the region, Western support should, I believe, take the form of a broad economic program, perhaps like the Marshall Plan. Also, it should provide for the rescheduling and consolidation of debt, be it Polish, East German, or Hungarian. In the new international situation it would also be possible to resume "political trade," something against which the report warns. Needless to say, this trade should not be as unconditional as it was in the 1970s, when, after all, Kissinger and Giscard d'Estaing did play a part in making trade as unconditional as it was. This time, such trade could considerably facilitate the entry of East-Central European countries into the circle of democratic states, making it difficult to install military dictatorships of an obscure ideological and political nature.

6

To end, one final general conclusion: If one recognizes the West's long-term interest in hastening the collapse of the totalitarian system in the USSR, and in making it easier for those former Eastern bloc countries who have already shed totalitarianism to decide their own future, then, despite certain correct appraisals of the situation, the strategy devised by the three famous politicians did not respond either to the current changes, particularly in the East, or to the spirit of the times already at the moment of its publication. The West must make a quick, explicit, and decisive choice. It must declare itself in favor of solutions that will facilitate change. Excessive procrastination and holding fast to the limitations of outdated beliefs could put the brakes on the process of the collapse of the really existing socialism. In that case, the evolution of East-West relations will also suffer. As never before in the postwar period, the key to wind the clock of the history of Europe as well as the rest of the world is in the hands of the West.

Note

1. V. Giscard d'Estaing, Y. Nakasone, and H. A. Kissinger, "East-West Relations," *Foreign Affairs* 63 (summer 1989). All page references throughout refer to this article.

5

Stealing Away in the Dead of Night

Krytyka, no. 34/35 (1991)

Marcin Kula

Political systems do not commit suicide. To be more precise, in the past they have often pursued suicidal policies, lost their power to see things as they really are or the will to act, but never have they consciously given up without even mounting a last-minute defense. Czarism drove a nail into its own coffin by going to war with Japan. The military junta in Argentina did the same thing by trying to take the Falklands/Malvinas. French aristocrats amused themselves as if nothing was happening, completely unaware of the approaching moment when many of them would have to face the guillotine. With the outbreak of the revolution, which was to deprive him of power as well as life, Emperor Nicholas II wrote in his diary that he had shot two quails. At the end of his rule, Emperor Haile Selassie busied himself with the immigration of Swedish gymnastics instructors. Even in these cases, the respective political systems put up a strong defense, usually stronger than that of their rulers.

Really existing socialism has gone into retreat without firing a shot and has done so of its own free will. Even if Gorbachev activated the forces over which he does not always exercise control nowadays, he obviously did not pursue his policies under the threat of a revolution aimed at his jugular. Really existing socialism has only made a handful of attempts to defend itself. The Warsaw Pact's intervention in Czechoslovakia belongs to the earlier epoch. The imposition of martial law in Poland was an attempt to block change, but it was inconsistent and irresolute. Without denying the suffering of a large number of people after 13 December 1981, one cannot help but notice that in similar situations in the past much more drastic measures were taken. Furthermore, martial law was a singular and serious appeal to new forces to come and join those in power. That appeal was absolutely unrealistic, as the victim never joins the tormenter-victor unless forced to. All the same, the invitation was made. The authors of the ideas underlying martial law were convinced of the need for systemic reform involving yielding part of their power, even if they still wanted to maintain their supremacy as a sort of enlightened absolutism. To achieve this aim, however, they chose a method that was doomed to failure because it was already obsolete. Nevertheless, their aim was clear. The Romanian *conducator* [leader] Ceauşescu demonstrated a strong will to defend really existing socialism. Even in Romania, however, it was striking that it was not a part of the population connected with the regime that defended the system, but first and foremost his secret police. For example, there were no reports of communist party officials barricading themselves in party committee buildings. Of course it is likely that the party apparatus abandoned the cause, seeing it as already lost (perhaps preserving some hope for the future). Yet despite the headlines there was no classic civil war in Romania.

A more classical defense of the ancien régime was visible in the decisive actions taken by the Chinese establishment. I shall risk saying that Deng was not alone in his decision to attack Tiananmen Square. I dare say that there was (is?) a conflict between social groups, some of which have defended—to date, effectively—really existing socialism.

Of course it is not obvious how things will develop in China. It is very probable that the Tiananmen massacre was the beginning, not the end, of resistance, and that the future development of the system could transform our picture of China. For the time being, China seems to be the exception that proves the rule. Other exceptions include Cuba, North Korea, and Albania. Little is known about the last two. The situation in Cuba has been shaped by specific circumstances: the conflict with the United States, the existence of an escape valve through emigration, a fairly recent authentic revolution in the process of consolidating its strength, and the authority of a leader (which seems to be greater than the strength of the system he personifies).

The relative ease with which really existing socialism has given ground is all the more surprising because, to a greater extent than other systems, the system had built-in protection against "defeatism." The communist movement was built on the pattern of a religious sect (the Leninist "party of a new type") whose dominant feature was its conviction in the mission it carried out in the name of the achievement of lofty goals. The entire education of its members was meant to prepare them for the fulfillment of their mission. They were made to believe that "defeatism" was among the most serious charges that could be leveled against a party member (that was, by the way, why so-called revisionism* was always treated more severely than so-called dogmatism*).

Really existing socialism was also very well prepared to defend its effective position of ownership. Although when compared with the underground corridors of Peking or Bucharest, the Polish helicopter decks built, if I am not mistaken, on top of the party voivodship* committee in Gdańsk and the Hotel Grand in Warsaw do not seem very impressive, the truncheons of the ZOMO* shock troops are, as we have seen, by no means toys. Warsaw Pact armored vehicles are much better than the cars manufactured by the same Eastern bloc countries. Yet this arsenal, all these public, secret, and semisecret police divisions, has not been used for some time. That a crowd seized Stasi* headquarters in East Berlin shows that Romania is the only country where the security police have taken defensive measures. How can one explain this unusual situation?

People have come forward with several possible explanations. Discussing them, I put aside the obvious, that the yielding of even some ground by the center inevitably demoralized the peripheral, concentric circles of power around it (the non-Russian peripheries of the Soviet Union, the "people's democracies," and the communist parties in the West). I do not mean to imply that really existing socialism in the periphery does not have local roots. To argue this in cases like China, Yugoslavia, or Albania—namely, countries where socialist transformations were brought about largely on their own—would be simply ridiculous. At the same time, one cannot deny that in certain peripheral countries really existing socialism was a mere reflection of the light shining from Moscow.

The first explanation for the phenomenon analyzed here assumes that the communists have consciously withdrawn in order to establish a better position to recapture the ground they have lost. This explanation is an extrapolation of the theory developed by Witold Jedlicki with regard to the Polish October* of 1956 (which paradoxically was later taken up in the propaganda of Moczar's* faction). Like all police interpretations of history, this one too is very catchy. Yet it has two weak points: (1) it is simplistic, and (2) it overlooks how the present transformations involve the disintegration of the very substance of really existing socialism, that is, the Leninist party.

Although I do not completely discount the possibility that historical Machiavellianism could be partially successful, I do have the impression that such an explanation does not fit very well with reality. If I see the possibility that Eastern Europe can become, according to the worst-case scenario, one huge Tiananmen Square and, in a more favorable scenario, an area under martial law like the one imposed on Poland in December 1981, this is not because of anybody's Machiavellian cunning, but because I cannot rule out the possibility that despite its disintegration the system will find enough strength to strike back in its final agony. It cannot be excluded that, as in *The Pharaoh* by Bolesław Prus,★ a secret Council of Priests will resolve to act as an emergency service and will command obedience as well. That was the scenario followed in Poland in December 1981. Today the implementation of such a scenario seems less likely, especially in the "people's democracies" where "the forces of law and order" are much less "reliable." It could still be workable in the Soviet Union. Even there, however, it could prove to be a short-lived solution. Martial law in Poland has shown the ineffectiveness of this as a long-term method of extricating the system from crisis.

When the Soviet army was retreating before Hitler during World War II, Stalin propounded the spring theory. Referring to Napoleonic wars, he compared Russia to a spring, which the more it is pressed the more it tends to return to its previous shape. Reality proved his theory, and the spring proved very resilient indeed. The truth was that, despite appearances, the spring still had quite a bit of bounce at the time. Although the German armies were pressing forward, deep inside Russia production was going on, new divisions were being formed, people were drinking to Stalin and to victory, and the system itself was working so smoothly that NKVD★ guards in the camps did not so much as flinch. Today foreigners are not pressing on the spring, but it has lost much of its Stalinist springiness.

Another explanation of why really existing socialism has been giving ground also assumes that it is deliberate, but with a different aim in mind: the desire to avoid widespread revolt (like the events in Romania, but encompassing the whole camp). To prevent a massacre, communists are letting off steam in a controlled manner, abdicating some of their responsibility, and maneuvering the establishment out of a very dangerous situation. Such an explanation assumes a full recognition of the situation as well as a far-reaching consciousness of goals. These two cannot be ruled out, considering that, under really existing socialism, political planning was the part of planning that was most accurate.

This explanation seems all the more plausible because the policy line pursued does not aim at self-abolition, but at the survival of the system through compromises. A miscalculation that permits change to get out of control does not preclude a policy of change formulated precisely in this way. On the other hand, the great similarity to the police version of history works against this thesis.

A third explanation argues that the leadership has realized the system lags behind the rest of the world and is incapable of catching up with the West in technology (military technology in particular) unless the existing institutions are changed. Such an explanation seems probable, especially if treated as a complement to the other explanations I discuss below. The argument against such an explanation is related to the risk involved. However, those who have taken the risk could either be unaware of it or have taken it consciously. That a ship is listing and the crew is in mutiny tells us nothing about the captain's motives.

The fourth explanation, the one I personally find most satisfactory (although not necessarily the only explanation), pays attention to the progressive transformation of the countries of really existing socialism and of their power elites. Contrary to the expectations of the classical literature of socialism, the communist movement won or seized power in backward countries. To triumph in this environment, the movement had to transform itself into Leninist parties "of a new type," which educated and brought to power activists very different from the common people. That vanguard was proud of itself, and its members praised themselves highly after the fact. However, with the evolution that took place after the new regime was established, the first group to be liquidated was precisely this vanguard. The process proceeded in various ways: through the Stalinist purges and new recruitment into the party or, as in Poland, by recruiting new party members from the Student Association. Each time, old combatants made room for people who, for better or worse, stemmed to a significantly greater degree from the nation than their predecessors. Initially, in the Soviet Union, these new people became the mainstay of Stalinism. The combination of the party "of a new type," which assigned activists the role of combatant, with the promotion of the youths coming from undeveloped villages had this effect. However, the country changed gradually as a result of, among other things, the development policies pursued by the system itself. Those measures had a great number of weak points and led in a number of cases down blind alleys—the system of education was not perfect, television was stupefying, and modernization as a process included a large number of traditional elements. All the same, the country became urbanized, industrialized, and every year great numbers of people were educated. It became a different country or at least a part of its population became different. It is not only true that Gorbachev has worked to modernize the Soviet Union. It is also, in a way, true that this partly modernized Soviet Union created Gorbachev the reformer. The system itself created the forces that have questioned the way it works today (in this way confirming the Marxist thesis that this is precisely one of the principal mechanisms of the transformation of sociopolitical systems).

Some of the people who constitute the mainstay of the regime, who were recruited from modernized social groups, became consumed by ambitions that could not be satisfied by arrangements up to that point. The same people were also more acutely aware of the need for modernization. Despite appearances, these people did not differ from the average citizen as much as the old activists had. Perhaps they had lost the zeal for standing up to society in the name of unattainable ideals, which under the system had little bearing on their ability to satisfy their aspirations for some time. Furthermore, as of late, because of the economic crisis, they have repeatedly turned their backs on the system. The monastic revolutionary of old would have made a much better defender of really existing socialism than the educated official who drives his own car to his dacha, or at least dreams about it. It has been observed that the ease with which the people connected with the system gave ground disproves Milovan Djilas's thesis on the existence of "the new class."

In each particular country under really existing socialism, the processes I describe here may have occurred in a slightly different fashion, but they all had the same effect. In Poland, the question of the modernization of society as a result of economic development was of lesser importance. Contrary to prevailing opinion, development and modernization had already begun in this country. The starting point was higher, in any case, than in the Soviet Union. In Poland, society's disappointment with the system was a result of historical events and the catastrophic economic crisis. The perception that conditions in the outside world were better than at home also played a greater role. It also seems to me that the close relations between the direct defenders of the regime and certain social circles played a major role here. The dichotomy between "those in power" and "the public" has for quite some time been only partly justified by the facts. Briefly stated, since Gierek's* rule, from both the point of view of its recruitment and the support it secured, the party-state apparatus did not differ or was not as isolated from the public at large to the extent implied in this division. The transition between "power" circles and "the public" was fluid, with the former absorbing a significant part of the latter. In terms of wisdom, stupidity, personal aspirations, and often even worldview, Gierek-era apparatchiks differed from the national average less than an older colleague of his from the time of Bierut* or Gomułka.* The younger generation of apparatchiks (and especially their wives) often did not like really existing socialism and wanted something better. They were interested in maintaining their positions, but in this they resembled the majority of people who normally desire the best job possible. These apparatchiks defended their positions but not the system. If they defended the system, it was for the sake of their positions, which was a weak basis for defense.

From a historical point of view, I would venture to say that the strongest defenders that any system ever had were the monastic orders of knights who acted out of broadly understood ideological motives. Another powerful motive for such defensive activity in history is the defense of property. It is my impression that the establishment under really existing socialism would have put up a much stronger fight had its private property been endangered. Its private property, however—contrary to popular belief—was quite meager and for all intents and purposes not endangered. Even if the members of the Gierek regime were "the owners of the Polish People's Republic," as they were popularly called, it was easier to lose the republic than one's own house or factory.

Last but not least, defense of one's life is a strong motivation for defensive acts. On that notorious night in December 1981, this motivation led many members of the *apparat* to defend the system. Their own observations, or information that was skillfully fed to them, led them to believe that their St. Bartholomew's Day was coming. The older members remembered the Hungarian Revolution of 1956, when the anger of the people centered on more than one communist. Dissipation of this fear became a major factor in the course of subsequent events in Poland. I think this was due to the prolongation of strife as a result of the imposition of martial law, to the loud repudiation of the Jacobin model of revolution by the opposition, to the church's sui generis position as a peculiar kind of patron in the struggle, and also to how the opposition engaged in struggle (which ensured the personal security and even to some extent the position of members of the establishment). However, to adopt tactics that did not drive the enemy to the wall where they had no choice but to defend themselves to the bitter end required the gradual maturation of the opposition, and this took time. From this perspective, the period of martial law turned out to be unexpectedly beneficial for the opposition. Such tactics could not develop in Romania, where conditions and the pace of events were different. If the system in Cuba is now so resistant to change, this is because, among other things, in the present situation (the powerful, materially attractive United States, which moreover has a large Cuban émigré community, is just next door) it cannot hope for evolutionary, partial change that could save anything of the present order.

With regard to the *apparat's* decision not to defend the system to the bitter end, its increasing similarity to the national average was significant for one more reason. The relationship of the "people's democracies" to the USSR was an important element of the system. And so, like the majority of society, the evolving cadre began to emphasize their nationality and the specific national road of their respective country. In extreme cases, this led to nationalism, but usually it just reflected the national norm. In Poland, little attention has been paid to this phenomenon, and the communists are seen above all as Moscow's tool. This is a gross oversimplification. I cannot resist quoting here the opinion of Sir Andrew Noble, the British ambassador to Warsaw, who on the eve of the events of October 1956 wrote, "Almost any Pole, and I include most of the members of the Politburo, is a Pole first and a communist second." Obviously, since that time things have gone much further. The evolution I am discussing here has diminished the cadre's commitment to the defense of really existing socialism as a world system, and more often than not has led them to question the system in their respective countries. It is true that the party apparatus did not question the system in all countries. The Romanian example shows that it was possible to build even a nationalistic version of really existing socialism.

By contrast, the recent victory of the system in its old form in China—in a country that is relatively backward and where moreover, since the time of the struggle with Japan, the communist movement has stood for the desire for national emancipation—emphasizes the significance of structural factors in undermining those old forms. The example of Yugoslavia too confirms the importance of structural elements, as selective modernization pushes this country along new roads, and the strong roots of the communist movement there prevent it from giving ground. It has to be acknowledged, though, in this particular case, that the abandonment long ago of classic "really existing socialism" by the Yugoslav communists, and the country's internal national conflicts, have been modifying the situation. This thesis on the structural conditions that are promoting change in Eastern Europe (if correct) is optimistic. It guarantees the permanent abandonment of really existing socialism with all its shortcomings. It does not mean, of course, that the process we are discussing cannot be upset; nevertheless, in the long term this thesis is strongly supported by social realities.

Yet even this thesis on the structural conditions does not permit optimism about what will follow the abandonment of really existing socialism. The prevalent sentiment in Poland, "Let the reds go away, because things can't get any worse," is glaringly false. Things can get much, much worse. Also, the opinion that if things do turn bad the situation will at least be normal ("Prewar Poland had many bad points, but it was a normal country") is also dubious. There are no sensible criteria of what constitutes a normal social regime, and, besides, Poland will certainly not become a Western-style, developed capitalist country any time soon. Although I would very much like to be optimistic, I cannot avoid certain misgivings. As I see it, in the immediate future we can, first and foremost, count on instability. The old system must fall apart and the new one will be only partially established, when the victorious camp finds it necessary to undergo some sort of internal restructuring. Such instability will be all the more serious because all the countries abandoning really existing socialism are in bad economic shape. Western aid will fall short of expectations, and the policy of laissez-faire economics, as a reaction to central planning, will not be conducive either to the lessening of social tensions or to quick extrication from the crisis. Countries who are led from really existing socialism by strong and experienced social movements, and where transformation is a step-by-step process, will find it easier to get through this instability. From this point of view, Poland's situation is better than that of other countries. The first symbolic change here occurred already in 1956, and Solidarity provided Poland with an alternative political elite. But even in Poland, Solidarity may be confronted by the threat of internal tension posed by the movement's dilemma of whether to support the government or to fulfill its role as a trade union—with all its consequences.

Generally speaking, one cannot rule out the emergence of governments with a strong hand, but not in the style of the "dictatorship of the proletariat" (this would be difficult in view of the disintegration of the communist parties). Such governments will rather resemble classic, populist authoritarianism, sometimes with paternalistic elements. One cannot rule out that such authority will be enforced by the present military elite and with the assistance of the army.

It is worth recalling here that the Soviet Union will continue to play a huge role in the region, no matter in what shape and under what name it emerges from its present turmoil. Many forces in the countries abandoning really existing socialism will continue to associate themselves with the USSR. The negative historical experience of Poland in its relations with Russia is not typical for the other countries of the bloc. For instance, during the collapse of really existing socialism in Romania, the Soviet Union seems to have strengthened its position there. One could even say that the Soviet Union is stronger there because it became more popular among the Romanian people. It very well may be that the Soviet Union has recovered what it lost owing to really existing socialism.

We can expect a considerable rise in nationalism in the countries of the old Soviet bloc. This is inevitable, considering the high degree of individual and public frustration, the great importance of national emancipation as a motive for the recent changes, the centrally controlled (that is, often hindered) development of national thought, the imprecise ethnic boundaries and the borders that Stalin imposed [to ensure that territories included more than one ethnic group, in order to use interethnic tension to maintain control], and large number of groups whom the fragmentary and defective socialist process of modernization left behind. The outburst of dissatisfaction in Bulgaria over the suspension of communist-era anti-Turkish regulations by the new authorities was, from this point of view, as sad as it was characteristic. I want to believe that the present positive change in Polish attitudes toward national minorities and the neighboring nations will be a lasting one.

We should expect that human reflection, which will constitute a major factor in the countries abandoning really existing socialism, will for many more years assume forms diametrically opposed to communist thought—with all the limiting effects this poses for its development (for instance, present economic thought in Poland is as doctrinaire as the concepts of Hilary Minc* once were, the only difference lying in its absolutization of the market instead of the plan). We should also expect that right-wing thought will become more influential. Under really existing socialism, the division between the Left and the Right lost all meaning because the ruling establishment monopolized the Left and excluded from it the concepts of human rights and antitotalitarianism, whereas everyday life brought people closer together through their common hostility toward the system. Under democracy, the old divisions are reemerging. Rightist thought lives off anticommunism, whereas the Left, after everything that transpired, is too weak and too reluctant to oppose the Right to develop and propagate its own vision.

With time, the situation might change. It is likely that the countries abandoning really existing socialism will come economically and socially to resemble the Third World with great income disparities, with a narrow luxurious and glittery market for Western goods available for only the well-to-do, and with poor masses excluded from that market. If such a situation develops, the Left may recover its former strength. It is not the Left who invented the slogans of liberty, equality, fraternity, and social justice. They seem to correspond closely to human needs. By failing to realize these slogans, the governments who described themselves as leftist reduced the appeal of the Left for the public; they even intellectually compromised it, but the slogans nevertheless remain. What disappeared, perhaps for the best, was a belief in humankind's linear progress, which was supposed to lead to its happiness. The rationalist Left adopted this belief together with the eternal myth of a golden age or the coming of the Messiah. As a result, they believed that it was worthwhile, possible, and commendable to force humankind to achieve that happiness, and this became the source of so much misery. Meanwhile, ordinary society will remain ordinary. Despite all the shortcomings of the ordinary, this was perhaps for the best, because had it not remained so, under the best circumstances, it would have been transformed into a society of happy idiots.

Section II

Sociology

6

The Transition from Authoritarianism to Democracy: The Case of Poland

Krytyka, no. 32/33 (1990)

Włodzimierz Wesołowski

Theory: Authoritarian and Democratic Regimes

There are two general concepts of the relationship between the state and society, and two corresponding philosophies of power. These concepts contain answers to these questions: What should take precedence, the state or society, and where should the source of the state power be located?

According to the authoritarian concept, the state has priority over society. It should take precedence because the state establishes the most general framework for society's existence. For example, it ensures society's external sovereignty and guarantees its internal order.

This concept involves a definite philosophy of power, which maintains that power stems from the very organization of the state institutions and from the power of the people who control them. The very existence of a state that rules over society creates a division between the rulers and the ruled. This idea has been expressed in its most open fashion by Gaetano Mosca. In every state organism there must exist, out of functional necessity, a ruling class and a ruled class. Theories of the revolutionary vanguard only generalize the belief that state power comes from organized force, that it is, in one way or another, imposed

A somewhat different version of this article was published in English in *Social Research* 56 (summer 1990). The editors express their thanks to *Social Research* in allowing us to refer to that version while making our own translation and to use a small number of passages verbatim.

on the majority. This is where Pareto and Lenin agreed, although they differed on many other issues.

In marked contrast to the picture presented above, the democratic concept presupposes that society takes precedence over state authority. The foundations of this concept were laid down by John Stuart Mill and Jean-Jacques Rousseau. Democratic regimes attempt to live up to this ideal. Rule by elected representatives is a pragmatic way to achieve it. Such an approach corresponds to a philosophy of power absolutely different from its authoritarian counterpart. According to the democratic concept, power is derived from society at large. Through the process of its self-organization and, then, the electoral process, society delegates its power to the organs of state. At the same time, it signals its preferences concerning the direction that the actions of the authorities should take. It tells those elected how power is to be exercised.

To differentiate these two, one can say that the democratic concept maintains that state power is "granted by society," whereas the authoritarian concept claims that power is "self-constituted."

The characteristics of both can be more precisely specified. One can enumerate four axioms concerning authoritarian systems:

1. The state is the fundamental mechanism of social integration and regulation.
2. The state is the organism that stands above all other forms of social organization and exerts control over them; it resorts to violence when necessary.
3. The state is always controlled by a minority; the rule of the majority is mere illusion.
4. The ruling minority knows how best to govern the state. Its wisdom may manifest itself in various ways: through discovery of the laws governing historical processes, through competence, through experience in government, through a flair for leadership; usually through all of the above.

The corresponding axioms of democratic systems are as follows:

1. The state is a product of society, which means that it represents the intentions and will of a concrete society; hence the citizens' fundamental attribute is their right to define norms and establish government.

2. The state should be constitutional in nature; that means its foundational legislative act defines the activities of the organs of the state and their competence. It thus makes clear which spheres of life are subject to control by the state and what procedures the state is not free to violate. One way to guarantee the constitutionality of the state is Montesquieu's notion of the separation of powers.

3. The accepted, and even necessary, connection between the state and the society is a number of different kinds of "intermediary bodies" (for example, parties, associations) formed by the citizens themselves with the idea of a collective defense of their interests and ideals. The free activity of these intermediary bodies must be guaranteed.

4. The individual members of society—the citizens of the state—must possess inalienable rights that belong to them as persons, both as "human beings" and as "members of society." The most important of these are freedom of thought, expression, association, and assembly. Protection of these rights against abuse by state bodies (such as the police or the bureaucracy) is an important aspect of "constitutionality."

Thus understood, authoritarian and democratic systems can be seen as ideal types in the Weberian sense. This means that not all actually existing regimes exhibit all the "axiomatic" characteristics mentioned here. After all, in real life, these characteristics are a question of degree. The two sets of axioms have an analytical and axiological character typical of every political doctrine or concept. Every political doctrine states how things are and how they should be. Therefore, advocates of particular regimes tend to "beautify" their constitutive characteristics whether they be fundamental or tangential. For example, some of the advocates of authoritarian regimes would say that a narrow power elite best expresses the aspirations and the will of the people at large, even without asking their opinion. On the other hand, some of the proponents of democratic solutions would tend to overlook the greater influence of the economically stronger classes on the direction of the government's actions.

My most general observation is the following: a political system is the result of a society's spontaneous collective experience, which is generalized in a schema of definite ideas. Thus theories about systems are something more than "generalized practice" and "objective knowledge." They show societies the path to further action, how their respective systems should be preserved or improved, because at more advanced stages of development every political system is a human invention.

Totalitarianism and Its Imposition on Poland

The system the communists tried to impose on Polish society by force did not have only authoritarian characteristics, because it was not only a political system. It was intended and planned as a totalitarian system; it was an intensification and universalization of authoritarian principles.

The communist version of totalitarianism—in contrast to Nazism, for example—was characterized by two phenomena: first, the complete subjugation of the economy to the political authorities by nationalizing the means of production and total planning of production and economic development; and second, an unusually developed ideology of universalistic ambition that was supposed to explain all aspects of reality. The expansion of this ideology into the cultural sphere was the "logical justification" of plans to subjugate individuals.

Communist totalitarianism had yet another unique characteristic. It presented itself as "socialism," the most humane of all systems that had existed until that time, and one that aimed at a historical transformation to a communism that in all respects would be practically ideal. This imaginary self-portrait included the seed of its own self-destruction because it invited a very high standard of evaluation which everyday reality could not meet.

Totalitarianism was in concept and practice imposed on Poland by the Soviet army. Perhaps for precisely this reason it was never to be completely assimilated and its specific features were never to develop fully on a mass scale. The population's resistance played an important part, but so—I should add—did the reluctance of some of those responsible for implementing it. This was especially true of the area of culture. However, it was the resistance of the people, the resistance of "the stuff of society," to manipulation that played the decisive role. The maintenance of full independence by the church and the survival of private farming are two well-known features of Poland's incomplete conformity to the totalitarian model, even in the darkest years of 1949–55. These phenomena, which limited the grounding of totalitarianism, made it possible early on to reject this foreign implant. This rejection began in 1956. This does not mean that today remnants of the old system do not remain. Their legacy is considerable, and to surmount it will be an ongoing task in Poland's transition to democracy. Nevertheless, it is worth stressing that in certain areas—for example, culture— owing to the endurance of the church and to the intellectual opposition, the elimination of totalitarianism does not constitute as great a problem as in politics or in control over society and economy. The concept that the Polish United Workers' Party* [PZPR] has a special role and place in the social system, the existence of the *nomenklatura*,* the powers of the police, and the level of party membership in the police are actual remnants of the totalitarian system.

History: The Processes of Change

How can Poland's situation in September 1989, at the time of the country's transition from an authoritarian and totalitarian system to a democratic one, be characterized? The rapid pace of change in the years 1988–89 has made the process of democratization uneven. A semi-democratic parliament was elected, and a government whose majority comes from forces supporting democracy was formed. But other structures and the institutional processes of extrication from the old system are less advanced. From the viewpoint of political psychology, Poles have a decidedly democratic orientation. However, the economic structure is already outdated, although the institutions typical of a civil society are not yet fully formed.

For the sake of the present analysis, the history of events in Poland and the process of democratization can be divided into two periods: (1) from October 1956 until 1988, with special emphasis on the years 1980–88 (the short interval of 1980–81, namely, "the time of Solidarity," was a sign of things to come), and (2) after 1988, when the process of transformation gained momentum. As a result of the Roundtable Talks held in the early spring, elections to the Sejm (Diet) and Senate were held in June 1989, and a Solidarity government was formed in August. The most important political events were crowded into the space of one year.

The Period between 1957 and 1988

Immensely important to the whole evolution was the relatively long initial preparatory period, during which the system proved itself to be inefficient and oppressive, a system that reduced people to "automatons" or to cogs in a machine. Many Poles perceived the system in this way as early as 1945. Successive generations came to know the characteristics of the system through their own experience. The lofty slogans and plans always stood in contrast to the institutionalized reality.

The "classical" Stalinist period in Poland lasted from 1949 to 1955 (the years 1945–48 were only a deceptive prelude). The year 1956—the period of the "Polish October"*—marked the beginning of the systematic undermining of the Soviet-inspired authoritarian system, which was connected with a project for the totalitarian reconstruction of society, as yet incomplete (the church, agriculture). An important role was played by the public disclosure and condemnation of the crimes of the Stalinist security apparatus as early as 1955. However, the greatest significance, because it persistently seeped into the minds of those who thought critically, was the erosion of the Stalinist ideology, which had been meant to justify the new order. Since that time, in intellectual circles [the authority of] authoritarian rule has been powerfully shaken and has eroded so much the faster, even though the regime's power has remained strong.

If the Polish October opened the way for intellectual reservations about the foundations of the system, even among those convinced of the value of socialist ideals, then those doubts spread through the younger generation and the intelligentsia in 1968. From that time on intellectuals no longer supported the Soviet model of socialism.

The strikes and riots of 1970 and 1976 discredited the system politically in the eyes of the working class. The events of 1980 were evidence of a decisive loss of faith in the economic foundations of the "socialist" model among workers and other social strata and groups.

After these experiences, 1980–81 had to become and became a period of multifaceted and general criticism of the system and of real opposition to it. Solidarity became such a strong antiauthoritarian force that the authorities felt compelled to impose martial law.

The Period from 1988 to 1989

In 1986 and 1987 authoritarianism still remained strong and well en-
trenched in the economy and the political system. Three factors seem
to have led to the situation that exists today. The first was the disastrous condition of the economy and the desire to push some of the
responsibility for it onto the opposition and to use the opposition to
obtain credits from the West. The second factor was the realization
that authoritarian government, which under martial law was as brutal
as it was ineffective, could not secure society's support for those in
power or generate the energy necessary to restore the economy. The
third and perhaps most crucial factor was change in the USSR. It
seems that these changes made negotiations with the opposition a necessity, so that events in the Soviet Union did not overtake the Polish
ruling team.

Just how authoritarian in attitude the ruling team was at that time is
demonstrated by how, at the time of their first contacts with the opposition, they did not foresee the possibility of relegalizing Solidarity.
Their only aim then, in line with the logic of the political system, was
to co-opt several well-known figures into the government. They
wanted to lure the opposition into the political system without changing its form or ways of functioning.

Social pressure (strikes) and the opposition's refusal to accept such a
solution led to the Roundtable Talks. At that moment, the first structural breaches in the authoritarian system appeared. The party-state's
concessions can be interpreted in various ways—for example, as expressions of their awareness of the desperate situation, as fear of remaining in Gorbachev's shadow, or as fear of a great social explosion.
They believed that the real changes would not be large. They expected
that the parliamentary elections "for which" they had legalized Solidarity would end in partial success for them and would allow them to
exercise power for at least another four years.

From the perspective of the most general characteristics of the transition from totalitarianism to democracy, that the Roundtable Negotiations were held and that, as a result, a social pact was signed is important. Pacts of this type are not unique to Poland. Latin American
military juntas have signed similar agreements with civilian politicians
before. Usually such pacts guarantee the relatively autonomous exis-

tence of their signatories. However, they create shaky equilibriums because they do not satisfy society's aspirations while they give the authoritarian side a chance to regroup their forces.

The pact signed in Poland did give democratic forces a certain place in the political system. It was certainly a step toward democracy. It is important to realize, however, that it was an undemocratic step—and that it would produce a system that was still authoritarian. The parties to the agreement appointed themselves representative of larger social forces, movements, organizations, and institutions. The contract they signed was not submitted to public scrutiny. Not all social forces were partners to that contract. In Poland part of the opposition remained outside the process. The result was a quasi-social contract and democracy "for partners" only, not for the whole of society. The representativeness of those sitting at the Roundtable was proclaimed, but in certain cases, the pact they signed could be seen as a usurpation of authority. That was not the case with Solidarity, but the government's claim to represent such large and active parties as the PZPR and the United Peasant Party* [ZSL] was the result of delusion.

In return for its legalization, Solidarity was obliged to take part in elections, which from the outset seemed to guarantee the victory of the old "PZPR coalition"—PZPR, ZSL, and the Democratic Party* [SD]. Only the elections to the Senate were to be fully competitive. This settlement was intended to enable the communist party to hold onto power, and to allow the opposition to express criticism, to press for "democratizing" changes, and to exercise limited control over government actions. It gave the authorities four years to repair the reputation of the authoritarian system and to introduce reforms under its auspices.

This negotiated political balance of power, which tilted toward the PZPR and its satellites in the system of power, was destroyed when the electorate refused to approve the pact. They decided that Solidarity would win by an overwhelming majority, because only its victory would make real economic and political reforms possible.

The authoritarian regime turned out to be arrogant, ignorant of the real public mood, and inept in competing for votes under real conditions. The ruling camp lost also because of the electoral tactics of the opposition. The Solidarity opposition backed particular PZPR, ZSL, and SD candidates in the second round of the elections, and as a result of this strategy some of the non-Solidarity deputies in the Sejm became real allies of Solidarity. This allowed Solidarity to form a "new" coalition—Solidarity with the ZSL and SD, the former allies of the PZPR. This was something nobody had thought possible earlier.

Then there were two frantic months. First, by a one-vote majority General Jaruzelski was elected the country's president, a position with extensive powers. Jaruzelski asked General Czesław Kiszczak, the minister of internal affairs and the PZPR's chief negotiator at the Roundtable, to form a cabinet. Prime Minister Rakowski* became the first secretary of PZPR. This was a sign that they intended to continue with a somewhat modified form of authoritarian rule. Yet after the damage the PZPR suffered during the elections, it could no longer control the country at all. The reluctance of all well-known politicians who did not belong to PZPR to accept ministerial positions made General Kiszczak give up his attempts to form a government.

This change was a result of other circumstances as well. Fraudulent attempts to free the price of food did not succeed. It only made prices skyrocket without alleviating shortages. People felt a real threat that Poland might continue to be ruled by the same old triumvirate—Jaruzelski, Kiszczak, and Rakowski. This is how things looked in the street and in the coffeehouses. This triumvirate represented too much "continuity." Social dissatisfaction had reached a critical point.

In this new situation, and despite the reservations he and Solidarity had expressed earlier, Wałęsa announced that Solidarity was prepared to form a coalition government with the ZSL and the SD. That great gambit led to a complete realignment of forces in the Sejm and fundamental political change. The ZSL and the SD betrayed the PZPR and formed an alliance with Wałęsa and the opposition. A new parliamentary majority, not foreseen in the pact, emerged. The new coalition's success should be seen as the result of unseen psychological and political processes that were occurring both in society and in the old power elite.

Following its electoral defeat, the PZPR fell into depression, chaos, mutual recrimination, and conceptual confusion. After the fiasco of the Kiszczak mission, the upper levels of formal power, especially the offices of the president, remained suspended in a political vacuum. No one was willing to stand up to defend authoritarian rule. For the PZPR there was nothing left to do but to join the actual alignment of political forces.

Meanwhile, despite the inner tensions caused by Wałęsa's gambit, the opposition elites proved to be integrated and resourceful. The Solidarity deputies from rural regions ultimately accepted the compromise with the ZSL, despite its association with yesterday's authoritarian regime. The public, having already played its part in the elections, now carefully watched the political scene where the drama of betrayal and change of partners played out. The public did nothing that could serve as a pretext for the use of force. The moment had been seized. A government led by the opposition, by democratic forces who had gained a mandate to rule in general elections, was established.

Sociology: Problems Arising after the Breakthrough

This initial breakthrough was limited to the parliament and the government. The changes preceded the emergence of fully elaborated structures of a civil society, and remnants of authoritarianism and totalitarianism continued to exist. This creates specific problems for a democratic evolution.

The Economy: Structural Problems

The economic restructuring of society is only just beginning. The shape that it takes will depend on the new forms of property adopted, on changes in investment priorities across different branches of industry, on new technologies, and so on.

Today the economic structure is in a period of disintegration. Group economic interests have a short-term character, whereas the formation of new classes, strata, and vocational groups strongly rooted in the system of production and services has not proceeded very far. The organization and crystallization of groups to promote the interests of particular industries or the large private and cooperative sectors have not clearly emerged. No one knows yet what will happen to large-scale state-run industry. Will it be self-managed, sold to the workers, or privatized? This makes it difficult for business and vocational associations to prepare programs. On a general level, it can be argued that a new and durable structure of interests has yet to emerge. Under normal conditions such interests would lead to the creation of organizations on a higher level, and above all to the emergence of a civil society in a political sense.

This organizational backwardness is a product of the neglect of economic reform. It is paradoxical that the PZPR, which until the democratic breakthrough had been responsible for economic reform, only managed to initiate one new process—the "enfranchisement of the *nomenklatura*,"* that is, the creation of a specific stratum of capitalists from the party-managerial cadre. Distribution or sale of stock to employees was only a foggy notion.

Political Fluidity

The political party structure, from which representatives to legislative bodies normally emerge—in this way signaling the distribution of public preferences—is also underdeveloped. The deputies from the Citizens' Committees, the representatives elected from Solidarity circles, have considerable internal political differences. It is not known whether they will continue to function as a loosely organized, multifactional political movement under the auspices of Solidarity, whether they will split into Christian-democratic, social-democratic, and peasant parties, or whether some other future awaits today's most influential "party organization."

The old parties of the authoritarian system are in a deep crisis. The PZPR, which has lost its political and ideological identity, is at the very beginning of a process of rethinking its program and establishing links with its future but as yet unspecified social base. Processes difficult to characterize at present are under way among the PZPR rank-and-file. Hiding their heads in the sand, the leaders want to defer their basic programmatic decisions until the party congress.

The ZSL, for its part, wants to return to its programmatic past—the Polish Peasant Party* [PSL], which was dissolved in 1947 as a party of kulaks opposed to socialism. Further, the ZSL wants to pull Rural Solidarity into this new PSL. Meanwhile, Rural Solidarity announced that it already is the PSL (alongside yet another PSL created by parliamentary deputies associated with the Citizens' Committees), although in parliament it was part of the same organization as the urban Solidarity.

The Democratic Party (SD), which has several well-worked-out ideas about the new constitution, wants to lead the constitutional debate, but it suffers from a narrow base of support. It remains to be seen whether the development of a medium- and small-size private sector in industry and services will contribute to a growth in the SD's members and an increase in its political significance.

The so-called extraparliamentary opposition includes several groups of unknown political strength. Perhaps a formidable party will suddenly emerge from among them, one possible candidate being the Confederation for an Independent Poland* [KPN]. The KPN demands complete independence for the country, that is, total and immediate autonomy from the Soviet Union. It organizes demonstrations against the continued presence of the Soviet army in Poland.

Nearly all political parties and movements are only now pursuing their bases of support and working out their platforms and general doctrinal orientations. The situation is peculiar, inasmuch as smaller parties, such as the SD or the KPN, supply more detailed (which does not mean more sophisticated) programs than the bigger parties, including Solidarity. Will this fact lead to a change in the relative numerical strength of the parties? Who will benefit? Beyond this—what will be the ultimate relationship of the party organization to social classes and strata, the interests of individual industries, or political tendencies not connected with material interests but springing from great ideals? This we do not yet know.

We need not simply to satisfy the intellectual curiosity of a few researchers, but to compile a relatively reliable list of political orientations within society and build a stable organizational infrastructure for the Sejm. Indeterminate or changing interests represented by political parties can, in the long term, lead to general political instability in the country and disturb the work of parliament. Such a course of events would hamper quick progress in the direction of democracy.

The Weakness of Associations

This indeterminacy is accompanied by the weak structuration of independent associations and movements. In many countries, associations of scientists, teachers, lawyers, engineers, and managers; trade unions in various branches of industry; artists' associations; numerous educational and regional societies; and consumer and cultural associations are very active in the public life. In Poland, despite hopes that this would come to pass, the re-activization of unions and associations—following the period of authoritarian control—is slow in coming, and their activity is hardly perceptible. They have yet to provide the expected sphere for everyday contacts between people for the satisfaction of mutual needs, aspirations, and interests. It is tempting to say that society was étatized for so long that it will take a long time to transform it from an anonymous mass into a civil society. The causes of this state of affairs are probably very simple: people are too absorbed in satisfying their basic economic, educational, and health needs. Here it is worth considering whether the greater development of independent associations would not more adequately guarantee social stability, a greater sense of participation, and greater satisfaction of particular needs. As yet, only the new movement for the establishment of private schools based on new pedagogical concepts shows a certain dynamism and appeals to the public.

Trade Unions and Social Instability

Trade unions are a unique form of association. They have at their disposal a more developed organizational apparatus and are capable of conducting large-scale, nationwide actions—of protest or support. There are two trade-union federations in Poland at present: Solidarity and the All-Poland Trade Union Alliance* [OPZZ], which was created by the authoritarian regime after martial law was imposed on 13 December 1981.

The fundamental questions are: Which of these federations will have greater influence in the future among the crews of the large factories? Which will become a force capable of supporting reform? Which will go the other way, deciding to instigate unrest and instability?

Solidarity at present has more than 2 million members, compared to nearly 10 million in 1980–81. There are various explanations for this. The simplest seems to be the most convincing: following Solidarity's spectacular electoral victory, and thus its "overall" political triumph, a large number of people were satisfied with the changes. In addition, these people do not see the Solidarity trade union as capable of effective action in the coming period of profound economic reform. Sacrifice by the working class is necessary. Thus people have begun to distinguish between Solidarity's function as a trade union and its function as a political movement. This distinction is the cause of the union's drop in members and of its waning influence in many factories. This, however, does not hinder Solidarity's top leadership—and herein lies a peculiar paradox—from exercising a decisive influence on the Citizens' Parliamentary Club [OKP], Solidarity's parliamentary caucus. This situation contains the seeds of instability both for the internal composition of the Solidarity movement as a whole and for the country itself.

On the other hand, the OPZZ is already a source of instability. The OPZZ claims to have "parted company" with the PZPR; nevertheless, the majority of its activists are still party members. It also claims to have nearly 7 million members—that is, many more than Solidarity. Before 1988, OPZZ had not staged any protest actions. Then, eager to change its public image (from the PZPR's obedient tool to a brave champion of the working people's cause), it began to oppose some of the policies of the Rakowski government. It is even more combative toward the Mazowiecki* government. It seems that its ongoing policy will consist of bandying slogans about defending workers' interests against the government, capitalists, "connivers from the *nomenklatura*," and all other possible "exploiters."

This demagoguery hardly ever refers to Marxism, which until recently was the official ideology of both the PZPR and the OPZZ. It cannot be ruled out that the federation will add anti-intellectual and anti-Semitic slogans to its demagoguery. In other words, the OPZZ is capable of sowing discontent and confusion. Solidarity will be able to extinguish fires started by the OPZZ only in the factories and regions in which it is strong. But there is also the possibility that the OPZZ will gradually compromise itself and become less popular. Then, in order to recapture its position, the OPZZ may try to form a populist party.

Inertia of the Old Bureaucracy

After Tadeusz Mazowiecki became prime minister, the weekly *Polityka* [Politics] published an article by Marek Henzler, "Wasz premier, nasz aparat" [Your prime minister, our *apparatus*], on the central state bureaucracy, 90 percent of which belonged to the PZPR. The article's title referred to a broad public discussion from which a fairly obvious conclusion was reached: the formation of a government by Solidarity could prove to be a Pyrrhic victory because the actual administration of the affairs of the state and all major spheres of life, from economic activity to culture and education, remains in the hands of the party's nominees, the *nomenklatura*. They have the ability to effectively block all policies, if only by failing to take action or by failing to do so in a timely fashion.

I, however, see the danger looming elsewhere: in the habits of the posttotalitarian bureaucracy. The bureaucracy of the authoritarian system does not function well, and it requires a titanic effort to make it work. The characterization of "backward" is not sufficient to describe this particular stratum. The bureaucratic *apparat* the young democracy inherits from the authoritarian system is servile. It is accustomed to obeying orders given by phone instead of the law, and it is incompetent because its members have not been promoted according to their expertise. It is rude toward petitioners because it is exhausted by unnecessary tasks and because, vis-à-vis citizens, the bureaucrat represents an all-powerful higher authority. Last but not least, it is rife with cronyism. It would be difficult to dismiss all of them or to remake them substantially. We must use the old bureaucracy, even though it is ill-adapted to the new style and new tasks of the state. I do not think they will be too inclined to sabotage the decisions of the new authorities. The majority of the bureaucrats have been "taught" to "adapt" continuously, so they will once again. The problem is whether good intentions, unsupported by good habits, will be enough.

Dismissal of bureaucrats could become dangerous. Those incapable of working in normal professions could constitute a powerful faction in the PZPR, which would press for political confrontation if the possibility arose.

Remnants of Totalitarianism and Authoritarianism

In discussing the problem of the administration, we face the problem of remnants of the authoritarian economic, legal, and even constitutional systems. Their evolution will be decisive in the transition to democracy.

Certain remnants of authoritarianism, some pervaded with totalitarian elements, continue to be a part of everyday life. Thus, for example, in a country where the former opposition has formed a government, communist newspapers predominate in supplying readers with information. Furthermore, everyone who buys a newspaper, even if it is published by the former opposition, does so from newspaper kiosks, thus increasing the profits of the PZPR-owned monopoly on press distribution. In the spring of 1989, the National Bank of Poland gave the PZPR a loan at 3 percent interest, when the usual rate was somewhere between 50 and 60 percent. These are just a few examples of how, under the totalitarian system, citizens were under the control of the communist party and how their work and sometimes their money helped the party to maintain control.

The army and the police are another example. Nearly the entire officer corps and all employees in the Ministry of Internal Affairs (MSW) are PZPR members. All instruments of force remain under the command of the people from the party. For this reason alone, the democratically elected Sejm and government are still in danger. They do not have the allegiance of a comparable force. The imbalance between the former opposition, who now control the government, and the former ruling team, who have distanced themselves from the government but still control the coercive apparatus, could create a permanent undercurrent of macropolitical instability. Yet things cannot be changed overnight, or even from decade to decade. In particular, it would be impossible to replace the old army cadre with activists from the *Wolność i Pokój* [Freedom and peace] pacifist movement.

In the MSW, all employees were required to sign a pledge of loyalty to the PZPR. New recruits do not, but theoretically the old guard should, as before, act at the behest of the PZPR. When the matter was raised in the Sejm, the responsible deputy minister of internal affairs resisted the demand to remove that pledge from his officers' personnel files by referring to the relevant legal regulations.

The office of the president, which has very extensive powers, is yet another relic of the authoritarian system. It is worth remembering here that the president was elected by just a one-vote majority, which was possible only because ten opposition deputies deliberately abstained on this vote. Thus he does not represent the people. Once elected, however, he is the only person entitled to call for the formation of a government. The president also controls the army and influences foreign policy. Everybody knows why this is so. It is not because Poles admire the French system (which in its Polish version is even more inclined toward authoritarianism). The Roundtable Agreement calls for the president to oversee the peaceful transition from authoritarianism to democracy. Yet the presidential office so tailored is itself a remnant of the old authoritarian system. The delegation of such extensive powers to a specific person—a member of the PZPR—would seem to guarantee that rule will have the character of "continuity" with the past. Of course, much will depend on the specific actions of the president. The quite smooth designation of Tadeusz Mazowiecki to form a govern-

ment coincided with the president's ostentatious reception of representatives of the PZPR hard-line faction and the executive board of the
disgraced Journalists' Association of the Polish People's Republic,
formed under martial law to replace the banned Polish Journalists' Association.

Evidence of the survival of authoritarian and posttotalitarian elements is abundant. For example, the PZPR defends its ownership of
its offices and the salaries its activists are paid by factories. Other parties do not have such privileges. Some elements of the authoritarian
regime may gradually disappear, others may persist, and others may
still change their nature and role. The study of the new social role
of people from the old *nomenklatura*, and the scope of their new political influence, will become rich subjects for long-term sociological
study.

In Lieu of a Conclusion

Authoritarianism's retreat is not an indicator of its decisive loss of
strength. Postauthoritarian elements, still present in the incipient democratic system, hold the highest office in the state—that of president—
and control the apparatus of coercion. Authoritarianism in retreat must
have an alternative to its fall into definitive and overall powerlessness.
It is possible to advance the hypothesis that the basis for this is the
great political and moral attractiveness of a competitive solution—parliamentary democracy. The attractiveness of this solution captivates
even people from the upper reaches of the authoritarian system. They
obey the outcome of the democratic process, which in itself is "powerless."

At this juncture, one should add an observation, which although it
supports the optimistic conclusion just presented, nevertheless reduces
the role of the idealistic motives for supporting democratization. The
modern world is divided into "centers" and the "periphery," into superpowers and weaker countries, which are connected with the former, not to say dependent on them. What is occurring today in Poland
cannot be discussed in isolation from what is going on in the USSR,
just as contemporary developments in Latin America cannot be analyzed independently from the political orientations prevailing in the

United States. In Latin America they too have begun to abandon authoritarian forms of rule.

It is at present a era in which the two superpowers have begun to advocate, and even promote, the idea of political democracy on a global scale. I shall not go into details about the sort of democracy they envision; it is the general line that matters. In the present situation, the elites of the "allied" countries have also opted for democracy, and yesterday's authoritarian practitioners have become converts—either out of a sense of realism or out of sincere conviction. Their motives need not be idealistic. Nevertheless, if we assume that the center influences the periphery, the thesis that authoritarianism is on the retreat seems increasingly sustainable. Here, however, a theoretical reservation must be made: transformation from an authoritarian regime to a democratic regime cannot be treated as historically inevitable. It is the result of a coincidence of a set of outcomes, a specific constellation of conditions. We can only hope that these circumstances prevail for as long as possible.

Early October 1989

7

The Polish Voter—Ten Years after August 1980

Krytyka, no. 36 (1991)

Jan Powiórski
[Krzysztof Jasiewicz]

Eight years ago *Krytyka* published my article, "Polacy '81: Opinia pub-
liczna w przededniu stanu wojennego [Poles 1981: Public opinion on
the eve of martial law]." It reported on a sociological study conducted
(as scholarly fate would have it) just three weeks before the declaration
of martial law. The report, though completed and printed, never
found its way into the hands of potential readers. Of the several hundred copies printed, some were delivered to high party and state officials. The authors each received a copy, perhaps as a gesture of kind-
ness or perhaps because of an oversight on the part of the thought-
police. For several years my article in *Krytyka* remained the only
source on the views and attitudes of Polish society just before martial
law. Several years later *Krytyka* published another article which reported on the results of our ongoing research: *Polacy '84* [Poles 1984].
This time one hundred copies of our findings were published. The
purpose of the second article in *Krytyka* was to publicize our findings
in condensed form to a wider audience. For a number of years now,

This text is based on the author's own research, including secondary analysis of survey data
and two collective research projects: *Polacy '90* [Poles 1990] a project sponsored by the East
European Research Group of the Stefan Batory Foundation, conducted by W. Adamski, I. Bia-
łecki, K. Jasiewicz, L. Kolarska-Bobińska, A. Rychard, and E. Wnuk-Lipiński (based on a
sample of 1,862 individuals, representative of Poland's adult population taken in October 1992);
and "*Wybory prezydenckie 1990* [The presidential election of 1990]," a panel study conducted by
A. Banaszkiewicz, S. Gebethner, and K. Jasiewicz (three waves of 848 individuals, representative of all voters, taken in November–December 1990). All judgments and interpretations
expressed in this article are those of the author alone.

Krytyka has published sociological research that would have been censored under the heading "sociology barred from circulation."

Today this is no longer necessary in sociology or any other field. There is no need to summarize to the readers of *Krytyka* the thick tomes of our results now available in every scholarly bookstore and library. Rather, I will discuss some of the issues explored in the most recent book in the series *Poles* and other studies. Also, I can now begin to sign my articles with my real name rather than the pseudonym "Jan Powiórski."

Have the Poles Gone Mad?

This should be the subtitle of this article. It refers to the 4 million of my compatriots who in the presidential elections of fall 1990 voted for Stan Tymiński. This is the burning question that this article must address. The point is not to repeat Leopold Unger's famous quip during television coverage—that it was not Tymiński (whose psychological health had been previously called into question), but those who voted for him, who should undergo psychiatric treatment. Instead, my purpose is to explain why nearly 25 percent of the electorate decided to trust their fate to a virtually unknown expatriate entrepreneur with holdings in Toronto, Canada, and Iquitos, Peru.

This phenomenon is hard to understand for both Poles and foreign observers, particularly those sympathetic toward Poland. The Poles who initiated change in Eastern Europe, who did not wait for Gorbachev or perestroika to rebel, who did not need totally free elections to remove the communists from power legally and democratically, whose solidarity and Solidarność amazed the world—those same Poles, having just embarked on a program of reform, turned against one another or followed the voice of a political charlatan. Again, it is irrelevant to us who Stan Tymiński really is—a charlatan, an agent, a fraud, or simply an ambitious man with a brilliant idea. I am not a psychiatrist or a detective. I shall approach this problem from the perspective of political sociology. I shall try to outline the values and attitudes of Polish society on the eve of the presidential elections in order to examine those elections and electoral behavior in terms of continuity and change, and to specify the differences between groups within the electorate.

The Landscape before the Battle

Some observers of the Polish political scene believe that the popular election of the president was the decisive factor in destroying the national consensus on reform and the direction it should take. According to others, the competition for Belvedere* was only the expression of tensions and conflicts that raged, if not on the surface, then certainly inside the cauldron of Polish politics. Sociological studies cannot answer questions such as these. They can, however, provide information about social expectations, attitudes toward political actors, and the potential for conflict and protest and link this information to political behavior.

Let us first look at some of the data gathered for the study *Polccy '90*. Table 7.1 presents data on confidence in public institutions collected from 1984 through 1990. The values are coefficients that range from −1 to +1 (−1 denotes complete lack of confidence, and −1 denotes complete confidence).

In the period 1984–88, the church, among all institutions, enjoyed the highest level of confidence. The central institutions of the old order enjoyed varying degrees of confidence, ranging from a relatively high degree for the Sejm (parliament) and the army, through a moderate degree for the government, to a negative evaluation for the police (MO, People's Militia*). The high confidence in the army and the Sejm

Table 7.1. Coefficients of confidence in institutions, 1984–1990.

Institutions	1984	1987/88	1989 (fall)	1990 (fall)
The Sejm	.31	.45	.58	.1C
The church	.65	.65	.58	.43
The government	.17	.26	.61	.21
The army	.39	.42	.16	.37
OPZZ	−.19	−.02	−.29	−.29
People's Militia (MO)/Police	−.19	−.08	−.37	.08
Solidarity	−.52	−.23	.61	.22

(which at that time was not, even in part, freely elected) can be explained by their perceived status as symbols of Polish statehood. Finally, the respondents did not express confidence in the underground and illegal Solidarity movement (although in 1988, not as drastically as four years earlier). In 1988 and 1989 there was a 180-degree turnaround. With electoral victory and the formation of a government under its leadership, confidence in Solidarity rose to a level previously reserved only for the church. The government (under Prime Minister Mazowiecki★) and the Sejm (in which Solidarity held only 35 percent of the seats) enjoyed similar levels of confidence. Confidence decreased in the All-Poland Trade Union Alliance★ [OPZZ], the police, and the army, which were perceived as institutions still under the control of supporters of the old regime. From the fall of 1989 to the fall of 1990 there was a rise in confidence in both the army and the police, who went through a period of structural, personnel, and symbolic change (including a change of name from the People's Militia to the State Police). The postcommunist OPZZ still had the lowest level of confidence of all institutions. During this period there were also sharp decreases in confidence in the church and the Sejm to the lowest levels ever recorded in such surveys. Analysis of more systematic data gathered by CBOS★ and OBOP★ showed similar results.

This rapid drop in social confidence levels for the Sejm, the church, and the government in the fall of 1990 indicates that the presidential elections took place at a time when the new political order was undergoing a serious legitimation crisis, but we are unable to state whether this crisis was intensified by the electoral campaign itself. It should however, be pointed out that at that time confidence rose in the police and the army, institutions which had been fully and decisively depoliticized and were scrupulously neutral in the presidential campaign. The opposite occurred in the case of the church, whose direct presence in public life was becoming increasingly visible at that time.

The issue of confidence in the Sejm merits separate consideration. The relatively high degree of confidence it enjoyed in the 1980s was due to its perception as a symbol rather than an actual actor on the political scene. After the elections of June 1989, once it had become a functioning parliament the Sejm became an object of hope and expectation. This produced the high degree of confidence that the Sejm enjoyed in the fall of 1989, and its swift dissipation later. The drop in confidence was not merely the result of the propaganda campaign directed against a "contractual" Sejm [the communists and their allies had been guaranteed 65 percent of the seats], since a similar drop is observable in the confidence level enjoyed by the Senate, whose members were chosen in free elections. Both institutions achieved high levels of confidence by opening themselves up to public scrutiny, including live television broadcasts of their proceedings, and both subsequently experienced sharp decreases in public confidence. Today the Sejm enjoys less confidence than the Sejm of 1984, which had not changed since Gierek,* or the Sejm of 1988, which was dominated by the Patriotic Movement for National Revival* [PRON].

Care must be taken in interpreting these changes in confidence levels. Do they mean that when the parliament stopped acting purely as a rubber-stamp body, when it became an important actor in the political process and was opened to public scrutiny, it suffered a loss of confidence? Or did the Sejm lose public support because it was no longer purely a symbol? Or did the withdrawal of support signify a loss of confidence in democratic institutions and the procedures that brought them into being? Existing data do not provide an answer to these questions. However, the complete loss of confidence in all political institutions, which was observed among all groups who voted for Tymiński and Cimoszewicz,* suggests a process more profound and complex than ordinarily seen in democratic systems. It may signify a retraction of the legitimacy granted to the new political order and could lead either to political apathy or to greater social protest.

Conflict, Protest, Reprisals

In our research conducted in the 1980s, we devoted a great deal of attention to the legitimacy of forms of social protest and state responses to them (see *Krytyka*, nos. 13–14 and 27). Table 7.2 displays coefficients of acceptance of protest and reprisals from the period 1981 to 1990 (+1 denotes complete acceptance, and −1 denotes complete rejection).

Comparison of the data from 1990 to previous years points to several conflicting potential hypotheses on the legitimacy of protest and repression:

1. The degree of acceptance of protest increased as channels of political articulation were unblocked and the real threat of severe reprisals came to an end ("It was easier to have courage"). Simultaneously, the acceptance of reprisals continued to decrease ("Our government should not be more repressive than a communist one"). The confirmation of this hypothesis would signify the creation of what could be labeled an *anarchic vision of the legitimization of protest and repression*.
2. Acceptance of both protest and reprisal increased ("People should be able to express their opinions, but the state should maintain law and order"). This we call a *liberal vision of protest and reprisal*.
3. The acceptance of both protest and reprisal decreased ("At last, we live in our own house—why quarrel?"). This is *a romantic vision of protest and reprisal*.

Table 7.2. Coefficients of acceptance of protests and reprisals, 1981–1990.

	1981	1984	1987/88	Fall 1989	Fall 1990
Protests					
1. Gathering signatures under petitions and protests	.33	.55	.52	.41	.59
2. Boycott of government decisions	−.17	−.05	.01	−.14	.05
3. Street demonstrations	−.34	−.01	−.22	−.28	.04
4. Strikes	−.02	.06	−.12	−.15	.15
5. Displaying posters	−.05	.01	.09	−.09	.29
6. Occupation of public buildings	−.39	−.63	−.61	−.63	−.58
7. Resistance of the police or other organs of law enforcement	−.41	−.38	−.48	−.41	−.43
Reprisals					
1. Using police units against street demonstrations	−.55	−.49	−.54	−.79	−.46
2. Application of severe court verdicts against demonstrators who did not obey the police	−.49	−.44	−.48	−.62	−.48
3. Promulgation of a law prohibiting public protests and demonstrations	−.31	−.32	−.30	−.50	−.46
4. Using the army to break strikes	−.72	−.68	−.85	−.81	−.79

4. Acceptance of protest decreased while acceptance of reprisal increased ("Since there are other constitutional means of interest articulation, there is no need for spectacular protest and the state should defend this principle"). We call this a *conservative vision*.

From table 7.2 it is obvious that in the fall of 1989 Polish society had a romantic vision of protest and reprisal. The acceptance of reprisals was at its lowest point in a decade, but it should be emphasized that it had been low throughout the decade. Acceptance of protest was at or near its lowest level. However, there was radical change from the fall of 1989 until the presidential campaign (fall 1990). The acceptance of most forms of social protest (with the exception of the occupation of buildings and resisting law enforcement) rose to a level not seen in the 1980s. At the same time, acceptance of reprisals grew slightly (particularly the use of police against demonstrators and reliance on stiff penalties by the courts), but did not exceed the levels observed in 1981–88. If we examine the attitudes of Polish society during the presidential campaign of 1990 next to the development of such attitudes earlier in the decade, it lies somewhere between the liberal and the anarchic visions of protest and reprisal, or more precisely, respective segments of the society favored one of these two visions. We can then risk the conclusion that, along with the strong signs of political apathy, as seen in the high rate of absenteeism in the presidential elections (almost 40 percent in round 1, almost 50 percent in round 2), Polish society at the end of 1990 contained a significant protest potential, which could have been expressed in the presidential elections.

However, this protest potential was not evenly dispersed across political camps. It was particularly strong among followers of Stan Tymiński. For example, their coefficient of acceptance for a boycott of government decisions was 0.19, whereas for Wałęsa's followers it was 0.13 and for Mazowiecki's followers it was −0.10. It is interesting that none of Tymiński's followers answered the question whether they had personally boycotted a government decision positively (in the whole sample, only 1 percent answered that they had).

Social protest is never an abstract phenomenon. The forms it takes depend on how people perceive the main axis of social conflict. In the 1980s, conflict was perceived as a dichotomy: state versus society, authority (the rulers) versus the nation (people, workers, peasants, the ruled, and so on). Compared with 1984 and 1988, more people ac-

Table 7.3. "There is talk of and there are articles about social conflicts in Poland. Do you think that such conflicts do indeed exist?"

	1984	1987–88	1990
Yes	56.7%	48.4%	61.0%
No	18.1%	14.9%	10.4%
I have no opinion	25.2%	36.7%	28.5%

knowledge the existence of conflict today (see Table 7.3). Undoubtedly, the end to the ancien régime's monopoly on information and the unblocking of various mechanisms for social expression have contributed to this perception. It should be added that the supporters of different candidates in the presidential elections do not essentially differ in their opinions on the existence of conflict. If, however, the majority of the society agree that social conflict exists, do they see it as they saw it three or six years ago? In response to an open question on the nature of conflict, asked in 1984, 1989, and 1990, we received the answers presented in Table 7.4.

The dominant perspective of political conflict in the 1980s, in which the party-state authorities were seen as one participant, gave way in 1990 to a perception of many different social conflicts. Many people continue to perceive political conflicts, but such conflicts are no longer seen as a simple dichotomy between the party-state authorities and others. In addition to conflict between the authorities and the nation, new conflicts have emerged (the old regime against the new, the var-

Table 7.4. "Who is in conflict with whom?" (in % of the entire sample).

	1984	1987–88	1990
Authority, government, etc. vs. nation society, etc.	24.8	22.4	4.2
City vs. countryside	6.9	0.7	9.8
Authorities (new or old) vs. Solidarity	5.2	2.9	2.9
PZPR, communists, party members vs. others	3.3	2.0	2.6
Rich vs. poor	—	5.9	4.5
Old authorities vs. new authorities	—	—	3.5
Various parties with each other	—	—	6.0
Conflict within the government, between the authorities	—	—	2.8
Conflict within Solidarity	—	—	3.5
Wałęsa vs. Mazowiecki	—	—	3.5

ious political parties against one another, and so on). More than previously, the data from 1990 register socioeconomic conflict, including conflict between the urban population (workers and the intelligentsia) and the rural population (peasants).

Even if the potential for conflict is significant, it seems to be no less significant than before. Unlike in the 1980s, it is not dominated by a single dichotomous relationship. There are different axes of conflict, as social discontent and frustration have turned in different directions. One way this frustration seems to have manifested itself (and was perhaps to some extent dissipated) was in the very act of voting. Voters for each of the main candidates emphasized different aspects of their perception of the essential nature of conflict:

> The followers of Lech Wałęsa, more so than any other group studied, perceived continuing conflict with the Polish United Workers' Party★ [PZPR] or its successor parties and saw the Mazowiecki government as responsible for this conflict.

> The followers of Tadeusz Mazowiecki were more inclined to see conflict between the government and Solidarity or conflict inside Solidarity itself; more frequently, they considered minorities (national, religious, and so on) as party to the conflict.

> The followers of Stan Tymiński more frequently perceived conflict between the authorities and the society (they defined conflict in the same categories as it was perceived in the 1980s) and also more frequently cited "conflict between Wałęsa and Mazowiecki."

> The followers of Włodzimierz Cimoszewicz★ and Roman Bartoszcze,★ more than the groups above, talked about a conflict between rural and urban areas.

> Undecided voters also pointed to conflict between various parties (a likely cause of their confusion) and finally, like Tymiński's followers, to conflict between the authorities and the society as well as conflict between the rich and the poor, and superiors and subordinates.

This may point to the factors that motivated electoral behavior. Wałęsa's followers hoped to settle accounts with the *nomenklatura*★ and to replace the constantly squabbling government and parliament with a strong leader. Mazowiecki's followers tried to defend the government against the threat from within its own camp. Votes for Stan Tymiński were definitely votes against the establishment—not only because of its alienation from society but also because of its internal squabbles (Wałęsa versus Mazowiecki). This may confirm the hypothesis that Tymiński's support came from people who were unhappy with the end of the myth of Solidarity's unity. Nonvoting seems to correlate with the following perceptions of conflict on different levels: macropolitical (authority versus the nation), micropolitical (superiors versus subordinates), and economic (the rich versus the poor). This perception explains the fluctuation of nonvoters' attitudes from apathy to aggression and back.

Continuity and Change in Electoral Behavior

The Polish political scene at the time of the presidential elections can be seen as the inevitable product of political pluralization. The situation was qualitatively different from the 1980s, which were characterized by a polarized, rigid conflict structure, where demands were articulated unidirectionally, toward the monopolistic party authorities. We can wonder if pluralization had to lead to the division of Solidarity and to conflict among its factions. We can ask whether the millions of votes cast for Tymiński were caused by the acceleration of pluralization, which undoubtedly took place in the period immediately preceding presidential elections, or whether there were continuities in the political behavior of this population with the polarization of the 1980s.

Most interpreters want to see the Tymiński electorate as a political and sociological novelty. Some went so far as to interpret the behavior of this group as an expression of the interests of the emerging Polish middle class. Our data do not bear this out. In fact, Tymiński's voters seem to exhibit strong continuity with their past political behavior. In addition, from a sociological perspective, it was not Tymiński's voters, but rather Mazowiecki's, who distinguished themselves from the rest of the electorate.

This argument is supported by two kinds of evidence. The first is a statistical analysis of the official electoral results from individual provinces. The second comes from an analysis of public opinion polls. A frequently used measure of the relationship between two variables is the Pearson correlation coefficient r. This measure tells us whether there is a statistical relationship between two variables. It does not, however, establish the existence of a causal relationship. The correlation coefficient ranges in value from -1 to $+1$. Zero signifies no correlation. We found correlations (on the provincial level) between the percentage of votes for Tymiński in round 1 of the presidential elections and electoral behavior in previous elections. In particular, we showed a positive correlation between voting for Tymiński and votes for the "national list"* [*lista krajowa*] in the "parliamentary elections of 1989"* ($r = .60$); voter turnout in the 1985 Sejm elections ($r = .52$); and voter turnout in the elections to the People's Councils* [*Rady Narodowe*] in 1984 ($r = .41$).

We found a negative correlation between votes for Tymiński and votes for Solidarity candidates in the Senate elections of June 1989 ($r = -.47$).

This analysis does not mean that the same voters who supported Tymiński in round 1 of the presidential elections also cast their votes for the national list and voted against Solidarity Senate candidates eighteen months earlier, or did not heed Solidarity's call for an electoral boycott in 1984 and 1985 and instead voted for PRON's candidates. The data indicate that in provinces in which the boycotts of 1984 and 1985 were less successful, or in which more votes were cast for the national list and fewer for Solidarity candidates in 1989, support for Tymiński was strongest. There is a clear element of continuity here. Constituencies more closely linked with Solidarity in the 1980s were more resistant to the charm (or demagoguery) of Tymiński in 1990.

The continuity in electoral behavior becomes more explicit if the analysis includes more variables, such as votes cast for other candidates in round 1, votes cast in round 2, voter turnout in both rounds of the presidential elections and in round 2 of the June 1989 parliamentary elections, as well as the combined vote for the candidates with Solidarity backgrounds (Wałęsa and Mazowiecki) in round 1. Using factor analysis, we determined whether and which of these many variables correlated in such a way that they could be explained by a common factor. (For example, in studies of eating, if people like halvah, cake, candy, and chocolate all this correlates in factor analysis to one explanatory factor: a sweet tooth.)

An analysis of the variables mentioned above allows us to isolate four factors that determined the strength of the relationship between a given variable and a given factor. The strength of these factors is shown in Table 7.5 (factor loads with values too low to indicate a relationship with the variables have been omitted).

The main factor determining electoral behavior in the presidential elections of 1990 was voters' attitude toward Solidarity. The votes cast for Lech Wałęsa in round 1 and the votes cast for Solidarity candidates correlate in an obvious way and do not need explanation or interpretation. Similarly, there exists an obvious negative correlation between the votes cast for Wałęsa and the votes cast for Tymiński, particularly in round 2. It is not equally obvious that locations where Wałęsa had strong support in 1990 coincide with locations where Solidarity did well eighteen months earlier (our data were collected at the provincial level). Also significant is that votes for Tymiński had more of an anti-Solidarity character than votes cast for Cimoszewicz, the candidate of the postcommunist forces. Here we see an element of continuity—among those who in 1989 voted for the national list and against Solidarity candidates in the Senate elections, Tymiński was clearly the most attractive candidate, outpolling even Cimoszewicz.

Table 7.5. Factors relating to voting behavior, 1989–1990.

Variable	Factor			
	I	II	III	IV
Solidarity—Senate 1989	.753	—	—	—
The national list 1989	−.841	—	—	—
Wałęsa 1	.924	—	—	—
Tymiński 1	−.809	—	—	—
Cimoszewicz 1	−.532	—	—	−.645
Moczulski 1	—	—	—	.760
Bartoszcze 1	—	—	−.879	—
Mazowiecki 1	—	—	.923	—
Solidarity 1	.874	—	—	—
Wałęsa 2	.939	—	—	—
Tymiński 2	−.942	—	—	—
Voter turnout 1989	—	.922	—	—
Voter turnout 1	—	.947	—	—
Voter turnout 2	.599	.712	—	—
% of explained variance	46.3	16.9	14.7	8.0

There also is a relationship between votes cast for Wałęsa in round 2 and voter turnout in that round. In round 2 Wałęsa was able to mobilize almost the entire Solidarity camp, a mobilization on the same scale seen in the June 1989 elections. In both cases it was a mobilization of, at best, a plurality of the potential electorate. Both in June 1989 and in December 1990, the number of votes cast for Solidarity did not exceed 40 percent of eligible voters.

This pattern was the only one we uncovered between voter turnout and electoral choice. That voter turnout in June 1989, November 1990, and December 1990 shaped up as a distinct factor and did not show a relationship to the merits of the decision to vote means that, on a national scale, certain factors were the basis for the decision "whether to vote" and other factors were the basis for "how to vote." Voter turnout was higher where there were well-integrated local communities with long (reaching back to the time of partitions) traditions of political and social activism, such as Wielkopolska and Małopolska. At the same time, both regions were (for reasons that would require another paper) the polar cases of support for Solidarity (highest in Małopolska, weakest in Wielkopolska). Finally, the two last factors help explain two extremely contradictory pairs of candidates: Tadeusz Mazowiecki and Roman Bartoszcze, and Włodzimierz Cimoszewicz and Leszek Moczulski.* In the latter case, we can, without great risk, talk about support for or rejection of communism as a factor. It is interesting that this factor does not coincide with support or rejection of Solidarity. It may also mean that some part of the electorate was inclined to support, and another to reject, these candidates and/or the programs of their parties.

It is more difficult, on the basis of factor analysis alone, to interpret the opposition between Bartoszcze and Mazowiecki. However, a superficial glance at an electoral map of Poland shows that Bartoszcze fared much better in rural provinces, whereas Mazowiecki did better in large cities. Thus, for the first time since the formation of Solidarity we see political preferences based on voters' position in the social structure. One of the most significant findings of our research in the 1980s was the irrelevance of social structure (broadly understood as occupational and class membership) as a determinant of attitudes and behavior. By the end of 1990 a relationship became apparent. Roman Bartoszcze's electorate is the peasantry, who although as politically polarized as the rest of the society in the 1980s, tried in 1990 to integrate themselves politically as a class in order to become a third force in

Polish politics. So far they have not been successful even in rural areas, where Bartoszcze finished third in the presidential race, behind Wałęsa and Tymiński.

The real novelty was Mazowiecki's electorate. To describe it accurately we must examine public opinion polls. The most representative samples came from exit polls conducted during both rounds by OBOP with the cooperation of a German polling firm (INFAS). The results of this poll presented on television on the evening of elections could and should have persuaded all those skeptical of the precision and predictive value of such polls. Tables 7.6, 7.7, and 7.8 present data on electoral preferences according to sex, age, and education. Table 7.9 presents the official data of the State Electoral Committee on voting by type of locality.

The novelty of Tadeusz Mazowiecki's electorate was that it was largely drawn from college-educated residents of large cities. In contemporary Western sociology this group is described as urban professionals. Half of the votes cast for Mazowiecki came from cities with more than one hundred thousand inhabitants, where one-third of the eligible voters reside. Mazowiecki also won among those with higher education, no matter where they lived. The intersection of these two groups is urban professionals, one of the social bases of the first noncommunist government in Eastern Europe, and for whom Tadeusz Mazowiecki became the natural and obvious political representative.

The situation in 1990 is something new, compared with the situation in the 1980s when the entire society was politically polarized, and at the extremes of this continuum one could find almost equal numbers of members of every social class, group, and category. "Urban professionals" were also polarized, although the pro-Solidarity orientation was stronger than pro-regime feelings. In the fall of 1990 most urban professionals supported Mazowiecki, and thus were the first group

Table 7.6. Voting in round 1 of the presidential elections according to gender (in %).

	Bartoszcze	Cimoszewicz	Mazowiecki	Moczulski	Tymiński	Wałęsa
Men	7.6	7.1	18.6	3.0	23.5	39.8
Women	5.0	9.7	22.3	2.1	23.1	36.5

NOTE: Figures do not add up to 100.0 due to rounding.

Table 7.7. Voting in round 1 of the presidential elections according to age (in %).

Age	Bartoszcze	Cimoszewicz	Mazowiecki	Moczulski	Tymiński	Wałęsa
18–25	5.9	7.5	20.8	3.2	31.2	31.2
26–45	6.6	8.7	20.1	2.9	27.0	34.4
46–60	5.8	8.8	21.9	2.0	16.5	44.8
61 & up	7.5	6.8	21.6	1.7	7.4	54.7

NOTE: Figures do not add up to 100.0 due to rounding.

Table 7.8. Voting in round 1 of the presidential elections according to education (in %).

	Bartoszcze	Cimoszewicz	Mazowiecki	Moczulski	Tymiński	Wałęsa
Elementary	12.5	5.6	10.5	3.2	20.3	47.6
Vocational	7.2	6.0	12.2	2.6	31.3	40.5
High school	4.5	9.5	22.7	2.4	24.3	36.4
College	2.8	12.4	39.7	2.4	13.2	29.4

NOTE: Figures do not add up to 100.0 due to rounding.

Table 7.9. Voting in round 1 of the presidential elections according to residence (in %).

	Bartoszcze	Cimoszewicz	Mazowiecki	Moczulski	Tymiński	Wałęsa
Rural communes	17.1	7.4	7.4	2.3	24.2	41.7
Mixed urban/ rural communes	8.9	9.3	15.2	2.6	27.3	36.8
Cities up to 10,000 inhabitants	2.6	9.4	21.8	2.8	26.8	36.7
Cities 10,000 to 20,000	3.1	10.8	18.0	2.5	25.3	40.3
Cities 20,000 to 50,000	2.1	11.3	20.0	2.5	25.9	38.1
Cities 50,000 to 100,000	1.8	11.1	20.5	2.9	26.1	37.6
Cities with more than 100,000 inhabitants	1.4	9.5	26.6	2.7	19.4	40.4
Warsaw districts	1.1	10.0	27.8	1.5	10.7	48.9
Voting abroad	1.7	3.8	36.6	2.5	10.7	44.9

NOTE: Figures do not add up to 100.0 due to rounding.

whose political preference was defined by its location in the social structure and its interests, not by its values and responses to political symbols. Something similar could be said about those who voted for Roman Bartoszcze, but only a significant minority, not even a plurality, of peasants and village inhabitants voted for him. Another interesting finding about Mazowiecki voters is that a positive or negative attitude toward Solidarity was not significant. This means that the social structural factor—the level of urbanization or modernization (modernity)—influenced the level of support for Mazowiecki more strongly than attitudes toward Solidarity and its political symbols. It might also mean that Mazowiecki drew support from some segments of the intelligentsia or urban professionals not previously linked to Solidarity.

The two remaining large blocs of voters—Wałęsa's and Tymiński's—are more difficult to characterize in terms of social structure. They do not, however, mirror society as a whole. Among Wałęsa's voters, people over sixty-one, and people with either elementary-school educations or lower, are overrepresented. Among Tymiński's supporters, young people, people with vocational or incomplete high-school educations, and the inhabitants of small cities and tiny towns are overrepresented. A plausible hypothesis is that Wałęsa's and Tymiński's supporters, although not very different in terms of their location in the social structure or their interests, differed in the degree to which they were exposed and susceptible to Solidarity's programmatic slogans and political symbols. Solidarity has traditionally had the least support in smaller cities and towns. Similarly, Solidarity had less support from those of the younger generation, who did not directly experience the great surge of 1980–81 and who throughout the 1980s lived in the shadow of a Solidarity myth it did not directly experience. Today it seems to have decided to live in opposition to it.

The Stubborn, the Unstable, and the Apathetic

Mazowiecki's electorate was distinguished from other groups by its location and its social position. Those who supported Wałęsa and Tymiński were distinguished by their attitude toward Solidarity's ideals. Each of these groups was, however, strongly differentiated internally.

This internal differentiation was frequently greater than that between different social groups. Therefore, one must be careful in generalizing about the ideological, social, psychological, or outright philosophical differences between the supporters of Wałęsa and Tymiński, or of Wałęsa and Mazowiecki. Those who voted for candidates who received less support are easier to categorize—peasants voted for Bartoszcze, people who remained loyal to the old communist system voted for Cimoszewicz, and certain staunch anticommunists voted for Moczulski.

Despite the very obvious relationship between Mazowiecki and the intelligentsia (or urban professionals) and between Wałęsa and Solidarity, support for each was heterogeneous socially, structurally, ideologically, and programmatically. Thus an explanation of the motivations for electoral behavior cannot be limited to a comparison of the voters for Wałęsa, Tymiński, and Mazowiecki but must include an internal examination of each group. We must not forget that there were two rounds of elections, and voters could support Wałęsa or Tymiński throughout, or abstain from voting twice, or change their minds between rounds. Many voters did change their vote in the second round because the choice was narrowed to either Wałęsa or Tymiński. Was there a difference between those who supported Wałęsa from the beginning and those who voted for him only in the second round? What led some of Mazowiecki's supporters to cast their votes in the second round for Wałęsa, and others to remain at home? Did exactly the same voters vote for Tymiński in both rounds? To answer these and similar questions, electoral sociology uses panel studies, which consist of multiple questionnaire-style interviews with voters over time in order to register changes in attitudes, views, or behavior. Stanisław Gebethner and I conducted such a panel study on the presidential elections. We interviewed subjects at three different times: (1) seven to ten days before round 1, (2) six to nine days after round 1, and (3) one to two weeks after round 2. Analysis of whether and how respondents intended to vote, and whether and how they voted, allowed us to distinguish several groups of voters. These data are presented in Table 7.10.

Let us begin with the characteristics of the two most strongly opposed political groups: those who voted for Wałęsa and Tymiński in both rounds. These groups, paradoxically, are similar in many ways. Their social composition differs slightly—those with vocational educa-

Table 7.10.   Patterns of voting in rounds 1 and 2 of the presidential elections.

Round 1	Round 2	No. of respondents	%
Wałęsa	Wałęsa	283	33.4
Mazowiecki	Wałęsa	116	13.7
Did not vote	Wałęsa	50	5.9
Tymiński	Wałęsa	32	3.8
Tymiński	Tymiński	85	10.0
Mazowiecki	Did not vote	39	4.6
Did not vote	Did not vote	66	7.8
Other cases		177	20.9
Total		848	100.0

NOTE: Percentages do not add up to 100.0 due to rounding.

tions and incomplete high-school educations are overrepresented among Tymiński supporters. Wałęsa's consistent supporters closely approximate the composition of society, with a slight overrepresentation of the elderly and those with elementary educations or less. Even more significant is the similarity of some views and opinions expressed by both groups. Both are unhappy with the speed and the direction of the economic reforms introduced by the Mazowiecki government. They have similar visions of what is a desirable socioeconomic order (egalitarianism, strong state intervention, aversion toward foreign capital), as well as some similar views on public order, such as reticence about minority rights.

Those who voted for Wałęsa or Tymiński in both rounds shared feelings of frustration and a belief that positive changes could take place quickly and painlessly, but differed over current political issues. Wałęsa's supporters favor the current political changes and view them as properly, but too sluggishly, moving toward democracy. Tymiński's supporters are inclined to view the current political situation not as a democracy but as a new dictatorship. Thus they have a negative view of the pace and direction of political change. The biggest difference between the two groups is their attitudes toward the Catholic church (Wałęsa's supporters are the most devout, whereas Tymiński's are the most critical) and certain issues raised by the church. Their attitudes toward the de-legalization of abortion place the two groups at the opposite poles of the sample: the prohibition is favored by 43 percent of Wałęsa's supporters versus 8 percent of Tymiński's (support in the entire sample was 28 percent). These differences of opinion stem back to the political histories of these groups. Wałęsa's supporters, to a greater extent than Tymiński's or anybody else's, were members cf Solidarity, both now and at the time martial law was imposed in 1981. They also participated with greater frequency in the May 1990 municipal elections and in the June 1989 elections when they more frequently voted for the candidates put up by Solidarity's Citizens' Committee. The data from our panel study confirmed official data gathered on the provincial level—Wałęsa's hard-core supporters were people who have been strongly tied to Solidarity and its leader for a long time.

Another tenacious and consistent group were those who did not vote either in round 1 or in round 2. Some of their views are similar to those of Tymiński's supporters—they are strongly dissatisfied with the direction of political and economic change. In other areas, such as social conservatism and strong ties to the church, they are closer to Wałęsa's conservative supporters. Their ties with Solidarity are not significant. They tended to vote in greater numbers for the national list, and less frequently for Solidarity candidates in 1989. Most important, and more than any other group, they admit to not voting in previous elections, both the parliamentary and municipal. These are not people who recently became politically apathetic—for example, as a result of disgust with negative campaigning or disenchantment with the Solidarity government. They are more consistently apolitical and uninterested in politics than others; they responded to questions more frequently with "it is difficult to say" and are unconcerned about ritual political behavior. In structural terms, they come from the underclass (the group at the very bottom of the social structure). People with only an elementary education or less, as well as the elderly, are overrepresented. The most striking thing is the scale of overrepresentation of women—there are three times as many women as men in this group. I am not familiar with any other case in sociopolitical studies where sex so strongly defined political view or behavior. The emerging Polish feminist movement appears to have a formidable task to perform.

There were individuals who did not participate in round 1 but did participate in round 2. The majority of these voted for Wałęsa. Sociologically, they resemble the "core" electorate of the leader, but their views were less strongly held, with one exception—they were just as critical of the direction and pace of change. This group was not strongly inclined toward expressing their opinions publicly, and most of them had not participated in previous elections (parliamentary or municipal). They can be seen as "the last rank of mobilization." They marched off to the ballot boxes only at the moment when, for one reason or the other, they recognized that their vote might count and that the elections were more than just a ritual to confirm the obvious.

Voters whose candidates lost in round 1 of the elections faced a different dilemma. They could either abstain or support the candidate who seemed closer to them or to be the lesser of two evils. Our sample was not large enough for a statistical analysis of those who voted for Cimoszewicz, Bartoszcze, and Moczulski. For the same reasons, we had to omit the few people who voted for Mazowiecki in round 1 and for Tymiński in round 2. We were able to analyze two groups of Mazowiecki's supporters: those who voted for Wałęsa in round 2 and those who decided not to vote in the second round. The groups were similar in many ways, including their social position as described above and views—acceptance of economic and political change, satisfaction with government actions, a vision of political and economic order based on pluralist democracy and a free-market economy, and a low level of national xenophobia. However, their political histories were different. Those who decided in round 2 to support Wałęsa were very much like his consistent supporters: they had almost as frequently been members of Solidarity, and had frequently participated in previous elections, casting their ballots for Solidarity's candidates.

Those who did not participate in round 2 appear to be a heterogeneous group. Compared with others, this group contained more former members of the PZPR and the old pro-regime branch-line trade unions, as well as OPZZ. They did not constitute a majority of this group, but their presence indicates that Prime Minister Mazowiecki did draw some support from the non-Solidarity electorate. For some of them, voting for Mazowiecki in round 1 could have been tactical— we support him because our candidate (for example, Cimoszewicz) does not stand a chance and, forced to choose between the two Solidarity evils, we prefer Mazowiecki's "thick line"* to Wałęsa's "hatchet."* Others may have voted for Mazowiecki in round 1 out of self-interest. This was consistent with the group interests of urban professionals who joined the party in the 1970s to advance their careers rather than for political reasons. In 1989–90 they may have identified with a reform process that allowed them to utilize their professional skills.

Among the Mazowiecki supporters who refused to vote for Wałęsa in round 2 were also vocal supporters of Solidarity. They saw Mazowiecki as a guarantor of the continuity of change toward a free-market economy and pluralist democracy, and Wałęsa as a threat to these processes. Taken as a whole, the Mazowiecki supporters who did not vote in the second round held very liberal views, in the traditional nineteenth-century meaning of "liberal." This group's political heterogeneity explains why, in the factor analysis above, votes for Mazowiecki were not related to the pro/anti-Solidarity factor.

The last group of voters, who cast their votes for Tymiński in round 1 only to abandon him two weeks later for Wałęsa, was probably the most interesting. Sociologically, they resembled Tymiński's consistent supporters (overrepresentation of young people with vocational and high school educations). They were even more impatient with the speed of change, although not as critical of the direction, especially in the political realm. This is perhaps because many of them have ties with Solidarity going back to 1980–81. They voted for Solidarity candidates in June 1989 and May 1990, but some of them may have regretted it. Their views are characterized by a very strong attachment to egalitarianism and state intervention, and they are more strongly ethnocentric than other groups. It appears that, for them, membership in Solidarity and support for its candidates in the elections was motivated not by the real or some imagined "ethos of Solidarity" but by hope for a quick improvement in their individual material situation. The Solidarity government failed to fulfill these expectations and, out of disappointment these voters turned to Tymiński and his promises. However, before round 2, like lost sheep, they returned to Wałęsa's camp. What caused this conversion?

The Power of the Screen

That television made Stan Tymiński, formerly a small businessman from Canada and Peru, a strong contender in the presidential election is indisputable. The best evidence of this comes from Leszno province, where he won the first round of the elections even though he had no campaign staff and his campaign posters were not displayed. Some have argued, though, that this was the result of an intensely negative anti-Tymiński campaign conducted before and during rounds 1 and 2 (though it should be recalled that Tymiński was the first to use negative tactics, calling Mazowiecki a "national traitor"). It is unclear to what extent the negative campaign damaged Tymiński and to what extent it had a "boomerang" effect ("Since they are attacking him, he must be dangerous to them, so we should vote for him"). There were no data collected that would allow us to answer this question definitely for the campaign before the first round. Available data indicate unequivocally that some lost sheep returned to the Solidarity camp under the influence of the campaign as it was conducted through the mass media, if not of a negative campaign. Let us look at the data in Table 7.11 from this point of view.

People who in the two weeks separating the rounds decided to change their vote to Wałęsa almost twice as often as any other group admit that their electoral decision was influenced by informational (as well as partisan) programs in the mass media (including television, radio, newspapers, and reports on public opinion polling). The socioeconomic and educational profile of this group does not suggest that they read the press or follow the results of sociological studies more frequently than others. We can therefore speculate that the intensely negative electoral campaign conducted against Tymiński between the two electoral rounds was somewhat successful. However, the loss of votes from Tymiński to Wałęsa could also have been caused by mistakes made by Tymiński. Table 7.12 presents the evaluations of Tymiński's refusal to participate in a televised debate with Wałęsa, and to

Table 7.11. The influence of mass media on electoral decisions (in % of answers that a given mass medium had a big influence on voting).

Round 1	Round 2	Polish radio broadcasts	Campaign shows on TV	Newspaper articles about the elections	Published results of public opinion polls
Wałęsa	Wałęsa	20.9	35.5	9.6	7.1
Mazowiecki	Wałęsa	18.1	31.9	20.7	9.5
Did not vote	Wałęsa	18.0	24.0	8.0	10.0
Tymiński	Wałęsa	40.6	62.5	31.3	18.8
Tymiński	Tymiński	16.5	44.7	12.9	3.5
Mazowiecki	Did not vote	12.8	30.8	20.5	10.3
Entire Sample		20.1	37.7	13.7	8.5

Table 7.12. Opinion about Tymiński's refusal to participate in TV programs (in %).

	Definitely right	Rather right	Rather wrong	Definitely wrong	Difficult to say
1:Tymiński 2:Tymiński	32.1	26.2	16.7	4.8	20.2
1:Tymiński 2:Wałęsa	6.5	12.9	29.0	32.3	19.4
Entire Sample	9.8	10.2	18.7	32.6	28.7

NOTE: Figures do not add up to 100.0 due to rounding.

appear on another well-known television show (*Interpelacje*). For purposes of simplification, the table provides only the results for consistent Tymiński supporters, those who voted for Tymiński in round 1 and for Wałęsa in round 2, and the results for the whole sample.

For Tymiński's consistent supporters, television was clearly a medium their candidate should have taken selective advantage of—to introduce himself (how else could even his strongest supporters find out about him?) but not to confront his rivals, the press, or the public. This is potentially a good strategy to retain support. Elections, however, are won by convincing the unconvinced. Television can bring stardom, but sooner or later it uncovers the weaknesses of even the crowds' favorite, especially if opponents highlight the negative. In the second round, Tymiński gained the support of some who voted for Cimoszewicz and Bartoszcze in round 1, but he lost support among those who had voted for him in the first round. Some of his first-round supporters did not vote in round 2, and an even greater number cast votes for Wałęsa. Even without the negative campaign and the mistakes he made, Tymiński could not have won the election. If not for television, however, there would have been no Tymiński. It is a lesson that not only he should remember.

Polish Elections, Polish Choices

In the late summer of 1980 Poles appeared united in their desire for change—or, as the authorities then described it, renewal. Several months later, on the verge of martial law, enthusiasm was already less universal, and one could with some precision distinguish forces interested in reversing the course of events. They came from the social base of the old regime, people connected to it through such structures as the party, the old trade unions, and the state administration. Nevertheless, 70 percent of the adult population of Poland identified, to a greater or lesser extent, with the reforms symbolized by Solidarity. These were the conclusions of our research in *Polacy '80* (Poles 1980) and *Polacy '81*. Successive studies (*Polacy '84* and other research conducted in the mid-1980s) investigated who continued to identify with reform and Solidarity and to what extent.

We discovered that a consistent proreform and antiregime orientation was held by no more than 20–25 percent of the population. A similar, or even slightly larger, number of people appeared to be determined defenders of the political status quo. The remaining population, somewhat lost, lay somewhere between these extremes.

These results made neither the authorities nor the opposition happy. Each side preferred, in its own interest, to believe that it had the support of a majority. In June 1989 it might have seemed that the question of who was right and who was wrong was definitively settled. In the semifree elections of that month Solidarity won an unprecedented victory. In this euphoria, few wanted to notice that only a plurality and not a majority voted for Solidarity candidates. In the elections to the Senate, the largest victory for Wałęsa's team occurred in Nowy Sącz province, where one candidate was supported by 57 percent of those entitled to vote (82.5 percent of votes cast with 69 percent voter turnout). This was the most support Solidarity received. On a national scale it was no more than 33–39 percent of those entitled to vote. That is all Solidarity and its leaders mobilized in this hour of ordeal.

In the municipal elections in May 1990, when the candidates of Solidarity's Citizens' Committee triumphed overwhelmingly, mobilization levels were even lower (75 percent of the votes with a turnout of 40 percent = a mobilization in the 30 percent range). In the summer and fall of 1990, the "war at the top"★ destroyed the unity of the Solidarity elite and divided its electorate. In round 1 of the presidential elections, Wałęsa received 23.8 percent of the votes and Mazowiecki 10.8 percent—together 34.6 percent of eligible voters. In round 2 Wałęsa was supported by a slightly greater number of adult Poles—38.7 percent. Solidarity—the main political force of democratic, postcommunist Poland, the symbol of the rejection of totalitarianism in all of Eastern

Europe—has never achieved the active support of more than 40 percent of the population in any election.

Forty percent is a large measure of popular support. Many successful U.S. presidents are elected by less than 30 percent of registered voters. Forty percent is certainly enough to, individually or as a coalition leader, govern a country under normal conditions. However, the conditions in Poland are not normal. The political, economic, and social systems are still not stable. Is 40 percent enough to rule a country like Poland today? Can anyone again mobilize such levels of support?

In the behavior of the Polish electorate to date there have been many elements of continuity. First and foremost, the polarized scheme of political reference, along the symbolic line of "for or against Solidarity," persists. It is likely that this sort of divide will figure in the next elections. Some will vote for post-Solidarity parties, motivated by self-interest, public interest, or attachment to its values and political symbols. Others will cast their votes for the anti-Solidarity forces, including postcommunist, Tymiński-like, and chauvinistic parties. Still others (half of the electorate?) will remain at home.

The voters will do what they are supposed to do on election day. The rest—the shape of the governing coalition, the definition of the function of the opposition, the model of the state, and the role of its various institutions (parliament, government, the president, the courts), and the type of democratic system (parliamentary or presidential?) we will have in the future—will be decided by those who are elected. So it will be, unless before then the electorate is compelled or encouraged to create on the streets of our cities and the roads that run through our villages some form of government other than, after all, so imperfect, democracy.

Translated by Alexandra Sachowicz

8

The Polish Intelligentsia: Departure from the Scene

Krytyka, no. 40 (1993)

Joanna Kurczewska

How we interpret the role of the intelligentsia in the Polish variant of the systemic transformation of Central and Eastern Europe depends to a large extent on how we understand the social and cultural phenomenon of the intelligentsia,[1] and on how we learn, while analyzing the current political discussion, to separate the intelligentsia's own illusions and myths from reality. Out of regard for the traditions of Polish sociology, and in view of the value that local color has always had here, we have accepted a concept close to one of the classic concepts of the intelligentsia. For us the intelligentsia is a group of people capable of devising ideas and defining an ethos (its main values being knowledge, responsibility for others, social mission, and spontaneous leadership in culture), which in conditions of backwardness, in the absence of (or limitations on) sovereignty, and in a weak democracy represents the interests of the entire nation, substitutes for the Western middle class, and accelerates the modernization processes.[2]

Our thesis is that the role of the Polish intelligentsia is coming to an end. The process of its disintegration, which began under really existing socialism, is almost complete. Its consequences include the differentiation of experts from intellectual ideologists, ambivalent relations between experts and intellectuals, and politics as the mediation of the specialized and the ideologically universal.

Before we analyze the phenomenon of the disintegration of the Polish intelligentsia and its consequences, several observations about what happened to the intelligentsia before 4 June 1989 are in order. What is happening to the intelligentsia now is largely a consequence of its condition at the moment the old structures of the state and the economy were subjected to radical change. In the new macrosocial situation, the intelligentsia (as defined above) was entangled in a complicated set of relations with the political authorities and with its own social basis, that is, with the aggregate of nonmanual workers with higher education, carrying out mental work in the social division of labor.[3]

Generally speaking, this intelligentsia was divided into "old" and "new" components. We do not agree with the thesis that in 1945, as a result of the Nazi extermination, the intelligentsia ceased to exist.[4] The "old" or "traditional"[5] intelligentsia did survive, although reduced in number, largely institutionalized by the church, without much influence over the public, making do with the remnants of its own prewar associations and clubs.

Unlike the "old," the "new" intelligentsia was initially socially and ideologically related to the communist party and its state and economic apparatus. It can be said that the birth of this "new" intelligentsia was related to the process of its desertion[6] from the communist party. This "new" intelligentsia's ethos was created by the continuing and growing intellectual and emotional opposition to political power and the doctrine that legitimated it.

Relations between the "old" and the "new" intelligentsia (irrespective of all the problems related to their composition and internal relations, especially before the "December events"★ of 1970) and the authorities were quite different. The "old" intelligentsia was at first severely persecuted and then effectively marginalized, whereas the "new" intelligentsia was first cherished, then tolerated, only to be eventually rejected. Conflict between the party and the new intelligentsia (predominately revisionists★) became increasingly open. It concerned control over historicity[7] and the state redistribution of material goods.[8] (It is worth stressing here that this conflict has been analyzed very well by Z. Bauman.)[9] This conflict had two kinds of effects. On the one hand, by allowing for further de-ideologization of their old members and supporters, the political authorities helped create a class of experts. On the other hand, by admitting the most competent, educated, and qualified representatives of selected professional groups to the highest levels in state and party organizations, the authorities laid the foundation of the system of *nomenklatura*,★ but according to new rules.

Concerning relations between the intelligentsia and its base of recruitment (some Polish sociologists regard this base itself to be the intelligentsia and have a great deal of data on this subject),[10] we must deal with questions of usurpation and mutual representation. Under really existing socialism, it was first and foremost members of the white-collar aggregate who usurped the attributes and tasks of the old and new intelligentsia by claiming to be a supraprofessional community, to represent definite axiological orientations, and to have opinion-creating and social-catalyst functions.[11] In empirical studies, they spoke of the need for a mission and authority and took their ideal visions of the intelligentsia's tasks for the attributes of their existing, loosely linked professional communities.[12]

Not only its social base, but the intelligentsia itself, manipulated its own image and the image of its base. Distinguished writers, great artists, popular columnists participating in numerous discussions on "the crisis of the intelligentsia," on relations between "the intelligentsia and the people," on "the intelligentsia and the working class," and on "the intelligentsia and the state," referred to larger communities of white-collar workers, to numerous professional organizations and associations while expressing their own opinions and beliefs in the name of an unrecognized larger community of "intellectual craftsmen." They spoke in their name, but without "democratic consultations," when they announced that the intelligentsia acted as vanguard or arbiter in service to the nation and culture.[13]

The intelligentsia emerged from the ancien régime victoriously: it was internally integrated and at the same time had strong ties with the public; it enjoyed relative material security and was the most important link with the West, with which it maintained direct cultural and political contacts. In this respect, the experience of Solidarity and of martial law was of considerable importance. Within the Solidarity movement a number of positive integrations occurred—of the old and new intelligentsia; the intelligentsia and its base of recruitment; the intelligentsia, workers, and peasants; and so on. The negative experience of persecution under martial law strengthened the internal ties of the intelligentsia, making it the intelligentsia "for the movement," the Solidarity intelligentsia. In the eyes of society, the intelligentsia passed its test as a collective independent of the communist authorities, as an intellectual and moral authority, as the opposition's architect and helmsman.[14]

An institutional revolution in the state, the economy, and the culture began in 1989. It was directed toward controlled pluralism, democracy, and the market. It destroyed the dichotomy between the state and civil society and laid the foundations for a new kind of relationship between them—the relatively agreeable cooperation characteristic of the democratic societies of the West. Thus the Solidarity intelligentsia, one of the highest authorities of the opposition to the state, and civil society's elite, found itself in a situation that is rarely encountered in modern history: it was offered new tasks and functions within the institutional structures of the state and civil society.

Above all—and this was the greatest *novum*—it was given the possibility of building state institutions according to the programs, strategies, and visions it had been creating and pursuing for years, but only in words and ideas, in conditions limited by the oppressive character of the ideological state and the canons of its national and political culture. In other words, the Solidarity intelligentsia was like an architect who got an offer to become a builder, to be a creator of the institutions of the state instead of a creator of ideas.[15]

Did they accept the offer? Yes, but at great cost—they lost their social and ideological identity. A considerable number of them undertook tasks requiring special professional skills, activities that put them on a par with the highly proficient nonmanual workers with higher education who are in great demand on the market. In this way some of the intelligentsia have been transformed into experts, into a group of state officials, into technical executors of somebody else's ideology and political will. Others, especially the leaders of the democratic opposition, are trying to become builders on a large scale. They take over or establish institutions in the service of their own political and ideological ends, use these institutions, and then discard them. They do not invest too much in them or treat them as significant elements in a larger strategy of economic, civilizational, or cultural change. Unlike a craftsman who takes care of his tools, they neither take care of the instruments of power nor think about how to create an efficient system of government or a new system of institutions that work well in general.[16] They can be called institutional nomads.[17] They are characterized by a moralistic orientation that prevents them from understanding the importance of the institutional order to the smooth functioning of society. Their organizational experience has been limited to underground or quasi-legal structures. To date, they have not created any new, significant national institutions. Rather, they use the institutions left over by the communist regime to attain their own political and economic aims. If they create anything at all, it is without any long-term perspective. Although it would seem to be the greatest need of the modern democratic state, they have not taken up politically responsible institution-building. Instead, they manipulate ideas, symbols, and images and are agitators, educators, and spokesmen for and participants in the process of the personalization of politics.

They are no longer members of the intelligentsia, and yet have not become professional politicians. They are no longer intellectuals because they were finally given a great chance to realize their earlier visions in a relatively unrestricted fashion—to implement civil initiatives and systemic designs, under conditions of limited state coercion. They have not yet become politicians, because the motivations for their actions are primarily moralistic and utopian. They are political intellectuals[18] who in their plans and actions are motivated by lofty intellectual and moral standards. However, they do not assume political responsibility for their standards or for the resultant decisions, only intellectual and moral responsibility. Neither do they represent the interests or ideals of any actual community. Political intellectuals offer themselves to the state and society—their axiological orientations, programs, or ad hoc views.

The dynamic of changes in the state is being decided by a whole range of factors. Of particular importance is the conflict between political elites, the completely open conflict between experts and political intellectuals.[19] The victory of experts in this conflict will mean disaster for the broader base of specialists from whom the intelligentsia is recruited, and a minor setback for intellectuals per se. The result of this process could be the creation of a class of experts who will produce and spread an ideology of efficiency and technocracy, a class that is subordinated to the state, its rationales, interests, and strategic aims.

However, the entire intelligentsia has not crossed over to the side of the state. The part of the intelligentsia who still act in the sphere of symbols and ideas[20] have stuck to their routinized mission from Solidarity's heroic past. They criticize the state in general, create stereotypes of reform, and make plans for and outline visions of the good state and society. In principle they are against state intervention in civil society—even when the means and ends of intervention coincide with the needs and interests of society's members.

Beyond that, they have been extending their critical attitude to their own institutions, group opinions, and lifestyles. Earlier, they tended not to do this openly for fear of being suspected of compliance and cooperation with the communist authorities. In their increasingly open criticism of the state, they constantly make use of the myth of Solidarity. They refer primarily to the concept of social self-organization. They fail to notice that the symbolical and organizational value of Solidarity has declined radically in the eyes of the public.

Attitudes and actions of this sort on the part of the intelligentsia promote a number of conflicts along the axis of civil society and the state. Taken together, all this leads to the impression that civil society remains the intelligentsia's refuge. However, this is no longer justified either socially or politically—first, because of changes in the state and the economy; second, because of the socialization of the state and a general change in the nature of relations between civil society and the state; and third, because of the political vindication of, as well as attempts to reactivate, the ethos of small-scale enterprise, which is repugnant to the classical ethos of the Polish intelligentsia to whom "bourgeois virtues" were alien and somehow "inferior."[21]

The intelligentsia has also been disappointing in its traditional and routine self-organizational activities in various kinds of scientific, professional, and social associations. Intellectuals remaining within civil society could reactivate the numerous associations that have existed since the interwar era. They could also modify the rules and semilegal institutions of social self-organization inherited from really existing socialism. Last but not least, they could form new associations oriented toward broadening and enriching the network of civil society's institutions with new organizations based on partnership with institutions of the democratizing state.

Numerous empirical observations[22] do not indicate that the associations and societies created in interwar Poland and later, in the era of really existing socialism, now play an important unifying role. One need only look at what has happened to such academic associations as the Polish Economic Society, the Polish Historical Society, or the Polish Sociological Society. Beside pursuing their strictly professional aims, these societies operate in the public arena, are committed commentators on public events, and also act as independent arbiters in political and moral disputes. In the 1970s and 1980s they were centers of independent thought and creative discussion and provided a forum for unrestricted debates on the state, society, and responsibility. At present they are invisible to the public and are experiencing a serious institutional and intellectual crisis. Their members have not devised new principles for their involvement in wider public activity. Members who were once very active are no longer interested in their activities.

Generally speaking, the intelligentsia has been disappearing from the social and political scene, because, it should be repeated yet again, the organizational and symbolic context indispensable to its existence and to the tasks and social duties it once had has disappeared. The state has become our very own, responsive and sovereign. This is so also because—as shown by the political debates accompanying the presidential and parliamentary election campaigns—the post-Solidarity intelligentsia themselves have questioned the fundamental distinguishing features of their ethos, those that differentiate them from other social groups. It is obvious that the intelligentsia was criticized, not just from "outside" for forgetting its own roots or for subordinating themselves to the interests of the communist party or the church. The criticism flowed primarily from within its own circles, and from the most influential circles in terms of shaping public opinion.[23]

The intelligentsia has lost its social and political importance because the innovative character of the current changes has reduced it to a normal participant, one of the many collective actors, and not the one at the rudder. The general collapse of political authority, and that of groups from the intelligentsia in particular, are evidence of this. If it still exists, it does so only among old and less ostentatious intellectual authorities—such as the circle around the monthly Więź* [The link]— who either have stayed completely out of the political struggle or do not participate in it openly. However, the public seems to show more respect for their past achievements than for their present activities and ideals.

It also needs to be said that the intelligentsia is no longer fundamental to the transformation of culture, the creation of new political styles, and the introduction of normative programs and visions, including new models of political language and the relationship between politics and morality.[24]

The intelligentsia's activities in the sphere of culture boil down to sustaining the old canons of national and universal culture and to mimicking the mythologized social and national mission of the old intelligentsia. It is not the actions of the intelligentsia alone that have diminished its cultural role, but also the increasing influence of the international context of culture. Americanized popular culture, as well as the power of the liberal and democratic political culture of the West, have played an important role.

As noted above, the intelligentsia has been dying a natural death, leaving its successful children, experts and critical intellectuals, behind. Both the quality of experts and intellectuals and the character of relations between the two will be important for the character of the ongoing changes. That these are not clearly defined is the greatest drawback. Their relationship does not as yet conform to the principles and rules recognized by the public and the state. Neither are they negotiating with each other on the shape of their relations. There is not much risk in saying that relations between experts and critical intellectuals are more often than not decided by chance.

Such a state of affairs makes the character of relations both within groups of experts[25] and within groups of intellectuals even more vague. Only the echoes of conflicts between lawyers and economists, or engineers and bankers, reach the general public. Even more common and less understandable to society are conflicts between intellectuals who serve as ideologues of the transition from socialism to democracy and pluralism. People know that intellectuals quarrel among themselves, but nobody knows exactly what they quarrel about. The most that people know is that the argument is about great programs. However, questions of strategy and tactics remain obscure. Generally, it is known that the dispute is between spokesmen for pro-society and efficiency options, or between supporters of liberalism and those of Christian-democracy or socialism.

The vagueness of the relation between experts and intellectuals has its numerous political repercussions[26] both for society at large and for both sides themselves. It makes it difficult to articulate fully the natural and stimulating conflict between people of narrow technical and scientific abilities and those of broad cultural horizons.

The policies of the government and parliament suffer most from the lack of this sort of debate. In politics there is no room for a regular and complete presentation of the group, professional, social, and political interests of experts employed in the state administration and in the private sector. These interests seem to be articulated only under the pressure of moral authorities, when they refer to their own problems or to those of experts who are dependent on them.

Those of us who research the Polish political scene usually agree that we still do not have professional politicians and that we have only a few responsible expert advisers.[27] Instead, the Polish political scene abounds in moralists, teachers, and utopian critics. As a result of the ambiguity that governs the new politics (because of the absence of a socially recognized standard of political competence), there are too many possibilities for easy and surreptitious passages from the role of expert to that of ideologue, whether as a critic or as a strategist. Ambivalent relations between intellectual ideologists and experts make the situation even less clear.[28]

Still, it does seem possible that ideologists and experts could take care of the things they should take care of for the sake of modernization, that the former could work out the most general forms of government, and that the latter could search for the most effective techniques and methods for implementing them. This depends in large measure on final intellectual liberation from the myth of Solidarity. One can presume that, once the community is given up as an ideal, the conflict between experts and ideologists will become open, and could possibly speed up the processes of the differentiation of interests, which are indispensable to the modernization of the sovereign state, the market economy, and independent culture.[29]

If this does not happen, politics will remain an area ruled by explicit ideals, vague rules,[30] and unclear social roles. It may become ready to accept a substitute for the intelligentsia—if they have a mission, superior knowledge, and are above society.

May 1991

Notes

1. Here there is no time, and this is not the place, to cite the numerous and important semantic differences over the notion of the intelligentsia in Polish scholarly literature. Its importance cannot be overestimated, considering that along with the concept of "nation," "the intelligentsia" has been present in Polish sociology since its inception and that disputes over it marked important moments both in the history of the science and in its relationship to Polish society and culture.

The literature of the subject includes first and foremost: J. Chałasiński, *Społeczna genealogia inteligencji polskiej* (Warsaw, 1946); F. Znaniecki, *Ludzie teraźniejsi a cywilizacja przyszłości* (Warsaw, 1934), and *Modern Nationalities* (Urbana, Ill., 1952); B. Cywiński, *Rodowody niepokornych* (Warsaw, 1971); J. Szacki, "Tezy o inteligencji polskiej," *Colloquia Communia*, no. 5 (1982); M. Zahorska, "Spór o inteligencję w polskiej myśli społecznej do I wojny światowej," in R. Czepulis-Rastenis, ed. *Inteligencja polska pod zaborami* (Warsaw, 1978). An excellent introduction to the discussion on the intelligentsia in Poland and abroad can be found in the preface to the book by A. Gella, *The Intelligentsia and the Intellectuals* (London, 1976). Also see Z. Wójcik, *Rozwój pojęcia inteligencji* (Warsaw, 1962).

2. See Marcin Kula, *Narodowe i rewolucyjne* (Warsaw, 1990), especially the chapter "Narodowo motywowani burzyciele systemu," 228–47, in which the author analyzes the role of the Eastern European intelligentsia in modernization processes.

3. See, above all, J. Szczepański, "Inteligencja a pracownicy umysłowi," *Przegląd Socjologiczny* 13 (1959). It must be said that the majority of postwar studies on the intelligentsia concern college-educated, white-collar workers. Before World War II, studies concerned white-collar workers with high-school diplomas, and this was also reflected in the collection of statistics.

In prewar statistics, the intelligentsia was smaller than the peasant class and the working class, but bigger, and showing a tendency to grow even bigger, than the landed gentry and bourgeoisie. See *Encyklopedia Powszechna PWN*, 2d ed. vol. 2 (Warsaw, 1984). According to the *Encyklopedia*, out of the total Polish population in 1931, 5.5 percent were members of the intelligentsia, 52 percent were peasants, 29.8 percent were blue-collar workers, 0.5 percent were landed gentry, and 2 percent were rich bourgeois. During World War II, the Polish intelligentsia lost 40 percent of its members.

Since the war the number of white-collar workers (both those with high-school and those with university diplomas) has increased. For example, in 1960 its number was four times larger than in 1931. According to M. Haller and B. Mach (in a 1988 report on social mobility in Poland), this was due to a revolution in the system of education and to generational upward mobility.

According to the *Rocznik statystyczny* (Statistical yearbook) for 1989, out of the total of 37.8 million Poles in 1988, the university-educated intelligentsia included 1.7 million persons. Together with high-school graduates, there were 8.4 million members of the intelligentsia. It needs to be said here that the intelligentsia (nonmanual workers with higher education) worked primarily in three sectors: the state administration, the state economy, and education and the health service. The most numerous group is the technical intelligentsia (graduate engineers, economists, and technicians).

4. W. Kwaśniewicz emphasizes this in his fine review article, "Sociological Dilemmas of Intelligentsia. The Case of Poland," presented to the conference at Radzyń, 27–29 November 1989.

5. It is usually termed "traditional" by researchers who stress the importance of the noble roots of the Polish intelligentsia, and who also characterize it in the categories of higher culture and high society. See, for example, A. Zajączkowski's introduction to *Główne dylematy kultury szlacheckiej* (Warsaw, 1965).

6. I refer here to the concept of "desertion" as presented by A. O. Hirschman in *Exit, Voice and Loyalty* (Cambridge, Mass., 1972).

7. A. Touraine et al., *Solidarité: analyse d'un mouvement social, Pologne 1980–81* (Paris, 1982).

8. Here I refer to the theses about the role of the intelligentsia under socialism, as put forward by G. Konrad and I. Szelényi in *The Intellectuals on the Road to Class Power* (New York, 1979).

9. Z. Bauman, "Intellectuals in East-Central Europe: Continuity and Change," *East European Politics and Societies* 2, no. 2 (1987).

10. See first of all A. Borucki, ed., *Polska inteligencja współczesna. Z problematyki samowiedzy* (Warsaw, 1980); S. Kwiatkowski, "Inteligencja 84," *Biuletyn CBOS*, no. 3 (1985); J. Babiuch-Luxmore, *Portrety i autoportrety inteligencji polskiej* (Warsaw, 1989). All these works

concern differences among the intelligentsia and show the main types of its self-representa-
tion in the 1980s. New studies are under way, but their results have not yet been published.

11. To be more precise, this was the claim of 37 percent of those polled by CBOS in a
national sample of college-educated employees. It is to this survey that S. Kwiatkowski refers
in "Inteligencja 84." Thirty-seven percent of the poll's respondents believed that the intelligentsia should act in behalf of society and offer values on society's behalf and in its name. In
J. Babiuch-Luxmore's study of the Warsaw technical intelligentsia in 1983 (published 1989),
42.5 percent of respondents declared their pro-social attitudes. Of those, 23.2 percent believed that they should take care of blue-collar workers both intellectually and socially.

12. While studying the systems of values to which college-educated white-collar workers
subscribed in 1989, S. Widerszpil came to the conclusion that particular professional groups
represented several, relatively coherent, axiological orientations. His studies showed that the
white-collar workers defined themselves in categories from a number of value communities.
He found that 33.3 percent represented the Apollonian orientation (pursuit of creativity,
knowledge, and innovations), that 24.3 percent represented the Dionysian orientation (lifestyle and comfort); and that 25.9 percent represented the Promethean orientation (work on
behalf of society). It should be added here that they believed that the Promethean orientation
was the most characteristic of the Polish intelligentsia.

I think that after 1989, the responderts' orientations and choices might have changed considerably. Yet no relevant studies have been repeated. See information provided by E.
Śmiłowski and L. Kuleszyński in *Biuletyn CBOS*, no. 2 (1991).

13. See J. Kozielecki, *Intelektualiści—miejsce na ziemi* (Wrocław, 1989); W. Markiewicz,
"Etos inteligencji polskiej," *Tu i teraz*, no. 12 (1984); S. Kwiatkowski, "Inteligent—kto to
taki?" *Polityka*, no. 13 (1985).

14. See, for example, J. Frentzel-Zagórska and K. Zagórski, "East European Intellectuals
on the Road of Dissent. The Old Prophecy of a New Class Re-examined," *Politics and Society*
17, no. 1 (1989): 89–113; J. Holzer, *"Solidarność" 1980–1981: geneza i historia* (Paris, 1984).
The post-1989 national press abounds in texts on the heroic role of the intelligentsia in the
time of Solidarity and martial law. The relevant articles primarily want to show the moral
and intellectual sources of contemporary powerholders. All the larger press articles on the
present political scene raise the problem of the intelligentsia as powerholders. Articles of this
kind aim to give legitimacy to the new authorities and to the new political system. These
texts speak about "Solidarity" and the "post-Solidarity intelligentsia" and link Solidarity to
the ethos of the intelligentsia allied with the whole of the nation.

15. See statements by sociologists-turned-politicians, such as J. Kurczewski, "Diabeł tkwi
w retoryce politycznej," *Spotkania*, May 1992. See also K. Pomian, "Inteligencja II
Rzeczypospolitej," *Rzeczpospolita*, no. 99 (1990).

16. See A. Z. Kamiński and J. Kurczewska, "Institutional Transformation in Poland: Actors, Strategies and Structures," *Journal of International Politics* (London) [forthcoming].

17. Ibid.

18. I refer here to the category of "political intellectuals" as coined by J. Szacki. He differ-
entiates between political intellectuals and cultural intellectuals, with the latter being oriented
toward solving the problems of relatively autonomous systems of knowledge and culture.
See J. Szacki, "Intellectuals Between Politics and Culture," in J. McLean, A. Montefiori, and
P. Winch, eds., *The Political Responsibility of Intellectuals* (Cambridge, 1990), 229–46.

19. This conflict has not been publicly noted to any great extent and has not yet been
studied. J. Staniszkis often talks about it as a major structural conflict in her public addresses.

20. Columnists, scientists who are also influential commentators, and politicians can be
recognized as such by their press and other public statements and by their participation in the
work of state and government institutions.

21. See A. Bocheński, *Rzecz o psychice narodu polskiego* (Warsaw, 1971), 61. I mean in particular the intelligentsia's attitude toward capitalism and production.

22. On this subject, local and national studies are almost nonexistent. There already are data concerning the period before 1989, but not many about the present situation. In my opinion, authors of the relevant studies too often refer to the concept of civil society without defining the term. In the present article, I refer to C. Bryan's concept of a sociological variant of civil society. See materials from the December 1991 conference "Democracy in Context."

23. It is sufficient to study the press connected to the Democratic Union and a part of the press related to Christian-democratic groups. This has been a subject of dispute between the "Europeans" and the "patriots" within the Sejm, and in other public discussions. This is also a subject of contention between parliament and parties with a Solidarity background who are not represented in parliament.

24. See the discussion on national culture in *Polityka* in November and December 1991. Especially important were the opinions of Professor M. Janion regarding the chaos in and the lapse of the canon of national culture. She was happy about the collapse of the romantic canon and the birth of a new, instrumental and civic one. She associated the first with the intelligentsia and the latter with new businessmen, the incipient middle class.

25. This is shown in the specialized professional press (for example, *Gazeta Bankowa* or *Życie Gospodarcze*), but not in the press addressed to the public at large.

26. Norms and opinions are influenced by Sejm debates and by public statements by ministers, especially those heading economic ministries.

27. Not much is being said in a detailed and systematic way about expert advising. Most often it is said that expertise is necessary, but no one discusses what is happening with experts and what their expertise involves. In other words, expert advice is merely an ideological postulate. The press and statements by government officials are the main source of knowledge on this subject.

28. Successive finance ministers, [Leszek] Balcerowicz and [Andrzej] Olechowski, have the reputation of experts but leaders of the largest parties represented within and outside the Sejm pass for politicians. Only the skills of the Liberals seem to resist any classification of this kind.

29. I encounter this opinion with increasing frequency. It has become popular, particularly since the last parliamentary elections. People not only object to the absence of any practical effect from Solidarity's ideals, but they often question the ideals Solidarity held in 1980–81. One is led to believe that an end to the disputes about Solidarity and its legacy is a major condition for the pluralization of the political discourse and the initial pluralization of the new state and civil society.

30. Here I mean the vagueness of the rules and politicians' insistence on acting as moralizers without specific political responsibility. This makes the political situation even less clear and promotes an uncritical faith in old patterns.

9

The Social Limits of Economic Reform in Eastern Europe

Krytyka, no. 36 (1991)

Edmund Mokrzycki

The Polish program of economic reform, named after Finance Minister Leszek Balcerowicz,* was implemented on 1 January 1990. The first aim of the Balcerowicz Plan was to stabilize the economy, especially to control inflation. Its ultimate aim was to transform the economic system, that is, to introduce a market economy.

The stabilization measures led in a short time to spectacular successes, such as a rapid reduction of inflation and rapid improvements in both market and budget equilibrium. At the same time, however, symptoms of a deep recession appeared—for the first time since the war there was unemployment while real incomes contracted.

In the second half of 1990, alarmed by the extent of the recession and the first manifestations of public resistance, the government corrected the stabilization program by making it somewhat less restrictive. The corrections did not mitigate the recession or soften resistance to the effects of the stabilization program, which hurt particular social groups. Actually, that resistance, with various fluctuations connected to the political situation, increased. In addition, inflation began to increase, reaching a rate of 12.7 percent a month in January 1991, before coming down slightly over the next few months. For technical (methodological) reasons, it is difficult to assess the real extent of the recession. According to the Central Statistical Office, in 1990 the output of the state-run and "cooperative" (that is, virtually state-run) firms fell by 25 percent, compared with the previous year. In the same period, the private sector's output rose by 8.5 percent. Private industry's share in industrial output also grew significantly; but it remained modest (13.4 percent).

Exact figures on unemployment in Poland are not available. The relevant statistical data are not reliable, first and foremost because of the problems with the unemployment compensation system. It can only be said that, by and large, in the second half of 1990 the steepest rise in unemployment was observed in industrial towns, but before the end of the year it was highest (10 percent) in the undeveloped regions of northern Poland.

It is also difficult to assess the drop in living standards. During 1990 salaries lost nearly one-third of their real value, but under current Polish conditions this is a very unreliable index. Economists and sociologists generally agree that the actual fall in incomes was considerably smaller.

Protest against the stabilization program emerged in the spring of 1990. Like a relay race of opposition, it successively encompassed different social and occupational groups. It began with the farmers, who were the first to suffer the acute effects of the stabilization program. It brought about a rapid decline in demand for food, a jump in the prices of agricultural inputs (imposed by monopolistic state-owned producers), and the withdrawal of cheap credits. In addition to farmers, in the spring and summer of 1990 other occupational groups protested, primarily those who had had a weak position under the planned economy and who thus entered the period of reforms without substantial material reserves or political strength. In the autumn, all major branches of industry came out against the stabilization program. By the end of 1990, opposition to the program encompassed all important occupational groups. For all intents and purposes Solidarity joined the opposition too, with the declaration that it was "closing the protective umbrella it had held over the government" and by its support for the general demand—made by almost all state-run industry (representing close to 80 percent of the industrial output) and the farming sector—to do away with the so-called tax on the inflated growth of wages. In Balcerowicz's program, this tax is the main instrument for fighting inflation. It is, in fact, an administrative tool to limit wages.

In February 1991 it became clear that Balcerowicz's stabilization program was in serious danger. The government became isolated, enjoying only the weak and rather passive support of certain elite intellectual and political circles, and facing the opposition of organized masses of workers and other wage laborers, farmers, and even private businessmen. Beginning in mid-1990, public opinion polls noted a consistent drop in the popularity of Balcerowicz, the government, Solidarity, and other leading actors in the political arena (including the church). Opinion on reform was becoming increasingly ambiguous, so that at the start of 1991 it reached a state of social schizophrenia. General and uncritical belief in the slogans of economic liberalism, and the belief that the Balcerowicz program was the only way to liberal economy, began to go hand in hand with the equally general, dramatic, and outright moral condemnation of the actual consequences of the reform program.[1]

The Social Context of the Reform

Neither opposition to reform nor inconsistencies in opinion toward it are peculiar to Poland. Nevertheless, the situation in Eastern Europe is quite different from the situation in, for instance, Latin America. Poland, as the case where reform has proceeded furthest in Eastern Europe, best demonstrates these differences.

From a sociological point of view, the reform program, whose aim is the establishment of a Western-type market economy in Poland, should take three problems into account (of which, only the first is similar to Latin America).

First, Poland has not completed a cycle of capitalist accumulation and does not have a tradition of a modern market economy. Before World War II its economy was largely based on backward agriculture. Modern industry, usually state-owned or foreign-owned, was only at the initial stages of development. Therefore, with respect to the economy, the slogan of a "return to Europe" finds no support in the country's history. Whatever one might say about Polish people, one thing is certain—the spirit of capitalism was not encoded in their consciousness.

Second, they have on the other hand been imbued with the spirit of socialism in the only version known to history, that is, really existing socialism. Here I mean the syndrome of attitudes and dispositions that is sometimes described as *Homo sovieticus*. The syndrome includes such significant characteristics as "learned helplessness" (loss of any enterprise), the recognition of state paternalism as something natural, and an aggressive brinkmanship. The last of these features is in part specific to Poland and is connected with Solidarity's success in the struggle with the communist regime.

Third, under really existing socialism, Polish society experienced structural changes, which turned out to be more profound and longer-lasting than previously believed. These changes involved not only the liquidation of certain social classes and the advancement of others, but also a change in the mechanisms of social differentiation and a radical shift in the structure of group interests.

I believe that the last problem is more important than the first two. First, structural changes constitute a stronger objective barrier to reform than the absence of a market tradition or a postcommunist mentality. Second, because the authors of the reform have failed to notice this particular problem at all, they have incorrectly explained the negative impact this has had on reform as the results of habits and irrational thinking acquired under communist rule. Let us therefore take a more precise look at this matter.

The Distributive State

After World War II, the social structure of Poland underwent two kinds of changes: (1) revolutionary changes, which were a result of "class struggle," postwar migration, and accelerated industrialization; and (2) organic changes, which spread slowly in the postrevolutionary period—that is, under really existing socialism—as a result of the new "socialist" economic order.

The revolutionary changes were spectacular, connected to expropriation, emigration, and violence, on the one hand, and to the rapid social advance of individuals and social groups, on the other hand. As a result of these processes, in essence planned and organized by the communist party, the landowners and the bourgeoisie were destroyed, the intelligentsia lost its elite character by incorporating the huge mass of the new "working intelligentsia," a considerable number of peasants moved to towns, the working class swelled, and social differences diminished. Postwar migration also diminished the significance of traditional regional divisions and made Poland a nationally uniform country. Generally speaking, a thoroughgoing homogenization of society took place, and its traditional structure was obliterated.

The organic changes proceeded slowly. Only today has their full extent become clear. These changes were based on a shift in the structure of group interests, which meant that the social position of individuals and groups was connected with their place in the state system for the distribution of goods.

At the symbolic beginning of the system there was outright distribution: a division of apartments, vacation time, free medical service, and the like. From a sociological point of view, that simple distributive activity (perceived in the West as one of the major attributes of really existing socialism) had a limited significance because it brought only superficial and short-lived social change. To create profound and lasting change, "centralized planning" was needed. Its essence was—as everyone knows—not so much planning as centralization of economic decisions.

State distribution of goods is an essential part of the system of centralized planning and a condition of its operation. From a purely economic point of view, it is a functional substitute for the circulation of goods on the market. From society's perspective, it is the basic tool for social differentiation. An individual or a social group keen to maintain or improve its social position tried to gain access to the best possible place in the system of distribution or tried to affect the system to make the place it occupied as lucrative as possible. One could pursue the first strategy by choice of career. Individual career choices in Eastern Europe were clearly different from those in the West. Examples of this include the degradation of the medical profession and the attractiveness of all sorts of "special services." Strong vocational groups, such as the army or miners (the case of the latter was more complicated and the product of the model of industrialization chosen), favored the second strategy.

It was that tacit mechanism of goods circulation, not a revolutionary "class struggle," that changed the social system in Poland and in other countries of the region. Ostensibly not much changed, if anything at all. A worker remained a worker, a peasant remained a peasant, and a doctor remained a doctor. Yet after years of the system's operation it turned out that every social group not only changed its position vis-à-vis the others, but itself became something absolutely different.

A worker remained a worker, but his social position was determined by the place the central planner allocated to industry in general, and to his industry in particular. A teacher remained a teacher, but his position vis-à-vis other vocational categories steadily deteriorated because the primary flow of the state distribution of goods bypassed "nonproductive" sectors. Officially, a peasant remained the nominal owner of his farm. In reality, however, administrative limits to his rights of ownership, administratively set prices, a state monopoly on the procurement of agricultural crops, and state rationing of agricultural inputs all made the peasant farm an essential part of the "socialist economy." As a result, the position of a peasant depended more on how the central planner managed resources, that is, on current "agricultural policy," than his own enterprise, energy, resources, conditions in the international food market, and so on.

The Dismantling of the Distributive State and Group Interests

Where the rational, long-term economic aim is possession of the most advantageous position in a system of state distribution of goods, adjustment processes that gradually change the entire economic and social infrastructure of the country develop. After more than forty years' experience with a "planned" economy, each occupational group in Poland has become connected to the system of central planning and dependent on state distribution of goods. For every enterprise, this dependence has very real dimensions: the structure and quality of production, its market, prices, the size and skills of the workforce, local and international cooperation, and so on. Private farming (which accounts for about 80 percent of the land under cultivation) also has in its own way adapted itself to a situation marked by chronic (systemic) food shortages, relatively stable prices, centrally organized procurement, clear signals from the center about what should be grown, and so on. Intellectuals, for their part, have for forty-five years lived in a world of soft financing and continuously expanding scientific and cultural institutions (which remained, nevertheless, a world of censorship and subservience).

Liberal reform intended to dismantle the distributive state strikes directly at the whole existing system of group interests. This is one of the most difficult problems of reform. There is no room here for the play of interests, for political maneuvering, or for betting on certain groups whose interests coincide with the aims of the reform. Even the private sector, that seemingly capitalist fifth column within socialism, was no less dependent on the distributive state than other sectors, although private business's dependence was less direct, related to—among other things—the general situation of shortage, corruption, and the absence of competition.

Hence the idea of creating a Western-style "middle class" that would constitute a solid social basis for reform and the driving force behind a market economy probably came from an intuitive understanding of the situation. To a sociologist, the idea is utopian; it is another example of how a planner tries to shape social reality. The Western middle class is as much a support for the market economy as it is its product.

How then should one interpret the initial unanimous and strong support for the liberal reform and society's exemplary patience for almost half a year? Sociological studies and other sources (such as programs of fledgling political parties and organizations) clearly indicate that support for reform did and continues to grow from ideological premises—from an ideological rejection of socialism and from an ideological belief in an abstract idea of capitalism. The average Pole was not aware of the real dimensions of economic reform. People accepted the "cost of the reforms" but understood them as only belt-tightening. After all, this was how it was presented, in good faith, in government propaganda and by the mass media.

The sudden rise in tension in the second half of 1990 and the mounting criticism of the reform were the result of "impatience" not so much with the protracted period of bearing the "costs" as with a growing sense of insecurity. People began intuitively to realize that the reform threatened not only their standard of living but their fundamental group interests as well, and that it entailed not only "belt-tightening" but the disintegration of the present economic and social order. After forty-five years the order seemed natural in its constitutive dimensions, just like a state distribution of goods and all its practical consequences (for example, unlimited, centrally organized demand for everything that has been produced).

The Vicious Circle of Postcommunism

The authors of the reform assumed that Polish society did not differ from Western societies in its basic structure and that it would react to tested economic instruments in the way that Western societies do. After the first revolutionary wave of structural changes, such an assumption was plausible. Had the communist system collapsed at the beginning of the 1950s, the situation in Poland would have been comparable to that of Spain after the death of General Franco. The market—or its Eastern European substitute—had already ceased to exist, but social barriers to the market had not yet emerged in the form of the "organic" structural changes I outlined above.

The strategic aim of the Polish reform was to liberate the social energy confined by the communist political system. In this way it was expected that "natural" market mechanisms would come to life on their own accord. The same strategy has been adopted in other countries in the region, but its advocates have underestimated the power (whether destructive or not is another question) of really existing socialism as an economic and social system. Market mechanisms, once blocked by the communist political system, are now blocked by the ingrained social and economic consequences of that system. The social energy that is released, instead of spontaneously creating market relations, is mobilized for the defense of group interests that crystallized under really existing socialism and are now jeopardized by the market itself.

By striking at the distributive state, liberal reform strikes at the foundations of the very existence of the primary social groups. The circle is closed: the distributive economic system has created social structures fated to defend this system. The only consistent advocate of the reform is the state administration backed by the active segments of the public, usually ideologically motivated columnists and intellectuals. The people to whom reform has already brought real benefit, most often small traders, as yet constitute a category that is both socially and politically completely amorphous. Maybe one day they will produce the germ of a middle class, and maybe not.

The erroneous conviction that the liberation of public energy was sufficient to break down political and legal barriers and create a powerful and spontaneous movement to initiate a natural process of creating healthy market relations led to a number of tactical mistakes. The most serious mistake was the state's unilateral withdrawal from the role of the owner of the means of production. This withdrawal was unilateral because it was not accompanied by the effective establishment of a new owner. As a result, Polish industry has moved with astonishing speed toward a model of managing nominal state enterprises whose workforces engage in plunderous exploitation and blame the state for the disastrous results. It is telling that toward the end of April 1991 the government announced it was going "to regain control" over state enterprises, presumably by putting them into receivership.

The Balcerowicz Plan, presented as a plan to transform the economic and social system, is in fact a program for economic stabilization. From the analysis presented herein one should conclude that it is too narrow as a program. I am afraid that the authors of this program—economists—have underestimated the depth of the social changes that took place under really existing socialism and have taken as the point of departure for this program sociological assumptions that do not correspond to the realities of postcommunist society.

The Polish program for reform reflects the prevailing way of thinking in Eastern Europe. Others will follow Poland, undoubtedly Czechoslovakia and Hungary. The technical corrections that other countries will probably introduce into the Balcerowicz Plan will not change the underlying philosophical assumption that if the political system was the cause of all of the miseries of Eastern Europe, it will be enough to abolish the system in order to bring about universal happiness. I am afraid that from the sociological point of view, this is a naive philosophy.

April 1991

Note

1. Only small groups of intellectuals who lean toward Western social democracy, such as Solidarity of Labor, moderately criticize the "naive faith" in economic neoliberalism. Their criticism extends to the Balcerowicz program. See, for example, Tadeusz Kowalik, "Piętnaście miesięcy Planu Balcerowicza," in Studia i Materiały, Ośrodek Prac Społeczno-Zawodowych Komisji Krajowej NSZZ "Solidarność" (Warsaw, October–December 1990). Generally speaking, however, the opposition to the Balcerowicz program is based on purely pragmatic assumptions. Adherents of neoliberalism give Balcerowicz their full support, even though certain consequences of this program (administrative control over wages, a fixed exchange rate, customs barriers) are in point of fact repugnant to neoliberals. Jan Krzysztof Bielecki, one of the leaders of the Liberal Democratic Congress, and [in 1991] prime minister, argued at a recent meeting of the Liberal International that a peculiar problem of the Polish situation was the necessity of achieving liberal aims by illiberal means.

Section III

Culture

10

According to Mackiewicz

Krytyka, no. 23/24 (1987)

Jerzy Surdykowski

A new figure of stature has been inscribed in the pantheon of opposition—the recently deceased writer Józef Mackiewicz. His voluminous
output as a writer of fiction and a publicist has been undergoing an
unusual revival after many years of marginal interest on the part of
those living in exile and those living in Poland. Underground publishers have vied with one another to issue the novels and collections of
essays by the "Great Uncompromising." The underground press, including the part that justifiably pretends to uphold the highest intellectual and moral standards, has been running a veritable festival of reviews and essays on Mackiewicz, praising him as a great writer and the
literary sensation of the day. The only thing they have not done is
express a rational opinion on the political legacy of the deceased and
the vision of modern history he represents. Therefore, I will undertake
this mission, hoping that my voice will not sink in the recent tide of
idolatry. Józef Mackiewicz's legacy is an exceptional one because it
justifies the well-known warning that the sweet sleep of reason
awakens demons.

I

I do not know whether Józef Mackiewicz was a great writer. This sort
of question is answered only by time and by specialists in literature
who are more competent than I. Perhaps Polish prose will honor his
descriptions of nature in the borderlands.* Or perhaps it will remem-

ber his openness to the areas of Polish consciousness and history that
have thus far been overlooked or seen as "unwelcome," such as the
drama of Poland's eastern frontier and Poland's eastern neighbors
(Lithuanians, Belarusans, Ukrainians, and Russians). Mackiewicz's
openness to history will certainly be remembered, despite how distorted and unacceptable his vision of history may seem to us. It is with
his vision of history that I want to take issue. We, with our obsessive
Polonocentrism, who derive morbid satisfaction from recollection of
our past sufferings, badly need this sort of openness—not only because
others may have suffered more than we have, or because we too have
made others suffer. We need it, first and foremost, to widen our horizons, to verify the old, hackneyed patterns of understanding history,
and to practice thinking, even if only to exercise it in polemics. Józef
Mackiewicz's "opening to the east" contains not only bitter nostalgia
in the face of loss and ruin of the sort depicted by Czesław Miłosz in
The Issa Valley or by Tadeusz Konwicki★ in practically all of his
novels. It is not limited to the tragic experience of Wilno★ in the years
1939–41 or 1944. Mackiewicz poses questions that are merciless for
Poles, questions that should not be asked too loudly. Such topics include the loss of Ukraine, the bloody rift between the two oppressed
peoples, and lost chances for Polish-Ukrainian understanding. He
raises these questions in the novel Lewa wolna★ [Make way on the left].
He also asks if it would have been better for Poland to cooperate
closely with Nazi Germany when caught between the Nazis and the
Soviets in 1939. He also poses the question of whether the soldiers of
the Russian Liberation Army★ (RLA), whom we see as a symbol of
treason, cruelty, and selling out to the Nazi crime machine, were not,
after all is said and done, ordinary Russians trapped in an unresolvable
dilemma posed by their hatred of Stalinist communism, on the one
hand, and their fear of the criminality and, even worse, of the political
stupidity of Nazism, on the other hand. One can ask numerous questions of this sort. Literature does not pose evil or incorrect questions.
Mackiewicz poses them in his novels and his journalistic writings. In
the latter, he brings back the forgotten, unspoken human drama of
Vlasov's★ soldiers. They too merit literary treatment because they,
even those who surpassed the Nazis in their cruelty, were people.
They were similar to Nazis who became entangled in the criminality of
their ideology. There are a number of literary works that try to penetrate the drama of the Nazi soul, although Nazism as such has not yet

seen its Dostoyevsky. The anti-Stalinist, democratic "Smolensk manifesto," which the Vlasov army issued in December 1942, was only the
futile voice of people of goodwill unaware that they were being manipulated by criminals of no less a caliber than Stalin himself. That
historians, both in the East and in the West, have discounted the role
of the RLA First Division under the command of General Bunya-
chenko in the liberation of Prague is a sad, Orwellian forgery justified
in the name of "freedom and justice." These are but two long-forgot-
ten episodes from the history of the Vlasov army. However, should
we call for that army's rehabilitation as Mackiewicz does? Should we
rehabilitate even those the Nazis used for "jobs" even they found too
revolting? Could Mackiewicz have been deaf to what the generations
of Poles born before 1930, who survived the war in their own country,
remember all too well? At this point I shall turn to one such problem
that exposes Mackiewicz's "tragedy of errors."

There is a huge difference between and a great distance separating a
call for understanding and judging fairly a human drama and a petition
for the rehabilitation of the people concerned. The neglect of this distinction is the result either of recklessness or of ill will. Thus Józef
Mackiewicz's failings as a historical writer are a product not of asking
the "wrong" questions, those one should not ask too loudly, but of his
answer to the questions, which are purposely formulated in a partisan
spirit.

II

In his many novels, Mackiewicz outlined his own answer, a vision of
the history of Poland and its neighbors from the October Revolution
to the present day. He systematically presented that vision and his
evaluation of events in the book *Zwycięstwo prowokacji* [The victory of
provocation], and he developed that vision further in some of his lesser
articles. Below, I try to present a faithful synopsis of history as seen by
Mackiewicz.

First there is a bitter description of the lost opportunity to defeat the
Bolsheviks by the combined forces of counterrevolution and foreign
intervention. Mackiewicz holds the West to blame for this, both because of its "wishful thinking" and because of its consistent readiness

to see the best, the familiar, and the civilized in communism. He also blames Piłsudski, the socialist for whom czarist generals and Ukrainian conservatives always were a greater evil than his ideological cousins, the Bolsheviks. He also blames the czarist generals for their personal squabbles. Yet he does not criticize them for their icy insensibility to those (including the Poles) who felt both nationally and socially oppressed, and for their clumsy march against the current of history toward a Russia that hardly differed from czarism at a time when the storm of the revolution had shaken the consciousness of the typically docile *muzhik*.

Mackiewicz treats Belarusan and Ukrainian nationalists as agents provocateurs or the dupes of provocation, because with the consolidation of the revolution and the establishment of Soviet republics for their nationalities, they saw greater possibilities for national development and turned their backs on Poland. It is pointless to look for the concrete ways in which the Second Polish Republic disappointed national minorities and Polish working people, failed to address peasant poverty, squandered the opportunity to carry out land reform, or repressed the Ukrainians.

Needless to say, that dreadful socialist Piłsudski was responsible for signing a premature peace with Lenin. The treaty was signed after the "miracle on the Vistula."* It once again suspended the death sentence on the Soviet monster, which Piłsudski held so dear.

Mackiewicz maintains that in 1939 Poland should have allied with Germany, because the countries drawn into Berlin's orbit, such as Bulgaria, Romania, or Hungary, did not emerge from the war as beaten and as ideologically disarmed as Poland. Nonetheless, he is probably right when he argues that on 17 September [1939] the Polish government should have proclaimed the Soviet Union an aggressor and should have started a desperate struggle on two fronts.

Sikorski* made a mistake when he collaborated with the Soviets. The case of the Home Army* [AK], which together with the Red Army had liberated Wilno, Lwów,* and several smaller towns, was even worse. The Warsaw Uprising of 1944 was not meant to defend the city against the Bolsheviks; on the contrary, it was meant to welcome them. In the eyes of Mackiewicz, one of the worst collaborators of the time was Stefan Korboński, the last delegate* the government-in-exile sent to Poland. The Home Army was after all pro-Soviet, inspired by a command that sympathized with the peasant and socialist parties, and by communist agents. Mackiewicz describes all this in detail in his novel *Nie trzeba głośno mowić* [It is not necessary to speak loudly]. At this point, one wants to cry "The Home Army, that spit-soiled dwarf of Bolshevism!" as A. Zięba did in his polemic against Mackiewicz's view of this aspect of Polish history (*Kontakt* [Paris], no. 10 [1985]).

Mackiewicz is ready to admit that the Nazi terror was horrible, but he maintains that it remained within the historical limits of terror during war with regard to the Poles. (One's hair stands on end when one reads such rabid nonsense.)[1] Although he maintains that war damage was considerable and that the Nazi policy toward Poland and Poles was stupid, he claims that the real extent of destruction was exaggerated and that Poland's part in the war was smaller than it seems to Poles. What is more, in the years 1941–44 the Nazi army was only a cordon to protect Poland against communist infiltration. According to Mackiewicz, Polish society's turn to the Left, which took place following the country's defeat in 1939 and the successes of the Red Army (this turn did not mean support for the Polish Workers' Party,* but a condemnation of Poland's post-1926 regime and support for the idea of some sort of People's Poland), was the result of infiltration that the frontier guards and the police had not been able to stop. The only political force that saw things correctly at the time was the National Armed Forces* (NSZ). Does this mean that the *General-Gouvernement** was better than the Polish People's Republic?

In discussing the case of Piasecki* and PAX,* the standard sources (Micewski, Majchrowski) are not sufficient for Mackiewicz. He makes up conversations and sources (*Zwycięstwo prowokacji*, 136), reserving the right to document them in the future. Yet this future never came. This is because—in Mackiewicz's opinion—only a right-wing underground had the potential to pose a mortal threat to communism in Poland after the war, and only Piasecki and PAX were capable of rescinding the new authorities' death sentence.

*Tygodnik Powszechny** [Popular weekly] and *Znak** [Sign] were also collaborators, or at least pharisees. Mackiewicz blames them for the disorientation and disarming of the religious masses, the episcopate, and even the Vatican. The "communist agent" Stefan Kisielewski,* who takes communist money to travel around Europe and foment trouble, exasperates him in particular. When all is said and done, the church's betrayal is uniquely evil; Mackiewicz even devoted a separate book to this theme, *Watykan w cieniu czerwonej gwiazdy* [The Vatican in the shadow of the red star]. The church's betrayal lies in its policy of openness and dialogue, and in reaching understandings with the state. Such agreements with the communist party would have still been heresy under the late, lamented Pius XII. This led to the ambiguous role of Cardinal Wyszyński,* and the open collaboration of such figures as Kisielewski, and also Jerzy Turowicz,* Stanisław Stomma,* Tadeusz Mazowiecki,* and all like them.

The movement away from Stalinism in the latter half of the 1950s and the condemnation of Stalin were merely a shrewd manipulation by Khrushchev. Similarly, the Polish October* [1956] was also a shrewd manipulation. Only the events of "June 1956"* were real. Everything else was a manipulation staged by the Soviet secret police, similar to the Trust* organization in the 1920s, which although allegedly anti-communist actually served the interests of the Kremlin (an incident that Mackiewicz cites continually). In all his writings, Mackiewicz commonly stretches the facts to support his own vision of events and history. For example, he maintains that *Po prostu** became critical only after Gomułka* had attained power (the party allowed its agents provocateurs to be critical), because his study of this weekly—which is, after all, also available in archives in London—indicates just the opposite. Similarly, all the manifestations of independent journalism in 1956–57, 1971, and 1980–81 were, according to Mackiewicz, controlled by communists and served their interests. Mackiewicz is above such nuances as the disintegration of the system, mounting public pressure, different stands taken by individual members of the power elite—all these, he maintains, are a mere provocation! This way, such people as Eligiusz Lasota,* Stefan Bratkowski,* Maciej Szumowski,* and this author, if not agents, were then at least involuntary supporters of the regime. The greetings sent by the Union of Journalists in Exile to their colleagues in Poland, who worked under the difficult conditions of limited freedom of expression and of censorship, was just a base act of treachery. I do not know how Józef Mackiewicz would assess the campaign in 1982–83 to provide relief for journalists sacked from the official press because of their close ties to Solidarity. No doubt he would treat this in the same manner.

The same can be said about his attitude toward writers. Polish literature in Poland ended in 1945 and since then has existed only in exile, just as Russian literature was created either before the revolution or in exile. Writing in Poland or the Soviet Union has become the hideous product of writers whose consciousness has been sovietized. It is conditioned not by the soul but by self-censorship. In *Zwycięstwo prowokacji*, whenever Mackiewicz refers to the literature of the Polish People's Republic (PRL) he puts the word "books" in quotes. He discusses this in greater detail. but in the same spirit, in his sketch, "Droga Pani . . ." [Dear Madam . . .].² He has the same opinion about supposedly independent writing; all *samizdat*★ only pretends to be underground literature. It only poisons the minds of readers both in Poland and in the West. I have never heard that Mackiewicz ever recanted this position, which he espoused in *Zwycięstwo prowokacji* (162). This statement is exceptionally painful and offensive to those of us who write for uncensored publications in Poland. Mackiewicz had ample time to make amends because between the time he wrote those words and his death much occurred, most significantly the creation of Solidarity. Yet he did not retract anything.

The fundamental instruments of communist subversion and the ideological disarmament of Poles, living both abroad and in Poland, are cowardly "Polish realism"★ [*polrealizm*], *poputnichestvo* [fellow-traveling], and the noxious influence of leftists. *Tygodnik Powszechny*, Paris *Kultura*,★ the so-called independent deputies in parliament, and the intelligentsia are agents of that communist plot. The Rapacki Plan,★ the overseas concert tours of the Mazowsze folk group, the work of Polish experts in less-developed countries, exports of Polish meat, and every move by a businessman who holds a Polish passport—all are communist plots!

To be sure, Solidarity too was manipulated by the communists, or at least served them indirectly—through its captive though authentically popular mass base—because it did not question Soviet control over Poland and instead entered into conciliatory agreements with the communists.

Mackiewicz had a particular dislike of dissidents. Solzhenitsyn, Sakharov, Daniel,★ Sinyavsky,★ Kołakowski,★ Kuroń, and Michnik were also Soviets, only even more dangerous, because they appealed to democratic ideals. After all, this was not the first time the party center entered into a tacit agreement with the leaders of certain movements in order to achieve their ends in an underhanded fashion. Why was Solzhenitsyn transported to the West in comfort instead of being sent to rot in a camp? Who helps dissidents smuggle their letters from prison?

Who gave the Catholics from the Lithuanian group *Auszra*★ the addresses of communist party centers in the West? Who smuggled their petitions out? Mackiewicz wrote: "I cannot treat anyone who tries to clean up or improve communism as my friend. They are my enemies. Potentially, they are more dangerous than unreformable communists."[3] In another column he wrote for *Wiadomości*,[4] Mackiewicz discussed the Polish democratic opposition, "which includes minor organizations ready to promise anything, who are not worthy of mentioning here, including the Workers' Defense Committee★ [KOR]." Perhaps the worst and most deceitful was Sakharov, the defender of "human rights" (in quotation marks). Why was he not arrested? Why did they allow him to write appeals and receive telephone calls from abroad? This was an obvious KGB plot! Mackiewicz's opinion of the Russian Nobel Prize winner, published in *Wiadomości*, no. 45 (1977), was wrong, particularly in the light of what next happened to Sakharov. [Sakharov was exiled, isolated, and held under house arrest in the closed city of Gor'kiy.] Yet, Mackiewicz never retracted this opinion on Sakharov, though he must have been aware of Sakharov's fate.

Mackiewicz opposed pacts with the devil. He wanted only to make war on him. Communism would evolve or collapse. Every year more people died in car accidents than would die in a confrontation with communism. The Warsaw Pact was five times weaker than NATO, even with its nuclear weapons (*Zwycięstwo prowokacji*, 232). Nothing remained to be done but launch the Pershings!

This is Mackiewicz's vision of history, reconstructed on the basis of his numerous works (presented in the most concise and journalistic fashion in *Zwycięstwo prowokacji*). His vision is oversimplistic, too narrow and partisan and, moreover, too blind both to facts and to social processes to merit any real discussion. To present this vision should be enough. One is tempted to sum it up as a victory of provocation over common sense. However, it is not my purpose to ruin this writer from the borderlands who tried to be faithful to the cruel fate of his home and who only expressed the truths of his experience and suffering. My purpose here is to compel the numerous contemporary followers of and apologists for Józef Mackiewicz to study his hideous vision of history carefully, if, of course, they have sufficient moral courage. I hope they do not find their own reflection staring back at them from the mirror.

III

There are no "wrong" questions, only bad and pigheaded answers. Reasoning in Mackiewicz's fashion, one must conclude that Hitler was clearly the best anticommunist ever, because only he managed to push the Soviet Union to the brink of disaster. Mackiewicz and many others are trapped by their own arguments. "Wrong" questions open up new horizons; they permit one to reexamine past situations and the consequences of the decisions taken long ago. Only if it is pursued in this fashion can history become the *magistra vitae* and not the source of myths to justify the present.

Could Poland have allied with the Germans? Did Józef Beck★ have any option other than a collapse with honor? If Poland had agreed to join the Nazi anti-Bolshevik Axis, would it have experienced less war damage, suffered perhaps one or maybe two million fewer deaths? Would it have had an efficient and large army that during the final stages of the war could have rebelled, defected from the Axis, and joined the Allies? First and foremost, that army would have been consistently and uncompromisingly anticommunist, free of the sort of collaboration that discredited the AK. These would have been the positive aspects of the collaboration with the Germans. We would have emerged from the war without Wilno [Vilnius] and Lwów [Lviv] anyway, but presumably without Szczecin★ and Wrocław,★ too—yet this does not matter.

However, one cannot agree with Mackiewicz's thesis that Polish participation on the German side would have led to the overthrow of Stalin and to the defeat of communism. Hitler's mad policy as espoused in *Mein Kampf* did not provide for the anti-Stalinist involvement of Vlasov's men, for the national aspirations of Ukraine, Lithuania, and Belarus, or for the sovereignty of Poland. The only fate offered to the Slavs was slavery. That was exactly why Hitler was doomed to lose the war against Stalinist ineptitude, and that was exactly why the leaders of the RLA or of the Committee for the National Liberation of Russia★ could expect nothing else but the gallows in Moscow, even if all other arguments favored Vlasov over Stalin. It is a shame. There was no other fate for the leaders of a Poland dependent on the Nazi lunatics. In this case the Gestapo would not have run the slaughterhouse, but it would have been presided over by our very own executioners, with the help of others imported from Moscow. It all would have been carried out under the banner of Stalin, just as it was in Hungary after 1948. History shows that the anticommunist resistance of the Bulgarians, Romanians, or Hungarians was no more determined than that of the Poles. In fact, the others seemed less determined, although it was Poland that had been cordoned off militarily from "infiltration" for a longer period of time, although it was Poland that had fallen victim to a plot that had spiritually disarmed the country.

However, most important and horrible, Polish participation in an alliance with the Nazis would have meant consenting to "the Final Solution of the Jewish question" as well as active participation in its execution. After all, it was on our territory, not in Bulgaria, Romania, or Hungary, where millions of our Jewish fellow citizens lived. It was with our country that they cast in their lot (although sometimes they were treated worse here than in other countries). It was here—no matter with or against whom the Polish government allied itself in 1939—that the Nazis would have established their death factories. If Poland had followed Mackiewicz's pro-Berlin option, we—as Poles—might not have suffered so cruelly, but our hands would have been permanently soiled with the ashes of Treblinka and Auschwitz. And so we paid an exorbitant price; the fates of the two saddest peoples in the world parted irrevocably. However, the price involved in Mackiewicz's option would have been eternally murderous.

IV

In his works and through his opinions, Józef Mackiewicz tried to justify his life. Many authors do this, and probably no writer is completely free from such tendencies. However, Mackiewicz's life was exceptionally dramatic and stormy. Only in our part of Europe, so mercilessly treated by history, can people live such lives. Happy are countries where similar experiences are not only impossible but even inconceivable! From Mackiewicz's posthumous memoirs, we know of his painful experiences in the east, his trip to Katyń* as a member of an investigative commission (it is another matter whether he went there with or of his own volition). However, almost none of his present-day apologists wants to raise an aspect of his biography that shocked the London émigré community after the war. This is specifically the odium of the death sentence that an underground Home Army tribunal in Wilno pronounced on Józef Mackiewicz for his collaboration with the Germans by the publication of a pro-German paper. Only very few of the authors and publishers of the "reptile papers" [the press sponsored by the Germans] in occupied Poland deserved treatment this severe. For a long time Mackiewicz lived outside the émigré community under the stigma of collaboration with the Nazis, and this was indeed an onerous burden. As time passes, old memories are forgotten, and Mackiewicz has reappeared as a "great writer." I am not going to throw all this at him in the grave. All are entitled to their errors and opinions. Today, however, when assessing the books of an author who described himself as the only true anti-Nazi because "everybody else was either anti-German or anti-Russian," one should remember what he lived through and how these horrendous experiences affected his thinking.

V

If one is opposed to communism as a matter of principle, one should treat our very own Polish communists, and not communism in general or foreign and far-off (for example, Soviet) communists, as the worst enemy. One's own, not somebody else's, sickness makes your life miserable. Similarly, a smarter, enlightened, and liberal communist is more dangerous than a mutton-headed hard-liner. This is why Mackiewicz so strongly disliked Dubček and the other figures of the Prague Spring, and why he even suspected them of being Soviet agents. He harbored the same feelings for successive generations of Polish revisionists.* Another trap into which Mackiewicz's anticommunism led him was his stubborn blindness to changes in the last decade. To attack this blindness serves no purpose. It was not some right-wing underground army, not national insurrection, not nuclear holy war, and not some Western doctrine of deterrence that became the only force capable of checking communism's expansion and has brought it to the edge of collapse. It is the internal decay of communism and its inability to adapt itself to the requirements of the modern world. It is precisely among the passive masses—supposedly sovietized and indoctrinated—that this resistance has developed. It is true that this resistance has been passive, often unconscious, ready to give ground and shun violence. But nevertheless it has been powerful and is capable of eroding the system like a silent, gathering river. Religious communities have begun to speak in their own voice, giving priority to truth over the interests of the totalitarian state. When opportunities present themselves, party people, increasingly contaminated by the curse of common sense, try to put a "human face" on the system through reforms, or at least to make it somewhat more efficient economically. These attempts do not produce the desired effects, but make the decaying machinery even more unreliable. Alas, there is no return to the time of the Great Linguist [Stalin], when everything turned out in the best way possible. Neither is there any prospect for successful reform. Thus under our very eyes—although in a fashion quite different from that for which its most unyielding enemy longed—the ship of utopia has begun to sink quickly.

VI

In *Zwycięstwo prowokacji* Mackiewicz wrote: "The death of a half of mankind in a nuclear war is not a catastrophe. The life of the whole of mankind under communist rule is a catastrophe." I do not think anyone has the right, in the name of mankind and its happiness, to choose between atomic fire and communist captivity, or ever to decide that megadeath under megatons is a fair price to pay for the sudden fall of utopia. Nobody had that right even when the utopia seemed much more attractive than it does today. It seems, however, that the slow course of history offers a possibility, the one I mentioned above, that remains outside this dilemma. This possibility will probably involve a process less devastating than war. All the same it will be protracted and ugly, full of unexpected collisions and related tragedies. It will be similar to the collapse of every empire that lives beyond its time and beyond its ability to perpetuate itself.

Yet it is at this moment, in the country that has done the most to undermine communism, that there is a surprising revival of Mackiewicz, a writer who bet on violence, brute force, and war, who, moreover, was blind to the changing of the times, and who was as unreformable as the regime he fought. This revival is a fact, and one does not dispute facts but just takes note of them. After all, Mackiewicz and his anticommunist consistency are necessary. First, they are necessary for all those great and small—from the banks of the Seine to the Thames, the Hudson and the shores of Lake Michigan—who refuse to compromise in order to justify their sense of superiority over everything that comes from the old country and that naturally must be contaminated by sovietization, self-censorship, and every noxious influence of the red Beelzebub. Second, they are necessary for the young people who have never tired or dirtied themselves living on the Vistula. Perhaps they need it as a drug to stimulate their fervent rejections, or perhaps as an argument against generations of their tired and soiled ancestors. Perhaps . . . For me only the local demand for Mackiewicz's message is significant, and I am interested only in what is going on in this country. It is here where history will be made. This is why I treat this phenomenon as an omen. Of what—I do not know; I am no seer.

Perhaps the renewed popularity of Mackiewicz's paranoid vision of history portends something very dramatic, something very violent . . . something that looms ahead.

October 1986

Notes

1. If readers want to check this I direct them to *Zwycięstwo prowokacji* (London, 1983), 122.
2. *Wiadomości* [London] 10 (1967).
3. "Okupacja czy coś gorszego?" [Occupation or something even worse?] *Wiadomości* 12/13 (1970).
4. "Na drodze wielkiego ześlizgu" [Down the slippery slope], *Wiadomości* 46 (1977).

11

At an Unbearable Crossroads

Krytyka, no. 34/35 (1991)

Andrzej Werner

Is this crossroads actually "bloodstained" or just "damned" in the sense that the English use "bloody"? Blanka Kuczborska, translator of Norman Podhoretz's book *The Bloody Crossroads*,[1] had to solve this unsolvable dilemma, which is unsolvable because, to all intents and purposes, Podhoretz wanted to be ambiguous. However one looks at it, he argues, nasty and dangerous things happen where politics meets literature. This means that he has not only a sense of threat but perhaps a bad conscience, a feeling of sinfulness, as well.

A clash between politics and literature is like a clash between a tank and a sparrow. The victim is obvious. We have been passing this crossroad every day, and not just for the last few years. For several generations it has been a particularly busy route. Sometimes it seems as if this has been the only route we could take. Thus we have managed to gain considerable experience, and a no less deeply rooted sense of guilt. There have been as many complaints as victims. It often seemed to us that we were particularly clumsy, that out of fondness or necessity we abused literature with politics, that we never expected spring to come, that we never saw anything but Poland. Having seen, however, what an American intellectual does at this crossroads, we can securely dispense with several of our own complexes.

What could have drawn an American neoconservative into such an unambiguous monomania with politics, to pose questions that obviously do not correspond to his subject, to the outright rabid reduction of every cultural fact to its "ultimate political meaning?" With us the situation was different; reality itself forced us to behave this way. In our reality, every sneeze had an apparent political meaning and conse-

quences. Laz Roitshvantz* learned this from his own experience at a
time when we did not dream that we too could suffer these consequences. Here every writer had to think about politics, and even if he
did not that was because of politics and was a political decision. But in
the United States, where reality can be depicted in all its colors?

Without any exaggeration, the more literary, ambiguous, and formally complex literature is, the more spectacular the accidents Podhoretz stages at these bloodstained crossroads are. Here, on the Vistula, I am probably not the only one who enjoys his description of the
procommunist snobbery of the patrons of the literary cafés of postwar
Paris, of the open hostility to which Albert Camus exposed himself by
The Rebel, and by his polemic with Sartre. Yet when Podhoretz
changes the subject of his analysis and turns to Camus's novels, my
sympathy turns into amazement and horror. Podhoretz is primarily
interested in the answer to one question—what historical (political) reality lies behind "the facade" of the allegory of *The Plague* and the
symbolism of *The Fall*? And he has not even the slightest difficulty
finding a completely unequivocal answer. *The Plague* is just an allegory
of the French Resistance during World War II. It causes us no distress
that Podhoretz pricks the balloon of that movement's myth. He does
this with visible pleasure, undoubtedly on account of the prevalence of
the left-wing or even communist elements in its ideology. To Poles, it
sounds exotic to hear that the Resistance's luminaries, or even heroes
of the movement, such as Camus or Sartre, published books and put
on their plays under the German occupation. However, this is not
enough for Podhoretz, who adds that Camus "agreed to the elimination of a chapter on Kafka from *The Myth of Sisyphus* because a book
celebrating a Jewish writer would not get by the German censors"
(43).

It was dreadful, but what does it have to do with *The Plague*? If it
does not, all the worse for *The Plague*. If we ask, as Podhoretz does,
"what a city in the grip of plague has in common with a country occupied by an invading army, the answer would seem to be very little.
The one is a natural calamity and, as such, morally and politically neutral; the other is a human phenomenon and is entirely moral and political in character" (42). But why did Camus choose such an inappropriate and misleading allegory? It appears that he had no choice. After he
has provided us with facts repugnant to Camus's heroic legend, Podhoretz explains:

With this background in mind, it becomes easier to understand why Camus could only write about the Nazi occupation and the Resistance in allegorical terms. Confronting it directly in a realistic mode would have required facing up to the element of (shall we say?) the absurd—the word applies here with cruel accuracy—in the idea that the French, and especially the French intellectuals, acted nobly and bravely during the occupation. . . . In treating the entire episode allegorically, Camus was able to take refuge from such issues in the posturing rhetoric that is for many of us the least attractive feature of the French intellectual style. But in translating the occupation into an outbreak of plague, and thereby inevitably making nonsense of the idea of heroic resistance, was Camus half-consciously struggling to tell himself, and the world, the truth? (43–44)

Horror! It does not occur for a moment to the American publicist that, maybe, *The Plague* does not code any specific reality, that it was no coincidence that Camus chose the form he did and asked questions in the form he did, because he could not do it any other way. And for that reason one should pose different questions both about Camus and about his novel and not just question his personnel file.

There are similar misunderstandings concerning *The Stranger* and *The Fall*. Does *The Fall* reflect the author's troubled conscience over Algeria and the National Liberation Front (FLN)? Or is it a "'satirical portrait of Sartre' and other progressive intellectuals, which would make *The Fall* an attack on the hypocrisy and their professed concern for the poor and the oppressed" (44)?

Podhoretz chooses a third explanation: the cowardice and hypocrisy of which Camus accuses himself "are the cowardice and hypocrisy involved in his failure to side as clearly with the democracies as Sartre was siding with the Communists—and all for fear of being dismissed as a man of the 'Right' and thereby losing his standing as a secular saint" (47).

Is all this interpretive nonsense merely the result of Podhoretz's literary deafness, or perhaps his deafness to anything that is not politics? It seems to me that in his political writing, in his very style of political thinking, there is something that inclines him toward similar oversimplifications. He discusses the books of others here with ingenuity and a sharp wit. According to Podhoretz, the settling of accounts with communism by former communists and fellow travelers (such as Koestler, Silone, and Gide, among others, in the book *The God That Failed*) runs into a wall of particular limitations because the authors maintained general leftist convictions. Yet they write with a certain strength, which those who lack firsthand experience of the siren charm of communist ideology also lack. People who never had anything to do with communism have a certain tendency to make light of its dangers, do not treat them seriously enough, whereas former communists behave just the opposite—their voices brim with the earnest cry of Cassandra. This only partially applies to Podhoretz. Although he was not a communist, Podhoretz nevertheless belonged to its broadly understood circle of sympathizers or, in other words, to the American intellectual left with which he now so passionately fights. He fights them from positions that are utterly external. One definitely cannot suspect Podhoretz of any sort of leftist leanings. On the other hand, when his anticommunism comes to the fore, one can hear the cry of Cassandra, although after some hesitation. All the same, Podhoretz's prophecies are gloomy enough: "This should have been clear even in 1950, and it should have been clearer still in 1980 when the decline of American power in the post-Vietnam era had left Western Europe more exposed than ever to the continually growing threat of Soviet power" (31). I guess that Podhoretz was not particularly unhappy when his prophecy proved to be not quite correct. I am not sure, however, whether the political reality is more important to him than the intellectual argument. Hence my hesitation in comparing him to Cassandra. Podhoretz shows a certain partisan spirit, which makes one fear that his primary task is to defeat his ideological adversary from the same part of New York. For him, the Bolsheviks and the democratic world of the West are mere black-and-white figures in a certain interesting situation on the chessboard.

Podhoretz's essay on Orwell is quite a piece of work. In this text, the reader finds many interesting observations concerning the author of *1984*. However, what seems to be most interesting to Podhoretz, what he devotes most of his attention to, is an absolutely empty problem—a "problem" in quotation marks because it boils down to a name, or rather to a label. This "problem" is whether Orwell was a man of the Left, and if so, to what extent and until when. Or perhaps he was a neoconservative, although, needless to say, he himself did not realize it. Could Podhoretz not find himself another victim? Why Orwell—who was less a party man than anyone else, and who was the most independent of all the writers?! At the same time it seems that Podhoretz is more concerned with "stealing" Orwell from his adversaries than with "registering" him among his own ranks.

The division into the "Left" and—presumably—"Right," although one visibly hesitates labeling oneself, is absolutely the most important thing for Podhoretz, the alpha and omega of his way of thinking about the world. This is so despite the similarity between this act of political division and the way policemen view the world. In this, Podhoretz reminds me, for example, of Piotr Wierzbicki,* although Podhoretz is less funny and his arguments seem better grounded than those of his numerous Polish counterparts.

Everyone who has tried to discuss politics with the so-called left-wing intellectuals of Munich, Paris, or New York can understand Podhoretz's mania. One can put up with a lot the first or second time—even their arguments about the superiority of the socialist economy, about life in the West being no better than in the East, about human rights being violated in the West in a manner that is no less objectionable but more perfidious, about the Soviet system being perhaps not ideal but certainly no worse than in the United States, and about there being nothing to choose between these two superpowers. If, however, one happens to live in the West and hold less "left-wing" views, it is indeed difficult to bear the incessant terror of "progressive" thinkers, especially when any "right-wing" deviation automatically reduces the delinquent to an inferior intellectual, moral, professional, and social level. This is why Podhoretz fights so passionately, stealing the other team's players, uncovering their doping affairs and bribery scandals. The fight is going on in the real world, and one cannot behave like an angel vis-à-vis opponents who have horns under their hats.

The battlefield should be as wide as possible; hence one cannot limit oneself to politicians or political columnists alone. In this battle, every soul taken away from your foe or at least captured counts. In keeping with the old tradition, the soul of an artist counts twice. It is of no consequence that he is interested in something else. You can always drive the poor devil into a corner and force him to confess who he is for: the Soviet Union or the United States. He must not be allowed any tricks. *Tertium non datur.* In this way politics becomes separated from thinking in terms of values and methods of their effective implementation, and the tactics of struggle with the enemy begins to prevail over the strategy of its goals. The wreck of literature haunts people at the crossroads, whereas political discourse, although justified as a reaction, becomes as fierce as it is futile.

Among Podhoretz's political-and-literary encounters, his polemic with Kundera holds an interesting position. Podhoretz's charge against Kundera is quite trivial and is frequently repeated in his book: why does Kundera stay away from politics, not wanting to take a firm stand in his books despite their clear protest against communist totalitarianism? There is something new here, however. Podhoretz's tone, which is full of reverence and admiration for Kundera's books, and at the same time full of astonishment—why, by God, do you defect from our camp if we love you so much? Why do you play into the hands of the enemy, whom you also hate? It is worth noting here why Podhoretz admires Kundera. That Kundera "gives a thrashing to the reds" is one obvious reason. There are also some vague aesthetic reasons. Nevertheless, in this essay Podhoretz demonstrates a greater understanding of literary subtleties than in the other essays I have discussed. Podhoretz realizes that his perception of literature misses certain real values. He seems to realize that he reduces literature to its ideological or political core. That which remains—one is led to believe—is limited to "aesthetic beauty." Here lies the crux of the whole misunderstanding. For Kundera the difference between literature (the novel) and a political dispute is fundamental and based on completely different cognitive aims, in a distinct epistemological perspective and ontology of expression.

Kundera's *Art of the Novel*,[2] in which he formulates his theory of the novel, gives Podhoretz an excuse for a confrontation. Podhoretz could not have known this book at the time he was writing *Bloody Crossroads*, although some of Kundera's essays had earlier appeared in French magazines. It does not matter a great deal though. In *The Art of the Novel*, the author of *The Joke* elaborates some of his impatient pronouncements, to which Podhoretz responded by writing "An Open Letter to Milan Kundera." The American critic gives examples of Kundera having been "stolen" by the Left, which desperately wanted to use his writings as proof that in the "free world" it was no better than in the communist Czechoslovakia—hence Podhoretz's bitterness about Kundera's declaration that he was never concerned with politics (for example, condemning Stalinism) in his writing. How should one understand such a declaration made by the author of *The Book of Laughter and Forgetting*?

To some extent it can be explained as a protest not so much against literature's political commitment as against the politicization of literature as demanded by the communist rulers of his native country, and by his left-wing "kidnappers," and by "right-wingers" like Podhoretz. Their demands and the way they look at literature are equally alien to Kundera, precisely because he lived for so many years in a totalitarian state and because as a young man he was enthusiastic about it. As a result of this experience, he has become utterly opposed to the idea of "literature that serves the party" (the term taken from Irzykowski*), no matter which party. This applies equally to the "party" of democratic antitotalitarian opposition and to the moral obligation to commit literature to a just cause, whose moral obligation is imperceptibly transformed into a moral blackmail that is onerous for an artist. By his resistance to imposed obligations (although he had fulfilled them by his own free will), he has incurred the ill-will of not only Podhoretz but his fellow countrymen as well. He is not very popular (to put it mildly) with the contemporary democratic opposition in Czechoslovakia. In some measure, this has been Kundera's own fault, because, as already noted, even a justified reaction to the behavior of one's "adversary" is not the best guide in matters of the spirit.

The Art of the Novel is a beautiful and wise book. It presents not only the author's theory of the novel but also an interesting and very competent analysis of the history of the European novel from Cervantes to the present day. Kundera does not believe in the crisis of the novel. On the contrary, he thinks that for quite some time now the novel has taken up reflection on being, something that has disappeared from philosophy and the humanities, to say nothing of everyday thinking. Therefore, the possibilities that lie before the novel are great, and to date have only been exploited by the greatest novelists. The program Kundera outlines looks very attractive. After all, its attractiveness is illustrated by Kundera's own output, which realizes one of the possible variations.

Kundera's program is based on the statement by Hermann Broch* that a true novel says what no other form of expression can. Kundera beautifully and persuasively analyzes and presents various "unique languages" of the novel, pointing out how they differ from other forms of communication. In view of the wealth of intermediary forms, Podhoretz's plain ideological approach appears just insolent—here comes a boor who does not know how to behave in polite company!

At this point, however, I feel the desire to protest against Kundera's

sometimes extravagant aristocratic tastes and to take the side of Podhoretz, who plays the simpleton lost in a world that holds too many
rituals for him and asks, Well, all and good, but what's going on here?
I understand Kundera when he protests against having his novels reduced to peculiar forms of political struggle, against the "terror of
commitment" to the struggle carried out by the more enlightened part
of his own society. He defends the basic rights (maybe also duties) of
the artist. He can meet social obligations in a form that suits him, but
he must not be forced into fulfilling them. He must not feel that he is
being morally blackmailed. Furthermore, Kundera does not agree to
"moral blackmail"; he does feel bound to tell inspiring stories or to side
with the virtues he otherwise praises. I understand Kundera's anxieties,
although I do not share all of them and do not always agree with his
choices. I understand him when he says that the novel is a form of
expressing one's opinion about the world. It is different from a simple
statement that something is true and something else is false; that here is
the source of good, whereas over there Satan holds sway; that the
question of who is guilty, either Anna or Karenin, is falsely posed. But
I do not understand him when he says that the novel does not make
judgments about the world, except about the existential dimension of
the fate of its heroes, whom historical reality affords only a certain
preordained field of maneuver, a limited number of options, which for
these heroes is like a shell for a snail. Last but not least, I do not understand him when he says that the only thing he is interested in is the
good of the European novel, that he never said anything about Stalinism or totalitarianism but merely told love stories and wrote regular
novels.

　　These declarations stirred Podhoretz not so much because of their
questionable truth as because of their function in the Western market
of ideas, because of the service they perform for the local lovers of the
best of all possible regimes, and the harm they do to his anticommunist friends. However, this time I am more interested in the strange,
ambiguous status of the novel's view of the world, and particularly in
that which is not worldly, beyond good and evil, and beyond the possibility of judgment. Therefore, it might be worthwhile to return to
Anna Karenina and her austere husband. We are going to speak not of
guilt but of the empathy with which the author treats the characters he
has created and their motives. To be sure, the answer will be neither
definite nor unequivocal. In this case we will be able to delineate a

range of unquestionable values that will inevitably collide with one another. The recognition of the equality of these values, that is, the creation of a tragic situation, can be recognized as a certain choice of worldview.

Situations of this type are by no means stable or timeless. They can be seen as a particular moment in a drawn-out process. Tolstoy wrote *Anna Karenina* at the beginning of that process, and Kundera wrote his novel when the process was already well along. It is no coincidence that the name of the beloved dog of the endlessly deceived wife of the hero of *The Unbearable Lightness of Being* is Karenin. In Tolstoy's novel, the opposite values (such as, to put it briefly, love and faithfulness) still belong to one system ("heavy" in Kundera's terminology). Yet one of these values (love, accompanied by freedom) seems already infected by a future lightness. Kundera is well aware of this, but Tolstoy had a similar premonition as well. Hence one can speak of the development of this notion through history. In this way the tragic encounter of conflicting values bears a germ of their future relativity.

Admittedly, by using the example of Tolstoy in formulating his rules of the fictional game, Kundera made his task easier. Had he chosen Dostoyevsky, whom he does not like, the thing would have looked different—although it would have concerned the same process, only in a form more contemporary than with Tolstoy. Given the full polyphony of Dostoyevsky's novels, it is not difficult to answer who is right—certainly not Raskolnikov, Verkhovensky, or Ivan Karamazov. One does not have to wonder too much about the author's position on "modern intellectual trends" in all his novels. Although, of course, to reduce the "sense" of the novels to those actually poor reasons is yet another crime against the greatness concealed in the art of writing.

When making his brilliant and convincing analysis of *The Sleep-walkers* by Broch, Kundera refers first and foremost to objective forms of the phenomenon of the process of the relativization of absolute values in twentieth-century reality. The heroes of the three parts of Broch's novel depict particular stages of that process. Kundera thus acknowledges that his ideal novel expresses the author's views of the contemporary world almost directly, and this in categories that express values. The process he describes is one of a spreading sickness, of equally sickly defensive reactions, and the creeping degradation of the world in crisis. This crisis acquires institutional forms that endlessly intensify the danger of individual deviation.

At this point I shall discuss the problems explored, only in part theoretically, by Kundera. Although Kundera does not know how to swear on all that he holds holy, he cannot deny the obvious: all his novels contain an analysis of a variety of fates that people entangled in the totalitarian system meet.

These people are reduced to the forms of existence generated by the system, or, much more often, they try to tear themselves free at least inwardly, and then they struggle in a net of illusory and hardly satisfactory solutions and artificial alternatives that result from their overpowering need to escape. Therefore, Kundera's description of things goes well beyond a simple picture of "tanks in the streets of Prague," political and social captivity, the mechanisms of exercising power, and the resulting human misery. In keeping with Kundera's theory, it demonstrates the existential (not psychological) possibilities of persons cast in a certain real historical situation (*in-der-Welt-sein*). All the same, it remains a description of this situation, first and foremost, in its human dimension. This is its truth and its judgment. This situation is the totalitarian system at its victorious, expansive, and ideological stages (*The Joke, Life Is Elsewhere*) and in its attempt to resist its disintegrating tendencies.

The value of Kundera's analysis lies, inter alia, in not treating totalitarianism as a fait accompli, in not treating it in isolation from the entire process of change in human consciousness, which to some extent called this institutional system to life. This is the same process already discussed here in *The Sleepwalkers* by Broch. It is the peculiar tragedy of Kundera's heroes that their attempts to escape from the totalitarian net are only other variations on the same feeling of metaphysical void. Making a deity out of humankind, as the creator of a future heaven on earth, was an attempt to fill this void. To escape from that paradise, which did not turn out to be heaven on earth, but a place of extreme debasement and degradation, is probably a more enjoyable but equally empty form of "the lightness of being." When all is said and done, this lightness is unbearable.

Podhoretz writes about Kundera's fascination with "erotic experience in its own right and for its own sake" (180). However, Podhoretz's next observation in his open letter to Kundera seems closer to the truth: "Sex also plays such a large role in your novels because under communism it became the only area of privacy that remained relatively intact when everything else had become politicized" (180). I would have expressed this differently, addressing Kundera's novels rather than the role of sex under communism and the resulting psychological conditioning. The sex lives of Kundera's heroes are a function of the life of the individual in a totalitarian society. Sex is an illusory escape, disappointing not just on account of totalitarianism but also because it remains part of a system that encompasses both totalitarianism and this sort of attempt to escape, part of humankind's metaphysical state in the modern world.

However, is not Kundera's aesthetic, his theory of Europe and the European novel, the next illusory escape, this time less conscious of its own limitation?

The question of why Kundera so stubbornly denies that his novels have any political meaning remains. Why does he try to lock himself in the world of the European novel, which has a very limited number of ways out? Although it is true, it is not enough to say that he is fed up with ideologies because he has lived in the world where everything is ideological (Podhoretz agrees). Similarly, it is not enough to say that his behavior is a natural reaction to interpretations of his novels, which attribute simplified, if not primitive, political sense to his writing.

Kundera has left his totalitarian homeland. *The Unbearable Lightness of Being* emphatically shows that his new reality does not seem to him essentially different from the apparent escapes his heroes practiced in his old country, when it was occupied by foreign armies and then by its own armies.

One can choose partial emigration by remaining, in spirit, in the homeland one left behind and living among one's countrymen, by continuing to live their problems, by thinking about them, and by working for them. Many, including a number of outstanding people, have done so. One can also break all spiritual ties, at least in the area most important to a writer, in one's creative work. One can take up the challenge and work to become a genuine part of the culture of his present readers. This challenge has been taken up by perhaps an even greater number of outstanding people. This may seem to be the case because the latter are better known to the public at large. One usually leaves a "smaller" culture for "the greater" culture.

Kundera is not a pure example of any of these prototypical positions. He was unable, and probably did not even want, to sever the ties with his past. His novels are full of tanks in the streets of Prague, in both the literal and the symbolic sense. He was incapable of casting off the burden of his experience. However, he did not want to or could not spiritually remain in that reality and share with his countrymen the obligations of space and time so badly suited to the writer's vocation. He divested himself of those obligations and the related (often false) splendors and (actual) restrictions. But he was also unable to strike roots in his new reality, exposing, paradoxically, its homely and even more grotesque—because it was unforced—proportions. Therefore, he had to invent for himself a certain myth, a myth of the best common denominator. Yet that myth, the myth of Central Europe (of European culture, of the European novel), looks strangely anemic even after everything that restricts and disturbs it is discarded. If the Europe of today is to mean anything more than an asylum for the tormented soul, it should encompass not only the legacy of the great spirits of the past, but also the history of European totalitarianism and the struggle against it. This means consciousness of the threat to and the actual degradation of the basic values of European culture. It also means arduous mental work to discover all the most secret threads leading to the catastrophe that became the most significant fact in the twentieth-century history of Europe. It means a real and always dangerous struggle on many fronts and different levels against thousands of incarnations of the monster. The Europe of today also means the history of subjection, of errors, and of fatal fascinations. Without this history and the present-day reality, the notion of European culture sounds, to be sure, noble but also somewhat hollow.

It is only from this diversity—not just from the cultural tradition, but also from direct social and political experiences—that a vivid culture of modern Europe, capable of resisting the wave of commercial trash that overwhelms us, can emerge. The novels of Kundera make use of these experiences in an exceptionally creative manner. In them, he processes these experiences into something that transcends their individual and private dimension. The writer's impatient gestures, where he tries to throw off this burden, do not affect the merit of his literary achievement. I do hope that in the future Kundera will not succumb to the temptation of literary self-sufficiency, of shutting himself up in the ivory tower of "European culture."

I am afraid that this viaduct over that dangerous crossroads leads nowhere.

Notes

1. Norman Podhoretz, *The Bloody Crossroads, Where Politics and Literature Meet* (New York, 1986).

2. Milan Kundera, *The Art of the Novel* (New York, 1988). Originally published under the title *L'Art du roman* (Paris, 1986).

12

The Autumn of the Ideologues

Krytyka, no. 34/35 (1991)

Józef Życiński

The "autumn of nations," understood as a mature counterpart of the earlier "spring of nations," can be grasped in the dazzling categories of the poetics of events. The charm of falling bulwarks, crumbling walls, and musty ideologies carried away by the wind of history has a beauty quite apart from the values of the variables specifying the condition of the crumbling concrete. One must not forget, however, the wealth of content to be found in reflection that goes beyond the simple cataloging of the events associated with the agony of the totalitarian ideology. On the one hand, this content reveals the disconcerting naïveté of a certain type of philosophy of history, and on the other hand it carries important moral and cultural obligations. Its importance does not allow one to limit an evaluation of the current transformations to the level of pragmatic concerns; it also means that one should raise a number of concrete issues that earlier attracted the attention of ideological visionaries who obliterated the line dividing fiction and reality.

Provincial Philosophies of History

As looking for new methodologies in the nineteenth century ensured fame, as well as originality, to writers, Ludwig Börne* proposed that writers resort to the free play of associations. His famous text has the attractive title "The Art of Becoming an Original Writer in Three Days." In initiating prospective writers into the secrets of this art, Borne advised:

> Take a few sheets of paper and for three days on end write
> down, without fabrication or hypocrisy, everything that comes
> into your head. Write down what you think of yourself, of
> your wife, of the Turkish War, of Goethe, . . . of the Last
> Judgment, of your . . . superiors—and when three days have
> passed you will be quite out of your senses with astonishment at
> the new and unheard-of thoughts you have had. This is the art
> of becoming an original writer in three days.[1]

No wonder this particular text was acknowledged by Freud as particularly inspirational in his psychoanalytic search for truth about human nature. Personally, I am afraid that many historical and philosophical visions and simple interpretations of social phenomena were
arrived at with the unconscious use of this particular method. The result is that original associations have been used to interpret the deepest
secrets of historical necessity and to develop an otherworldly vision of
the future. This play of artistic associations, unconstrained by traditional logic, led to a situation where patrons of the exclusive cafés of
Paris or Vienna cultivated the illusion that they had discovered the
deepest mechanisms of history and went into rapture over the achievements of Stalin or Mao Zedong. The seventy-year-old Sartre, writing
philosophical dithyrambs in honor of the Chinese Cultural Revolution,
which presaged a redemptive destruction of the state, can serve as a
symbol of a certain type of intellectual who will not forsake any absurdity if it only ensures him a reputation for originality and gives the
impression that he is someone who has uncovered important social
mechanisms.

Those who wanted to teach others about the deepest sense of history
did not learn much from the drama of the gulags, the genocide in
Kampuchea, or the Chinese gerontocracy. Historical and philosophical
fantasies constantly bloom in thousands of new flowers presented as
the results of "the only correct" method of rational cultivation adopted
by the newest generation of sympathizers with Börne's methodology.
The scariest thing seems to be that in a period when we appreciate
rationality and criticism new ranks of admirers of historical and philosophical gurus, who reserve for themselves the monopoly on the only
correct interpretation of social phenomena, constantly appear. Barely
two months before the tragic massacre in Tiananmen Square, I spoke

with a social scientist from Stanford University, which in contrast to neighboring Berkeley is seen as relatively conservative, favoring balanced and objective interpretations.

First, the man expressed a deep regret that the pope was critical of liberation theology without actually knowing what authentic Marxism was. When I asked him which of the existing states was the most advanced in the pursuit of the ideals of the "authentic Marxism," I learned that it was the People's Republic of China. His opinion was by no means acquired in some coffeehouse; he had spent two weeks in China and proudly trumpeted this as the empirical basis of his judgment. This brought to my mind Simone de Beauvoir's peepshow-like impressions of the various countries she had visited for several days. Tourism practiced by radically minded representatives of the social sciences has, however, an exceptional epistemological value. This is why the pope, who was not allowed even to fly over Chinese territory, would stand almost no chance against my Stanford friend in properly evaluating the liberalism of the Chinese authorities. Only professional liberals can see the liberalism of the Chinese.

The shots the official liberals fired into the people soon exposed the "authenticity" of ideal Marxism. Nonetheless, I do not think they will dampen the interpretative zeal of those who complacently reserve for themselves a monopoly on uncovering the most profound laws of humanity's freedom, dignity, or dreams of social justice. One reason why developments in Poland in recent years seem very significant to me is that they offer extremely valuable material that, when analyzed theoretically, demonstrate the groundlessness of many of the visions created by Western academic gurus in coffeehouses. The dramatic quality of the autumnal "flight of ideologues" requires that we should look back into the past and take note of a number of factors that facilitated the presentation of ideological illusions as profound truth about reality. It also means that we must free ourselves from a certain type of visionary philosophy of history, for the same reasons that earlier in human cultural development we freed ourselves from astrology and alchemy.

The events that shook Europe in 1989 definitively shattered the illusions of many visionary theoreticians who had believed that the history of the world had to adhere to the simple rules they had discovered at their desks. Even the texts by a thinker as mature as Alain Besançon * read a year after their publication, shock the reader with their lack of imagination in assessing Polish realities. On this score one should not bear Besançon any special grudge, because even when observed "from the inside" the speed of events in Poland often far outraced the limits of yesterday's imagination. The theoretical significance of the events we are witnessing today requires thorough analyses that not only record the facts but also try to establish general regularities.

The Ethos of Pragmatists

Today in the Polish intellectual landscape, urgent questions of pragmatism are linked with a perspective that creates the opportunity finally to repudiate the many myths that persist in philosophical reflection on society or history. We must not disregard pragmatism, which requires vigorous immediate measures, because the public's moods and interests tomorrow may depend precisely on the effectiveness of such measures. Yet I am apprehensive about a pragmatism that, out of necessity, would limit itself to the immediate psychological needs of particular social groups and lacks a broad ethical or axiological vision.

Reflection on history should be free of blank spots, as well as new taboo subjects about which we maintain a polite silence out of nothing more than a sense of tact in the face of an opponent who is uncomfortable with such discussions. In the spirit of elementary responsibility for the truth, the public should be told, for example, who edited the notorious "dialogue" between Wałęsa and his brother [to insinuate that Wałęsa embezzled and hid a substantial sum of money] and that a certain Colonel Przymanowski in an address to parliament fed the audience this cultural bestseller of the martial-law period. A whole range of decisions that placed absurdity and primitiveness on a pedestal should lose the discreet charm of the semiobscurity of anonymity, and their authors should be offered a chance to explain what inspired them in those days of ideological rapture. However, to avoid contamination with the ethical legacy of Marxism, this sort of information should be revealed free of the spirit of revenge and free of an atmosphere characterized by personal strife. I believe that, after the dose of brute force and nonsense we received after December 1981, we can afford to reconstruct the anatomy of absurdity in the style used, for example, by Jan Józef Szczepański* in his *Kadencja* [Term of office]. His style presents the hard facts, but with dignity. The dignity lies in his depiction of the gulf separating the ethics of Solidarity and the methods adopted by the world's ideological repairmen.

I am skeptical, for example, of the impatient advice offered to Andrzej Drawicz [the head of Polish television under Premier Mazowiecki]. Irritated authors tell him who should disappear from television and who should appear on the screen, and that his "Christian-ecumenical" approach could lead to incalculable damage. These warnings seem to suggest that the principles of Christian ethics are very good when adhered to as ceremonial embellishments for official speeches. You can refer to them, for example, during solemn meetings in commemoration of [the constitution of] May Third, as in earlier times people referred to proletarian internationalism on May First. However, once the solemn occasion has passed, one should put away and safeguard these principles, and concentrate on the determined struggle free of any contamination by Christian ethos in the manner of Drawicz or Szczepański.

These opinions invariably bring to mind discussions I was unable to avoid when I visited a number of expatriate Polish communities in 1987. The angry young men I met between Montreal and Minneapolis always made the same accusation: "You should have fought in December 1981. Had we shot at that time, today we would still be in Poland and feel at home there." The morality of the shots never fired or a balanced evaluation of the chances for victory in that uneven struggle were not of interest to them. Radical regrets about the struggle was a pitiable expression of their desperate state and absolute determination. Both the determination and the despair caused by separation from their country are understandable, but one cannot acknowledge the normality of personal strife that brings no wider reflection on values. I see the exceptional virtue of Solidarity's moral legacy in precisely that effective combination of a tradition of nonviolence with a subtle theoretical analysis that breaks with the recommendations of the well-known theoreticians of revolution. This combination not only illustrates the rule *plus ratio quam vis* (reason before force), but also obligates us to cultivate this legacy in a way that is at the same time both difficult and original.

A lesson of history should not serve only to alleviate the psychic needs of the moment, or be limited to intoxication with the short-lived success of the present day. It should lead to reflection on a deeper sense of our experience "yesterday." An absence of historical consciousness combined with reflection on the experience of the past is bound to lead to intellectual provincialism. The provincial mentality manifests itself in focusing on a narrow selection of events and in ignoring everything else that does not fit with this selection. This provincialism has its equivalent in the deformed consciousness that for the sake of peace, ignores past experience and pays attention only to the events of the day. I am afraid that the history of the modern era includes many morally disquieting phenomena that speak of a very selective grasp of the experience of yesterday.

I want to mention here the pre-December [1981] attacks against Michnik and Kuroń, accusing them, for example, of Trotskyism. Excelling in those attacks were not only veterans of "principled" journalism but also people from whom one might expect a certain minimum of objective thinking, especially since attitudes resembling those of the young Lev Davidovich were quite common among ideologues who treated martial law as a normal form of "dialogue" with the public in 1981. Michnik and Kuroń were accused of being Trotskyist fanatics and of accepting terrorism. No one took too much trouble to present the basic facts that would have substantiated those charges.

Now these principled critics seem to have become quiet and turn to other subjects. As yet none of them has written about a Trotskyist faction in the Polish parliament. Nevertheless, I have not been lucky enough to find a text in which the authors of that earlier libel have admitted their error or engaged in self-criticism of their earlier habit of inventing enemies. Normally in the civilized world one says "I am sorry" in order to show that libel and insinuation are not a means to arrive at the truth. The inability to say "I am sorry" is a clear sign of the lack of political culture. I mention Kuroń and Michnik just as examples. One could just as well mention [Czesław] Miłosz or [Jan] Nowak-Jeziorański* or many other important figures in Polish culture who in the past were targets of special campaigns organized in the name of ideological principle. The organizers of those campaigns show a strange reluctance to say "I am sorry." In their philosophy of society, pluralism probably consists of allowing certain people to be executioners while giving other people a full right to be their victims.

The Methodology of Removing Splinters

The legacy of "socialist creativity" in the successive reconstructions of the Polish People's Republic is not only found in the chimneys of Nowa Huta.* Nowa Huta's zealous builders also imposed their ethical legacy, which took the devastation of ethical or, even more generally, cultural life for granted. When I look over Soviet publications promoting reconstruction, I get the impression that they pay much greater attention to ethical questions and to the mechanisms that produce strongly unethical behavior than we do. Perhaps this Polish reluctance to write about morality is a reaction to television sermons by specialists in moralizing. Yet if we accept a basic responsibility for the conditions of our culture broadly understood, we cannot ignore the effects of the moral devastation that accompanied the captivity of our minds.

In his *Dziennik* [Diary], Gustaw Herling-Grudziński* reflects on the devastation of our cultural environment when he describes a conversation with a vacationer from Kraków who spent his well-deserved holiday in the South Seas. Talking to a friend of Herling, the gentleman admitted that in the 1950s one of his official responsibilities was "law and order." He admitted also that in extreme cases of breach of that order—for example, by young soldiers from the Home Army*—it was necessary to resort to harsher interrogation methods, including breaking the prisoner's fingers, in order to protect the achievements of the revolution. In a voice full of concern, the distinguished traveler assured Herling's friend that if it was again necessary to defend the interests of the revolution, he would act the same way he did years ago. This defense carried a serious risk of suffering, however: "when you chop wood, splinters fly. . . ."

Herling-Grudziński adds bitterly that the gentleman most probably meant the splinters forced under the fingernails of the interrogated men. The event he describes does not differ in its essentials from the pathology demonstrated by the people interviewed by Teresa Torańska.* In the zigzags of their dialectical excuses, these people represent a type of mentality that one cannot observe without horror. At the level of basic human sensation, it is not possible to be silently indifferent toward minds so captive that basic human feelings have atrophied. Inevitably, the question of whether such processes are reversible comes to mind. Are there no measures to restore, at least in some rudimentary form, the loss of human feeling? Can a matter-of-fact discussion of the autumn of the ideologues expose the illusory nature of the vision pursued by professional devotees of the totalitarian idea? Would it not be possible, in an attempt to restore their lost humanity to them, to learn from the experience of others who have passed from the moving vision of the loving Soso [Stalin's childhood nickname] to a discovery of the manifestly antihumane content of the vision that once moved them?

A common search for an answer to similar questions might present an opportunity to outline the mechanisms that, despite the stylized humanity of incessant declarations, lead to the instrumental treatment of humanity as a mere decoration for leading doctrines with a monopoly on truth. An uninhibited discussion on these mechanisms might make great sense humanistically; it can contribute to the unmasking of the hidden roots of evil; it can neutralize some of the bitter fruit of this ethical corruption. To effect such a reconstruction, however, we must dispose of superficial formal explanations and restore the correct proportions to the images deformed by this developed system of funhouse mirrors.

We must discard the illusion that we can be obscure and talk reality away. That was the illusion harbored by the optimistic builders of the Polish People's Republic, who believed that it was enough not to see certain things, and that then those things would automatically become unimportant. This programmatic ignorance was meant to make it easier to demarcate the line between being and nothingness, and to accelerate "the ultimate victory of the forces of progress." Today, the consequences of this ignorance recall the atmosphere of the works of Kafka or Mrożek.★ Socialist surrealism, which has aroused little interest among theorists, performed an exceptional service in creating the reality of which the ideologues dreamed. Its effectiveness was the result of a disregard for the facts and the elevation of appearances to the rank of the most profound truths. "Sham life" constituted the most effective means over time to reach the shining future.

The campaign waged by the authorities against the church's desire to send a copy of the image of the "Holy Mother of Częstochowa" around the country is a good example of the surrealist element in Marxism. The campaign, worthy of Kafka's pen, was particularly fierce in the Dąbrowa Basin [a coal-mining region]. That a campaign existed was obvious to all concerned through complications that obstructed the celebrations and destroyed decorations, and decisions to cut off electricity. For many months, however, that knowledge had no effect on the perpetrators. It was only their own error that constrained them. The slip was due to their overzealousness. When the painting was visiting the parish of Sosnowiec-Zagórze, the authorities ruined decorations on the house of the mother of the party first secretary. After the mother complained to her son, Colonel Juszczak was summoned to Warsaw. He was not reassigned to his previous responsibilities. His visit to Warsaw was enough to stop the ugly war with Our Lady. However, what mechanisms led to the acceptance of this grotesque as an ideal form of stylized reality for so long? I am afraid that irrespective of all the changes to date in what is broadly understood as the provinces, between Sosnowiec and Mława [a small town, proverbial for the parochialism of its residents], horrible organizations still operate and haunt people as before. To make things worse, even the greatest optimists do not believe that rational measures can eliminate the grotesque.

We delude ourselves if we optimistically believe that the years of surrealist activities by the ideologues have only left a trace in our psyche. The horrible heritage of those years permeates not only our subconscious but also our institutionalized social structures. Quite often we do not even discern the traces, because we have grown accustomed to the idea that our world simply must include elements similar to those found in the world of Gombrowicz's* or Mrożek's heroes. Only a critical reflection on the ritualized elements of our everyday reality will make it easier for us to notice the legacy bequeathed to us by the imitators of Mrozek's Mr. Lucus, who managed everywhere to demonstrate a style that corresponded to his level of intelligence.

Several years ago I asked an American friend about this legacy. He had been on his first visit to a "really existing socialist" country, and as he left Warsaw he expressed enchantment with Poland and its culture. I asked him at what point in his European fascinations he had felt the wind of Asia in Poland. Immediately at the airport in Warsaw, he said, when he noticed that the border guard checking his passport wore several rows of medals on his chest.

That was the time when the lack of such medals would have inevitably weakened the vigilance of the Warsaw Pact at the expense of our fraternal alliances. At that time, medals played a role no less important than that of the press in the principled creation of a new Orwellian reality. No doubt one can criticize these medals out of the fear that a fondness for decorations, once acquired, will yield a new crop of medals meant to act as a cultural substitute. This is why I emphasize the need to discuss the legacy of ideological visionaries, something that could easily go unnoticed at a moment when we are experiencing inner satisfaction at the autumn of ideologues.

Kraków, 19 December 1989

Note

1. Cited in I. B. Cohen, *The Newtonian Revolution* (Cambridge, 1985), 286. [The original German title of the text, written in 1823, is "Die Kunst, in drei Tagen ein originaler Schrift-steller zu werden."]

13

Three Fundamentalisms

Krytyka, no. 36 (1991)

Adam Michnik

Our political reflection must confront an urgent problem—Polish historical awareness. One need not explain the great significance of the Polish conception of history to our political positions and commitments. It seems that now the time has come to reflect quietly on Polish stereotypes of the past, in particular the history of the interwar Second Republic. To date, the entire history of the Second Republic has been a victim of myths and stereotypes, be they the black legends of official communist propaganda or the white legends of those who tried to defend themselves against the communist falsification of history. It seems that we need to pose new questions about our past.

First and foremost, we need to reflect on what happened in 1922 when President Gabriel Narutowicz* was assassinated. What type of process was then set in motion? In what sort of atmosphere was the attempt on the president's life made? What were its historical consequences? Why did this particular date become a milestone in Polish historical consciousness, and why was this fact so happily forgotten?

It also seems that we should reexamine the entire literary output of the political camps of the time, that we should look anew at the political scene of that era as an arena of conflict over the shape of the state and democracy, and that we should answer the question about which twists and turns led to the antidemocratic evolution in the thought of the "Belvedere Camp,"* the National Democrats,* and the Polish Socialist Party* [PPS]. Also, we should reanalyze the interwar history of the Catholic church. Without such reflection we are doomed to idealize our own past, to a historical consciousness burdened by mythology, to a lack of sober judgment, and to a certain helplessness in the face of something one might call the revenge of memory—memory that has for years been completely submerged into the subconscious.

It is necessary to speak about the recurrent threat of fundamentalism as a new phenomenon, one that has been periodically emphasized or deemphasized, that sometimes appears openly and sometimes remains secret and yet is always present in our political debate. Fundamentalism is nothing but the conviction that one has a concept of how to arrange the world for the good, which would free the world of all conflicts other than the one between good and evil—and thus, for example, free it of the conflicting interests or points of view that are an inescapable element of the democratic order. I perceive three fundamentalist threats to Poland.

First, there is nationalistic fundamentalism. A temptation exists to subordinate all areas of public life to something that can be described as national interest. National interest is defined in each case from the perspective of some political viewpoint. For the sake of national interest every good Pole is obliged to be in solidarity with, for example, the Polish minority in Lithuania. It does not matter whether this minority conducts itself wisely or stupidly or whether they take a pro-Soviet or pro-Lithuanian position. We must support them because they are Polish; that in itself is enough. Every attempt to criticize the course of action followed by the leaders of the Polish minority in Lithuania is labeled "anti-Polish." This kind of thinking presents Poland as a country free of any conflicts except the conflict between "well-understood, Catholic" national interest and nihilistic-cosmopolitan-leftist tendencies. National interest so defined sees discussion of anti-Semitism in Polish political debate or discussion of pogroms against Gypsies as harmful to the Polish nation.

Here I am speaking of the fundamentalism characteristic of a certain formation of nationalistic movements and doctrines which at present seems to play a significant role not just in Poland and the other postcommunist countries. In the contemporary world, this kind of fundamentalism has, for example, reemerged in the Arab countries, appeared in Israel, and also, on the right, in Western European countries. In French discussions on the phenomenon of Le Pen or in the German historical debate on Nazism, one can see a fear of the return of this kind of fundamentalism. For this reason it merits examination not just as a Polish phenomenon but as an international one.

Second, there is religious fundamentalism. This is related to the new situation in which the church finds itself in Poland, and the sacred in the world in general. It is no revelation that one illness of the modern world is the decline of the sacred—that is, the decline of the sphere of values common to the whole community, to which the community can refer. It can be compared to the smashing of the tablets on which the Ten Commandments were written. This destruction could signify the destruction of the very foundation of the values we all share.

This tendency has not as yet elicited a definitive response from churches or religions. One can question whether such a response is possible at all. However, attempts have been made. One such attempt was the Second Vatican Council, the opening to the world and the acceptance of the fact that certain authentic values can originate outside my church or even outside my own faith or cultural circle. Fundamentalism, however, presents quite a different response, which in this case is an attempt, once again, to obliterate the line between the sacred and the profane, between natural law and criminal law, between moral principles and the legal norms of the state. On these matters, we are in for a debate no less paramount than, say, the one about the call for a return to Europe. Different people mean quite distinct things and events when speaking about the return to Europe. It seems, for instance, that when certain members of the Catholic hierarchy speak of the return to Europe they have in mind a Europe that no longer exists, the Europe that preceded the French Revolution.

Last but not least, in today's Poland there is also a third fundamentalist trap into which people from the democratic opposition of the 1970s and the Solidarity period, the present author included, are most prone to fall. Here I refer to the blurring of the distinction between moral norms and the rules of political struggle. Because of our involvement in the underground, this distinction hardly existed for us. All political conduct was translated into the language and norms of moral standards. In a democratic order, things work differently, and this fundamentalist mentality—let us call it "moralistic"—can become the cause of considerable confusion. I do not want to say that in politics or in a normal political discourse there is no room for morality. Similarly, I do not believe, now that we have spoken about religious fundamentalism, that there is no room for the church in politics. Needless to say, there is a specific place for the church. We must realize that just as the church may not be a political party, just as a religious norm may not become a legal norm, so a Manichaean moral norm established in the anticommunist underground may not automatically translate to the rules of the democratic game. It may prove lethal to the game as well as to itself. Morality can very easily become fanaticism, which can be instrumental to ends that are by no means noble.

Populism constitutes another threat that should be considered. Although populism is nothing new, it should be reexamined. For example, it would be worthwhile to reconsider the lessons of Peronism. What was Peronism? What sort of language did it employ? What kind of procedures did it favor? Which mechanisms contributed to its rise to and fall from power? And finally, which mechanisms kept it alive?

It has to be said explicitly: populism in Poland was the language of the workers' rebellion against the totalitarian state. It was clearly a rebellion in defense of their freedom and dignity, but both these values were expressed in the language of populism. The well-known distinction between "us" and "them" was typical of populist discourse, not of political analysis or the social play of interests. And so one could say that an egalitarian consciousness, which for decades had legitimated communist rule, lay at the base of this rebellious populism. In this sense, one can say that this was a rebellion against communism in the name of the egalitarian principles it preached. It was thus a rebellion in the name of principles that were not completely consistent, but social justice was one of its essential ideas.

The market, which Poland is now building, is not an order in which there is room for social justice as the essential idea. It is the place to see efficiency and creativity, not social justice. Social justice can be achieved through the redistribution of wealth, but certainly not through the market mechanism. All the same, that egalitarianism—with which people were imbued under communism and by Solidarity's anticommunist revolt—continues to live on today and is equally present in the populist discourse of both trade unions, be it the All-Poland Trade Union Alliance★ [OPZZ] or be it Solidarity. It is fascinating to compare the language that both use today with the language they used a year ago. This language is something new, and we must approach it that way.

It is also time to admit to ourselves that the very effective rebellion against communism in Poland was a rebellion of the masses. As long as the communists were confronted by elite groups, they could ignore their voices. As long as they were concerned with democratic legal procedures, the communists did not take them into account. The communists only began to take the opposition seriously once the crowd sided with it. They had to talk with the crowd. This situation led us to believe that we were effective in a crowd, or rather that we were effective when we spoke the language of the crowd.

However, the language of the crowd is the language of the populist discourse. Today, we seem to be witnessing a return to that language of the crowd—namely, to the behavior we learned during the anti-communist resistance, to behavior that was rational within the confines of an irrational system because it was the only way to deprive the political system of legitimacy. Today, however, it is the parliamentary system that such behavior deprives of legitimacy, paving, instead, the way for authoritarianism. This is because as we move to create a democratic order, we still lack the political culture specific to democracy. It is a little bit like setting a man from the bush down in front of a computer. I do not mean to say that a man from the bush is inferior; in the bush, he manages much better than a civilized American. Yet in the bush a computer is not of much use.

There is a danger that people will become disenchanted with democracy. Such things have happened in European history. There is a threat of a return to the language we already know. When there was talk about the incompetent rule of the Sejm (*sejmokracja*), that was the language of the *sanacja*.★ When there was talk about parliamentary idiocy, that was the language of communists. When there was talk about the rotten "demo-liberalism," that was the language of the fascist movements.

With the anarchization of public life and the lowering of standards of living and personal security, there is a danger that democratic procedures will be undermined by a crisis. It is possible that we will increasingly hear calls to put an end to all that mess and corruption, calls for a strong hand to restore order. Such convictions can be "sold" as the idea of presidential rule or stable democracy. They can be supported by historical analyses that demonstrate that eighteenth-century Poland collapsed because of anarchy, pervasive license, and the *liberum veto*,★ and that lead to the conclusion that it is necessary to put an end to the similar situation now. In other words, there is a risk—which we have already faced in the past—that in a moment of deep crisis people who will to some extent propose an answer to this crisis will appear. When traditional cultural patterns and procedures fail, when the sources and mechanisms of social communication cease to be trustworthy, then a savior comes along who fills people with the hope that he will prevail over the chaos and save them.

Again, this phenomenon is neither specifically Polish nor new. Nevertheless, it needs to be reexamined; we should study how this type of authoritarian temptation emerges and what its effects are. We must establish what the authoritarian regimes can and cannot solve.

The answer to this question depends not just on the spiritual condition of the Polish intelligentsia—which today seems just as lost as in the worst of times, as if it had lost its ethos, its self-image, and its place in society. Something more depends on widening the scope of this reflection—a chance to counteract fundamentalism with democratic thought in which there is no room for any sort of fundamentalism whatsoever, be it nationalistic, religious, or moralistic. Democratic thought provides that no one is privileged by nature. In democratic discussion there is no room for authorities. If someone says that a matter cannot be put to a vote—for example, in a referendum—but must be one way or another because this is what natural law or national interest demands, that is a violation of the basic principles of the democratic discussion. For that reason, the democratic order maintains that everything that concerns everybody may be subject to a referendum.

Whether populism, which is a language of revolt, will stand against the language characteristic of parliamentary democracy and lawful government may depend on this sort of reflection. Furthermore, whether the authoritarian temptation, or the cult of the strong hand, will stand against the rational democratic order, or the cult of the strong mind, may also depend on it.

17 July 1991

Section IV

Economics

14

Sources of Opposition to Market Reforms in Centrally Planned Economies

Krytyka, no. 31 (1989)

Jerzy Osiatyński

Introduction

Opposition to market reforms in centrally planned economies (CPEs) has attracted the attention of sociologists and political scientists rather than economists. Economists often devised market-reform projects, disregarding the findings of the first two. Meanwhile, empirical sociology has made an important contribution. It has led to the abandonment of the comfortable economic paradigms of micro- and macroeconomic analysis, where whatever is intended is achieved, and also introduced group interests, political premises, the consequences of economic reforms, and the distinction between projected reforms and actual social and economic change. As will be seen, my intellectual debt to the Polish school of empirical sociology goes well beyond the references I have provided. My main purpose in this article is to bring together the thoughts of economists and sociologists on economic reforms and opposition to them.[1]

The version of the article presented here has been assembled from the original version published in *Krytyka* and a subsequent version published in English as "Opposition against Market-Type Reforms," in János Mátyás Kovács and Márton Tardos, eds., *Reform and Transformation in Eastern Europe* (London: Routledge in association with the Institut für die Wissenschaften vom Menschen, Vienna, 1992). The editors express their gratitude to Routledge and the editor responsible for the book, Alan Jarvis, for permission to make use of their version. The author wishes to express his gratitude to J. Kofman, T. Kowalik, and A. Rychard for their helpful comments on an earlier draft of this article.

My starting point will be Włodzimierz Brus's seminal typology of the three fundamental features of "traditional" CPEs (TCPEs). If we compare these features with the fundamental features of a full-fledged market economy, we can understand the implications of market-type reforms of TCPEs. The first fundamental feature is the monopoly of ownership of the means of production. The second is the centralized system of organization and management of the "socialized sector" of the economy. Third, and at the heart of the system, is the "institutional" role of the communist party and the dominance of politics over the economy. The essence of this third feature is the supreme role of the party in managing the economy, and "the double subordination system whereby the party apparatus, particularly at its center, [has] the incontestable right of supervision and interference at every level of the economic structure" (Brus 1986, 100).

At the enterprise level the party's interference is exercised through its executive organs both outside and inside the enterprise. One of the supporting pillars of this role of the communist party is the *nomenklatura** system of appointment to and dismissal from specified posts.[2] The institutional role of the party is based on communist control of all organized forms of public life (with some exceptions, such as the Catholic church in Poland). Moreover, since this control is outside any explicit legal framework, it does not entail formal public accountability.

In the system of economic planning and management of the sector composed of socialist enterprises, five spheres of economic decision-making are usually distinguished in economic theory and practice:

A—current ("routine" in János Kornai's parlance) operations

B—investment

C—pricing

D—foreign trade

E—money and banking

These spheres of decision-making enable one to describe the differences between TCPEs (in *A*, *B*, *C*, *D*, and *E* all decisions are centralized except for work regulations and the like in *A*, which are left to enterprise management) and, for example, the Hungarian New Economic Mechanism of 1968 (in which *A* is completely decentralized; *B* barely; and C, D, and E are partly decentralized on the enterprise level) or the Yugoslav system (in which A is completely decentralized; B, D, and E are mostly decentralized; and C is partly decentralized at the enterprise level). Furthermore, this typology offers a convenient framework for examining the nature of projected economic reforms.

The Main Types of Economic Reforms in the TCPEs

The following typology is one of many possible classification schemes. Its fundamental criterion is the change (or changes) that a given reform introduces into the fundamental spheres of decision-making elaborated thus far, and the relation of the projected new system of economic planning and management to the market economy. Four main types of economic reforms will be distinguished.

1. Reform without Reform

Here there are no institutional changes in the system of economic planning and management, but only a reorientation of economic policy. The essential element of reform without reform is an attempt to manage economic and sociopolitical problems within the old system, and its philosophy is: "Although the system is perfect, people are not." Since mistakes were made in economic policy, policy changes are a necessary and sufficient remedy.

This type of "reform" usually aims to restore more balanced development through (a) deceleration of economic growth; (b) reduction of the relative share of investment in national income; (c) reallocation of investment from the capital-goods sector to the consumer-goods sector, and from industry to agriculture; (d) restructuring of existing productive capacities (in particular, partially converting the arms production to civilian uses); (e) relaxation of forced collectivization and tough procurement measures, and also encouraging private agricultural production; and (f) easing of discrimination against the private nonagricultural sector.

There are many examples of "reforms" of this type. As a rule, they represent the first reaction of the communist authorities to social and political unrest or open revolts. They include the "New Course" policies of 1953–55 in Eastern Europe, as well as the deferred counterreaction to economic reforms of type 2 [System Improvement], which were attempted in the USSR in 1955 and 1965, in the German Democratic Republic in 1963, in Poland in 1964, and in Bulgaria, Albania, and Romania in 1965 (Brus 1986, chaps. 24 and 25). They are usually accompanied by a short-lived political liberalization. If easily accessible reserves exist in the economy, such "reforms" can indeed bring tangible improvements in standards of living, and bring them quickly (as in Poland in 1956–57). However, if one disregards internal reserves (which, as a rule, are used up before the crisis starts), conditions that favor reduction of military production, access to foreign credit, and the like do not necessarily emerge at the same time as domestic economic troubles. Even when they do, such policies, needless to say, merely buy time unless genuine systemic reform is undertaken.

2. System Improvement ("Perfection")

This type of reform leaves fundamental features 1 (monopoly ownership) and 3 (the role of the party) intact; and in feature 2 (centralized planning and management), decision-making spheres B, C, D, and E are also unaffected. With respect to current operations (A), more autonomy is granted to enterprises (often, in fact, to their immediate supervisory agencies), the number of obligatory targets is slightly reduced, gross-output plan targets are substituted for net ones, and some forms of managerial and worker profit-sharing are introduced. The essence of such reforms is a limited shift from direct, mandatory planning of the output of individual enterprises in physical terms to individualized planning in financial terms. However, the central planner, not the market, continues to decide what, how, where, and when to produce (sell, buy, and so on). The plan is implemented by means of old, quantitative instruments, but also partially by new, quasi-price mechanisms.

In practice, reforms of this type soon revert to the traditional system of economic management (Bauer 1986) with one important difference —namely, mass political terror, coercive allocation of labor, and outright violation of work and pay conditions are replaced by financial incentives for the workforce and enterprise management.

3. Central Planning with a Built-In Market Mechanism

This term was invented by Brus, as was, by and large, the underlying theoretical model (Brus 1972). Its essence is the abandonment of the obligatory targets imposed by superiors on their subordinates in the system of planning. Hence the allocation of inputs in physical terms is also abandoned. Annual plans continue to be drawn up but are not binding on subordinate members of the economic hierarchy (however, firms must meet specific output targets related to foreign-trade deliveries and government contracts). Whereas decision-making in sphere *A* is decentralized down to the enterprise, the central planner continues to assume responsibility for investment decisions (although the ability of firms to invest is somewhat increased).

This system is also called "central planning with regulated markets." "Regulation" is carried out by the central planner through a system of financial incentives that link micro- and the macroeconomic interests (via profit-sharing schemes), through parameters that affect financial results of the enterprise (and hence financial rewards for its workforce and management) such as taxes, subsidies, interest rates, foreign exchange rates, and, of course, prices. The Hungarian New Economic Mechanism (NEM) is a close approximation of this theoretical model, as was the Polish reform of 1981.

In addition to these changes in the second fundamental feature of TCPEs (centralized planning and management), there are also some minor changes in the fundamental features 1 (monopoly ownership) and 3 (the role of the party). The cooperative sector is granted greater autonomy, and perhaps even more important, there is some increase in the share of private business outside agriculture (because of methodological difficulties, the data are not wholly reliable, but this share seems to have increased in Hungary and Poland by a few percentage points).[3] With respect to the role of the party, some observers of the Hungarian scene point out that under the NEM the importance of technocratic expertise increased at the expense of the party's interference in the routine operation of firms.

There is no need to discuss here the achievements and shortcomings of the Hungarian NEM (see, for example, Kornai 1986 and Laky 1980). However, some problem areas should be noted. For instance, pricing, which—while balancing supply and demand—serves as an instrument of government policy options, is constrained by public protests against increases in the prices of basic consumer goods and services. Another problem area is ad hoc tax exemptions (subsidies, and so on) and ad hoc changes in foreign exchange regulations (aimed at export promotion). Yet another problem is caused by the concentration of output of individual goods in a small number of firms and the resulting monopolistic rather than competitive behavior of firms in the market.

In effect, it is sometimes argued that the NEM is little more than a shift from individualized planning in physical output to individualized planning by financial indicators (Granick 1975, 309) and that it did not significantly alter the behavior of enterprises (for example, Kornai 1986). Although the failures of NEM have been attributed mainly to the inconsistency of its introduction, recently it has been questioned whether it is capable of generating a viable market. As in reforms of type 2 (system improvement), the central planner continues to determine what, how, when, and where to produce (and so on), but financial "persuasion" is used in preference to administrative coercion. The market mechanism is supposed to follow the planner's preferences and choices, not the signals provided by the market. However, the scope of the central planner's interference is limited.

4. Radical Market Reform

This concept comes from the concept of "crucial reform," which was developed by Kalecki and Kowalik (1971) to describe the reforms introduced in the aftermath of the world economic crisis of 1929–33. They considered them crucial because they contributed to the further dynamic development of the capitalist system yet did not undermine its fundamental features; indeed, they *stabilized* it. Later the concept of "crucial reform" was used by Kowalik (1986) to refer to a socialist economy. He proposed that fundamental features 1 (monopoly ownership) and 2 (centralized organization and management) of CPEs should be replaced by market relations. With respect to fundamental feature 3 (the role of the party), "crucial reform" in a socialist economy called for the limitation of the *nomenklatura* (elimination at the enterprise level) and the introduction of various forms of pluralism. Nonetheless, the one-party system was to be retained. Thus the crucial reform would have stabilized the "leading role" of the communist party. Would this have been equivalent to stabilizing the essence of a socialist

economy in any sense similar to that in which the crucial reform stabilized the essence of the capitalist system? And, more important, is a
full-fledged market reform at all compatible with the retention of the
leading role of the communist party? Any answer to these questions
will by nature be highly speculative, especially after 1989.

A "market breakthrough" reform is "crucial" in a more ordinary
sense, in that it aims to replace *all* fundamental features of the CPE and
thus to *destabilize* the essential components of the communist economic
system and replace them with a "market socialist" system. Its goal
would be (a) to establish a truly pluralistic structure of ownership of
the means of production, with the private sector being large enough to
influence the pattern of microeconomic behavior in the other sectors;
(b) to replace the vertical links between the economic units with hor-
zontal ones (and to de-concentrate and de-monopolize the economy to
provide freedom of entry and exit); and last but certainly not least, (c)
to eliminate the institutional role of the communist party (or of any
other political party, though not of the government) in the economy
The new system would probably include a large public sector in
which most state enterprises would be subject to workers' self-management; the share of the cooperative sector would be higher than in a
typical market economy; there would be many types of "mixed" property firms; and there would be workers' participation in the management of private firms. Clearly, the socialist character of such a system
would not be a question of its microeconomic operation or of the
property structure of capital assets mentioned above, but rather a question of its macroeconomic policies with respect to national income distribution, personal income differentiation, the regulation of working
conditions, the system of wage bargaining, unemployment policy
(measures preventing other than frictional unemployment, especially
among youth), the social security system, and so on. Although this
concept of a socialist economy is an "open-ended" one, it differs from
the blueprints of the social-democratic parties in the multisectoral pattern of ownership, as well as in the role of workers' self-management
and various forms of labor participation in the organization of production and distribution and in the extensive powers granted to local
councils.

Until this time, most economic reforms in the CPEs were limited to
changes in elements of fundamental feature 2 (centralized organization
and management), with no attempt to enact a market breakthrough

reform. In three instances, however, some revisions of the other two fundamental features were also attempted. An expansion of the private sector and genuine autonomy for the cooperative sector were explicitly postulated in the draft of the Czechoslovak reform in 1966–68 (Brus 1986, 211), as well as in those of the Polish reform of 1981, where under the pressure from Solidarity the equal treatment of the private, cooperative, and state property was proclaimed (*Kierunki* 1981, thesis 16). With respect to the monopolistic role of the party, this was directly rejected in Czechoslovakia after January 1968 when Dubček came to power. In the Polish reforms of 1956 and 1981, the party's role was to be curbed by workers' self-management; furthermore, this was also the essence of the struggle Solidarity waged and lost in 1981 against the *nomenklatura* system.

All these initiatives were quickly neutralized by force rather than by political measures (for example, Czechoslovakia in 1968, Poland in 1981), or quickly degenerated into reforms of either type 2 or 3, as in Poland in 1956. The failures seem to indicate that unless a market breakthrough reform is undertaken, the other kinds of reforms must sooner or later revert to the traditional system of economic planning and management.

Opposition to Market-Clearing Prices

Another trait characteristic of the CPEs is repressed inflation. Periodically, it must give vent to price rises if consumer goods (and services) are allocated through the market rather than through administrative rationing. Such a restoration of market-clearing prices is by no means tantamount to the introduction of the market mechanism (which would also require that supply be made price-elastic), but it is a necessary condition for market-type reforms. Market-clearing prices invariably meet with opposition that often undermines the economic sense of price increases. What are the sources of this opposition?

For the public at large, repressed inflation means that consumer goods are allocated not through prices alone but also through time lost in lines, favoritism and corruption, and supplementary payments in kind (coal allotments for miners, meat allotments for employees of slaughterhouses and meat-processing plants, and the like). If the supply

of consumer goods and changes in inventory are given, their total consumption in physical terms is given too, and a rise in the price of consumer goods to market-clearing levels cannot change it. If forced savings (which may be treated here as the money equivalent of repressed
inflation) represent, say, 10 percent of household incomes (the size of
the gap between household income, on the one hand, and the value of
supply on the market and voluntary savings, on the other hand), a rise
in prices that would absorb this gap would not affect total consumption even if the real income of households fell 10 percent. From this
premise the conclusion is sometimes drawn that the opposition of the
public to such price rises is unfounded and based on the "socialist monetary illusion."

This conclusion is not entirely correct. Introducing market-clearing
prices implies changes in the distribution of consumer goods from
households where time rather than money is abundant (households of
three generations, retired people, women on maternity leave, and so
on) to households with higher monetary incomes (for example, with
high labor-force participation rates). Therefore, the consumption of
large sections of the society will be affected. Moreover, as the example
above shows, the "monetary illusion" encompasses one of every ten
units of currency spent. Thus, in practice, it rather resembles a game of
"musical chairs," in which all participants have a high probability of
success if not in this round then in the next.

The opposition of the public to price increases undermines the foundations of "commodity production" and pushes economic relations
back to precapitalist modes of production. Moreover, this opposition,
to which relatively little attention has been paid both in the theory of
economic reforms and in their practical implementation, has been in
the past and may well continue to be in the future a very important
obstacle to market reforms in the CPEs.[4] It cannot be effectively allevi-
ated without winning the public over to such reforms, which in turn
requires the political democratization of the system and institutionalization of some form of participation of the public in political life—
namely, a "market breakthrough" reform. An integral part of this is a
social revolution: the establishment of institutional foundations for parliamentary democracy. Will this be enough to alleviate the opposition
against prices rises? At any rate, the process of reaching this end will be
long and politically painful.

Repressed inflation also implies preferential rationing of consumer goods through privileged access (special shops and delivery systems) and special entitlements to purchase consumer durables (cars, plots of land for houses and recreation, and additional supplies of rationed goods) below market-clearing prices. The opposition of the beneficiaries of these privileges against market-clearing prices is often pointed out, but its actual political importance is uncertain. However, it is clear that the narrower the social and political base of the power system, the more elaborate the system of formal and informal privileges needs to be. This is reflected not only in wage rates, working conditions, retirement age, health care, holiday facilities, and various "fringe benefits," but also in the kind of preferential rationing mentioned above (Staniszkis 1972 and, especially, Narojek 1986).[5]

Opposition to Reform without Reform

Among all the types of reform, reform without reform meets with the weakest opposition of all, since by nature it does not alter any fundamental feature of the TCPEs. Despite this, any reallocation of inputs and restructuring of capacities is at the expense of some and to the benefit of others. Thus such reforms are opposed by sectoral and industrial interests that have to foot the bill of such policy reorientations—mainly heavy industry, metallurgy, machine building, armament production, nonresidential construction, and so on (Kozek 1986). The more permanent the change in priorities seems to be, the stronger the opposition will be. It will come from all segments of economic administration affected, from the bottom to the top of the organizational structure of the economy.

Because of strong personal ties the economic administration has to the government and party apparatus, its opposition is significant. Beyond that it can present its particular interests in an ideological form, saying, for instance, that the "principles of socialist reproduction" and the "law of the faster development of department I"* are being violated. They can label the termination of forced collectivization and diminished discrimination against the private sector in general as the reintroduction of capitalism, and better terms for private farmers and nonagricultural business as undermining the leading role of the working class.

Similar opposition stems from the workforce of enterprises whose privileges are endangered (and from local public opinion in the areas where new investment projects are expected to be abandoned, and thus new employment opportunities and infrastructural investments would be lost). This kind of opposition also appears whenever sectoral and/or industrial wage and income differentials are to change. This was particularly clear in the early phase of the NEM in Hungary, when in order to mitigate the rising income differential between state industry, on the one hand, and between the cooperative and private sectors, on the other hand, state employees were granted a large, tax-free, preferential increase in wages in 1973.

Similar patterns of conflicting interest, which will not be easy to solve either, are bound to emerge under a system of parliamentary democracy. Under the one-party system of the CPEs, however, they necessitate exceptionally strong determination at the highest political levels to counteract the interests of those groups, which constitute the natural power base of the authorities and are capable of neutralizing the reform efforts.

Opposition to Revising Fundamental Feature 1 (Property Reform)

Without much harm to the argument, we may now turn to opposition to a market breakthrough reform, as it also includes those who would oppose reforms of type 2 and type 3. The sources of this opposition can be conveniently categorized under the three fundamental features of the TCPE.

Changing the property structure of a TCPE is clearly a formidable task, not only because of the vested interests involved but also for "technical reasons" (these are discussed by Berg 1987). The state sector is too large and the domestic private market is too small (and operates within a restrictive legal framework) to permit the kind of rapid re-privatization that for other reasons seems warranted.[6] As in many less-developed countries, the government is willing to dispense with the state-owned enterprises that are not economically viable, rather than with the profitable ones. Divestiture may then simply mean closing the least viable firms and scrapping their plants. Moreover, since CPEs are usually small countries, transforming a public-sector monopoly into a private-sector monopoly is not very attractive. For all these reasons (and the ideological ones), the domestic political constituency for such measures is usually small.

Another option is to lease a part of state-owned assets, or areas of state economic activity, to the cooperative and private sectors. Where rigid price controls are likely to continue, a change in the legal framework of firm operation and the introduction of private competition may be more important than privatization of state monopolies.[7] Another potentially preferable option might be to contract out certain public-sector services (for example, waste collection or street cleaning). Another option would be to break up large state enterprises and monopolies (so that cooperation between their individual plants, factories, and so on, would be on a commercial rather than administrative basis). Clearly, all measures aimed at increasing the competitiveness of the economy would be opposed by the beneficiaries of the old system—both the workforce and the management of inefficient state enterprises (Rychard 1988). Such measures would also be opposed by adherents of an instantaneous and comprehensive privatization of the whole economy.

Changing the property structure means that while the public sector shrinks, the private sector would be reintroduced or expanded. This is easier said than done. The reaction to the new rules, which since May 1987 have allowed for some private economic activity in the Soviet Union beyond the agricultural sector, was particularly striking in this context. They were met with distrust and a lack of interest. There was little trust that new statutes would remain in force for long, and fear of a change in the political climate. In other countries (for example, Poland and Hungary) the tax regulations that accompanied reform were unclear and often decided on an ad hoc basis after the fact. The system of granting concessions to private economic activity invited corruption, as did the system of input procurement for the private sector. All this causes the position of private business to be extremely shaky. (Despite this, expansion of the private sector into "no-man's-land" is usually easier than privatization of the state-owned enterprises.)[8]

In CPEs there is also opposition, partly genuine and partly engineered by the official propaganda, to increased income differentials that benefit the private sector, as well as by populist egalitarian demagoguery directed against "privatizers" and "commercialization" of social life. Polish empirical studies show, however, that egalitarian values are accepted less often by workers than officially claimed, and that when egalitarian views are indeed advanced they often express opposition against income differentiation and privileges that the workers find unjust (Kolarska 1985). In light of these findings, it has been argued that claims about "the egalitarian preferences of the public" have been misused, primarily to legitimate the existing power structure and the traditional economic system (52).

All this undermines the stability and economic viability of the private sector in CPEs. It also partly explains why it shares so many negative features of the state sector (waste of inputs, low quality, insufficient innovation, and so on).

The arguments above also apply to the cooperative sector. It was treated by central authorities with distrust, as "incompletely socialist" even after it had been completely controlled and subordinated to central planning. Granting genuine autonomy to cooperatives is opposed by those who favor comprehensive centralized planning and fear the "anarchy of the market." It is also opposed by agencies that supervise cooperatives whose existence would no longer be justified, as well as by management and members of the cooperatives that hitherto have enjoyed preferential allocation of rationed inputs. Finally, it is also opposed by management and the local administration in places where the genuine autonomy of cooperatives would no longer permit misuse of their resources for satisfying private needs in exchange for patronage, and the like (the same holds true for some state enterprises—for example, in construction, food processing, consumer durables, and auto repair).

The importance of this opposition does not appear to be very significant because it can be undermined with a change in the regulatory environment and by greater openness in the business practices of the cooperatives. This demands, as in the case of the state sector, political change.

Opposition to Revising Fundamental Feature 2 (Decentralization)

As I have written about the sources of this type of opposition elsewhere (Osiatyński et al. 1985), I shall only reiterate here the main con-

clusions concerning individual and social- and occupational-group opposition to this type of reform.

First and foremost it is opposed by the intermediate level of economic administration and the agencies that allocate raw materials and
other inputs to state enterprises and cooperatives. Clearly, as a result of
such changes they would be deprived of power, if not wholly eliminated. Since there are strong personal links between this apparatus and
the middle-level party apparatus, this opposition is capable of effectively blocking measures that undermine its social and political position unless they are accompanied by appropriate changes in the political system.

Also ill-disposed to revisions in this area is part of the central economic administration—for example, the "branch-line ministries"*—as
well as the central and regional government and party administration,
whose powers would diminish in relation to autonomous enterprises.
The thorough change in the methods, scope, and instruments of central economic planning necessitated by such revisions requires not only
new attitudes and habits on the part of planners but, more important,
new professional qualifications, perhaps even a new generation of personnel.[9]

Such revisions are also opposed by risk-adverse and less-dynamic
enterprise managers whose attitudes, motivation, and decision-making
criteria were completely molded by the "command economic system."
Furthermore, such changes are often blocked by the political apparatus
at the enterprise level and higher up, not only because it represents the
interests of the social groups mentioned above (whose party membership is relatively high), but also because in the traditional system of
economic management the enterprise is both an economic and a political institution. Since this opposition overlaps to some extent opposition to revising the third fundamental feature of CPEs, we shall discuss
it in the next section.

Opposition to Revising Fundamental Feature 3 (Depoliticization)

The politicization of the CPE is deeply rooted in ideological and political doctrine, as well as in the fear of the "anarchy of the market" and of

the resulting cyclical fluctuations in employment, prices, and incomes that underlie the doctrine.[10] It requires that the government administration, guided by the directives of the party's executive agencies, approve the plans formulated by the economic units (or simply impose plans on them), create favorable conditions for their implementation, and control them.

Paradoxically, this politicization of the economy "from above" is reinforced by a similar trend "from below": when there are no other ways to articulate and realize the interests of workers, they use enterprises for this purpose. Consequently, the enterprise becomes a battleground for economic as well as political, social, and other interests (Morawski 1986). This, in turn, leads to a double interdependence between the rulers and the ruled in exercising a "negative authority." There emerges "not only a dependence of the 'governed' on the power elite . . . , but also an equally strong reciprocal dependence, that often leads to the 'incapacitation' and paralysis of the authorities" (Adamski 1985, 37).

Moreover, the question arises whether the higher levels of the system of economic administration are at all capable of controlling their subordinates. Even in the early phases of the CPEs, when the powers of supervisory agencies over their subordinates were much greater than now, it could be legitimately asked who ultimately controlled whom.[11] Thus, the struggle for distributive shares in the allocation of inputs, profits, wages, social benefits, and so on pervades the system, and it becomes increasingly incapable of reconciling these interests (Zienkowski 1986).

That the ideological and political doctrine requires total subordination of economic decision-making to the political apparatus is an important factor that works against market reforms in the CPEs. It is certainly more important than the interests, material or otherwise, of the party and government administration. However, depoliticization of the economy, especially at the level of state-owned enterprises, becomes a political question par excellence. The same applies to the establishment of clear rules subject to authentic social control for coordinating various branch, regional, and other interests (in place of informal and secretive deals that in practice make economic calculation impossible).

Conclusions

It is sometimes argued that microeconomic efficiency does not necessarily need to be combined with parliamentary democracy, and that autocratic rule may be equally effective in achieving dynamic improvement in standards of living, provided that the economy is left to the market. The experience of some newly industrializing countries is cited in support of this proposition.

Be that as it may, the question facing the CPEs is entirely different. Some years ago a report of the Polish Sociological Society raised a specific and dramatic characteristic of the situation in Poland: the social groups that are likely to support the reform programs put forward by the communist leadership neither trust it nor enjoy its confidence, and those who trust the political leadership and enjoy its confidence are on the whole opposed to reforms (Executive Committee 1987, 61–62). This is unlikely to change without a market breakthrough reform and the far-reaching democratic changes connected to it.[12]

It remains an open question, though, how such reform can be initiated and accomplished. I tend to agree that it must be both inspired and partly engineered from above, and partly engineered and supported—within a newly created institutional framework—from below (Morawski 1986; Kowalik 1986). Unless such reforms are implemented (whereby a crucial reform could be treated as a "halfway house"), the CPEs would face prolonged stagnation and relative decline.

Maybe the Polish experience of the Solidarity and post-Solidarity period is of some relevance in this context. First of all, it testifies to the strong preference of the adherents of reforms for a "peaceful revolution." Second, it shows that determined mass pressure may induce some expansion of market relations and some forms of licensed pluralism. Clearly, Poland of the late 1980s—with genuinely independent economic associations promoting private entrepreneurship, an association of workers' self-management activists, political discussion clubs, two regional student organizations, and with the communists' partners in the ruling coalition gaining increasing independence from the Polish United Workers' Party* [PZPR], with attempts to form "an Anti-Crisis Pact" with the opposition, and with the December 1988 Plenum of the Central Committee of the PZPR pledging to drastically reduce the *nomenklatura*—was a different country from Poland of a decade before.

In Poland and Hungary we have seen the old political and economic system disintegrate rapidly under pressure from below, leading to somewhat different attitudes on the part of the respective ruling elites. In Hungary the social pressure was less intense, or at least less vocal than in Poland, because the Hungarian ruling elite appeared to be more reform-minded and cooperative. The Polish ruling elite was deeply divided about the nature of and need for radical reforms, as well as about their political survival, but pressure from below, mainly from Solidarity members and sympathizers, was stronger. The intense political struggle in these two countries has clearly shown that the opposition to the kind of market breakthrough reform discussed in this chapter can be overcome only if it is accompanied by democratization of the political system.

Although any discussion of the conditions and manner in which communist rule comes to an end is beyond the scope of this paper, the experience of the Central and East European countries since 1939 clearly indicates a strong positive correlation between the public conviction that "the Great Transformation" is tantamount to an end of the communist system and public support for breakthrough reform, including the readiness of the population to accept even large short-term losses in standards of living. This banal truth explains why, for example, the first postcommunist government in Poland could preside over a 30 percent reduction in real wages after the reform was initiated in January 1990, but its communist predecessor did not survive a reduction of about 8 percent only a year earlier (Osiatyński 1991).

Translated by the author

Notes

1. This analysis is meant to apply to the six CPEs of Eastern Europe and the USSR. The sources of opposition to market reforms in Yugoslavia and in the non-European CPEs may well require a separate investigation.

2. Exact data on the scope of the *nomenklatura* system in the economy of any CPE (for example, on the ratios of positions covered by this system to total numbers of managerial positions in the state and cooperative sectors of the economy) are not available. For lists of posts, in the economy and elsewhere, falling under the *nomenklatura* of the Polish United Workers' Party's Central Committee (CC PZPR), regional committees, and district commit-

tees, dating from 1972, see MacShane 1981, Appendix 5. For a list of posts falling under the *nomenklatura* of the CC PZPR, its politburo and its secretariat, dating from August 1986, see "List" 1987. Interestingly, in spite of strong pressures in Poland in the early 1980s to limit the scope of this system, it continued to include even the position of foreman. The *nomenklatura* system in the economy was seen by a senior Polish sociologist as an instrument of surplus appropriation due to monopoly in the ownership of the means of production (see Szczepański 1987).

3. For doctrinal reasons, the output and employment of the genuinely private firms, for example, in some supply and purchase contracts or in subcontracting, is often included in the cooperative sector's official statistics, and thereby in those of the "socialized sector" of the CPEs. Also, for other reasons (for example, tax evasion), the share of the private sector in total output and employment are underestimated. This probably holds more for the Hungarian economy before the 1968 reform than in subsequent periods. In 1986, the relative shares of active earners in the Hungarian private and cooperative sectors outside agriculture and forestry were 6.3 percent and 11.2 percent (see Hungarian Central Statistical Office 1988, table 4.4, 68–69).

4. This was strongly demonstrated by the Polish referendum of November 1987, in which the more ambitious plans for introducing market-clearing prices were vehemently rejected. It should be noted in passing that the public at large, lacking everyday personal experience with the market economy, often does not clearly perceive the link between market-clearing prices and the introduction of market mechanisms. However, the reformers did not seem to take much note of this.

5. Although similar phenomena also exist elsewhere (for example, with respect to the police, army, or the fire department), they are kept in check by a system of genuine public control over government spending.

6. The participation of foreign capital must be limited so that privatization does not lead to the loss of economic sovereignty.

7. Berg (1987, 11) argues, for instance, for allowing private competition for passengers in public transit, instead of a change of ownership, if the price structure remains unchanged.

8. Iván Szelényi (1989) correctly notes that a political coalition of the state and party elite, and certain other social groups (the retired, disabled, and nonworking poor), who have little or no private income, could constitute a political force capable of blocking such changes. Nevertheless, he observes, the Hungarian Socialist Workers' Party favored "the expansion of private business, rather than the transformation of government-owned firms into joint stock companies."

9. For a more detailed analysis of the tasks of central planners under a system where the market determines output and capital expansion, see Józefiak 1988.

10. As long as the market system, regulated or unregulated, is unable to cope with unemployment, this fear is justified. Although unemployment, other than frictional, appears to me to be a social pathology, it is, I believe, largely a value judgment whether unemployment outside factory gates is preferable to unemployment on factory floors, and what the trade-off is between the microeconomic inefficiency of a CPE and the economic and social welfare it secures, as compared to the macroeconomic inefficiency (unemployment), and the economic and social welfare of a market economy. I shall not go any further into this matter since the subject of this chapter is not to argue for market reforms (which in themselves may or may not be a sensible idea), but merely to discuss sources of opposition to them.

11. Staniszkis (1980) claims that control from above is not possible. Rychard (1987) argues that it leaves the would-be controllers at the mercy of the controlled.

12. Therefore, I find any position that counterposes "democratic socialism" and "market socialism" (see Nuti 1986) rather misleading in the context of economic reform of the CPEs.

References

Adamski, W. 1985. "Aspirations, Interests, Conflicts" (in Polish). *Studia Socjo-logiczne* 2.

Bauer, T. 1986. "Reforming or Perfecting the Economic Mechanism in Eastern Europe." *EUI Working Papers* 86. Florence.

Berg, E. 1987. "Privatization: Developing a Pragmatic Approach." *Economic Impact* 1.

Brus, W. 1972. *The Market in a Socialist Economy*. London: Routledge & Kegan Paul.

———. 1986. "Institutional Change within a Planned Economy." In M. Kaser, ed., *The Economic History of Eastern Europe, 1919–1975*, vol. 3. Oxford: Clarendon Press.

Executive Committee of the Polish Sociological Association. 1987. "Report on Polish Society in the Second Half of the 1980s" (in Polish). *Dwadzieścia Jeden* 4.

Granick, D. 1975. *Enterprise Guidance in Eastern Europe: A Comparison of Four Socialist Economies*. New York: Princeton University Press.

Hungarian Central Statistical Office. 1988. *Statistical Yearbook 1986*. Budapest.

Jòzefiak, C. 1988. "Factors Blocking Economic Self-Regulation." In *Tendencies for Systemic Changes in the Second Phase of the Polish Economic Reform*. Wrocław: Polskie Towarzystwo Economiczne.

Kalecki, M., and T. Kowalik. 1971. "Osservazioni sulla 'riforma cruciale.'" *Politica ed Economia* 2–3. Published in English under the title "Observations on the 'Crucial Reform,'" in M. Kalecki, *Collected Works*, vol. 2. Oxford: Clarendon Press, 1991.

Kierunki reformy gospodarczej (Directions of economic reform). 1981. Warsaw: Komisja do Spraw Reformy Gospodarczej.

Kolarska, L. 1985. "Social Interests, Egalitarian Values, and Changes in the Economic Order" (in Polish). *Studia Socjologiczne* 2.

Kornai, J. 1986. "The Hungarian Reform Process: Visions, Hopes, and Reality." *Journal of Economic Literature* 24, no. 4: 1687–1744.

Kowalik, T. 1986. "On Crucial Reform of Real Socialism." Research Report 122, The Vienna Institute for Comparative Economic Studies.

Kozek, W. 1986. "Reasons for the Breakdown of the Polish Economic Reform" (in Polish). *Studia Socjologiczne* 3.

Laky, T. 1980. "The Hidden Mechanism of Recentralization in Hungary." *Acta Oeconomica* 24, no. 1/2.

"List of Posts Which Require Consultation, Recommendation, and Approval by the Central Committee, the Politburo, and Central Committee Secretariat of the Polish United Workers' Party" (in Polish). 1987. *Dwadzieścia Jeden* 4.

MacShane, D. 1981. *Solidarity: Poland's Independent Trade Union*. Nottingham: Spokesman.

Morawski, W. 1986. "Economic and Political Reforms as Counter-Crisis Measures." In J. J. Wiatr, ed., *Satisfying Needs under Crisis* (in Polish). Warsaw: Instytut Socjologii, Uniwersytet Warszawski.

Narojek, W. 1986. *Prospects of Pluralism in Etatist Society* (in Polish). London: Aneks.

Nuti, D. M. 1986. "Michal Kalecki's Contribution to the Theory and Practice of Socialist Planning." *Cambridge Journal of Economics* 10, no. 4.

Osiatyński, J. 1991. "Opposition against Market Breakthrough Reforms Re-visited." Paper presented to the conference "Positive Legacy. Obstacles to the Transformation in Eastern Europe." Vienna, Institut für die Wissenschaften vom Menschen.

Osiatyński, J., W. Pańków, W. Federowicz, and M. Federowicz. 1985. *Self-Management in the Polish Economy, 1981–1985.* Bologna: Biblioteca Walter Bigiavi.

Rychard, A. 1987. *Power and Interests in the Polish Economy in the Early 1980s* (in Polish). Warsaw: Uniwersytet Warszawski.

———. 1988. "Social and Political Preconditions for and Consequences of Economic Reforms in Poland." Research Report 14, The Vienna Institute for Comparative Economic Studies.

Staniszkis, J. 1972. *Pathologies of Organization* (in Polish). Warsaw: Ossolineum.

———. 1980. "Systemic Conditioning of the Functioning of an Industrial Enterprise" (in Polish). *Przegląd Socjologiczny* 30.

Szczepański, J. 1987. "Economic Values" (in Polish). *Życie Gospodarcze* 10.

Szelényi, I. 1989. "Eastern Europe in an Epoch of Transition: Toward a Socialist Mixed Economy?" In V. Nee and D. Stark, eds., *Remaking the Economic Institutions of Socialism.* Stanford: Stanford University Press.

Zienkowski, L. 1986. *The Struggle for Distribution of Incomes* (in Polish). Warsaw: Główny Urząd Statystyczny.

15

Civil Society and the Market under Real Socialism

Krytyka, no. 34/35 (1991)

Piotr Ogrodziński

They say that a weasel can suck the contents out of an egg without leaving any visible trace on the shell. That apparently was the source of the Shakespearean metaphor "I can suck melancholy out of a song as a weasel sucks eggs." On the basis of this, the Americans (supposedly Theodore Roosevelt) coined the expression, "weasel word," meaning a word that through excessive use suddenly becomes meaningless and empty. Hayek refers to this expression in his uncompromising criticism of the overuse of the noun "society" and the adjective "social." These words not only became empty, he argues, but they also are a sign of the fatal vanity of a constructivistic rationalism that considers human reality to be consciously created by and the object of the thoughts that devise it.[1] Though Hayek does not write expressly about "civil society," his critical remarks may be relevant for this concept as well.

In the context of the last few years, especially in Poland, where this expression appears not only in academic papers and conference proceedings but also in journalism and in the ideological declarations of competing political forces, anxiety about the loss of meaning and the emptiness of this expression is fully justified. This does not mean that we should necessarily reject the concept of "civil society" as meaningless or false. However, it does mean that its use should be clarified.

First of all, the concept of "civil society" appears on three different levels: (1) in the history of social thought, (2) in ideology, and (3) in social research, as a critical tool.

The ideological career of the concept of "civil society" is a product of the acute crisis of the Eastern European political systems. As long as the system of real socialism seemed indestructible, the lack of a social alternative was expressed in the opposition of socialism and capitalism. Furthermore, a return to capitalism was assumed to be impossible and inadmissible. Depending on the economic and political situation, ideologists argued that socialism meant either the pursuit of the ideal (communism) or that this "best of all possible worlds" was somewhat defective and needed improvement—even "renewal." The loss by this ideological algorithm of its power to convince forced conservative forces to replace "socialist system" with another term—"civil society." In turn, historical experience and the excessive development of the apparatus of coercion in real socialist states forced the radical opposition to search for an evolutionary strategy of change and a way to avoid revolutionary uprisings. For the opposition, civil society became an ideal that replaced the antinomy of "socialism vs. capitalism."

In critical research, the present approach toward civil society is in need of fundamental revision. Until recently, the most important question was "Does civil society exist under real socialism?" Today the key issue is whether the concept of civil society helps to describe dynamic processes of the transformation now under way. To make sense of this new situation, the concept of civil society must take account of four moments that also constitute the historical periods of the socialist system: (1) *genesis*, namely, the relation of the socialist revolution and the preliminary (as János Kornai calls it) heroic period[2] to civil society; (2) *endurance*, namely, the presence (or absence) and place of civil society under socialism in its classic form; (3) *dynamics* (reforming socialism), thus a question about the factors that brought about change, but included in the concept of civil society; (4) *prognosis*, deliberation on the possible outcome of the changes now under way, namely, civil society as a goal of transformation. These four points do not imply that the solution to this issue lies in the past. It can still be argued that real socialism in its classic forms (Stalinism and post-Stalinism) denied the existence of a civil society, and that the process of change could be interpreted as the creation of social structures included in the concept of "civil society." Or it might be argued that even in the Stalinist period civil society was present, though distorted, and that change is a product of its revival.

The features outlined below constitute civil society in its classic form. They are closely linked to the foundation of the capitalist world order, an order that was shaped, as Fernand Braudel put it, during the turning point of the "long sixteenth century" (or perhaps during an even longer period—from 1400 to 1800).[3]

1. *A fully developed division of labor and system of needs.* The division of labor is older than written history, but until the critical "long sixteenth century" it always had a local character; it had been confined to micro-systems (such as the Greek *oikos*, the Roman *domos*, or the feudal manor). The division of labor expanded beyond microsystems only to the extent that they produced a surplus. Basic needs were met locally. The turning point meant a widening and deepening of the division of labor, so that most human needs came to be met in an indirect fashion. Goods are produced to meet the abstract needs of unknown recipients, and producers depend on products of the labor of other producers whom they do not know. Under this system, production develops in a highly dynamic fashion. The division of labor becomes more subtle and needs more diversified, and this creates both greater diversity and greater uniformity.

2. *Formally differentiated subjects—natural and legal persons defined through property.* This turning point is connected with the process of individuation and the awareness of the individual self. Society becomes a collection of individuals in which everyone owns one's own abilities and that which one gains through their employment.[4] At the outset all individuals have equal rights, in formally defined law, to use their abilities. That is why freedom is described in a negative sense—not as the action itself, but as the possibility to act or not to act.[5] Cooperating individuals have the power to create group subjects—legal persons who are defined through property just as natural persons are. Civil society appears as a sphere of interaction where the subject (as a human being, as a natural or a legal person, as a citizen) is "let free," is capable of undertaking any action that does not violate the rights of other subjects to self-preservation and self-protection.[6]

3. *Formal rules of interaction—civil law.* Civil society constitutes the domain of the spontaneous, horizontal, constantly organized and reorganized cooperation of differentiated subjects. In these activities individuals do not identify directly with the whole; they make independent decisions at their own risk to achieve their own egoistic goals. They do this within the framework of a set of general rules that are consciously accepted as universally valid and equally binding for everyone capable of participating in civil society (a society of citizens). These rules do

not define objectives, but only methods of activity; they primarily protect property and define the procedures for its acquisition and transfer. On a general level, these rules constitute the ethical basis of civil society, and their institutionalization has the form of universal law, especially civil law, which establishes the norms for relationships between equal subjects.

4. *The cosmos of the extended order and the exteriorization of the state.*[7] Civil society constitutes a self-organizing and self-reproducing order. Its organization is not the result of a project or the control of one decision-making center, but the involuntary result of "human action, but not of human designs."[8] Belief in the power of the logic of "an invisible hand" presupposes the exteriorization of the state. The major task of the state is to protect property and ensure general respect for formal rules of interaction. The activities of the state are subject to constitutional limits; one classical form of this limitation is the division of legislative, judicial, and executive powers. There is a seeming paradox in that the crucial sixteenth century was the time of origin of the modern state,[9] which drew its uncommon political strength from the disposition of powers such as monopolies on the use of direct force or the issuing of money. Thus the limitation of the scope of state intervention in the private life of citizens (for example, the form and types of taxes) becomes the major political issue of civil society.

5. *Civilization without a world political center.*[10] In the period preceding the crucial sixteenth century, there was a trend toward the establishment of empires within the boundaries of the civilized world—for example, the division of labor of the redistributive economy in the ancient world was accomplished within the framework of the Roman Empire, and in Europe in the Middle Ages within the framework of the Catholic church. During this time the dynamics of political power substantially outpaced and contained within itself the development of economic life. Feudal anarchy and the lack of a dominant state in Europe in the early modern period had an important influence on the formation of contemporary civil society. The predominance of dynamic economic development and the expansion of the market, over political dynamics and imperial expansion, became the foundation for the clear separation of the economic sphere and the establishment of the ontological independence of civil society.

6. *Internal differentiation and corporations.* The five previous features present civil society as a product of the logic of the market—a com-

mercial society. Within this society, formally assumed equality through interaction results in a diversification of wealth and social position. It created a system of social stratification, which is expressed in the conflict of interests between classes and estates. However, not all social differentiation is derivative of the division of labor. Religious communities, national minorities, family—these are communities that are genetically independent of the market. Intermediate forms of socialization, such as political parties, associations, trade unions, churches, marriages, and so on, acquired various institutional forms. These institutions are partially influenced by market logic, and they partially defy it, or simply do not have a place within it. For example, a family—or more exactly a household budget—constitutes the basic unit of individual consumption, and through procreation it is the source of reproduction of labor power. The family is at the same time an institution of cultural continuity and of human spiritual support. Without these intermediate forms of socialization—partly inherent in market logic and partly outside it—it would be impossible for civil society to function. These problems are of special importance particularly to conservative tradition.

7. *Social justice and the police.* In the eighteenth century the term "police" was understood as the administrative activities of the state from municipal sanitation to public works.[11] It is sometimes impossible to fulfill general interests through the market mediation of individual interests. These are the circumstances under which even strict liberals allow for state intervention. However, the maintenance of the conditions that permit the spontaneous sphere of interaction to continue to operate also includes the prevention of sharp conflicts based in the disadvantaged position of some social groups, such as the poor. The reproduction of civil society requires provision for minimal standards of social justice. Social welfare cannot be realized within the logic of the market. These functions are usually performed by the state under the pressure of social-democratic ideas.

These seven points constitute a somewhat eclectic synthesis of the opinions of a number of authors on the nature of contemporary society. The first five points define commercial society and are most fully manifested in the theories of liberalism (though point 5 is the basis of dependence theory). Points 6 and 7 are special "objections" to the concept of commercial society, and as such constitute the domain of par-

ticular interests in the conservative and socialist traditions. At the turn
of the eighteenth century and at the beginning of the nineteenth, it is
possible to observe the emergence of these concerns in the descriptions
of the social situation, beginning with liberalism and proceeding
through conservatism to socialism. These concerns were synthesized
by Hegel in *Philosophy of Right*, which was first published in 1821.

In this article, Hegel will remain in the background, because I want
to escape his dogmatism (which is structured in a fashion similar to
that of Marxist dogmatism), which is based on the substitution of a
knowledge of social reality with an attempt to make the "course of
worldly affairs" fit the outlines of great theoretical concepts. It should
be added, though, that Hegel was actually the only theoretician who
used the concept of civil society consistently and placed it in a strictly
defined position (as a special type of ethics) in his social philosophy.
Naturally, the problems of civil society—as defined above—were considered by many authors—but implicitly, requiring additional interpretation. These authors sometimes use the term precisely, but they
often use synonymous notions such as civilized society, Great Society,
commercial society, open society, or extended order. When priority is
given to civil society, as in the works of the young Marx or Gramsci,
it points to the strong influence of Hegel.

Finally, an almost banal note, but one that in view of the trend to
idealize civil society, is necessary. The concept encompasses a reality
with unbelievable possibilities for development—material, social, cultural, demographic, and so on. It creates conditions for immense individual freedom, respect for personal dignity and integrity. On the
other hand, this same order, because it is so dynamic, creates acute
conflicts—poverty and war on an unprecedented scale, and even the
ability to destroy humanity. It is the cause of human loneliness; it often
degrades and compels in an extreme way. It is precisely this dynamism, brimming with conflicts, that led certain twentieth-century
thinkers to change their understanding of civil society. Gramsci and
Habermas (as interpreted by Jean Cohen and Andrew Arato)[12] consider
civil society as a sphere of mediation between state and economy, culture and civilization, and the system and everyday life. And I only
hope—if I consider the features encompassed in this concept as dominant in contemporary society *tout court*—that the self-sustaining powers of civil society will cause its lighter side to prevail over its dark
side.

I shall now address the fundamental issue of whether the concept of civil society makes sense in the reality of real socialism. The answer to this question must account for four moments (periods) of the development of real socialism. In its genesis, real socialism was to be the forceful implementation of a mental project. This project, derived from the part of the socialist tradition stemming from the October Revolution, was a clear negation of the idea of civil society as outlined earlier. For the young Marx, the social reality he experienced was torn by the contradictions of a political state and a civil society, of the citizens of the state and living individuals, of a class of owners and a class without any property.[13] His very sharp criticism was to a large extent correct. He tried to pinpoint the mechanisms that led to human alienation and to outline a means of eliminating this alienation. At the same time, he tried to create a theory with far-reaching practical consequences, a theory already inscribed in a foreseen revolution. In this context it does not seem surprising that Marx later (still demanding an end to human alienation), in the name of theoretical clarity, ceased to use the notion of "civil society" and replaced it with the term "bourgeois society."[14] In his vision of communism there was no place either for subjects defined by private property or for civil law, or for an exteriorized but strong state. Naturally, social differentiation was to be radically liquidated.

The basic mechanism that coordinates cooperation in civil society is the market—the principle of the realization of general well-being through individual egoism. In cooperation of this type many objectives are defined on the individual level. Commonly, means are priced on the basis of their marginal utility. In this sort of cooperation, because of individual egoism, individual needs exceed the means available to fulfill them (and shortages ensue), and the particularization of activity creates information disorders.[15] Cooperation is possible because principles of just behavior (*Recht*), which grow out of the material conditions of individual activity, are observed.[16] Individuals try to gauge their actions in a general perspective (Smith's "impartial observer"), because only in that way are they capable of realizing their own objectives, preserving themselves, and ensuring the material reproduction of their existence. The liberal tradition—beginning with Smith and ending with Hayek—contrasts civil society with the state of nature, savagery. This contrast, which could be called "not-civil society," is characterized by a direct (not mediated through individual subjectivity) identification of individuals with the general. Socialism, already as the

Marxist-Leninist project, postulated eliminating alienation through the reconstruction of the identification of individuals and society. The revolutionary act and the preliminary, heroic period of real socialism signified the domination of ethical coordination in human actions and postulated and demanded identification of individuals with the general interest even up to the loss of individual identity. In that period the creation of a new civilization, a new culture, a new human being— "not-civil society"—was attempted.

The real socialism of the classic period is, from our point of view, the key, fundamental issue. This is because here and now the reality still does not give a full answer to the question of whether the ongoing process of change, regardless of its spectacular character, constitutes an irreversible exit from the systemic framework of the previous period. From this perspective Stalinism and the post-Stalinist period, the classic period and the period of reforms, belong to the same social reality, a reality (as a perception of a social entity) whose shortcomings are obvious enough for its radical rejection to be demanded but whose actuality is so strong that it forces caution in the formulation of prognoses and leaves room only for partial optimism. Classic, real socialism, on the one hand, is endowed with an ontological peculiarity (it requires a description in systemically immanent categories, not by the lack of capitalism but by distinctively socialist features) and, on the other hand, is not ontologically self-subsistent (which means it is a system in a state of ontological contradiction). Such a theoretical evaluation points to the inevitability of radical change. History, however, often mocks theoretical inevitabilities, and for those who have lived until recently under real socialism it has forcibly endowed everyday life with a surrealistic character because of its [ontological] contradiction.

The author who put forward this thesis on the ontological peculiarity of real socialism, as well as on its inability to see to its own self-subsistence, is Jadwiga Staniszkis.[17] Her book, *The Ontology of Socialism*, demands in-depth analysis. Here, though, I would like to concentrate on one thesis of her work that is crucial for my deliberations: how the absence of civil society is constitutive for real socialism. In Hegel's categories the inability of real socialism to see to its self-subsistence means that, in order to render reality under state socialism sensible, reference must be made to things external to its presupposed reality. The impossibility of realizing its posited presuppositions manifests itself in reality. This presupposed reality includes, on the one hand, the acceptance of collective ownership of means of production (namely, the abolition of private ownership and agents of individual property), and on the other hand, the institutionalization of the communist party, the avant-garde of the working class, as a substitute for fundamental historical social subjects (and thus the liquidation of democratic institutions). The realization of these presuppositions results in an economy that lacks economic agents, an economy without economics, and prerogative authority without politics. By prerogative authority Staniszkis means that sovereignty does not have a legal character, because law is subjugated to authority (in this sense socialist bureaucracy has a non-Weberian character). This means that the rationality of the market has been totally replaced by the rationality of control. However, this rationality never fully materializes because the party-state, despite its theoretical control of all means of power, does not fully control social reality because of the lack of essential information, the play of interests, and mechanisms enabling such control.

On one level, I find myself in agreement with Staniszkis. I came to similar conclusions in my own work on how the actions of the socialist state to maximize its control were counterproductive. Instead of increasing its control, it diminished it.[18] Despite this similarity, however, Staniszkis and I differ in our conclusions concerning civil society under socialism. I was and still am of the opinion that the sphere beyond and opposed to the state, the sphere of horizontal interactions, is evidence of the existence of civil society under socialism, although in a distorted form. At first this difference did not seem very important to me. It struck me as a problem of semantics—namely, that it was not a question of different understandings of civil society, but rather a question of the scope of the concept's use. Today it strikes me that the difference in conclusions may be the result of different theoretical approaches.

The absence of civil society in Jadwiga Staniszkis's theory of real socialism is significant. A similar omission with reference to traditional primitive society, or generally about any premodern, precapitalist society, has different ramifications—it would mean either that civil society does not exist or that as yet it has not been established. However, civil society is absent under real socialism *despite*, *following*, and *alongside* its existence in the Western world. But this absence is not simply noncapitalism (explaining socialism through the absence of the characteristic features of capitalism). It derives from the immanent description of real socialism, and it has important ontological consequences: the phenomenon of the self-enclosed totality of the system, and the absence of a universalizing principle—because of the inability of the rationality of control to fulfill this function. For this reason precisely, on the level of reality, I do not see the absence of civil society, but rather a shortage (that is, an underdevelopment).

The issue of the shortage or absence of civil society under real socialism can be explored in relation to its condition "despite," "following," and "alongside" civil society in the West. I speak of "despite" because the projects of socialism and communism (expressed in a presupposed reality) were designed to abolish civil society. I speak of "following" because the constitutive features of real socialism originated in civil (market) society. The phenomenon of homogenization described by Jadwiga Staniszkis is the result of the uniformization of social spheres by the market in a civil society—the absence of the market interaction of those uniform spheres and subjects under real socialism, and in consequence the lack of (though I prefer "shortage of") universalization, lead to homogenization. Further and more important, the power and scope of the rationality of control of the party-state under real socialism is a development of (and not simply a contrast to) a modern state established on the basis of a civil society. It is enough to realize that Hobbes's Leviathan is a theoretical concept based on a keen recognition of the features of a market society. A hypothetical construction of the state of nature, where the isolated individual is in conflict with all others, serves as a justification for a state with almost unlimited power. The main principle of the Leviathan is its own sovereignty, and thus we have the origins of the concept of a prerogative state. Hobbes's state is also not an axiological value, because it was derived from the market.[19] Its function is to impose the rules of the market game on individuals, to civilize them. In that sense the Stalinist state goes beyond the Leviathan, but in accord with its inner logic, although rejecting the market as a point of departure.

The problem, however, is that Stalinism (or, more broadly, totalitarian regimes) is not a historic coincidence but a possibility immanent in the structure of a modern state. The state includes civil society, in the sense that we speak of "national" civil societies and also in the sense that the state is the general interest. At the same time, the state is established by civil society, and in this dimension cannot escape particularization. This is clear from Arrow's paradox—that it is impossible to aggregate individual utility functions into social welfare functions without somebody deciding on how to aggregate them.[20] This, however, is mostly a consequence of the construction of the democratic state itself—it is supposed to represent everyone's interests in order to legitimate itself. According to Anthony de Jasay, this leads to a mad redistribution (churning), where something is taken away from everyone and everyone is given something in order to get them to consent to the exercise of power.[21] Under such circumstances the state must become alienated, and becomes yet another subject of a civil society that defines itself by the rationality of power and a desire for a maximum of discretionary authority.[22] In this sense, even that most "ideal" of states, Hegel's ethical *res publica*, contains the threatening potential to develop into a prerogative state. Also in this sense, the incompatibility of theory and practice in the communist tradition—the concept of the withering away of the state and the systemic totalization of a prerogative state—is not proof of the aberration of reason, but rather a real paradox of civil society.

The issue of the absence or shortage of civil society in real socialism also exists "alongside" its presence in the Western world. The original project presupposed socialist revolution on a world scale, but at first the new order encompassed only one country, and revolution was exported only to other areas of the periphery, not to the world center. Thus the whole history of real socialism is connected to a world outside, which was more or less hostile and was treated in the same way. That external focus made dynamic development essential. This race to develop more rapidly than the outside world, from today's perspective, has been lost.

The syndrome of rapid development is closely connected with the problem of reform in real socialism. Today the commonly posed question of whether socialism is reformable seems incorrect. It was more political than theoretical, and it actually concerned the permanence of the system, which seemed beyond doubt in the Brezhnev era. The question was a peculiar reflection of the powerful tendency in real socialism to stagnate in a spiral of sham reforms, changes in bureaucratic structures aimed at the revitalization of rationality of control, and the strengthening of the prerogativeness of power. The authorities, who were unable to assert control over economic reality, tried to regain it by demonstrating their command over the instruments of power. Such reforms in the economic dimension only confirmed the lack of a spe-

cific type of rationality in planning. Planning became only an instrument for exercising centralized power, an artificially differentiated
fragment to manage the national economy.

Serious economic reforms would have meant seeking new means,
other than bureaucratic, to coordinate the economy. The Yugoslav
model and the cultural revolution in China could be seen as attempts
at this that relied on ethical coordination. In both cases the reasons
for introducing the changes were political, not economic. In the case
of China, the cultural revolution attacked both elements of capitalism
(all market institutions) and the bureaucracy. Its aim was to strengthen
the faction around Mao. Its economic and social results were pitiful. In
the case of Yugoslavia, the introduction of the new system served to
differentiate Yugoslavia radically from the Stalinist model and to
strengthen its political independence from the Soviet Union. This
model, in fact, was a mix of ethical, market, and bureaucratic coordination, and today it exhibits a number of economic (inflation, unemployment, flight of labor overseas) and political problems (nationalist
tensions).[23] Another path to serious reform is the attempt to resurrect
market coordination of the real socialist economy. With reference to
historical experience, János Kornai has argued that the seriousness of
reform projects of this sort is connected to their commitment to transform the economic system of real socialism into a market economy.
Kornai has noted three different attitudes toward market reform in
Hungary: (1) naive reformers who, like Oskar Lange,* believed the
market could be used as an instrument for central management of the
economy; (2) Galbraithian socialists who thought that past development had led to a convergence of contemporary capitalism, with its
intertwining of economic and political interests, with socialism; and (3)
radical reformers who advocated the establishment of the market economy largely through changes in ownership.[24] All this leads to the conclusion that crucial reform[25] can be achieved only by a real transition to
a market economy.

In this way the third period of socialism, the era of reforms and the
dynamic of civil society connected to it, was closely bound up with the
market. To the extent that the genesis of real socialism (its theoretical
idea) included the abolition of the market—that the revolution and the
heroic period aimed at destroying the market, and that during the era
of classic socialism the imagined reality did not allow for the existence
of the market (of course, a quasi-market existed), the period of reform

has meant the transition to a market economy. The history of the great transition currently taking place in the socialist countries is yet to be written. The course of events is different in each country, characterized by greater or lesser pressure from below, different external conditions, and different centralized decisions taken from on high. However, the general pattern of these transformations is the same—reforms ebb and flow near the boundary, which when crossed means not only realization of the market but also the liquidation of prerogative power. The thesis above that the state under a civil society tries to maximize its discretionary powers does not contradict the thesis that the dynamics of the market limit the scope of the state power. The West has escaped totalism because of the advantages of the expansion of the market over the expansion of the state, of the domination of the rationality of the market over the rationality of control.

What is the relationship of the market to real socialism? The market in a narrow sense (hard budget constraints) is incompatible with prerogative power on the level of the presupposed reality. However, the reality of socialism is devoid of economics and politics only in appearance (this is where I fundamentally differ with Jadwiga Staniszkis). However, its economics and politics are distorted; they are incomplete in comparison to the Western model. The process of desubstantialization, the dissolution of subjects, is a continuous process in a socialist economy. However, just because this process is continuous does not mean that it ever reaches the point where a socialist economy consists of one factory, where management becomes a purely technical issue, and where the only manager is the central planner. The national economy is based on a full division of labor and characterized by a certain dynamic (whether development or regression). It is certainly subject to Hayek's theory that knowledge of the economic conditions under which its elements operate must remain immanently dispersed despite the absence of a market in a strict sense. This fact alone bestows some subjectivity on economic entities (the elements), creating a certain basis for negotiating with the center, thus limiting the prerogatives of authority. It is true that state ownership results in a patrimonial attitude on the part of the center toward enterprises and in soft budget constraints. But the center, the state under real socialism, is most intensely immersed in the madness of redistribution, which de facto is the redistribution of shortage. Thus maintenance of the minimum cooperation necessary depends on the entrepreneurship of firms—they must, on the basis of the knowledge at their disposal, undertake actions that will enable them to continue producing and thus to keep production going in the national economy in general.

Kornai's definition of a market in a broad sense[26] is therefore not an empty semantic operation; it refers us to the horizontal regulation present in real socialism on a rudimentary level within the framework of dormant regulation.[27] Although one can speak about the market, as Hayek would like, only as regulation where differentiated subjects become aware of the best use of their resources through price signals, even on the level of vegetative regulation one may talk about an exosomatic pattern (that is, resulting from the interaction of independent elements).[28] In real socialism the absence of economic compulsion creates chronic shortages, an economy void of the rational function of demand, the indefiniteness of effective demand—the phenomena of runaway excess demand.[29] But due to the absence of price signals, the activity of enterprises is regulated horizontally (apart from orders from the center) to ensure the continuity of cooperation.

It is a distorted economy, parallel to a distorted civil society.[30] The distortion has two dimensions. On the one hand, it is completely part of the process of the reproduction of the system. It is a specific reflection of the distorted nature of the system and paradoxically complements the system. It ensures that the system will persist, that it reproduces itself (at least from an intermediate-term historical point of view). This phenomenon has already been described in many different ways: as "a dormant structure"; as the nontransformative character of revolts which due to the absence of the expression of real interests strengthen the authorities instead of weakening them, because they appeal to the authorities and request that they intervene; as shortages that strengthen the position of the center as the distributor of shortage; and finally, as the circumvention of spheres—the economic and political, and the natural and arbitrary—which resolves systemic conflicts.[31] This distorted process allows prerogative authority to implement its reality on the level of overdetermination, in accordance with a formula of action of an instrumental reason that outsmarts reality. On the other hand, we confront a self-enclosed totality caused by the illusory character of the universalization of this type of rationalization of control. The expansion of power limits power itself. It leads to its own desubstantialization through the disappearance of the sphere of generality (the market and law), indirectly creating social interactions of the extended order. The defense of a certain "biological" minimum—that is, the instinct of subjects (natural and legal persons, individuals, institutions) to preserve themselves—leads to the re-creation of a sphere of mediation outside the system on the level of everyday life. And let us also add holidays, because the Prague Spring or the birth of Solidarity had the character of a holiday that sprang from the grassroots, from outside the system. That sphere of mediation outside the system had a paradoxical character—it was divided into gray everyday life and holidays; into the economic entrepreneurship that created the black market, the redistribution of goods, and the shortage economy; and into moral protest that re-created general norms of behavior outside formal law in the ethical, religious, and cultural spheres.

Thus the presence of civil society under real socialism is deeply paradoxical. It is distorted and is evidence of the distortion of the system. Its dynamics cause the system to expand and contract. It manifests itself on the level of sublime spirit and down-to-earth materialism. The paradoxical presence of civil society also means that its surprising, somehow contradictory dynamics leads to substantial confusion among observers of the history of real socialism. On the level of the presupposed reality, there can be no alternative to prerogative authority, and to the degree that it constitutes reality, this lack of alternatives had to be manifested as reality (an obligatory outlook on things). But ontologically and to some extent geographically, the alternative was continuously present—civil society in the form of the rudimentary elements of the civilization of the countries under real socialism and the ever present influence of Western civilization. That is why change came as such a surprise and so "easily." It was enough, that the rationality of control caused the authorities to suspend their prerogatives and to try to save themselves through the "enfranchisement of the nomenklatura,"* for the events to turn into an avalanche. The destruction of the Berlin Wall was sufficient for the unchanging world of real socialism to suddenly find itself at its end, beginning with the end of the real socialist state in Germany.

The rapid changes currently taking place in the socialist bloc are, generally speaking, the effect of the proven advantage of the dynamics of civil society over the state. The rationality of the market may generalize the variety of human activity in a much more effective manner than the rationality of control. It achieves it by rejuvenating diversity rather than extinguishing it. Thus the present events constitute the re-

turn of the countries that experienced real socialism back to civilization. It is a situation where the formulation of a prognosis (the fourth
moment of civic society in real socialism) is both easy and extremely
difficult. It is easy because we are experiencing a movement forward
by a return,[32] a peculiar repetition of the history of civil society. It is
difficult because it is not clear how a distorted civil society can re-
create its fully developed structure. Until it became impacted in the
system of real socialism, its distorted character was its strength—its
existence was proven by almost every horizontal social interaction. At
the moment of the disintegration of prerogative authority this distortion becomes painful and extremely dangerous. In this form civil society is unable to coordinate social life.

Above all, this means the reconstruction of a market that actually
regulates the economy in an autonomous fashion, making the economic activities of subjects fully possible, where they make decisions
at their own risk, basing them on the calculation of the alternative
costs of using the resources they have at their disposal. This is obvious,
but the reality presents a number of difficulties.

First, market reality is not implemented from above. It is a process
that inherently escapes control from above. It grows par excellence
"from human actions, but not by the execution of human designs."
On this score the position of the neoliberals is exaggerated, but it certainly is not unjustified, because the process is subject to control, but
only to a limited degree.

Second, the market is not an earthly paradise—it has its good and
bad sides. The difficult situation in the socialist states now undergoing
reform has led to wishful thinking, to looking only at the advantages
of the market and not its problems. In realistic processes the trend may
be reversed. For example, the market is a sphere where the prisoner's
dilemma is present in a particularly clear fashion. The problem boils
down to the choice of two possible strategies of action under uncertain
conditions. Either the subject trusts other players and bets on cooperation, or chooses the attitude of a "free rider" in order to ensure short-
term but more certain benefits. The predominance of attitudes of the
first type creates a long-term foundation of mutual trust, business
ethics, and a powerful market where honesty and reliability bring mea-
surable benefits. Unfortunately, during the early stages of the restoration of the market economy the second type of attitude—speculation—
is likely to dominate.

Third, control of the process of restoration of a market economy is possible only in a developed civil society. The state, even if based cn completely democratic structures but suspended in a vacuum, is doomed to carry out empty redistribution, the sort of churning described by de Jasay. This may dangerously incapacitate the market. Control over the market is possible only through the institutionalization of structures for the articulation of interests. For example, Adam Przeworski describes how control over the market was established through social-democratic policies on the basis of Keynesian revolution. In countries such as Sweden, a long-term consensus has been reached, based on the limitation of consumption by employees in return for a constant level of investment by the employers.[33] The formation of such a consensus requires not only the presence of market mechanisms but also the presence of institutions that represent both parties. In Poland, the parties to the conflicts within civil society have not yet crystallized, and the institutionalization of a realistic structure of interests is practically absent.

Fourth, Poland, like other socialist countries, will once again have to establish its position in the world market. It is an especially difficult problem because a very unfavorable starting point—economic crisis in combination with external debt—leaves limited space for maneuver. The ability to steer the process of dependency is a crucial issue.[34]

Fifth, and most important, the anarchization of social life caused by the distorted character of civil society during the preliminary stages of transformation may result in a regression to a prerogative state, though perhaps in a different form. The only protection from this may be the rapid revival of a civil society that is capable of controlling the dynamics of the market.

Translated by Hanna Husak and the author

Notes

1. F. A. Hayek, *The Fatal Conceit. The Errors of Socialism*, (Chicago, 1988). The verse is from Shakespeare's *As You Like It*, and is quoted by Hayek (116). His arguments concerning the overuse of the words "society" and "social" is in chapter 7 ("Our Poisoned Language").

2. See J. Kornai, "Bureaucracy and Market: Introduction to the Political Economy of

Socialism," lecture notes to an economics course presented at Harvard University in fall 1986–87, lecture 2, "The Mechanism of Coordination," 30–31. Kornai proposes the following division of the historical implementation of socialism: (1) the heroic stage, (2) classical socialism, and (3) reform socialism.

3. I. Wallerstein writes on Braudel's "long sixteenth century" in *The Capitalist World Economy* (Cambridge and Paris, 1979), 37. It seems that Braudel himself treats the breakthrough as an even longer period, from 1400 to 1800, and believes that the full development of the division of labor took place on the turn of the eighteenth and nineteenth centuries. See F. Braudel, *Afterthoughts on Material Civilization and Capitalism* (Baltimore, 1979).

4. "Society becomes a lot of free equal individuals related to each other as proprietors of their own capacities and of what they have acquired by their exercise. Society consists of relations of exchange between proprietors." See C. B. Macpherson, *The Theory of Possessive Individualism* (London, 1970), 3.

5. See I. Berlin, *Four Essays on Liberty* (Oxford, 1969), lx.

6. "The sole end for which mankind are warranted, individually or collectively, in interfering with the liberty of action of any of their number is self-protection." J. S. Mill, *On Liberty* (Harmondsworth, 1979), 68.

7. The concept of "cosmos" is used by Hayek to describe a social order created in an unintentional manner as opposed to "taxis"—an order organized in a conscious manner. See F. A. Hayek, "The Confusion of Language in Political Thought," in *New Studies in Philosophy, Politics, Economics, and the History of Ideas* (London, 1978). The concept of extended order comes also from Hayek and denotes social cooperation that is not subordinated to one, preconceived aim (as in small groups). See Hayek, *Fatal Conceit*, 15–18. The concept of "external state" is Hegelian. See G.W.F. Hegel, *Philosophy of Right*, par. 183.

8. "Nations stumble upon establishments, which are indeed the result of human action, but not the execution of any human design." A. Ferguson, *An Essay on the History of Civil Society* (Edinburgh, 1966), 122.

9. A. Vincent even believes that the history of the state originated in the sixteenth century. See A. Vincent, *Theories of the State* (Oxford, 1987), 10. In Max Weber's conception the conditions that create the modern state are the following: (1) monopoly of the means of domination and administration based on (a) the creation of a centrally directed and permanent system of taxation and (b) the creation of a centrally directed and permanent military force in the hands of a central governmental authority; (2) monopolization of legal enactments and the legitimate use of force by the central authority; and (3) the organization of the rationally oriented officialdom, whose exercise of administrative functions is dependent upon central authority. Reinhard Bendix, *Max Weber. An Intellectual Portrait* (New York, 1963), 383.

10. This is an important feature of the modern world described by Immanuel Wallerstein as the capitalist world system, divided economically between peripheries dependent on a center. See Wallerstein, *Capitalist World Economy*, 4 and passim.

11. This is how Adam Smith defines police. See A. Smith, *Lectures on Jurisprudence*, ed. R. L. Meek, D. D. Raphael, and P. G. Stein (Oxford, 1978), 331. The police and corporations constitute the third element in Hegel's understanding of civil society. See Hegel, *Philosophy of Right*, par. 188.

12. See J. L. Cohen and A. Arato, "Społeczeństwo obywatelskie a teoria społeczna" (Civil society and social theory), in A. M. Kaniowski and A. Szahaj, eds., *Wokół teorii krytycznej Jürgena Habermasa* (On the Critical Theory of Jürgen Habermas) (Warsaw, 1988), 317 and passim.

13. See K. Marx, "Debates on the Law on Thefts of Wood," and "On the Jewish Question," in K. Marx, *The Early Texts*, ed. D. McLellan (Oxford, 1971).

14. See L. Kriwuszin and S. Owczarz, "Kategoria 'społeczeństwa obywatelskiego' i jej

przezwyciężenie w myśli Karola Marksa" (The concept of "Civil Society" and its overcoming in the thought of Karl Marx), *Człowiek i światopogląd* 12 (1985).

15. See F. A. Hayek, "The Mirage of Social Justice," in *Law, Legislation and Liberty* (London, 1979), 2:116 and passim.

16. Typically (and in agreement with the line of argument of this paper), Marx rejected *Recht* in the name of the emancipatory morality. See S. Lukes, *Marxism and Morality* (Oxford, 1985), 29.

17. See J. Staniszkis, *Ontologia socjalizmu* (The ontology of socialism) (Warsaw, 1989). I reflect on the arguments from the first chapter, "The Ontology of Socialism: An Initial Approach."

18. See P. Ogrodziński, "Dwanaście kroków w kierunku modelu społeczeństwa obywatelskiego zastanego socjalizmu" (Twelve steps toward a model of a civil society under given socialism), manuscript (1985), and P. Ogrodziński, "Reality at Utopia's Gate (An Attempt to Outline a Doubly Dual Model of Real Socialism)," Working Papers, no. 8 (1989), Institute of Philosophy and Sociology, Polish Academy of Sciences, Warsaw.

19. Thus my understanding of Hobbes is different from that of Staniszkis. See Staniszkis, *Ontologia socjalizmu*, 143 n. 33.

20. See K. J. Arrow, *Social Choice and Individual Values* (New York, 1963).

21. "A cascade of gains whose costs must be borne by the gainers themselves, ultimately breeds more frustration and more turbulence than consent." A. de Jasay, *The State* (Oxford, 1985), 232.

22. Ibid, 247. "Instead of saying, tautologically, that the rational state pursues its interests and maximizes its ends, whatever they are, I propose to adopt, as a criterion of its rationality, that it seeks to maximize its discretionary power. Discretionary power permits the state to make its subjects do what it wants, rather than what they want."

23. See Kornai, "Bureaucracy and Market," lecture 8, "The Yugoslav Reform," and lecture 10, "The Chinese Reform."

24. See J. Kornai, "The Hungarian Reform Process: Visions, Hopes, and Reality," *Journal of Economic Literature* 24 (December 1986): 1728 and passim.

25. The concept of "crucial reform" was introduced into discussions on real socialism by T. Kowalik. See T. Kowalik, *Reforma przełomowa realnego socjalizmu* (Crucial reform of real socialism) (Vienna, 1985).

26. "The concept of market is interpreted in two ways. In the broad sense it includes all processes of transaction based on the direct, horizontal relations between the supplier and the recipient of goods, even if price or money play a small or insignificant role in these processes. In the narrow sense it is limited to processes of exchange in which an important role is played by prices that react to supply and demand." J. Kornai, *Niedobór w gospodarce* (The economy of shortage) (Warsaw, 1985), 178 n. 1.

27. Ibid., 206. For a philosophical interpretation of J. Kornai's economy of shortage, see P. Ogrodziński, "Ontologia niedoboru. Filozoficzne implikacje teorii ekonomicznej Janosa Kornaia" (The ontology of shortage. A philosophical interpretation of Janos Kornai's economic theory), *Studia Filozoficzne* 4 (1990).

28. "Indeed, maintaining communication within the order requires that dispersed information be utilized by many individuals, unknown to one another, in a way that allows the different knowledge of millions to form an exosomatic or material pattern. Every individual becomes a link in many chains of transmission through which he receives signals enabling him to adapt his plans to circumstances he does not know. The overall order thus becomes infinitely expansible spontaneously supplying information about an increasing range of means without exclusively serving particular ends." Hayek, *Fatal Conceit*, 84.

29. "Everybody in the firm and in the bureaucracy wants to expand, and nobody fears

insolvency. Taken together these two facts provide a sufficient explanation for runaway excess demand." Kornai, "Bureaucracy and Market," lecture 15, "Shortage: Causes," 326.

30. In September 1986 I had suggested the term "deformed civil society." See Ogrodziński, "Reality at Utopia's Gate." A year later, at a conference in Ryn (September 1987), I presented a paper, "Distorted Civil Society under Real Socialism." In Polish, the most apt term ("ułomne społeczeństwo obywatelskie") was proposed by W. Wesołowski in "Czytając Narojka: wokół problematyki upaństwowionego społeczeństwa" (Reading Narojek: On the problems of etatized society), Krytyka, no. 26 (1987): 85.

31. See Staniszkis, Ontologia socjalizmu, 12, and Kornai, "Bureaucracy and Market," lecture 14, "Shortage: Symptoms and Consequences," 314; and Ogrodziński, "Reality at Utopia's Gate."

32. See L. Kołakowski, "Jak być konserwatywno-liberalnym socjalistą?" (How to be a conservative-liberal socialist?), in Czy diabeł może być zbawiony? (Can the devil be saved?) (London, 1982), 203.

33. See A. Przeworski, Capitalism and Social Democracy (Cambridge, 1985), 7 and passim.

34. H. Szlajfer discussed the need to steer dependency at a conference at Kazimierz Dolny in January 1987.

16

Toward a Market Economy—
Two Positions

Krytyka, no. 31 (1989)

The Minimal Political and Economic Changes Necessary for the Transition to a Market Economy
Jan Winiecki

1. No matter how radical the rhetoric, all change will be illusory if it affects only the economy. Under the present system, politics and economics are symbiotic. No real economic change is possible while

—the *nomenklatura** system, which uses criteria of loyalty (and in fact obedience) in making appointments, gives the communist party the exclusive right to fill positions in the economy;

—the priority given to obedience makes efficiency, profitability, and other economic criteria unimportant because the managerial cadre is rewarded on the basis of obedience. This is what creates "soft" budget constraints, when party apparatchiks pressure economic bureaucrats to open the sluice gate of subsidies and loans to enterprises. Both those who provide and receive subsidies and loans depend on those who have the final say on who holds what position;

—the system is structured so that the ruling elite, in particular, apparatchiks and bureaucrats, parasitically live off the economy (owing to the *nomenklatura*, they have easy access to goods and services in great demand). The elite defend this wasteful system, not because of its alleged ideological merits but simply because they profit from its arrangements.

This is why the first necessary reform measure should be to cut the totalitarian umbilical cord connecting the political and economic systems. This should be done by *abolishing the nomenklatura* in all enterprises and economic institutions.

2. Logic tells us that, together with the abolition of the *nomenklatura*, we must regulate *property relations* in the "post-nationalized" sector [the sector of the economy formerly under the direct administration of the state bureaucracy].

2.1. Taking into consideration the adverse effect on the efficiency of the whole economy of the largeness of this sector relative to other sectors, reform measures should aim to

—transform forms of property in this sector (for example, public utilities should become municipal property, and worker self-managed property could become joint-stock companies);

—reduce the size of the "postnationalized" sector at the beginning of the process (for example, through bankruptcy, the auctioning of assets, the sale of enterprises, and so on).

2.2. In normal economies, not only do various forms of ownership enjoy equal legal status, but owners also have the ability to change the type of ownership of a particular enterprise. Therefore, among the many proposals put forward we should accept only those that guarantee the possibility of changing forms of property. Only under such conditions will financial markets be able to play their role in resource allocation, directing them to the most profitable enterprises.

3. The creation of independent enterprises under authentic owners requires *the liquidation of the Stalinist institutions of the centralized economy*. These include:

—institutions of hierarchical control: the Planning Commission; industrial ministries; associations; monopolistic pseudo-companies such as Megat [electrical power engineering], Elpol [electronics], and so on; and pseudo-unions of cooperatives and small businesses (whether organized on an industrial or territorial basis) and

—institutions with monopolistic powers: not only the abolition of the central supply, procurement, and sales institutions, but also abandonment of the very principle of a state monopoly in the distribution system.

4. The adequate performance of authentic enterprises in a market economy requires *a rapid "opening" of the semi-autarkic economy*. Because the

Polish economy is not large in scale but has a highly monopolistic industrial structure [certain firms have monopolies or near monopolies on the production of certain goods in the national market], certain enterprises have the ability to use their market position to earn profits not justified by their efficiency. This leads to waste. In the initial period (during the first three months), the złoty should be made convertible within the country.

5. Because different economic options are not yet under consideration by parliament, it is necessary for organized political forces, who are not identified with the postwar system of rule, *to make the process of change politically credible*. By this I mean that

—Solidarity should be relegalized, and people should gain freedom of association. In this way institutionalized pressure on the system's evolution toward the market and democracy will become possible;

—a Council for National Economy should be established. During the transition (until the parliament assumes an authentic role in the economy), this council should monitor government activity in the spheres of economic reform and policy. The council must have *real* influence on economic reform, or at least have the right to postpone for a fixed period the legislation of the Sejm and the decisions of the government.

In this way we can improve the results and lower the costs of the new economic system. Faith in *the permanence* of the process of change will lead some people to take new initiatives, and it will dissuade others from activities oriented toward short-term profit—which are, on balance, harmful (such actions were commonplace under the old financial system, which lacked accountability).

6. We must also be aware of the costs of a democratic-collectivist orientation. The impoverished countries of Eastern Europe, worn out by the effects of forty years of a totalitarian-collectivist orientation, are simply unable to bear the heavy cost of the lower productivity involved in a democratic-collectivist orientation. Only rich Western European countries—and they too for a limited time only—were able to afford it, because they had something to give up, both with respect to their material wealth and with respect to their work ethic.

I Favor a "Social-Democratic" Option
Ryszard Bugaj

I believe that a plurality of forms of ownership—the market, workers' self-management, and political democracy—should be the principal objectives of reform. To be sure, political democracy does not have to be justified in terms of economic need, but I find this need to be irrefutable. I believe that these general objectives are universal; that they must constitute the main line of transformation of every communist economy.

In 1981, Poles (certain factions of the establishment included) were close to a consensus regarding a reform program, but the demand for the plurality of forms of ownership had not yet been expressed. Then "somewhere at the height of the second stage" [of reform], we came close to national consensus again, this time including a plurality of forms of ownership. Now, once again, we are moving farther away from consensus. A rival concept is currently being propounded, that of universal privatization (ruling out workers' self-management). Some advocates of this new concept are ready to drop the demand for political democracy, finding it inconsequential or even a threat to the economy.

We can thus see that the program I once recognized as universal is no longer as banal as it seemed. Now we have two options: we can call one of them Social Democratic, and the other Liberal. It is worth noting here that the line dividing the partisans of these two options does not correspond to fundamental political cleavages. Partisans of both these options can be found in the opposition as well as among the supporters of the authorities, although the latter do not express their "Liberal" views directly.

In both cases, the choice is not purely professional in nature. Social values play a great role in individual positions—the acceptance or rejection of considerable differentiation in standards of living, attitudes toward social welfare, economic coercion of individuals, and so on.

Social values are expressed, first and foremost, on two basic issues: in the choice between a plurality of forms of ownership and universal privatization, and in one's stand toward self-management. Economic theory does not provide any universal answer to these choices. It is deceitful to quote any authoritative opinion as a law of economics. It is true that all rich countries are capitalist. Yet it is also true that only a small proportion of the capitalist countries are rich. On the other hand, there is no reason to identify the communist economy (characterized by universal nationalization, the replacement of the market by a command-and-quota system, and totalitarian or authoritarian state institutions) with a nonprivate economy in general. There is an absence of empirical evidence on whether an economy that is largely nonprivate but subjected to market mechanisms and ruled by the democratic system will be as effective as the capitalist and market economies. However, there is no reason to dismiss such a hope as groundless. Similarly, one can sensibly challenge the hope that a private economy in Poland would turn out to be more or less as effective as those in Western Europe.

Therefore, opting for privatization seems to be unambiguously ideological. With respect to a plurality of forms of ownership, things look quite different. This option seems to be [ideologically] indifferent. It does not rule out universal privatization, but it does not provide for it either. The essence of the demand for a plurality of forms of ownership boils down to ensuring truly equal conditions for the growth of all sectors of the economy.

Nevertheless, professional analyses (although in economics, these do not prove anything in an irrefutable manner) can be useful when trying to answer questions about the possibility of universal privatization carried out in a relatively short period of time (within several years). It can be convincingly argued that there is no practical way to carry out such universal change either through distribution of property or through the sale of nationalized assets to citizens, even if all political obstacles were removed. This is why among the champions of the plurality of forms of ownership one can find so many people who otherwise believe that only a private economy can provide for high levels of productivity. Positions toward workers' self-management are also ideologically conditioned. The theoretical literature on this subject does not offer any decisive conclusions, and the relevant Yugoslav experience is highly controversial.

To be sure, the resolution of conflict between private ownership and hired labor is the great hope of the advocates of workers' self-management; on the other hand, however, there is no doubt that self-managed firms cannot have all the same property rights a private owner usually has. This creates doubts about whether all the institutions that comprise a market economy can function under worker self-management. Many economists are afraid they cannot.

Yet the choice of the self-management option is not an autonomous one. If we assume that there would be a predominance of nonprivate enterprises in the economy, then there is no other sensible alternative. In this situation, only an enterprise managed by its workers can offer some hope that it will be independent and that its staff will be interested in its performance.

There is no controversy over whether to move toward a market economy. On this question there is so much indisputable experience as well as conclusive theoretical work (disregarding the remnants of the communist apologetics) that we can agree that ideological orientation does not have decisive meaning here. However, arguments about the potential effects of a "partial" market mechanism remain in dispute. Here I must address the question of the development of a capital market. To establish one in an economy where nonprivate enterprises predominate may well be difficult or even impossible. Some people, myself included, believe nevertheless that this will not necessarily translate into poorer economic performance, provided that certain elements of the decentralized planning can effectively substitute for market institutions. At present, there is no way to settle this difference of opinion.

With regard to the demand for political democracy as the essential element affecting the implementation of reform and of the effectiveness of the reformed economy, I have only two observations. First, the distress that the transition to a market economy will cause the public, and also the lack of people interested in this transition among the supporters of the communist party, means that the transformation can be implemented only under the pressure from the forces outside the system, who must secure the support of a considerable part of the public for their program. This is unimaginable without reliance, even if only to a limited extent, on democratic mechanisms of decision making. Second, both historical as well as analytical arguments support the proposition that with market economies the selection of an economic policy and the resolution of conflicting interests is easier and more effective if accomplished within a democratic political system.

I do not know whether, say in fifty years, the Polish economy will be private. I am convinced, though, that it will not be fully privatized within the next twenty years. At the moment we face the question of what should be done in order to improve the effectiveness of the non-private economy. This is a question that all communist countries now face. It is my contention that a "Social Democratic" option provides a universal program for extricating ourselves from the communist economy. This does not preclude a comprehensive transformation of forms of ownership in the long term, but rather makes them possible.

Section V

History

17

In Every Situation I Look for a Way Out

Krytyka, no. 25 (1987)

Janka Jankowska Interviews Jacek Kuroń

JANKA JANKOWSKA: What is your impression of Jerzy Holzer's* book?
JACEK KUROŃ: I was very positively surprised. I was afraid he would repeat the legends our union press had created, but there was nothing of the sort. As far as I can tell, Holzer stayed amazingly true to the facts, making for an excellent book. It is an achievement that he has been able to write it. I admire him greatly. How did he compile so much source material? He must have done so earlier, otherwise he could not have written the book. What he presents is astounding. In the introduction, he writes about his book's failings. It is not a history of the movement. In writing the history of Solidarity's leadership, he was unable—and this is understandable—to undertake the mammoth task of interviewing a whole multitude of people and to verify and present how all sorts of decisions were made. Solidarity deserves its history as a movement, but I do not think it is possible to do this on the first try. However, it should be attempted.

JJ: Holzer has been accused of adopting the vision presented in the official press—that Solidarity was divided between moderates and radicals—doves and hawks.
JK: But there was such a division.

JJ: But the same people, depending on the situation, could be classified as belonging to both groups.
JK: Sometimes this was the case. Yet there were people who never changed. The superexpert Siła-Nowicki* always maintained that the

authorities were good and that we should come to terms with them, whereas Patryk Kosmowski* always claimed that we should kick them while we could. You could be sure that that was what each of them would say. Also, you can expect that both Modzelewski* and I will always be more or less close to the center. Sometimes he is there and I am here, and on another occasion he is here and I am there. We change places, sometimes more radical and less conciliatory, on others less radical and more conciliatory. This is a constant with us.

Returning to Holzer's book, one might object that he did not try to divide the Solidarity period into stages. This is connected to the division between radicals and moderates, but this was not the only division. In the union there were not alliances or factions in the conventional sense. For example, during the Solidarity Congress the participants divided themselves into fundamentalists and pragmatists. If you accept only one division, it makes the history of Solidarity look like a long, homogeneous course of struggle for compromise with the authorities. However, it was not so. There were a number of stages. From the perspective of the union's attitude toward the authorities, one can identify a rather long initial period when Solidarity wanted the government to govern and the union to control and defend the interests of the working people. In that period, Solidarity frequently appealed to the authorities to implement the August agreements, particularly the parts that pertained to society's subjectivity, to self-government, and to economic reform (namely, first and foremost to the reconstruction of the country's economy).

JJ: The authorities resisted those demands, arguing that the union was avoiding responsibility. The authorities complained to the union, "You only know how to make demands."

JK: Of course the union was making demands. It did not want to take the authorities' job. It wanted to do what the August agreements, and thus the authorities themselves, authorized it to do. The problem was that at the time the authorities were doing absolutely nothing to reform the economy, to build a new system. Some people said that the authorities were acting this way to be difficult, whereas others maintained that the collapse of the system was paralyzing the authorities. I usually agreed with the latter. I was convinced that the authorities were simply unable to do anything, but it later turned out that they were doing harm as well, which, I must admit, I did not expect of them. From month to month, the situation got worse. At a certain point we ran into a brick wall, when demands no longer made any sense. I spoke about this during a meeting of the National Commission. Holzer did not notice that during the meeting Andrzej Celiński* and I made the opening addresses. I mention it because for me it was a turning point. That meeting ushered in a new period in Solidarity's history.

JJ: Do you mean the National Commission meeting of July 1981, when the union finally put the problem of self-management on its agenda?

JK: Yes. At that time I said that whether the authorities were acting deliberately or not, the effect was the same. They were not implementing the most crucial part of the August agreements—the creation of a new system of government. The old system of control had collapsed, and it was necessary to build a new one. Solidarity was incapable of doing that because it would have turned into a party even worse than the existing one and, besides, the union's main role was to defend workers' interests. What should have been done then? There was nothing else but to establish a broad self-management movement, which meant that society had to begin to restructure the system on its own. Self-management was to save Solidarity from the task of building a new system, because the union had other tasks to do. This should have been the task of the self-management movement, which, however, the union had to initiate. This was a necessary step and could not be avoided. This is when the division between radicals and moderates began to change. The ultraradicals were demanding, "Let them give everyone two kilograms of meat; let them increase wages," to which the moderates were replying, "That can't be done; we must change the regime." In this way moderation became political radicalism. Holzer does not mention this in his book.

JJ: Let's discuss his chapter titled "Origins." Were you mentioned outside the union?

JK: No, I was not. Holzer does not notice—it is his privilege, I am not complaining—my essay from 1976, *Myśli o programie działania* [Reflections on a program of action], which in some ways foresaw the program for the construction of such a union, such a movement.

JJ: In August and September 1980 you opposed the establishment of one national union.

JK: I opposed it until the end of the negotiations. From time to time Adam Michnik reminds me, "How lucky it was that they locked you up, otherwise Solidarity would never have been founded!" Needless to say, this is only a joke—its founding was a necessity. At the time, I was not in the Lenin Shipyard in Gdańsk but in Warsaw, and therefore did not grasp certain things. I kept telling Gwiazda,* "Remember, the demand for free trade unions is our initial bargaining position." At the time, I thought that the Central Council of Trade Unions* [CRZZ] should not be replaced by new unions, because that would have involved the creation of an extensive bureaucratic apparatus, which unless it collapsed on its own accord would turn into a monster that would gobble everything up.

At this point I want to express a reservation. It is hard for me today to say to what extent what I say now is what I thought at that time, and to what extent I arrived at those conclusions some time later. One thing is indisputable—my conviction, which I expressed in *Myśli o programie działania*, that the system could be changed and transformed only by a multitude of social movements, from both the inside and the outside—from the outside by establishing institutions like KOR [the Workers' Defense Committee*], TKN [the Society for Academic Courses*], and SKS [the Student Solidarity Committees*], and so on; and from the inside by being active in various kinds of associations and institutions that were not yet compromised. Together, this could outwit the old system, transforming it piece by piece. I also wrote this at the very beginning of Solidarity's existence, in September 1980, in my article "Co dalej?" [What next?]. I was afraid when I wrote that article. I think I had the same fears earlier, when the negotiations on the foundation of the union were in progress. When Solidarity was created, I recognized that a state within a state had emerged. It was a vast organization, a powerful movement, and it was clear that no one would now try to form other organizations, but that everyone would try to pursue their agendas through Solidarity. In this way we would make the state our enemy. From that moment, everything that was to happen later was already obvious. Such a new "state" was bound to paralyze the old one. And those two states did paralyze each other. They did not allow us to do anything positive; they were strong enough to see to

that. And we, for our part, did not allow them to do anything positive—we were strong enough to do that.

JJ: Let me also remind you that you yourself are partially to blame
for the social explosion of the summer of 1980. KOR activists struggled mightily to transform the scattered work stoppages in July into
a wave of strikes. Your apartment became the information center,
and at that time information was dynamite.

JK: I was not the only one to work there. My apartment became one
huge office. People from all over Poland called to tell us what was
going on in their workplaces. We regularly passed the information
on. *Robotnik*★ [The worker] came out more frequently, and it
printed a chronology of the strikes. We tried to send the paper to all
centers of strike activity. To begin with, every day the radio broadcast [Radio Free Europe] the names of the plants on strike and the
strikers' demands. Last but not least, in certain plants, there were
people connected with KOR. In terms of demands, the Ursus [trac-
tor factory] was first to issue a slogan about the necessity of establishing workers' commissions. There was a locomotive roundhouse in
Lublin that fought to transform its workers' council. Later, they suc-
ceeded in electing a new council. Then there were the demands of the
Gdańsk shipyard. We published all those demands and circulated them
nationwide. In subsequent strikes, workers made the same demands.

It was obvious to me at the time that the organization, whose
emergence I had anticipated in my *Le Monde* article, would elect
workers' delegates to informal bodies—namely, workers' commissions. Initially, I thought that if we won over the workers' commissions in the majority of plants, that would be a major success for the
strikers.

JJ: Yet what happened in the shipyard went even further—

JK: Wait a minute, wait a minute. Before all that emerged out of the
shipyard, I had dreamed up a gathering of all workers' commissions
from all over Poland. I remember very well that on the same day the
Interfactory Strike Committee★ [MKS] was established, *Robotnik*'s
editors held a meeting, during which I proposed a slogan on organizing a congress of workers' commissions, to which they jokingly
responded that this would be another Congress of Soviets. However, on the next day we got the news that Gdańsk had managed to

organize a commission of strike committees on a regional scale. And I had dreamed that what we would ultimately achieve were workers' commissions that the authorities could tolerate. What would such workers' commissions do? They would control trade unions, the official ones, and would also represent the workers in negotiations with management and even with the industrial ministries, because these unions would be organized from the ground up even though they would not have secretaries, offices, and so on. Do you understand?

JJ: Not quite.

JK: They were to deal only with welfare problems—how much people are paid, how much things cost, how high prices could be increased, and with working conditions. That's all. They were in no condition to do more than this. Needless to say, in certain situations, they could stand up for arrested activists. The appointment of such commissions would open the floodgates because all of a sudden people everywhere would begin to organize themselves. And then we would be able to start a movement, something about which I dreamed and on which I had elaborated in "Co dalej?"—a movement for economic reform. What does this mean? Various guys—managers, the socially concerned, people of syndicalist views, concerned workers—all of them together would start a movement for economic reform. This movement could have its technocratic and syndicalist wings, which might fight with each other but which at the same time would all have the same hard nut to crack: workers' commissions opposed to the lowering of wages! This is what I call a healthy and sensible struggle between equal partners, with the shape of economic reform as the main object of their struggle.

A large number of such movements could take root. If this had been the case, the authorities would have felt less threatened. The number of objectives and axes of struggle would have made the process much more time-consuming. The process of arriving at solutions would have been slower and thus more effective, which would have made it easier for the bolder and more reasonable people in the party apparatus to agree. What actually brought Solidarity to disaster? The absence of sufficiently strong forces for reform in the party. A strong movement for reform within the party was Solidarity's only chance. This did not occur because we did not give them enough time. Everything became one assault on "the reds," so that not only the hard-liners but even the majority of party members, who were maybe even open to reform, closed ranks in the face of such pressure. When I gained the reputation of being a "red," every member of the *apparat* probably thought, "I'm already hanged!" Why did it happen this way? Because in no time there came into being a vast, powerful organization that no one could possibly withstand and that at the same time could not demand a higher standard of living. The plummeting standard caused people to run amok. Had all this been spread out over two or three years, the people would have acquired a greater maturity and the possibility of finding forces of reason within the party would have been much greater.

All this is hypothetical reasoning—"What would have happened if . . . ?"—but I dwell on it because it seems to me that it explains the logic of later events. After all, what happened was inevitable. I'll even say that it was good that it happened this way because it contributed to a great social revolution in Poland, whose highest achievement was the creation of social elites among the masses. If we are, however, to explain the course of events and to answer the question about our mistakes, then I regret to say that we made a great many mistakes. But none of those mistakes taken separately nor all of them taken together, brought about 13 December 1981 [the day martial law was declared]. One thing did that—we established the Independent Self-governing Trade Union "Solidarity," but that was no mistake.

JJ: What you say seems to imply that it was. After all, you wanted informal workers' commissions, not one big huge trade union—isn't that so?

JK: No, not exactly. I admit that this construct is a bit strained. But when it first occurred to me, it was realistic. What is more, everything seemed to be going in that direction—

JJ: —apart from the fact that it went in quite another direction—

JK: No, not quite in another. After all, the union proved to represent a multitude of different movements. In this sense, everything I had ever dreamed of came true more than once. Much, much more was accomplished. But it seems that in our geopolitical circumstances "much, much more" meant "too much." I am very sorry to say this, but if in September 1976 I wrote *Myśli o programie działania*, where no matter which way you look at it I anticipated the emergence of exactly such a social movement, then I can think of Solidarity as my brainchild too.

JJ: All right, you had already begun to think about reforming the republic in 1953, and since then it has gone through various stages. You represent one of the most effective movements of the Polish postwar intelligentsia, KOR. However, you yourself are a strong personality. It seems that both these factors affected the shape of the union. How? This exactly is the topic of our conversation. Where you came from (in the deepest sense of its meaning) and how you developed are not inconsequential. I remember you in the dock in June 1985. That was the last time you were put on trial, on a charge of organizing the May Day demonstration. You said then that the atmosphere of May 1985 reminded you of the prewar demonstrations you watched as a child on your father's shoulders. . . .

JK: If you are interested in my family, my grandfather Franek, who was really the one who raised me, was a member of the Polish Socialist Party's* [PPS] Fighting Squads. His brother Władek was deported to Siberia, and Staszek was hanged. Staszek's pseudonym was "Julek," and I was brought up in the cult of "Julek" and of the 1905 revolution. Dad used to take me on his back, march around the table, sing workers' songs, or recite poems. I remember *Reduta Ordona* [Ordon's redoubt]* until this day. He used to sing *The Internationale* in German, Russian, and French. If you asked me then what I would become, I would have answered, "A revolutionary." I was fifteen and began to smoke. My father told me, "You know what? It isn't good to smoke." "Why?" I asked. "When you go to jail, they will take your cigarettes away, and then you will be lost." It was said as if it was only natural to end up in jail. As a result, years later when I did indeed land in jail it was no shock to me. I observed a number of people who had committed economic fraud. Their whole world had collapsed. For me, a normal thing had happened. People treat handcuffs as a stigma. When they handcuffed me for the first time in 1965, I was moved. Until this day I offer my hands for handcuffs with a sense of satisfaction and say, "This is the only jewelry I wear." A handcuffed man is really something. I sort of worship handcuffs.

My father, or maybe it was my grandfather, told me about a friend who went to visit her son in the "Tenth Pavilion"* and took her grandson with her. The child was scared and began to cry. She told her grandson, "This is the Tenth Pavilion. Your grandpa was kept here. Your dad is kept here, and so will you be." When Gajka [Kuroń's wife] brought Macius [Kuroń's son] to me in Wronki,* I told him that story.

The one thing I feared was pain. During the occupation my father used to tell me, "The less you know, the better it is. When they torture you, you will talk. What good will that do you?" But I wanted to know everything. I thought up various tortures to see how it was to be subjected to them, and each time I was scared. That became my obsession. That lasted until 1967, when I got an attack of acute nephritis in jail. The doctor told me that was the most severe pain known to modern medicine. I lay there in jail with all that pain and thought about whether I would compromise myself. No. I was so proud of myself that I heaved a sigh of relief. Only later did I realize that the most acute pain known to medicine is not as acute as the pain that people can inflict. Therefore, I still do not know how it would be if I were tortured, but I have already inured myself a bit. I once visited Aniela Steinsbergowa* in a hospital. Her leg had been amputated and she was feeling dreadful phantom pain in the leg. She said to me, "Do you know what I think, Jacek? I think that if this was torture I would give away all the underground's secrets. It hurts me so much. It is all I think about." She was ninety. Our attitude toward pain was the same. I think pain is a very significant part of our national history.

JJ: Why did you join the Union of Polish Youth* [ZMP]?
JK: I joined the ZMP and became a communist because there is a day when a person inevitably rebels. I did that quite early.

JJ: You rebelled against your own father, against "Julek" and the PPS legend?
JK: I made it more consistent. I did know that I was embarking on an incredibly inconsistent and intricate life history. Where did my rebellion come from? Ideology is only one element in the climate of any great social movement in which one participates. There is something I would call spirituality. The word that most closely approxi-

mates this is "ethos," though ethos also embraces customs as well. My grandfather was a revolutionary, and my grandmother was a church patriot. They were intertwined in this combination. Their children took a bit from one and a bit from the other, but the spiritual dimension was always inconsistent. Life lays layer upon layer; this is a work of generations. In other words, this is the spiritual culture of the nation, and since it is born out of great movements of the Left and the Right it has various shades and points of contact. Let me present an example. People who have a leftist spirituality are much more tolerant of adultery. On the other hand, the family as an institution plays a prominent part in the values of the Right. With leftists, love seems to be more important. I discovered inconsistencies in the spirituality of my home. To me it was somehow inconsistent that in 1920 my father, being only fifteen, went to the front as a volunteer.

JJ: Why?
JK: In Russia, a proletarian revolution was taking place. Both my father and grandpa believed this.

JJ: In Poland, after 120 years of partition, the borders of the new independent state were being decided.
JK: Because of such patriotic feeling I perceived them as inconsistent. Remember, the PPS was a revolutionary party. I was brought up in a cult of revolution. In 1949 my generation received an attractive offer—a vision of a revolution in Poland that would settle all our nagging problems once and for all. This appealed to the imagination of a fifteen-year-old. This is what the communists were proposing, and it was simple and extremely attractive. I admit that it fascinated me. This is a very general answer about how I moved toward communism. Right after I graduated from high school, I began to work for the apparatus of the Warsaw ZMP and became a full-time employee.

JJ: In 1953 they expelled you from the party for the first time. Why?
JK: Because of my stupidity. It was out of stupidity that I joined the party, and out of stupidity that I was ousted. The Propaganda Department, which I headed at the age of nineteen, was commissioned to undertake an analysis of the work of ZMP circles. This analysis

was a disaster because the organization was dying out. And I wrote that. What is more, the chairman of the ZMP Executive, Jurek Wolczyk, bought it; the presidium ratified it; and thus our analysis of the questionnaires became the official opinion of the presidium, and Wolczyk took it to the relevant politburo meeting. He came back with instructions for me that I should immediately make a new analysis. That was it for me. I refused. Remember that at the time I was constantly quarreling with my father. It was a permanent row. My father sneered at my being a dignitary. I had rejected his point of view, but what he said somehow sank in my mind. Maybe that was why I stubbornly refused to change the results of the questionnaire. They suspended me and began the process of expelling me. It was difficult to fire me for seeing things negatively because the presidium had originally unanimously endorsed my opinion. However, it turned out that I had recommended people with improper social backgrounds for the *apparat* three times, and they found something else against me as well. As usual with dignitaries, when I got a knock on the head I began to think. I called the rector of the Pedagogical College, Kaluski, who always was at the party's disposal, and told him, "Comrade Rector, I feel like studying with you." He replied, "Oh, please do. Stop in one day to arrange the formalities." I answered, "I'll be there right away." That was how I began studying history at the Pedagogical College. Why didn't they expel me when I lost my job as head of the Propaganda Department, or my party membership? I think I owe it to Wolczyk, who having been, so to say, the architect of my brilliant ZMP career somehow felt responsible for me.

JJ: As a nineteen-year-old you had your first experience with power and also the first taste of defeat. That must have made you think.

JK: Yes, I began to analyze everything I had experienced. My experience, contacts with factories, with ZMP circles, and my attendance at organization meetings led me to the conclusion that people were not taking advantage of the opportunities they had to govern. At that time I did not yet know that, if they had tried, everything would have been done to prevent them from doing anything. I saw people's reluctance to accept any post. When it came to electing the chair of a ZMP circle, one man ran away, another did not attend the meeting, another did not listen, someone proposed something, and everybody voted unanimously. It was possible to disagree and to propose one's own candidate—from that point of view, formal democracy in the ZMP was all right. I came to the conclusion, then, that people had to be brought up to govern, and from that moment the long attempt to create a socialist pedagogy began. I tried to create a scouting movement that was fully self-governing and that would educate people to be socially active. These were the "Walter scouts."* That was my first attempt to reform the system. There is no getting away from the fact that five members of KOR had been Walter scouts.

JJ: How did you envision changing the world through the scouting movement?

JK: By introducing children to the world with all its conflicts. By bringing them up in the struggle to change this world. This is the way to build a social movement. In order to have any effect, a movement must be big—it must include children, youth, and adults. Communists reason in a similar way. The party's political line is extended to youth and children's organizations. With us, it was the other way around. The program for changing the world prepared in the scout movement was meant to attract youth organizations and then adults. Today I think the same way, with one reservation—the program should on no account be political, and by this I mean subordinated to the policy of this or any other ruling group. But without regard to my worldview, if under the totalitarian system I want to change the social order my activities will always be seen as political.

JJ: How did you meet Karol Modzelewski?

JK: That was in 1955. I remember it very well. At a ZMP department conference at the university, I began to launch an assault on the ZMP system. I did this from the position of a faithful reader of *Po prostu** [Simply speaking]. That was when ZMP department organizations were meeting to prepare for a national conference of student activists. Karol took the floor too, and as a result the two of us were elected delegates. After the stormy department meeting, we left and walked the streets together, talking for a long time. He was a young kid at the time. He had gone to the university straight from school. I was his elder, not only because of my age but also because of my experience as an *apparatchik,* an educator, and a man who had al-ready earned a living. The delegates selected an editorial commission to prepare the position the university would present to the Warsaw conference. Krzyś Pomian* and I were among the commission members. Other people, including Teresa Monasterska and, later, Jędrek Garlicki, my best friend since childhood, began attending the commission meetings. Karol joined in too. Quite soon, during a discussion on what the student organization should be like, we be-gan to discuss the broader idea of the renewal of the entire youth movement. We drew up a program—we would establish contacts with factories in order to establish a worker-student alliance; we planned to create a joint newspaper and a workers' university and to organize rallies. It was, in a word, a maximalist conception of the developing struggle for power in the country. We were not seeking power for ourselves, but for a certain line that from today's perspective I would call "socialism with a human face." First, we planned to take over the university ZMP and to present our program to the entire country. Workers' councils were most important to us. That was when I rejoined the party.

JJ: When did you realize that the authorities were abandoning the re-form line they adopted in October 1956?

JK: This is an extremely complex question. What was society's view of October 1956? It was an unwritten pact between society and Gomułka,* recognizing that there were limits to independence after the Hungarian experience. We believed that he would carry out poli-cies to preserve Poland's distinctness to the best of his ability. "You give us—society—a certain leeway, and we will give you our sup-port." That agreement opened the road to people of traditional, broadly understood, rightist standards—to various public-minded men, to Catholics, and to Home Army* veterans. For us—the radi-cal left—it cooked our goose. The public, who valued that "leeway" in their everyday life, in the more relaxed atmosphere, in publishing policy, in new films, and so on, sided with the authorities. We were quickly cut down to size. "Enough of these discussions, get to work." But we wanted to redeem the world, to purify socialism, to replace bureaucratic socialism with a new, humane, true workers' socialism. We lost because we became completely alien to society, we became useless to the people, not because the authorities did a number on us. "I'm going to play bridge," my friend Pomian said. I returned to scouting. And there I became silly—busy with scouting. I ignored the outside world and did not notice the abandonment of the ideas of October. As I said, I understood the scout movement as a way to reform the system. In the scout movement, we were fighting a struggle on two fronts: against scouts who, according to us, were socially and educationally of the Right—

JJ: Many people later, particularly during the Solidarity period, reproached you for how you acted at that time.

JK: I am criticized for it all the time. It's funny that every time it is the party, almost never the scouts themselves, who reproach me for it. Our other front was the struggle against the bureaucratization of socialism. We tried to create a large organization to change the world for the better, which meant that our organization was "counterrevolutionary" and that we were bound to fail. We were bound to fail not only because the authorities were prepared for us but also because the majority of instructors were loyal to the regime. At the same time, I was such a fool, an idiot, for not seeing that by fighting other scouts I was digging my own grave, because what I was doing was possible only when there was a certain measure of pluralism. Once this was suppressed, I was not able to act. However, at that time, the understanding of such mechanisms was beyond me.

JJ: The dissolution of the Walter scout group was already after the end of the spirit of October. What about Karol?

JK: When I was stirring up the scout movement, Karol got a research grant to study in Italy. He returned full of enthusiasm, calling for us to do something. He went around, only to hear from everyone, "Are you out of your mind?" He came to me. I was also full of enthusiasm. Together we came up with an idea of creating a debating club affiliated with the university Union of Socialist Youth★ [ZMS].

JJ: How did that go?

JK: Despite the abandonment of October, in 1962 it was still possible, at a party meeting at the university, to hear Kliszko★ say, when asked about the greatest danger to the party, "The greatest threat to the party is lethargy." Adam Schaff★ told Adam Michnik, who at that time was setting up his "Club of the Seekers of Contradictions,"★ that "a Marxist thought, even if revisionist, is worth its price in gold." A party that thinks lethargy is the worst thing that can happen to it? Even revisionists seemed to be welcome. Do you understand? The party was lapsing into narcolepsy. The leadership felt safe. The people still loved Gomułka. The post–October stabiliz-ation had worked, and the standard of living was rising. Who threat-ened them? Totalitarianism had lost its teeth. The period of *Sturm und Drang* was coming to an end. However, the authorities kept dreaming that a part of the masses would support them out of ideo-logical conviction. Therefore, when Karol proposed setting up a de-bating club, the party and the ZMS said, "By all means, you may open such a club." They looked at him in surprise, because at that time, people did not say anything at party meetings. The club got under way. We selected a topic for discussion. Our Walter scouts, who at that time were already students, told their fellow students that something was going to happen. People came and strongly at-tacked the existing situation. Our debaters made feathers fly. A crowd of people came to our next meeting. And all of a sudden there was a thaw at the university. We again tried to implement our old plans of winning over the university ZMS organization. We suc-ceeded very quickly, and everybody spoke of us very favorably.

JJ: The political leadership too?

JK: When they finally saw us as an enemy, they acted with utmost incompetence. We met with Załuski★ and just smashed him in the discussion. He was the standard-bearer of the Moczar★ group. Then the leadership decided that our club was a hotbed of the Puławy★ group and launched an assault on us. The relevant press organs claimed that on the eve of May Day leaflets were distributed at the university. Only the officers who brought them to the Party Uni-versity Committee, however, saw even one such leaflet. Karol stole one, which is how we learned what they said. It was a clear provo-cation. The very day they allegedly found the leaflets, they began interrogating whole dormitories. They had prepared rooms in ad-vance and even established a jail in one of the dorms. They read students' personal letters. As we found out later, we had been infil-trated by a security service officer who pretended to be a student. We even nominated him as chairman of the university ZMS Com-mittee after we took over ZMS after a fierce battle. Still, the authorities closed our club. They kept close tabs on us, and Gomułlka delivered a speech in which he stated that revisionism was getting out of hand, and he mentioned both Michnik, who was presiding over the Club of the Seekers of Contradictions, and me by name. I met Adam in the street in August and said, "The boss himself spoke about you." But Adam was running somewhere, very fretful. "L-leave me alone, I-I have no time now to m-mess around, I must repeat a test in physics." [Michnik speaks with a stutter.] So I went around telling everybody that Gomułka had time to mess around because he, unfortunately, didn't have to repeat any of his exams. At that point we ceased overt activity and tried to act informally and clandestinely.

JJ: What ultimately led to this decision?

JK: When it became apparent that there were crowds of people at the university who were fighting the system and were attracted to us. Until then, people were only aware of a critical perspective that opposed the present reality to prewar conditions—namely, the anti-Soviet, pro–Home Army position. In this situation, we decided that it was necessary to spread our leftist, Marxian critique of the system. First we had to expound it—this was why Karol and I began to write a paper, which we hoped to duplicate secretly. Our preparations were very well thought out, but the security forces intervened just as we were about to print our text. They seized two manuscript folders but did not find any printing equipment. They thus put an end to our clandestine activities. We then decided to circulate our paper in an "Open Letter." At that moment we were already prepared to go to jail.

JJ: Was the "Open Letter" another of your attempts to fix the system?

JK: We tried to incite a proletarian revolution to overthrow the authorities; thus it was a peculiar way of fixing things. We sought the absolute sovereignty of society, which was to be guaranteed solely by the system of workers' councils. That was our first mistake. We did not identify the problem of national sovereignty as it was beyond the limits of Marxist theory. That was a sign of our isolation. A year later, when both Karol and I returned from prison, we agreed to make that correction.

JJ: Did that occur to you when you were in jail?

JK: During talks with people. If everybody thinks something, you cannot disregard it. In 1968, we drew practical conclusions from the mistakes of that earlier theoretical diagnosis. When all is said and done, March [1968] began with a battle over the play *Dziady*★ [Forefathers' eve], over national traditions. All the same, I believe that Marxism is an important school of thought. Those who effectively reformed capitalism benefited from Marxism. Unfortunately, Marx did not appreciate the strength of the workers' movement under the regime he described, or capitalism's reformatory forces. We also made that mistake in our "Open Letter," and therefore, all of our diagnosis was wrong. However, if you use a model consistently, you can discover something. We discovered the mechanism of the system's cyclical crises, and we even predicted that new crises would arise at the end of the 1960s.

JJ: When did you abandon Marxism?

JK: When I was serving my second sentence. It was a purely intellectual decision. It seems to me that it is in the seventh of the *Theses on Feuerbach* where Marx expressed the thought that the entirety of social relations is the essence of man. That thought had fascinated me since my early youth, because if things were as Marx wrote, one could make a journey in the opposite direction as well—to depart from what he called the essence of man, psyche, personality, everything that we knew about man, and from that try to construct social relations. I had never had time to deal with this because it is a gargantuan task. But in jail I had plenty of time. Gajka sent me books, so I was working, sitting, making this intellectual journey and arriving at—a different conclusion. If this is so, then Marxism is not worth a tinker's dam. That was a purely intellectual adventure. And by a strange coincidence, I made the decision to abandon Marxism at the end of 1970. At that time Poland exploded with the "December events."★ "I'm always unlucky," I told Gajka when she visited me in prison. "When I was a Marxist, Marxism didn't prove correct. When I stop being a Marxist, it does." We had predicted such a crisis in our analysis of the system.

JJ: Can one tell oneself, "I'm no longer a Marxist," and stop using the conceptual instruments used for eighteen years of one's adult life to describe the world? This is not a reproach. Even today people find and complain about, in particular, in your writing style and in your written statements in particular, traces of a Marxist way of looking at the world. It is also a fact that you sense social processes and are quick to draw conclusions about the methods of action. In our society such an active attitude sometimes arouses immediate distrust. I'm sorry to have ignored the next two attempts you made to improve the world: the events of March 1968 and KOR, the Workers' Defense Committee. Surely, you'll write about them in an autobiography. I want to make only one remark on the KOR period. I think what made that formation so unique—a brave, ideologically committed and socially integrated group of marvelous people—also led to its isolation. To those who did not have the right connections, KOR was inaccessible. This is perhaps where the view of KOR as an elite oriented toward its own goals came. Don't you think that something of this relationship toward KOR was passed on to Solidarity?

JK: I don't think so. Attitudes in the union toward KOR depended on a number of different factors. The one you mentioned was maybe tenth on the list. You're right when you say that we were in some sense isolated. I think that was an inevitable cost. After all is said and done, we did not have any police spies among us, not even one. We could not accept the principles of formal membership and of openness. There are difficult tests to join every clandestine organization. Our test was simple and very informal, but it proved more reliable than any other. I agree with you that there was a certain element of exclusivity in it, but that was, I believe, an inevitable cost.

JJ: At this point in our conversation I would like to ask who Jacek Kuroń was and what role he played as an expert and "professional revolutionary" in Solidarity? You were a man whose demeanor and wide experience in social activism endowed you with the highest authority, on the one hand, but on the other hand, saddled you with a stigma as an "enemy of socialism" and made people suspect you of an inclination to manipulate them. To some people, you were the man who incited radicalism; others attacked you for a readiness to compromise. Both the former and the latter belonged to the same movement. It is a complicated matter.

JK: This can't be explained in just a few words. I must honestly say that I was no expert, but an activist who acted as an expert because nobody would elect me. Of course, in practice the differences between activists and experts disappeared, but it was nevertheless obvious that I was an activist. At the start, I was preparing the National Commission's meetings, which meant that I was teaching people how to conduct meetings—that when you take the floor your statement must end with a conclusion, that you must plan what subjects you want to discuss, that the relevant documents must be prepared before the discussion, and so on. Moreover, I raised my own voice, delivered speeches, and tried to convince the audience.

JJ: Were you always able to persuade people to see things your way?

JK: You can't say that. If those had been situations where I had my own ideas and had prepared to present them at the meeting, I probably would not have been able to convince people. Our ideas were generally accepted; we arrived at them together. I was so involved in formulating them that they also became mine or, I should say instead, that they met my expectations as well. As is usually the case in such situations, I often let myself be persuaded. My reasoning was sometimes more sensible and sometimes less. On various issues, I had to keep a low profile; I couldn't address them directly. All the same, I quite regularly spoke out when I shouldn't have, because it was impossible not to.

JJ: You were invisible during the first national meeting of delegates from Interfactory Founding Committees on 17 September. You stayed in the background, remaining in Anna Walentynowicz's* apartment, with the safe-conduct pass of an expert of Solidarity's Gdańsk region in your pocket. Why?

JK: Here, I must start from the very beginning. On that very day I was released from prison and traveled to Gdańsk. I met with activists from the "Free Trade Unions"*: Anna Walentynowicz, Lech Wałęsa, Andrzej Gwiazda, Alina Pieńkowska,* Bogdan Lis,* and Bogdan Borusewicz.* We worked all day and all night. The next day, at the meeting of the delegates from all the Gdańsk enterprises, the first draft program was presented, and then in the afternoon I was made their official adviser. I obtained, as you say, a safe-conduct pass so that from that point every action taken against me would be a violation of the 31 August 1980 agreements. I was very proud of that distinction. I returned to Warsaw, and there the whole uproar started. How could I go to Gdańsk without having first discussed it with Mazowiecki*?! Celiński came to me with the text of the statement calling on me to relinquish my position as an expert because as an adviser I served only to discredit the union, that I burdened it with the weight of my past and KOR. That evening a meeting was held during which Celiński released a draft statement from KOR that condemned my willful action. Everybody rejected it. That was the beginning of my conflict with Mazowiecki and his group of experts. Adam [Michnik] and I asked various people to mediate between us.

JJ: What was the major point of conflict?
JK: At that time it was my negative reputation that led them to believe I wanted to radicalize the movement. In conflict, you often suspect the other party of bad intentions. They thought I wanted to cause trouble, but in reality I wanted nothing of the sort. I understood them perfectly well. They recognized that the August Uprising was over and that what they needed now was the skill to incorporate the union into the system. From that perspective an activist who had been stigmatized as an "enemy of socialism" was potentially dangerous. On the other hand, I was convinced that the uprising was only beginning, that the union would become more radical, and that making Solidarity a part of the social order was our most important task. That was possible only if that order was significantly reformed. That required great patience on both sides. I had no influence with the other side, but on our side I could have some. I was convinced that I was one of the few people in the country who understood the social movement, and I also believed that Solidarity needed me and the other KOR people because we could afford to take a conciliatory position.

When I arrived in Gdańsk on 17 September, Wałęsa told me that I had better not show up at the hall, because there was a stink about me. I was to remain an expert; he wouldn't let anyone force him to get rid of me, but it would be better if I stayed at Anna's apartment. The whole Gdańsk presidium, led by the Gwiazdas, came to see me. They would end the debate at the hall and then come see me at Anna's place. Something began to emerge that I was very pleased about. I asked various people to tell Mazowiecki that he was pushing me into forming a faction even though I didn't want to. The people who were coming to see me later continued to meet without me. That was the beginning of the Gwiazda group, which later played a role in internal conflicts within the union, particularly with Wałęsa.

JJ: The meeting on 17 September came to the decision that there would be one national trade union called Solidarity. We already know that initially you were against it. You were in favor of a loose federation of regions. When did you change your mind?

JK: Even before that day, Modzelewski, who was a delegate to the meeting, came to me and said that there should be one union. Then, there was a meeting at the apartment of Bujak's* sister, which the representatives of the largest enterprises attended. Heniu [Henryk] Wujec,* Jaworski,* and some others also came. Jan Olszewski* strongly supported the idea of one union. Karol [Modzelewski] and Jan's arguments appealed to me. I cited them to Wałęsa and to WZZ people, which neutralized the initial resistance of the Gdańsk presidium, which only wanted to register a Coastal Trade Union. Although in the relevant discussion they did not support the concept of the national trade union, they didn't oppose it either. Had they opposed it, Karol's proposal would have been torpedoed as the Gdańsk and WZZ people had a majority in the presidium, and their authority in the country was absolute.

JJ: As soon as the union applied to register as a national organization, the registration crisis began, and your conflict with experts came to a happy end.

JK: Earlier, we had been divided by our different views on the so-called Wałęsówka.* I noticed that in the August agreements, the clause about pay increases was so confusing that it could have led to spiraling demands for pay increases from which we might not be able to extricate ourselves. I had called for a uniform "Wałęsówka" and, even more, a freeze on future raises. To that end, it was necessary to prepare materials and to negotiate on this issue with the government. We would have said that it was necessary to work out a uniform, coherent, and simple program that would have tied wage increases to improvements in the economy. The government was to name the period over which it would be implemented, and the union would have supported that program. At that point we could have come to terms. However, the experts, who were extremely suspicious, thought that I wanted to incite people to press for higher pay because I had some cunning plan to radicalize people's attitudes. What is more, they treated my descriptive statements as normative. I said, "A wave of radicalization is coming," and they said, "Kuroń is trying to radicalize attitudes." On the other hand, in no way did the government want to end pressure for higher wages. There were maybe five telephone conversations between Gwiazda and [Prime Minister] Pińkowski, during which Gwiazda shouted "Only the 'Wałęsówka'" and then "Freeze all pay increases!" I was sitting next to Gwiazda, so I know. Each time Pińkowski answered, "You know, this is an interesting idea," and nothing happened. During the subsequent conversations, Wałęsa, with the support of the National Commission, raised the issue again. Holzer writes about it. But through the old industrial-branch [government-sponsored] unions, the government forced higher and higher new pay demands on us, because the government always yielded to these unions' pay demands. They thought they could crush us this way. We—the eleven members of the National Commission—were doing nothing except opposing those pay raises.

I also had some misconceived ideas. Because I was deathly afraid that the party-state machine would devour the movement, I thought the interunion factory councils should take care of organized holidays, distribution of apples and onions, and other benefits. My idea was that the members of the factory committees should be elected by the entire workforce from electoral lists (as in parliamentary elections). The Gdańsk region embraced my concept. Mazowiecki argued, and rightly so, that this was tantamount to the radicalization of the union, because instead of dealing with strictly union problems the union would delegate this task to another body and have to run an electoral campaign in the struggle against the state-sponsored unions. I was in the wrong, but Mazowiecki thought this was an element of some cunning plan I had for radicalization. To make things worse, Solidarity in the Gdańsk shipyard began to complain that although they had led the struggle for the union they had not gotten a raise. At that time, the WZZ had influence in the shipyard, so in the eyes of the experts it appeared that I was trying to destroy the union. Finally, I had had enough of all that, and together with

Gajka I left for a vacation in the Tatras. When we returned, the alarm bell summoning me to Gdańsk immediately began to sound because a serious conflict had erupted there.

JJ: That was the beginning of the registration crisis. On 24 October Justice Kościelniak arbitrarily added a sentence to Solidarity's statute on the leading role of the party. That aroused strong indignation. On the eve of the National Commission's meeting, the Gdańsk presidium resolved to transform itself into an Inter-Factory Strike Committee. On 27 October the National Commission summoned Prime Minister Pińkowski to talks in Gdańsk. The prime minister refused to come. [Deputy Prime Minister] Jagielski arrived in Gdańsk, although not in the shipyard, and proposed talks in Warsaw. Gdańsk was ready to strike immediately. The members of the National Commission had a number of different opinions. WZZ and the shipyard people still had overpowering influence on the rest of the country. Wałęsa was isolated on the presidium. That was the prevailing atmosphere when you arrived in Gdańsk on the second day of the meeting of the National Coordinating Commission (KKP).

JK: The first thing the Gwiazdas told me was that the Gdańsk presidium was already moving to the shipyard in order to strike. Horror! I went to Mazowiecki, who surprisingly received me. We had both decided that, considering the situation, we had to come to terms. It turned out that our opinions on the whole affair were similar. Karol Modzelewski also had a similar opinion. It was necessary to go for talks to Warsaw. If the talks produced no result, then the union should announce a warning strike. Mazowiecki drafted the final resolution to that effect. Then we had to win the support of the whole KKP for our position.

JJ: That meant persuading the Gdańsk presidium and the shipyard. That task was assigned to you.

JK: Yes. First, the debating hall—everybody who opposed the strike began his statement with "Poland, the mother country, for Poland. . . ." A roly-poly kid—to this day I do not know who—stood up and said that Poland—that the fatherland—and that was why the strike was necessary—because the infantry cadets on "November Night"* did not ask what would happen next, they just staged the uprising. The audience was awestruck. As a result, he sounded as if he opposed the strike because if we immediately acted without thinking about what would happen next— Well, he provoked the audience perhaps to consider the situation. I then took the floor.

JJ: But it wasn't enough, was it?

JK: I don't think it was enough. During the break, Wałęsa (who was against the strike), people from the shipyard and the presidium, primarily WZZ men, and I gathered in a small room. It took me a long time to persuade them. They entered the hall. The shipyard representatives were the first to take the floor. "I agree with you," said the speaker, turning to me. "What's your name?" I replied, "Jacek Kuroń." "Oh, then I am even more at one with you," he said. As a result, they resolved to go to Warsaw.

JJ: Gdańsk's authority was collapsing, and Wałęsa's was growing.

JK: Wałęsa insisted that I join the delegation to the talks with Pińkowski. "Take it easy!" I told him. "Let's see whether the Eleven will agree to have me on the delegation." They agreed. I waited until they copied the names of the delegates, and then I took the list to typists, crossing off my name on the way. I knew I couldn't go, but I needed the vote on that question. As everybody knows, those talks did not produce anything, but my conflict with Mazowiecki was over. That was a load off my mind. Later, we were able to work quite closely, primarily with Bronek Geremek★ and Andrzej Wielowieyski.★

JJ: Are you aware that by willfully crossing your name off the list of delegates you violated union democracy?

JK: Let's save words like a "violation" of democracy for decisions that a manager or someone else takes contrary to the will of the majority. I failed to obey discipline. At the time, it didn't even occur to me that I was breaking discipline—but had it occurred to me, I wouldn't have hesitated even for a second. I have no such inhibitions. I think that in the last instance I myself must decide what I will do.

JJ: But by reasoning and acting this way, you—Jacek Kuroń—placed yourself above those people, in some way countermanded their decision.

JK: No. A lack of discipline does not place one above others. Had I crossed out somebody else's name, then, yes, then I would have taken a decision above them, in their place. But I decided about myself. In general, I believe that one should submit to the majority's will. Nevertheless, there are situations where one must not do this. This is all I have to say on the matter.

JJ: Who in the union had any influence on the decisions made?

JK: That was a complex issue. On the most general level, decisions depended on the intensity of the pressure exerted by the trade union rank and file, on social pressure filtered by a large body of activists. Ultimately, the problems discussed at the National Commission meetings were already highly concrete. Yet the union leadership and its advisers influenced the form in which resolutions were adopted. As a rule, the leadership and advisers tried to mitigate the tone of the National Commission's resolutions. However, the possibilities of toning down these resolutions were very limited. Only rarely did the advisers manage to shape decisions, and this was only through persuading the decision-makers. This was the case, for example, with the appeal to the rank and file to work eight Saturdays that year, which had been negotiated as work-free. It took a real battle to persuade the National Commission, and we won. The final text of the relevant statement was decided by agreement among those who drafted it—since things shouted out still have to be put in written form. This does not mean that those who put the ideas into words were directing the union's policy. That could scarcely be called manipulation; it was taking the sting out of decisions whose intent remained unchanged.

JJ: But in those circumstances, didn't form play the crucial role? Activists wanted to bring matters to a head.

JK: They did. I remember a statement that, because of its form and also its content, could have plunged the union into a conflict. It was in connection with the "Sienkiewicz affair"★ in the Jastrzębie Solidarity. He gave an interview to *Perspektywy* [Perspectives] in which he "cut himself off" from Gdańsk. The National Commission called him to appear and make an explanation. He didn't come. He sent Bogdan Kuś★ instead. On the eve of the National Commission's meeting, when the Eleven were drafting the agenda, Kuś put a tape recorder on the table and we could all hear: "Lech, speaking as one leader to another, we can come to terms . . ." It was an oral letter to Wałęsa. The Eleven went berserk. I suggested that we appoint a commission, including sensible men from Warsaw, Kraków, and Katowice, who would go to Jastrzębie, talk to Sienkiewicz and other people there, and then report to the National Commission. My proposal was accepted. A lawyer from Kraków was supposed to write a resolution to be presented to the National Commission the next day. The next morning, just before the meeting, I got an inkling. I read the text only to see that it was already a verdict. "Who wrote this with you?" I asked the lawyer. "Gwiazda," he said. "Man," I told that fellow from Kraków, "you're a lawyer. How can you appoint a jury and dictate the verdict to them?" We quickly wrote a short, prudent statement, which he then submitted to the meeting. Then Gwiazda, however, said there was another text and he demanded that it be read. I took the floor to explain that we appointed a commission to avoid an ex parte proceeding. The commission supported me. They were ready to take the matter to a vote. Kuś asked to be allowed to speak. We couldn't refuse him. He defended Sienkiewicz and attacked practically everybody else, including [Andrzej] Rozpło-chowski,★ over some mine situated on the border between regions. Rozpłochowski jumped up, demanding to answer Kuś. Well, he had to. He did, and so it started—everybody was against Sienkiewicz. In the twinkling of an eye they endorsed Gwiazda's statement, which meant an open conflict with Jastrzębie. I sat dejected; other points on the agenda had already been discussed, when Sawicki, the leader from the Lublin region, ran up to me. "Jacek, we can't act this way. They are miners! Man, understand that this statement will agitate all the miners. Jastrzębie still has great authority. We mustn't. What can we do?" I signaled that I had to say something on the preservation of the union. I delivered a speech. Silence. I asked for Sawicki to be allowed to speak. He voiced his reservations. They withdrew. As a digression, I want to add here that Sienkiewicz called me to wish me Merry Christmas and then, through intermediaries, proposed a meeting with Żabiński. He understood nothing.

JJ: Ultimately, the Sienkiewicz affair was resolved by the region's activists themselves. The commission did not have time to go there. Who finally decided?

JK: *Vox populi.* But the statement the National Commission fortunately did not issue could have led to a serious conflict within the union and thus made the situation in the region difficult. Each statement had its own particular history. You have to remember the circumstances under which these decisions were made. Even now people hardly realize this. Solidarity *already* had several million members when it came into being as an organization. It was created in a vacuum. From the start, the leadership bodies, including the National Commission, had to make a number of decisions without which the union could not have functioned. Those decisions concerned nearly everything, beginning with questions of membership dues and ending with economic matters and the rule of law. That was beyond the capabilities of any democratically ruled body, and in this case the leadership was particularly large because it was composed of representatives of more than thirty regions. Each region had sent two or three people, and everyone wanted to say something. It was even more difficult because none of them had any experience in mutual deliberation. Even if you had picked the leading experts in the procedures of democratic institutions, they couldn't have produced more than 10 percent of what should have been done.

I remember the National Commission meeting devoted to establishing a principle on how to distribute the money received from dues. The union would have been paralyzed if it could not settle this. Sugar-factory workers were threatening to strike, and something had to be done because the sugar-beet harvest was near. The industry had been starved of investment for years. The textile-workers were ending their strike and had settled their grievances, but because they were supporting Narożniak* they were repudiating the agreement they had just signed because they had found a political demand. In Warsaw, the Narożniak affair was a burning question— we had to reply to the authorities. There was the problem of dividing Solidarity into regions. There were thirty-five founding committees, including one from Nowa Sól [a town with a population of about thirty-nine thousand], and at the back of the hall sat fifty other committees demanding to be recognized as regions. Moreover, worker-activists from specific industries wanted to organize themselves to promote their particular interests. The engine-building industry had already signed an agreement with the ministry and demanded that the National Commission should give them the power to negotiate. But the commission had not yet decided what to do about unions organized around specific branches of industry. The authorities did not want to release the movie *Workers*★ [Robotnicy], so the film's director arrived and demanded to be allowed to speak immediately. How could we refuse him? He delivered a speech in a tone more appropriate for a call to seize the Bastille and demanded that the National Commission defend him. Meanwhile, Jastrzębie preoccupied half of Poland, and Sienkiewicz gave an interview in which he said that he didn't "give a damn" about Gdańsk and that it had been a mistake to release the KOR people from prison. At that point everybody was reaching for their knives, prepared to stab Sienkiewicz. All this took place in the same place at the same time. But these were not people who could afford to debate endlessly; all of them faced similar problems in their home regions. Meanwhile, decisions had to be made. The National Commission usually met on weekends, regardless of the importance of any given issue. On Saturday everybody had something to say. People chatted with each other until midday. On Sunday, when the debate was over, everyone was in a hurry to catch his train home and thus was ready to vote for anything. At that point some visionary always got up to propose doing away with any industrial organizations within Solidarity. A resolution would be passed. Try to convince someone who has to catch a train that liquidation of the branch sections is the death of the union. Try to convince them when they have a train home in a minute.

JJ: Nevertheless, you often were able to persuade them. What did you want to achieve within the union?

JK: I wanted to influence its policy to allow the authorities to operate—that is, to prepare a program for the reform of the economy and of the system. I wrote that Solidarity was an independent and self-governing train in a centrally controlled system. That was a handy phrase that I still like. The very fact that Solidarity existed gave independence and self-government to other organizations as well. Such a situation was bound to lead to a clash. The problem was the following—either abolish self-governing and independent trains, or change the traffic control system. The government had to do this. Therefore, we had to demand this of the authorities and at the same time make it possible for them to govern. Therefore, we could not plunge the country into anarchy, demanding everything which appeared anywhere.

JJ: You yourself know what happened when aspirations and grievances that had been suppressed for forty years exploded.

JK: I know. This is exactly why I maintain that, after all, Solidarity as a mass movement acted with incredible moderation. There were some escapades though. The other side talks about the occupation at Ustrzyki Dolne!* What are we talking about? A revolution was under way, and ten guys sitting in a gmina [the smallest unit of local administration in Poland] office are holding a grudge against us. Others sat in the club room of a cultural center somewhere near Jelenia Góra. How was it possible to appeal to them not to go on strike in such a way that they wouldn't? Needless to say, there were also conflicts that posed a threat to the union, too—in Bielsko-Biała and Zielona Góra. I swear that they were provocations. In general, the union behaved in a way that gave the government room to govern—if they had only wanted to do just that. The miners' case was the best example. They accepted the union's appeal to work on eight free Saturdays. It should be remembered that the miners were not against working, just against it on free Saturdays. Their stance was justified. In Gierek's day, they worked seven days a week. Repair work was neglected, and this affected mining output. Thanks to the repairs done on Saturday, the calorie-content of coal increased. The volume of coal mined declined, but its quality increased. They stopped adding stones and began to produce decent coal. I insist that general productivity improved under Solidarity. One of our failings was that we were unable to prove it. We faced too many problems. Ultimately, in response to the union's appeal, the miners did begin to work free Saturdays. Then the government passed Resolution 199, which awarded special bonuses, and all hell broke loose. That is perfect proof that the authorities didn't give a damn about coal, that their only aim was to set people at odds with each other.

JJ: All the same, today the struggle for free Saturdays is generally seen as one of the union's mistakes. Can we ask whether that was economically feasible?

JK: It wasn't. Nevertheless, the Jastrzębie Agreement* provided for free Saturdays. Don't forget that the rank and file were becoming increasingly radical, and that National Commission meetings were hence also getting more radical as the economic situation deteriorated from day to day. Regional activists remained under pressure from people who asked, "What has this Solidarity won? We've got a union, and so what? Things are getting worse and worse." That was why it came to the question of free Saturdays; everybody demanded that all Saturdays should be free of work. Horror. I told them that if we were to get free Saturdays, everything that happened in the country would be blamed on us. I was against free Saturdays. I proposed that the union organize a referendum on the issue. I thought we had an obligation to persuade people. If the activists remained under pressure from the rank and file, we should make our appeals to them directly. Even today I am convinced that if we had asked people then how many free Saturdays there should have been, and at the same time explained the country's economic condition and related problems to them, the outcome would have been positive. People would have given up some of their free Saturdays. People were in despair but had a great sense of responsibility.

I spoke in favor of the referendum several times. Yet I couldn't persuade my audience. Everybody was against it, and my proposal was voted down. Then they agreed to an emergency agreement, which sacrificed the Saturdays the union had won earlier as days off. The government made the union look foolish. Later, I had to defend this agreement before a mass meeting of representatives from factory committees from Gdańsk. They were indignant. At a certain moment, a guy stood up to say that a bad agreement had been signed and that nothing was going to persuade him otherwise, but there was something more important than our free Saturdays and our work, and that was the unity of the union. He got an ovation and—the audience voted for the agreement.

JJ: Meanwhile, conflicts began to appear at the "top" of the union, primarily between Wałęsa and the WZZ circle—the people around Gwiazda. You were involved in that conflict on account of your old friendships and your role as an expert. Some people accused you of lack of loyalty to your friends.

JK: Perhaps first I'll talk about the sources of the split. Remember 17 September 1980 and my meeting with the presidium at Anna Walentynowicz's apartment. In my opinion that wasn't the only reason for the split. With the official registration of the union, Wałęsa became the union's undisputed national leader. Yet the WZZ people still treated him as one of the boys. And that was wrong, because he wasn't the same—but they didn't understand. At the same time. a conflict between the veteran activists began. The younger ones, who had printed *Robotnik wybrzeża** [Coastal worker], had distributed it and had been routinely detained for forty-eight hours—how well I know it from my 1905 revolution—grew embittered. The victory was snatched from under their noses. They grew dejected, went to the beach, and cursed Lech. Lech? After all, he was one of them, so why did he put on airs? Meanwhile, Lech felt threatened by the authority of Anna Walentynowicz and Gwiazda. After all, it was he who said, "There cannot be two suns in the union," which rather bluntly settled the question of her membership in the leadership. On the other hand, Anna, a wonderful woman and of great value to the union, was not suited for a leadership position. She really was not. Gwiazda's group exerted absolute authority on the Gdańsk presidium. Yet as the movement spread across the whole of the country, the significance of that presidium declined, particularly after the registration conflict threatened to lead to a general strike. We shouldn't be surprised at their frustration. Activists like Borusewicz and Kołodziej* withdrew into the shadows, but the sharp conflict with Anna Walentynowicz was coming to a head. Wałęsa became the union's "Number One."

JJ: And you stood by him, which led to your personal conflict with some members of KOR.

JK: Not completely. Earlier, I urged KOR's dissolution. The majority of the members were opposed to the idea and suspected that I wanted KOR to dissolve to further my own career. I believed that the time for KOR's activities was over, that KOR activists should join Solidarity, which needed them. When it came to an open conflict between the Gwiazda people and Wałęsa, I sided with Wałęsa, but nearly all the other KOR colleagues sided with Gwiazda. My old colleagues believed they should defend the people who had been first to say no. As they saw it, our old, honest, and fine comrades who had taken great risks earlier, who had fought alongside us, and so on, were now being harassed.

JJ:	Those were moral reasons.

JK:	Yes. Andrzej Gwiazda and KOR were people of high morals. They were people who thought in purely moral terms. That was a mistake, also a moral one. Imagine making shoes for only moral reasons. To be sure, the moral criteria are supreme. But within the boundaries of what is morally acceptable you must assess what is politically effective. You cannot act otherwise. Yet it can happen that you run into the boundary between what is effective and what is moral. These are situations of moral dilemma. This is why, I should add, why I was closer to Mazowiecki and Geremek than some of my KOR colleagues. It is obvious that you must not discriminate against people of merit, but at the same time you can expect them under certain circumstances to understand that their imprimatur can only bring harm to the cause. That was why I crossed my name off the list of delegates to the talks with Pińkowski. Later, when I spoke about a national government, I made it clear that such a government could not include anyone known for an anti-Soviet stance. Does this mean that I wanted to discriminate against anyone? To be a cabinet minister is not anyone's civic right. To occupy an important office isn't either. It is as in the case of Anna Walentynowicz. It was sad that she was dismissed the way she was, but I could not defend her a priori, irrespective of circumstances, just as I could not defend Andrzej Gwiazda. He's a wonderful man. Please, God, let me be as strongly moral, as straight, and as high-principled as Andrzej. But he wasn't suited to a position that required politicking, precisely because he is a man of morals. This should not be mistaken for the term "a moral man," which every democratic politician must be. When Andrzej was leaving for talks with the government, I used to say, "You are sending an underage virgin to play poker in a brothel." To which Joasia Gwiazda [Joanna Duda-Gwiazda*], his wife, used to reply, "Andrzej is very good at poker."

JJ:	Internal conflicts got sharper at the time of the election campaign for the union's new leadership.

JK:	The election brought significant change on several levels of our movement. Previously, one's position in the union had depended on personal commitment. People who were more dedicated to the cause, who devoted more time to it, also had a greater say. This is typical of the initial stages of every movement. Certain movements remain at this level, and this is an excellent situation because the group is united by their common goal, everyone is active at his post without establishing a central structure. However, if you have a mass movement with difficult obligations, then a loose structure based on mutual agreement between its members will not do. You need formal structures. And this leads to a paradox—formalization of structures, the precise definition of individual prerogatives, duties, and so forth, diminishes members' influence on the union, and at the same time it is the only way to allow the members to maintain influence. I remember that at the beginning in Gdańsk, it was impossible to hold debates because everybody standing in the corridor felt entitled to take part. Whenever you introduce formal structures, you always feel that something is going wrong. The organization runs into red tape. Unfortunately, democracy requires red tape, even if only to obey the rules previously agreed upon. The more difficult and complex the tasks a given organization faces, the more red tape there will be. Many people who had spontaneously joined the movement felt, several months later, that there were barriers, formulas, rules, and regulations that excluded them. This is what happened, and we could not ignore it. Just then the elections began, and successful candidates could get full-time positions. That was how we came to the situation where a decision to run did not require any effort. You just got a full-time job with the union. For many it was a promotion.

JJ: A trade-union job at one's enterprise made the activist concerned independent of the employer.

JK: It was, of course, necessary under the circumstances, but not too healthy. What is more, the union was just beginning to formulate its program. Thus differences between candidates did not touch on their positions on the union program. We did not know how to assess candidates. Therefore, the elections followed the rules of street entertainment. A guy appeared on the stage, gave a sharp speech, and if the audience liked him they elected him. Simply put, it became a demagoguery contest. This mechanism eliminated many committed, genuine activists and instead promoted crowds of people who had the potential to become activists one day but would have to work long to achieve this, and who might not put in this sort of work because they had become full-time union employees.

JJ: Through this mechanism a sudden antipathy for KOR emerged. Why?

JK: What permitted somebody to become a union activist? One's performance earlier in Solidarity, but also one's record of struggle before 1980. KOR was a most visible and dangerous rival in the struggle for promotion. That was why, all of a sudden, there appeared an anti-KOR front. KOR was a relatively narrow group of people who unexpectedly became prominent and thus constituted a threat to others. Thus it became necessary to discount their past service, and thus an assault on our position was launched.

JJ: The assault was an outright frontal one in the Mazowsze Region. Was that the reason for the division of the region's Executive Board into "true Poles"* and KOR-people?

JK: Had that been the only reason, the assault wouldn't have been so successful.

JJ: The security forces also played a role here, by exploiting national feelings—

JK: The security forces? They too wouldn't have mattered if not for another phenomenon. At the very beginning of Solidarity, those who first joined were, without doubt, people broadly associated with KOR. At the same time, those people had the widest experience. Hence the significance of those activists was out of proportion to their numbers. As KOR was perceived as a leftist organization, this could not help but arouse the distrust of people of rightist leanings of all sorts, people whose experience made them distrustful of the Left, people who joined the party for reasons of convenience, and, last but not least, people for whom the left wing meant the PZPR. This is how the anti-KOR front was set up—uniting certain church people with certain party people, and with all sorts of extreme and also moderate nationalists. And this front profited from a certain general public distrust caused by ignorance. "What's going on? There is so much talk about that KOR, but what is KOR? Does it exist? No, it doesn't. Did it exist? They're Freemasons. They are a secret organization that acts without showing its face. Just like the

Freemasons." You said that certain people distrusted KOR because they maintained that KOR acted as a closed circle of friends. Until 1980, their distrust had not been of great significance. Perhaps some people had felt rejected, but not many. In Solidarity, however, such distrust was significant. Non-KOR people saw a certain mechanism at work in KOR—that KOR members had known each other for a long time, that they trusted each other and had a sense of solidarity. In a word, they constituted a "mafia." I realize that it was possible for many new activists to see us in this light.

JJ: Let us return, however, to the most distressing internal conflict within the union. In Gdańsk—

JK: This is what I've been aiming at all the time. In Gdańsk, there was sharp conflict between Gwiazda's group and Wałęsa. It was my firm belief that the former were in the wrong. If I had to say where the Gwiazda group was coming from, I would say that it was a revolt against the inevitable formalization of the union. To be sure, there were certain manifestations of bureaucratization and an emerging status based on high position. Remember Żabiński's earlier speech to party activists: "I do not know people whom power does not corrupt. Provide them with as much luxury as possible." What he said did not prove true for even a small percentage, but to a certain diminutive extent he was right. One could begin to see traces of privilege and a caste system in the union—which repulsed many sensitive people, such as those from the Gwiazda circle, people with a strong moral sense. To that you should add their consciousness as veterans of the struggle and their unquestionably justified sense of great service to the movement at the time of the strike. They were the Free Trade Union movement, and Wałęsa was one of them. All this led to conflict, and each conflict has its own logic. You had to deal with an attack by the Gwiazda people, by a part of KOR, against Wałęsa who was the undisputed leader of the workers. At that point distrust of KOR was bound to grow rapidly. My role became incoherent—I was a symbol of KOR, and yet I sided with Wałęsa. People just couldn't figure me out.

JJ: Then the Gwiazda people said, "Kuroń has betrayed his friends."

JK: Their demands on me were of that classic type that old combatants make of one another. I think that when a political decision is involved, and it is demanded of me that I should act on the basis of solidarity with old friends, we are dealing with a classic misunderstanding based on the ties between old combatants. I did not want to forsake old friendships. Despite my profusion of union activities, I still spent many nights talking with Gwiazda. And because of our friendship from the very beginning I warned him against a conflict with Wałęsa. I tried to persuade him.

To finish with our discussion of KOR, I want to add here that even when KOR was at its most unpopular its significance must have been great if the delegates to the Solidarity Congress, despite the racket and noise made by our enemies, passed a resolution thanking KOR. Our authority was still significant enough to overcome our enemies.

JJ: In his book, Holzer pays considerable attention to the "Bydgoszcz crisis"* and to the mechanisms by which emergency decisions were made. How do you see that conflict?

JK: What interests me about the conflict in Bydgoszcz is the situation within the union. What was the position our negotiating team should have taken? At that time [March 1981] I thought we needed to negotiate further but still sign an agreement all the same. I did not believe that we could afford a general strike. Thus I wanted the same thing the negotiating team did, only I wanted to achieve it in a different way. It was my opinion that the National Commission should go to Warsaw and hold open negotiations while staying in contact with factories and regions by telex. So the decision the negotiators made was seen to be the opinion of the entire movement! Unfortunately, my expert colleagues and my colleague Wałęsa believed that the National Commission could not control the strike. To be safe, they preferred not to summon it.

JJ: Were they afraid of the National Commission?

JK: They constantly feared the National Commission. We differed in that I was not afraid of the people. On the contrary, I have a deep faith in my ability to convince them. This does not mean that I never lost.

JJ: In Bydgoszcz?

JK: In that case also, I didn't manage to persuade my colleagues. The argument that there was no time was weak, because even after the general strike was announced, there was still time to call it off. That people were remaining in their factories? They were. That it was hard on them? It was. But nobody can tell me it was easier on them because of that shitty situation. You could have publicly delayed the date of the strike, called the commission to Warsaw, and met while remaining in continuous contact with the KKP. Just as the other party was under Soviet pressure, the union delegation would be under pressure from the KKP and the whole movement. That demands tactical consideration. Yet at that time I was guided not by tactical reasons but by the conviction that under no circumstance should we break the principles of union democracy. Leaders had to stand at the head and lead the union.

JJ: But only a few months later you persuaded the KKP presidium to compromise on the issue of workers' self-management. They did so, contrary to a resolution passed at the first round of the Solidarity Congress. That was exactly the opposite of your views on the democratic participation of the masses in the decision-making process.

JK: It was.

JJ: Didn't you just say that "that under no circumstance should we break the principles of union democracy?"

JK: I find my position regarding self-management at odds with the principles I profess. Are you happy now? Well, those were different circumstances. At the time of the Bydgoszcz conflict that principle was sacrificed out of the KKP's fear. I did not fear the Congress. You must also remember that the circumstances at the time were unusual. All of a sudden, the Sejm proposed an agreement on self-management. We could not put our decision off, because the Sejm was scheduled to recess shortly. At the same time, Solidarity was under heavy fire in the official propaganda, and it was clear that the authorities were preparing an attack. I was certain that their proposal was meant as bait to attract us. They knew perfectly well that we could not resolve anything in the period between the two rounds of the Congress, and that therefore we would turn down their proposal and become—in the eyes of the whole country—the party that did not want an agreement. And this was on an issue as fundamental as self-management! Then the authorities would attack us in the name of self-management! I constantly repeated, "Let them attack us on a matter where we are obviously in the right, not one where there is some ambiguity." At the same time I was sure that they would never pass such a law, because even with amendments it was our idea. My main critic at the time, Grzegorz Palka,★ said not long ago, "These are good laws." At the meeting of the presidium I supported approval of the Sejm commission's amendments. Everybody cried, "How will the Congress receive this?" I answered, "They will endorse a law that isn't too bad, and we will get it in the neck. That's okay. We deserve it. This is how it should be." I believe that democracy lies in our doing everything to see that decisions are made by the entire movement. However, there are situations where this is impossible. Then you must be able to take complete responsibility. I accept this and bow before my critics. If for doing this I will have to "drop out," I will. Everybody will know why.

JJ: Were you prepared for that when trying to persuade the presidium?

JK: The records were read out to the Congress. Wałęsa asks, "If the Sejm passes this law, how shall we go into the Congress?" To which I answered, "No problem, we can back our way in." Then my colleagues reacted as if I had passed that law in the Sejm. The entire Congress was against me. I violated the Congress's will. I understand that for many people that was the only moment in their lives when they could feel like subjects—not objects. They caught me! Okay. That was necessary. All the same, when someone called me a "manipulator" it was a most unjust accusation. My style is to step forward and say what's on my mind without mincing words. That is what I did then. As a result, God must have helped me, because we now have the self-management law, which the authorities do not know what to do about. However, no real reform will come out of it—this is already beyond our control. We pushed through as much as we could. This is what remains after us.

JJ: What is your opinion on the *Message to the Workers of Eastern Europe*★?

JK: When I heard it, I felt like I had been knocked down. That was a time for restraint, and that was why sending such a message was not politic. However, looking at it from the perspective of the years that have passed, this message is an important legacy.

JJ: You deserve the credit for preventing the Congress from debating a draft resolution on deleting a sentence on the leading role of the party from the annex to the union statutes. Hardly anyone remembers this today.

JK: That was Sobieszak's [delegate from the Gdańsk shipyard] halucinatory idea. Every solution was bad. Had the Congress accepted that idea, it would have been an empty gesture that could only have given the authorities an excuse to move. You can be sure of that! It would have become the excuse for the coup d'état of 13 December [1981]! Had Sobieszak's motion passed, it would have been even worse.

JJ: Didn't the union make mistakes with regard to the party?—I mean even the careful monitoring of what was happening inside it?

JK: Solidarity had a chance to find within the party forces that could have initiated changes in the system. The "horizontal structures movement"* was such a force, and in March 1981 they entered into an alliance with us. Iwanów [the influential leader of the horizontal structures in the city of Toruń] maintained that by losing the Bydgoszcz conflict we had lost them as well. At that time they still had a chance to win. We should have taken the risk. At the time, I argued that we could not go on strike because we did not have a program. Looking back on it today, it was not a moral dilemma comparable to the one that plagued Abraham. It was a question of choosing a more effective, better solution. Despite all the arguments, people did not realize at the time how much they lost by giving in. On the other hand, people did know what they were going to lose by giving in. Was it possible to make a different decision? Only someone irresponsible could have.

JJ: All the same, couldn't you have somehow supported the forces for reform in the party, particularly during their pre-Congress [the PZPR's Ninth Extraordinary Congress in the summer of 1981] campaign?

JK: It was not possible. I have heard or read horizontal activists who say that Solidarity did not help them. They are wrong. It could not

help them. Hostility toward the party was too great. The "comrades" from the security apparatus exploited and fed hostility toward
"reds." The "comrades" who advocated conciliation also fanned that
hostility to achieve their immediate aims. This was natural. Politicians have no right to complain about a bad situation. Why
shouldn't they have taken advantage of the situation? Solidarity did
not have any chance at all to directly support party people.

JJ: Cooperation was established in cities like Poznań or Toruń.
JK: And that was all that was possible. If there was any chance, it
was during the Bydgoszcz conflict. With the Warsaw agreement this
chance disappeared.

JJ: Why didn't you take part in the National Commission's meetings
following the Solidarity Congress?
JK: It is as I have said before—until the last commission meeting I
had no new proposals.

JJ: You are speaking with respect to the union politics. Elsewhere
you were very active—for instance, your involvement in the WSN
[Freedom, Self-Government, Independence] Clubs for a Self-Governing Republic.
JK: I had been committed to that idea as early as July. The clubs were
"wrested" from the union in order to improve its internal atmosphere. When a sizable number of the union activists began rallying
around antileft slogans, we found only one method to counter this—
to make the Left visible, to make clear who they were, what they
wanted, and what they were doing. Otherwise, we would have
lived in a witch-hunt atmosphere where no one knew anything,
where everybody would have fought with everybody else, and no
one would have known why. For what other reason did we establish
those clubs? We believed that the public needed the development of
Solidarity's programmatic thought in a number of areas, including
activities that were not strictly trade-unionist. The ideological struggles that broke out in the union, except those stirred up from the
outside, had solid foundations. We needed a place where new ideas
and concepts could be formulated, articulated, polished, and titled.
That was the role the clubs were to play.

JJ: At the beginning of our conversation you said, "We did not give them [the party] enough time." Was it within the power of the leadership to spread the escalation of public demands over two to three years?

JK: No, it wasn't. No one was strong enough. On this point I disagree with experts who maintain that the union was too radical. It certainly was not. The whole problem is that the emergence of Solidarity destroyed the system. Only the authorities could build a new system; however, they did not build it and that was the whole problem. It was like a Greek tragedy where everyone is doomed to do what they are fated to do. Solidarity defended its existence, and that was something it had to do. And the party, once they assumed that "the system had to remain intact," was also doomed to do what they did—to fight the union and ultimately to impose martial law.

JJ: Nevertheless, you always tried to defy the conventions of Greek tragedy. Until the Solidarity Congress you acted like a fire truck. You traveled around the country extinguishing fires, like those in Radom, among miners, in Olsztyn, just to name a few. After the Congress, you proposed the idea of a national government, which the general public saw as a radical idea. Did you believe that this was a potential way out?

JK: I always believe in and try to find a way out. During the famous July meeting of the National Commission, I said that to extricate ourselves from crisis we had to tighten our belts and get to work. I believe that society is capable of this, but that it must be sure that what it produces won't be wasted. However, it can only be sure of this if it can trust the government. The Program for a Self-Managing Republic was a compromise offer to the government. When all is said and done, you cannot create self-government without the government. But what can you do if the government refuses all cooperation whatsoever? This is what happened after the Solidarity Congress. Therefore, I tried to find another way out. I explained this position in my article "Rząd narodowy" [National government], which was distributed during the last meeting of the National Commission. It was a response to the conditions that had emerged, a logical conclusion from the totality of relations between Solidarity and the authorities.

JJ: People remember that you said "Power is lying in the streets."

JK: I did not say that it was "lying in the streets," but that it was not being exercised. People remember things poorly. The only persistent strike was staged by the government and the administration. This does not mean that they were unable to put us in prison or even to kill us. They had the repressive power, yet the authorities did not perform the basic tasks of the state. This is what I meant at the time.

JJ: Your reasoning must have contained miscalculations, considering that just a few hours after you presented your idea of national government several thousand people landed in jail.

JK: My major miscalculation involved two erroneous assumptions, about which I will speak in a minute. The imposition of martial law was the only operation in the whole history of communism that the authorities carried out in a planned and effective manner. The idea had occurred to them much earlier, as Holzer demonstrates very clearly. I would also bring attention to the registration crisis, the events in Częstochowa and Olsztyn [security apparatus operations that in retrospect seem like training exercises for martial law], which coincided with Sienkiewicz's statement—his letter to Wałęsa mentioned earlier—in which Sienkiewicz appointed himself union leader. I think that originally the authorities planned to mess some people up and to put others in their place. In 1980 they were not yet strong enough, so they began to make systematic preparations. To this end General Jaruzelski became the prime minister and then the party first secretary; provocations occurred more frequently, including the desecration of monuments [to Soviet soldiers], poison scares, and so forth. They painstakingly worked to create a threatening political atmosphere.

JJ: Wasn't the creation of military operational groups in autumn a clear sign of such a plan to you?

JK: It was. I realized that these groups were a part of their preparations for a planned attack. I thought that as long as the general had us in his sights he would stay his hand at the last minute, as he had done before. I also considered the possibility of a military putsch. The error in my last address to the National Commission was that I did not foresee an immediate attack. I believed there was still time for the authorities to respond to the proposal for a national government. In this government every member would have needed the approval of three parties—the ruling party, the church, and Solidarity. It was a way out.

JJ: Did you really believe that such a government was possible?
JK: Perhaps it was. No, it wasn't possible, because they were preparing for war, but I did not know that.

JJ: How could a government that in August 1981 clearly wanted to break off negotiations, and that after the Congress only pretended to talk while actually stalling for time, agree to anything like this?
JK: They are saying this only now, when you know that they were ready for war. Had they been willing to try everything before resorting to an all-out war, such a government would have been their only chance. By this I want to say that if I were in the same situation again I would make the same proposal. This was the only way out, save a war on us. If there was any miscalculation on my part, it was a failure to believe that they could be so crazy! All the problems that existed then still remain. They have not accomplished anything.

To sum up—my principal mistake involved two wrong assumptions. First, I was sure that every use of force on their part would be met in kind by the public. I underestimated—to this day I don't understand why—how strongly people were convinced that they should not resort to force under any circumstances. With the use of force we would have undoubtedly beaten them.

JJ: How? Fraternal tanks would have crossed the border in no time.
JK: They could have intervened no matter what the course of events in Poland. That was why I believed they would not decide to make a frontal assault on society. That was my second erroneous assumption. I believed they were completely unable to make a decision. I still cannot understand how Jaruzelski was finally able to make a decision. Both before and after the event, Jaruzelski played the role of a classic Hamlet. Now, I understand him; it was a situation with no way out.

JJ: Now—my final question. In the article you wrote in Białołęka* prison, "Tezy o wyjściu z sytuacji bez wyjścia" [Theses on the way out of a situation from which there is no way out], you spoke of staging a general strike in the spring of 1982. That too was received as a totally unrealistic proposal. [Like almost all Solidarity activists, leaders, and experts, Kuroń was interned after the declaration of martial law. He had the article in question smuggled out of Bia-łołęka.]

JK: First, a mistake was made. I affixed a note to that article reading: "To be published only with the endorsement of the underground leadership." When all is said and done, you have to admit that it is difficult to discuss whether or not to stage an uprising in an underground publication. I simply understood the slogan "Zima wasza, wiosna nasza" [The winter is yours and spring will be ours] as the underground's slogan. I thought the leadership was planning a general strike and needed someone to justify their position. That was caused by my isolation in prison. I was also deeply convinced that we should strike in spring. The climate was auspicious.

We shall never learn whether I was right or wrong. However, we shall learn whether I was utterly wrong. If we end up covered in our own blood, then it might mean I was right. If we emerge from all this in peace and quiet, then it means I was certainly wrong. We should then thank God for that.

June 1986

18

On Niewiadomski

Krytyka, no. 25 (1987)

Anna Bojarska

The Myth

He botched his own death. Facing the firing squad, the man who killed the first president of the Republic of Poland tried to make a speech. He did not shout "I die for Poland!"—which would have sounded so beautiful in his future legend. What a shame. The last sentence he said before his death was: "I am dying for the Poland that Piłsudski is bringing to ruin!"

The killer's interests were painting, shape, color, light, not words. An actor or a writer would understand that complex sentences do not make for famous last words. A politician would not reduce his own last act to a petty party game by uttering the name of his enemy. To die with one's enemy's name on one's lips—what an absurd death for the nationalist! There were more absurdities in Niewiadomski's case, so many that it was easy for one side to disregard what happened, and impossible for the other to turn Niewiadomski into a martyr. A mad painter assassinated the president, that's all. It is strange. To tell the truth, it continues to baffle everyone even today.

Alas, this was quite likely the most important event in the postpartition history of Poland. The three gunshots fired in Warsaw's Zachęta gallery on 16 December 1922 still echo.

The facts are well known. One hundred twenty-three years after being partitioned by three foreign powers, Poland recovered her independence. Józef Piłsudski, the "head of state," held the dominant position of authority in the first stormy period. Meanwhile, a constitution was adopted, and elections were held. The parliament chose a president who was then sworn in and, on that same day, assassinated. The killer acted on his own; there was no plot. Nevertheless, there were powerful forces behind him. The attempt on the president's life was preceded by a fierce campaign of hatred waged by the parties of the Right, who had supported another candidate. They accused the winner of having been elected by the votes of national minorities. (Actually, it was the Piast [a moderate peasant party] deputies who held the balance when in the last, fifth, round of voting they chose Narutowicz. Yet no one expressed hatred of peasants during the campaign.) Without the votes of the minority deputies, Gabriel Narutowicz would have received twenty-two fewer votes than the Right's presidential candidate. A real storm raged about that difference of twenty-two "pure Polish" votes. It came to street disturbances, to assaulting members of parliament, to demonstrations "for" and "against." There were casualties. Lumps of dirty snow were thrown at the carriage of the president-elect as it drove across the town. Newspapers dreamt of "a lump of snow that will change into an avalanche" and about removal of that man-"hindrance," that man-"obstacle." Then, afterward, a great fire would at long last be able to illuminate "the twilight of Piłsudski and the dawn of a new Poland." The infamous ride through the streets of Warsaw was a ride down death's lane. Someone hit the first president of the republic in the head with a stick, someone else waved brass knuckles in his face, and then suddenly he hesitated. That was how the first day of Narutowicz's presidency went. After reportedly fruitful talks with Cardinal Kakowski, he arrived at noon for the opening of an art exhibit at the Zachęta gallery. There a bald painter and art historian, Eligiusz Niewiadomski, shot him in the back three times. What happened next?

Ah, next there were new "facts," just as unambiguous and oh so logical! The shots by Niewiadomski marked an end to the week of hatred. Poland suffered a shock—even the Right did. National reconciliation bloomed like a thousand flowers. The president's funeral became an occasion for a deeply disturbed society to demonstrate. Half a million people walked in the funeral procession! People were deeply moved and wept openly. The angelic soul of Poland again reappeared from under its coarse skull! It is true that after the election of the next president (once again with the help of "minority votes"!), one Sejm deputy yelled at the benches of the Right, "When will you kill him?!" That, however, was only an expression of bitterness and pain. Hearts and minds were clean, people were good and loved democracy in their hearts, whereas Niewiadomski was a lunatic. Madmen exist everywhere. The whole country shook hands and danced a polonaise at Narutowicz's coffin. How can one doubt their noble-mindedness?

It is indeed difficult to doubt their nobility. Works of history, whether prewar or postwar, local or émigré, all refer to it as a "shock of redemption." Brought up on this history meant for imbeciles, I was shocked with horror when I tried to read the famous poem by [Julian] Tuwim★ ("You had a crucifix on your chest and a Browning in your pocket, / they formed an alliance with God, and a pact with the killer") through the eyes of the people from that time. How they must have turned red with shame, how moved they must have been! Why should I not believe that? Close at hand, I had someone who was just bursting with shame, slapped in the face by the words "Don't turn your eyes! Just stand and look, you cutthroats!" During the Hate Week, my own grandmother, a teenager in 1922, had the time of her life, up from dawn to late at night, running from one demonstration to another and shouting slogans at the presidential carriage until those three shots in the Zachęta gallery were fired. Then, only shame and pain remained, to the end of her life. "I too killed the president." My God, who ever thought it would end like that! Everyone who has blood, not whey, in their veins likes it "when something is happening." Everybody likes to shout, to sing a bit, to express their feelings. People are not cucumbers to pickle in a barrel; they need their Hyde Park and holidays. But then someone shoots someone else in the back—that is not fair. That was not the way it was supposed to be!

After all, many things seem to confirm granny's optimistic recollection—the living witnesses, serious scholars, and literature. In a novel by [Pola] Gojawiczyńska★ (a realist of the first rank), a well-to-do pharmacist and perfect model of an object for manipulation, repeats on the morning of Narutowicz's funeral: "It could not have ended any other way! . . . He was elected contrary to the people's will; the people were insulted because he was elected by Jews, communists, and socialists!" But by noon, confronted by the pathos of the great demonstration of mourning, he changed his mind—"Something happened. It was committed by a madman. No one is to blame." This comment was typical.

However, a much less well known book by Szemplińska-Sobolewska, *Narodziny* [The birth], presents a different picture:

"Murdered," people with horrified faces were saying. Others were shouting, "The Jewish flunkey has been put to death! We found a hero!" They were beaming with joy.

An embittered nihilist commented with *Schadenfreude*: "The Black Hundreds commit their outrages just like at the height of czarist rule! This is what independence has brought us!" At school, girls from the best families were dancing with joy (soon after the killer's execution, they ostentatiously carried flowers to his grave, while their Latin teachers "in the middle of the declension of Rome or reindeers" suddenly remarked, "Yes, God's mill grinds slow but sure." Is this picture exaggerated? Not much. Wojciech Kossak,★ a diehard present in the Zachęta gallery at the time of the murder, in a private letter described the event as if he were describing the killing of a bug. "For a long time we were not allowed to leave. Everybody was searched and his or her identity card checked." What a nuisance! When all is said and done, had not the press called Narutowicz a "hindrance" and an "obstacle" and the "larva of red-bearded Satan?" That larva, that bug—crush it without giving a damn; it is not even human! Until the end, Niewiadomski emphasized that that was the only way he had seen the victim. This expansive tradition of hatred was hysterically falsified by myths of "Unity, Concord, and Reconciliation." One of my friends remembers that his kindergarten teacher in 1935 ecstatically told the class of four-year-olds, "Children, we have been blessed with a great joy today: Piłsudski died!" What about the slogan "Quiet over the coffin!"? Even its author, Stroński,★ never forgave himself for this phrase. It was eagerly taken out of context, misrepresented in myth, and misunderstood. Besides, why mention the coffin? A struggle was under way, and hatred was brewing; and in politics, as a great dictator said, there is no room for sentiment. It is all very well that an enemy was shot in the back. Only children brought up on Westerns can condemn it. Yet, there were no such children in 1922.

Those who felt ashamed when reading Tuwim's poem were few and of no consequence—the eternal dung of history. Regular people who read the poem flew into a fury. That poem earned Tuwim the undying hatred of thousands, perhaps ten of thousands, or even hundreds of thousands of people. The counterargument was simple, and the press was only too eager to advance it—here is a Jew who dares to kick "golden-haired Wanda" in the face! Had anyone else written the poem—[Władysław] Broniewski,* for instance—the press would only have redirected its invective somewhat; their hatred would have remained. Whoever dared to see a horrible crime in the crushing of that larva Narutowicz was a wretch who deserved a fate a hundred times worse than the one that befell Poland's first president. Throughout the interwar era, public feeling—concentrating on that event in 1922—seethed with rage. However, history, written both in Poland and in exile, talks of the event as "a redeeming saving shock," "a turning point," and "a reconciliation." The words used by Paweł Zaremba in his *Historia dwudziestolecia* [The history of twenty years] (Paris: Instytut Literacki, 1981) are characteristic: "It was a shock that shook the whole society. Some people even maintain that it prevented civil war." But to what end?

The Two Messieurs N

It was all the same to Niewiadomski, whom he shot. People said that the man he chose as his victim was a person beyond reproach—good, wise, and high-minded. But it did not matter. It did not make any difference to Niewiadomski, who was not interested in shooting any particular man, but only the president.

To be sure, it did not matter to Narutowicz who shot him. The identity of the killer was of no consequence. It was an enemy with a thousand faces who shot the president. It did not matter precisely who wielded the gun. One political orientation killed another; totalitarianism killed democracy; the nationalist killed the liberal; an assassin killed the president.

But obviously people are individuals. Gabriel Narutowicz, a descendant of patriotic country squires, a scholar who had held a chair at the Zurich Federal Institute of Technology, a respected engineer, was also an expert on Western Europe (its economic relations in particular). Swiss democracy had shaped him politically. As a "European" who belonged to no party and was above all of them, he was rare in Poland. Poland would never have anyone like him in power. He returned to his liberated mother country, to imperiled Warsaw, in the hottest days of 1920. He treated his political activities as a service to the nation. Reportedly, the salary of a Polish minister was half of what he had paid to his Swiss cook. He was a member of the Polish delegation to the Genoa Conference.* He formulated a plan for the autonomy of Eastern Galicia (the vexing Ukrainian question!) and strove fervently for its implementation. As president he intended to form a government that stood above the parties. He was killed at the moment it seemed as though he would succeed.

His unblemished reputation helped make the conflict even sharper. He was beyond reproach both personally and politically. Yet he was attacked, even if only for the benefit of the mob. One objection was obvious. Narutowicz was religiously indifferent; in any case, he did not go to church. Among the rumors planted during the stormy week preceding his assassination, there was one that he had seen to the removal of the crucifix from the Sejm chamber. A second objection was that he was a Freemason. A third nonsensical one was that he was Jewish, which was a charge from which no adversary of the Right was spared. Thus Narutowicz too was a "Jew" for several days (after all, his first name was Gabriel). However, all that quieted down quickly. As soon as he died, he stopped being a Freemason and a Jew, and the question of his church attendance lost all significance whatsoever. He disappeared from the political arena with an insignificant wave of the hand. No one had held anything against him! Maybe he was a paragon of virtue, even a good politician, but that was not the point. It was not the man or the politician who had been killed, but an abstract idea. It was that unhappy difference of twenty-two votes that was murdered.

Eligiusz Niewiadomski, the killer, should have been a more complex character. Was he a nobody who was only noticed because of several shots? It was not quite so. Inasmuch as the first Mr. N. was the perfect model of a liberal, a democrat, a "centrist," and a "European," then the second Mr. N. was a model fascist. He too—like Hitler, Goebbels, and other lesser people of that sort—was a failed artist. A graduate of the St. Petersburg Academy of Fine Arts, he started his career impressively by winning three medals and having a successful first showing of his paintings in Paris. But that was where his career ended. He became a drawing teacher. Specialists valued a manual he authored, but the rest did not count. Nevertheless, he kept working, stubbornly and priggishly. He painted portraits, nudes, and landscapes. He gave his compositions such titles as "Polonia," "Lech" [according to legend, Poles are descendants of a Slav named Lech], or "Angel of Death." Art was his passionate but unreciprocated love.

When Poland regained independence, he got a job in the Arts Department of the Ministry of Culture. Nobody liked him there, and he did not like anyone. His relations with his colleagues were the worst possible. He was continuously fighting with someone. He already had a reputation for not being mentally stable. Summoned to court as an expert once (in the case of a painter who sued a customer for failing to accept the portrait she had commissioned him to paint), he gave an opinion so chaotic that nobody understood it. In delivering a lecture on [Stanisław] Wyspiański★ at the Zachęta gallery, he suddenly interrupted himself and said, "Why should I bother to explain anything to you, ladies and gentleman? You will not understand anything anyway." He wrote incoherent and completely confused letters, but they were written in red ink, and every character was "sculpted." He claimed to have a plan to solve all political and social conflicts and demanded audiences with ministers and premiers to reveal those plans to them. Then, all of a sudden, he decided to kill Piłsudski, the founder of "Judeo-Poland." He carried a gun and practiced shooting. He postponed the execution, though, because he wanted to finish his book first. By the time the book was almost ready, Poland had elected its first president. Niewiadomski went to the exhibition the president was visiting, stopped behind him, took the gun out of his pocket, and shot three times. In jail he wrote manifestos offering prescriptions on how to regulate life in the entire country. He designed his own tomb and the inscription with which the grateful country was to honor his memory. He demanded that the fifth regiment of the legions,★ in which he had served, should pay him military honors before his death. Finally he was shot, uttering those awkward last words: "I am dying for the Poland that Piłsudski is bringing to ruin!"

The book for which he postponed his attempt on the life of the chief of state, which he never finished, is good. It is titled *Malarstwo polskie XIX i XX wieku* (Polish nineteenth- and twentieth-century painting) and was issued by Arct Publishers in 2,700 numbered copies. My grandfather, a supporter of Piłsudski, bought copy number 1,733. I still have it. It is a mere guidebook, but written with a true, even pathetic, love for the arts and beauty. It is full of often clumsy attempts to express admiration for other people's artistry. For example, he says of Grottger★: "How very beautiful his colors are: you simply see the *shade* of the white shirt, the darker shade of the woman's skin; still different are the shades of the room's walls, the man's pants, and his overcoat." The final fragments are written in great haste ("I was bent on finishing this work"), almost in telegraphese, without the use of verbs. The last sentence of the unfinished paragraph on Mieczysław Jakimowicz* reads: "These are lovely harmonies of black and gray spots, peaceful, simple in line and tone."

He himself was far from harmony, peace, and simplicity.

This is a classic biography. An unsuccessful artist who lacks talent is to be immortalized by an Act, just as Hitler and Goebbels became immortal. This serves as a warning to the world that it should not disregard artists, yet the world never heeded this advice.

Niewiadomski's Legacy

The killer created his own legend, but ineptly. In documenting Niewiadomski's catatonia in a special brochure, Maurycy Urstein, a psychiatrist of the Kraepelinian school,* made one incisive statement, comparing the defendant's speech to the court to "an orchestra without a conductor." The speech was nevertheless interesting.

What did Niewiadomski tell the court?

Niewiadomski actually wanted to kill Piłsudski. Piłsudski, however, declined the position of the president, so killing him "would only kill his body"; Piłsudski's ideas, spirit, and popularity would continue to triumph. Thus, he killed Narutowicz.

Piłsudski? Why yes, he used to admire him. Piłsudski had been a hero! He had been admirable until he returned from Magdeburg [where he had been imprisoned by the Germans at the end of World War I]. But then? The people "had been waiting for a slogan, for a word of command, brave and powerful, that would unite the nation and lead them in heroic effort." In a word, they had been waiting for dictatorship, and instead they got democracy, which boils down to anarchy.

Piłsudski did not want to be a dictator. Instead of a kick in the mug, the anarchic, feverish, and strike-bound country had received "a Sejm elected according to a five-point electoral law" [that is, by universal, direct, equal, proportional, and secret ballot]. That meant that "instead of one head, there would be four hundred rulers, and what they were like was revealed by those five-point elections. The most complex matters of state had been entrusted to stable-boys and shepherds."

Sejm! Clearly such a democratically elected Sejm was half composed of "spiritual illiterates" and another "quarter or fifth . . . who stood beyond the border of Polishness and citizenship." Independent Poland, which equated "a Polish citizen" with "a Pole," made representatives of national minorities—"stable-boys and shepherds"—citizens. It dispensed with educational requirements. The proletariat, that is, "the most ignorant masses," were given as many rights as the people who until then had been privileged. All parties were allowed to operate. In a word, Poland introduced democracy! Niewiadomski could not reconcile himself to that. Many others also could not reconcile themselves to it either. It was in the name of those people that Niewiadomski fired those three shots.

Thus Narutowicz died as a symbol of democracy. He died because he accepted the choice of the majority, without regard to who comprised that majority. That majority consisted of "enemies of the Polish state." That was the democracy, that anarchy, which Poland introduced after the radiant coup by Mussolini, whom the Poles should have seen as a model and an example! The spirit of socialism seized the country. And what do socialists consider the Motherland? "The Motherland is all of us." Bah!

After all, Niewiadomski reminded the court—and this was the main line of his defense—the historical tragedy of Poland was the result of weak government. "That had been confirmed by all historical research in the nineteenth century." And here again Poles wanted a weak and benevolent government, a soft rule! "Who needs a soft rule? Honest citizens, people with clean consciences, do not fear an iron hand." Those who need democracy and freedom are "thieves, profiteers, bandits, tax-evading peasants, Jews, plotters, traitors to the state," and the like. In those circumstances, he, Niewiadomski, was defending the Polish Reason of State. He was defending "the majesty of the Republic from the abuse of small-fry." He also "wiped disgrace off the face of living Poland." Thus he did not regret anything. He told the court, "On the contrary, I express a certain hope that the echo of my shots will reach the most remote parts of the country and knock at every cottage and every heart."

He developed this point in *Kartki z więzienia* [Notes from prison], published after his death. The book included a large portrait of the author framed in black, giving his dates of birth and death, with the latter embellished with the word "fallen."

First, he developed the theme of the Jewish plot and also presented a plan for solving the Jewish question. His plan was interesting, especially if one considers that he developed it right after Mussolini's coup d'état and directly before Hitler's first putsch. Niewiadomski's plan was nearly identical to Hitler's, the one carried out in the Final Solution: take no notice of international law—the damned Treaty of Versailles was "only a piece of paper." He advocated depriving Jews of their rights as citizens, separating them by a "Great Wall of China" from the rest of society, imposing on them a lump-sum tax equivalent to half of all other state revenue, and punishing crimes and offenses committed by Jews several times more severely than normal. These were just "interim" proposals. Later, other measures would be adopted as necessary. The reasons for all this did not require any explanation. It was obvious that one should fight the "Absolute Evil." Nevertheless, Niewiadomski advanced two arguments for those not in the know: The Jews had given the world both "Marx and Kautsky" (it is difficult to understand why he mentioned Kautsky) and had adopted a treacherous position in 1920. However, when anti-Semitism is used as bait, it is always worthwhile to look for both the hook and the fishing-rod. It is rare that such talk pertains to Jews alone. In this case too it is clear that Niewiadomski had something else in mind.

If we look at Poles through Niewiadomski's eyes, what do we see? Physical and spiritual degeneration, depravation, "protruding ears, sunken noses, dim eyes, shoulders that stick out too high, monkey-like movement"—in a word, we see "the people." This loathsome people, because of Piłsudski—who could have imposed dictatorship at any time he chose—was granted full civil rights. This was wrong. Let's be frank— not only Jews should be deprived of these rights. Democracy is unacceptable. It is not acceptable that people with protruding ears and dim eyes should elect their own leaders and decide on the type of government and the conditions under which they will live. Universal franchise should be immediately abolished. The ignorant masses, children, and avowed enemies of the state must not be allowed to decide the fate of all, and thus even their own. "The intellectual horizons of the shepherd, the stable-boy, the illiterate worker, the maid, and so on, do not authorize them (save exceptions) to perform the task of citizens in this area, to decide on the fate of Poland." Likewise, the idea of twenty-one-year-old kids voting is just preposterous! If they are to vote at all, the age limit should be raised to at least twenty-five; they should, moreover, be required to meet educational requirements, and furthermore the list of offenses that would deprive them of the right to vote should be expanded ("antistate agitation," giving false political information, and so forth—in fact, any oppositional activity). Once this sort of order is established, it will be necessary to kindheartedly and humanely raise the people's standards—though in such a way as to beat politics out of their heads once and for all—to give them health services and cooperatives, theater and choirs, to show them paintings by [Jan] Matejko★ and the two Kossaks,★ to organize dancing-parties and picnics for them, but without drunkenness, brawling, or "sexual wantonness." If to these you add excursions, sports (boxing, best of all), movies, and community centers, "the worker himself will reject all those 'ideological' parasites."

So much for Eligiusz N.'s political legacy. Perhaps one could add here his appeal to Poles to wake up from the hypnosis spread by that mean and incompetent founder of the Polish Legion [Piłsudski]. Poland, awake!

According to one newspaper (*Gazeta Poranna 2 grosze*), "a crowd of up to ten thousand" marched in Niewiadomski's funeral procession. That was fifty times fewer than at the funeral of his victim. Among the inscriptions on wreaths, one reading "Honor to the Immortal" was common. At his graveside, the mourners sang the anthem *Rota*.★

Killed as a Proxy

As stated above, the "Niewiadomski affair" cropped up between Mussolini's and Hitler's coup. Italy, Poland, and Germany had one significant factor in common: all three gained (or regained) their respective statehood late and not without difficulty, after a long period of division and partition (in Poland, combined with loss of independence). Was it impossible to preserve what they had gained without totalitarian slogans that appealed to the public in those newly united states, and the public's readiness to accept the heel of the master's boot, the knout, and grabbing the nation by the throat? Or was it just a natural inclination to exaggerate hysterically the role of the state?

It is true that in the interwar era Poland did not become a fascist or national-socialist state. It all played out in a somewhat different way.

To begin with, there was Piłsudski in Poland. Right after Narutowicz was assassinated and the Right (who else?) took power, Piłsudski
retired from political life. In his last, embittered address, he quoted
what the first president had told him after that hideous ride through
the streets of Warsaw: "You are right, this is not Europe. These people
felt better under those who trampled on their backs and punched them
in the mouth." It was not the shock that the masses experienced that
turned out to be significant, but the shock to Piłsudski. He decided
Poland's interwar history. That shock led to the May [1926] coup, and
Brześć* and Bereza.* When the only man who had the power to take
dictatorial power in Poland at the time of his choosing, returned, when
he made his coup, he was no longer enthusiastic about democracy at
any price; he no longer was the kind of politician Niewiadomski had
wanted to kill. Niewiadomski did indeed kill him as a proxy. The
former head of state from 1918 to 1922 reconciled himself (he believed
that he had no choice) to the elimination of his federative ideas, to the
frustration of his military plans, and to many other defeats. After 1926,
in his capacity as the minister of defense, he began—much too late to
be effective—to impose his own will. When all is said and done, he did
this with a delicacy that was uncharacteristic for a time of brutal total-
itarianisms and bloody dictatorships. The Brześć trial and the Bereza
camp, compared to trials and camps in other countries then and in
subsequent years, seem like child's play (as well as fatal and unexplain-
able errors precisely because of that). There is no doubt that democracy was violated, but not on a mass scale or "with particular cruelty."
How awful could a dictator be who had the army occupy parliament
and then withdrew shamefacedly following a conversation with the
Speaker, who as a man of principle was not going to bend to bayonets,
pistols, and swords! Yet that was not and could not be the same Poland that came into being in 1918. The chance had been lost.

The same history that tries to convince us of the "shock to society"
unleashed by Niewiadomski's three shots marvels at the marshal's
metamorphosis. It contains so much hatred and contempt for an opponent it once called a Bolshevik-nationalist, for so much foul language,
and for the outright ostentatious fashion in which he imposed his will!
Commentators went as far as to explain the marshal's metamorphosis
with deadly seriousness as a product of grave illness. That romantic,
that unyielding fighter from the most desperate period of slavery, the
Siberian exile, the prisoner of so many prisons, the commander of the

Legion, once convinced that Poland had to be a country of democratic freedoms and human rights, the head of state who suddenly begins to sneer at "constitution-prostitution," to laugh at the indignation of the arrested and beaten Sejm deputies, and to revile his opponents publicly in the harshest language. Why?

Piłsudski probably knew the statements Niewiadomski made before the court and in jail well. He never lowered himself by uttering Niewiadomski's name. And yet he finally did what Niewiadomski had expected him to do. He grabbed the state with his own hands. He curbed the democratic disorder—only in a different manner than thousands of Niewiadomskis expected. In the days preceding the assassination of the president, nobody prevented people from shouting at will, singing, or venting their anger. Now, their freedom of expression was curtailed "a bit." With that perpetual "a bit," which settled things by compromise, Piłsudski saved himself in the eyes of posterity. His words were more violent than his deeds, and his form was more violent than his content. And above all this hovered the ghosts of the two Messieurs N.—one shot down and one killed by a firing squad.

During his voluntary exile at Sulejówek★ in 1925, Piłsudski wrote his book *Rok 1920* [The year 1920]. He dedicated it to Aleksander Prystor,★ "a man who looked at Polish sordidness and disloyalty and reached for a lash," asking for his fond remembrance. A year later, already after the May coup, he told *Kurier Poranny* [The morning courier], "The last straw, which forced me to make my decision, was the formation of a cabinet that reminded me of the infamous government that led me to retire. I did not want to lend my name and services to the people who, in my opinion, had been accomplices in the most revolting crime ever committed in Poland, the assassination of the president of the Republic, Gabriel Narutowicz." Piłsudski must have meant the government of [Wincenty] Witos.★ Piłsudski did not level his accusation concerning "the most revolting crime ever committed in Poland" at the bald painter with the gun or at the tub-thumpers of those December days. He saw the crime's "moral perpetrators" elsewhere. They were not only on the Right. They included "national-Bolshevik types," the "spit-soiled, freakish dwarf . . . , who was beaten about the mouth by each of the invaders who partitioned Poland, sold from hand to hand, and paid for this." This level of invective explains both Brześć and Bereza. This is how Piłsudski saw his enemies. Was his picture false? Was his definition too broad? Did he give in to his neurotic feelings? This is not at all certain. One should keep in mind not only the rule of the colonels [Piłsudski's men after his death in 1935] but also wartime, the 1940s, 1950s, and the subsequent years. . . . One can hardly find a better description of the enemy of democracy in Poland than Piłsudski's "national-Bolshevik type." It had to have consequences. . . .

As a matter of fact, the feelings of Piłsudski, the politician and statesman, corresponded to those of the teenage girl who after the magnificent street festivities sobbed, "I too killed the president!" To him that sob would be not a naive and exaggerated self-accusation but an honest statement of fact. It is true that the most revolting crime in Poland was committed not by Niewiadomski, not by just the National Democrats.* Its perpetrators were larger in number. They were so many that one had no choice but to take a lash into one's own hand.

The occupation of the Sejm by the army, the dissolution of the Sejm, Brześć, and Bereza—all these actions incited rebellion and protest even among those loyal to Piłsudski. If only these moves had been merely wrong! Alas, they were also stupid; they were a mistake. Piłsudski could have governed "without the lash." He did not have to go as far as he went. Brześć and Bereza were not necessary. Years later they seem to be a rather unnecessary demonstration of power, mean revenge, and a reckless mangling of his own legend. Cold political calculation would have allowed him to avoid blemishing his magnificent image. Yet it was not a cool political calculation that mattered here, but something else—a knot tied and twisted many years earlier, perhaps as many as two centuries earlier.

One more of the family stories: that girl who "too killed the president," later married an employee of the notorious Department II [military intelligence]. At home her husband spoke about his work only once, after he came across something that exceeded his abilities to cope. He spoke of it in tears. On the last national holiday in the marshal's lifetime—that is, right after Bereza—the couple were standing on a review stand. The army was marching along the street, and music played, while those standing on the reviewing stand were silent. Praetorians stood motionless in their icy disapproval. Piłsudski watched and saluted the troops. Behind him reigned the empty silence of people who were resentful, people who were now opposed to him. According to the family legend, that Department II employee—who had recently fallen ill from shock having studied the pictures from a certain "operation" shown to him by a colleague from another department—could not stand that silence and raised himself up and shouted, "Long live Grandpa!" [That is how many Poles referred to Piłsudski.] Piłsudski turned to him with his fingers raised to the peak of his army cap and thanked him with a smile that suddenly exposed all the age and wear of his face, the countless wrinkles of the dying man. . . . Reportedly, at that moment those on the review stand broke their silence. Supposedly, both junior and medium-level dignitaries jumped up, shouted, cheered, and flung their hats in the air. It was as if that first, spontaneous shout lifted the imposed pressure to keep silent. It was as if they were finally "free" to shout. This is only a tiny part of the myth of Piłsudski. But it is not only this. It is also a distant reflection of the case of two Messieurs N.

In the final analysis, Piłsudski imposed only as much dictatorship as was necessary to guarantee democracy. Niewiadomski's ghost must have wrung its hands, seeing that sneering reversal of his most sacred principles. People who adhered to his legacy, who made it their credo, were the first to land behind the barbed wire of Bereza. Earlier, the moral perpetrators of the murder in the Zachęta gallery, although not them alone, found themselves in the Brześć fortress, in the dock, in jail, and in exile. Were the people waiting for a great and bold command? Perhaps Niewiadomski was right. In this case they lived to witness to it, but it was not the one of which they had dreamed.

Anarchy and Dictatorship

Niewiadomski's views were as simple as the crack of a whip. "Anarchy" is not to be tolerated. If it has already been allowed to develop, things must be put to right—anarchic elements must be pacified and iron-hand rule introduced. Niewiadomski was merely a symbol that expressed the views of many. In [Andrzej] Strug's *Wielki dzień* [A great day], a grotesque novel about a nationalist coup, the Niewiadomskis sing in ecstasy: "Truncheon! Truncheon! Rubber truncheon! Just say the word, and the thing is settled." That was it! Strug may have seemed to be mocking this, but he was dead serious. "Truncheon, truncheon, lead us forward! Hurrah! Hurrah! Club, club, club!" Why not? Everything depends on supreme values. For

Niewiadomski, these were the State and the Reason of State. For Piłsudski supporters, liberals, and the like, it was Liberty, Justice, and
other nonsense. One just had to puncture that balloon!

When addressing the court, Niewiadomski revealed his ties to a political current much older than the nationalist movement with which
he ultimately identified himself. (He differed from them by his readiness to accept Piłsudski as dictator—the only acceptable one—but that
was of secondary importance.) He defined his own position when he
reminded the court what "the great nineteenth-century historical
studies had confirmed"—that the historical tragedy of Poland was a
result of weak governments. "Today every school kid knows this, but
the head of the state did not want to know it." The idea that the partitions were a just historical punishment meted out to Poland for excessive civic liberties and democracy has been repeated here for generations. Who would give its correctness a second thought? A slick
formula about enslavement as inevitable punishment for liberty has
from the beginning played an obvious ideological role. [Adam]
Asnyk* poked fun at these views as propounded by the nineteenth-
century New Historical School:

> . . . the partitioning of Poland
> Took the baptism of the apostolic mission.
> In the full light of its proceedings
> Despotism shines as a bright star,
> And Targowica's* patriotism
> Often comes out . . .
> As Kościuszko* was a maniac
> Who stirred up the proletariat!
> And so on . . . and so forth . . .

That's it—and so on and so forth.

Who needs the great historical studies of the nineteenth century to
discover that Poland collapsed because she had been reduced to anarchy? After all, the treaties of partition stated that in black and white!
How did the three neighboring states justify the invasion of 1772? —*A
complete disintegration of the state and a spirit of factionalism that reduced
Poland to anarchy.* Yet the first partition by no means sobered up those
obsessed with freedom. It was necessary to form the Confederation of
Targowica [1792] and to ask foreign armies to intervene to partition

the country a second and a third time. . . . Even a history addressed to idiots cannot conceal that this death by installment was in part a suicide. After all, Poles destroyed their country themselves. Poles asked foreign armies to help them fight other Poles, the Polish Sejm ratified the partitions, and the Polish king signed the partitioning treaties, including the last one, which brought the existence of the Polish nation to an end. It is of minor importance that someone stood with tears in his eyes on that occasion, that someone was "sorry," and that someone had chosen the lesser of two evils. Had there been strong internal resistance to "anarchy," Poland would have not fallen, or would have fallen in a different manner. However, many preferred to see Poland wiped out of existence to seeing the country lost in anarchy because of the arrogant belief that every country squire was equal to a count and that all estates were equal. So, Poland ceased to exist.

During this whole period of enslavement, two currents existed alongside each other. One produced the New Historical School and many similar accomplishments; the other resulted in uprisings. To the first, death was better than democracy—the death of Poland, needless to say. However, the other current prevailed. Its victorious leader, though, did not know what *every school kid* knew—that freedom and human rights equaled ruin, that War equaled Peace, that Freedom equaled Slavery, and that Ignorance equaled Power. Do the shots in the Zachęta gallery now seem so strange? And what about how short-lived a victory they were?

Before the court, Niewiadomski wrung his hands at the ghastliness of the reborn republic. He was a representative of those who tried to shatter the dreams of freedom fighters by asking the reasonable and exclusively valid question "Poland, what sort of Poland?" He chastised those for whom a free Poland was most important, even if it was imperfect, poor, and conflict-ridden. Meanwhile, the state had been reborn with the anarchic freedoms it had defended until it had fallen apart. Some 123 years later the course of history started anew, but where it had left off. A country was reborn where people were free and equal, in fact more equal than at the moment of Poland's disintegration. As if nothing changed in the interim, the free play of political forces resumed as well. But there were new elements too: the people's government, Moraczewski's* militia, a multiparty system, demonstrations, and strikes—an absolute frenzy of strikes! The height of it all, Niewiadomski argued before the court, was the strike of hos-

pital workers. "Patients lay in their own excrement, and Messrs. Piłsudski and Wojciechowski* were unable to devise a way to put an end
to this outrage." Even that was not a good enough reason for them to
establish a dictatorship! And what was going on in 1920 in the defense
sector, where Niewiadomski worked, at the time of the greatest danger? They had caught a student distributing communist leaflets. The
obvious thing would have been to shoot the reptile! Yet Niewiadomski's superiors—at such a moment!—showed unpardonable leniency. He was young and capable, so they let him finish engineering
school. That was out-and-out treason! There were other cases of such
disgraceful leniency. That those people had won the war did not excuse them. In Niewiadomski's eyes, harshness and leniency were not
methods to be considered each time with regard to their effectiveness.
One should always be severe. Then the election of Narutowicz, that
"European," democrat, idealist—what did that all mean? "Leftist circles in cooperation with the Jews standing at the head of the open
enemies of the State" wanted "as before to keep the country in a state
of anarchy." It was exactly against anarchy, and in the name of the
Polish raison d'état, that Niewiadomski let fly those three shots in the
Zachęta gallery.

Prosecutor Rudnicki challenged all Niewiadomski's attempts to justify his actions as a fight against "anarchy." Rudnicki called the argument false and demagogic. Anarchy? Two hours after the assassination
of the president, the funeral of the worker killed in a clash with a
National Democratic paramilitary group turned into a demonstration.
Crowds of people walked in the funeral procession. Only two hours
later! It would seem that in such a moment all that was necessary was a
spark . . . And what? Not one violent act was committed in Warsaw
that day! The public passed the test. In the face of these facts, to speak
of anarchy was pure demagoguery. Nevertheless, a widespread myth
of anarchy exists and lingers on.

That social strife, a dreadful evil, had broken out justified every
countermeasure in Niewiadomski's mind. But what was wrong with
that? "What is wrong in the struggle for rights, for the future, and
wanting them today?"

Those were the words of the public prosecutor in 1922. At the
beginning of the next year, the painter Eligiusz Niewiadomski was
executed. Those who identified with him and who sang *Rota* above
his grave continued to use the myth in their fight against vile individ-

ual liberties and rights. That myth, rooted in the terms of the treaties of partition, proved to be stronger than one might have thought. In May 1935 [when Piłsudski died] a kindergarten teacher, face beaming with satisfaction, said, "Children, a wonderful thing happened to us today . . . !"

From then on, Niewiadomski began to carry the day.

19

Jews and Communism

Krytyka, no. 15 (1983)

Abel Kainer [Stanisław Krajewski]

Introduction

One day a friend told me, "You know, people of Jewish origin should not get involved in the activities of the opposition so as not to provide the authorities an argument against the opposition." I cannot treat his remark as anything but a warning: "Listen, Jew, don't. . . . " This puts me in the clutches of a dilemma that perplexes me just as it perplexed previous generations of assimilated Jews and their offspring. Why, I protest, should I take into consideration the faith of my forebears and not the importance and rightness of the opposition's activities? All the same, I begin to feel the power of my friend's argument. It is true that one encounters a certain reserve toward the democratic opposition, or rather toward some of its factions, because of its allegedly large Jewish membership. Some people want to believe that because the problem boils down solely to anti-Semitic bias there is nothing to talk about, because anti-Semitism is an ugly thing. Although I recognize the noble intention behind such a position, I still see in it a desire to flee from reality. There certainly is something to talk about. First, too much attention is being given to the presence of Jews—not only in the opposition—to let one pretend that what we are observing is a mere trifle. Second—and this is something I shall consider below—at the foundation of the present phobia lies the memory of Jewish connections with communism. Here I am referring to the role that communists of Jewish origin played in postwar Poland, as well as the influence some of them or their children have had on the shape of the present-day opposition, or at least one of its currents.

Conventional opinion holds that Jews were the major support for communist power in Poland (and elsewhere) or readily offered their services to that power and received certain privileges in exchange.

How much truth is there in this common belief, and how much is a false stereotype? Although this problem did dramatically—and tragically—come to a head in March 1968,* until this day it has not been raised *sine ira et studio*. There are no serious studies, because Jewish topics are taboo in official life, and even though the situation in the underground press has begun to change, no really serious investigations have yet been published. For example, in his book about the Left,[1] Adam Michnik does not mention Jews at all. This is allegedly because it would be difficult to address the Jewish question in sufficient depth when writing fundamentally about something else. Out of fear that you will not be up to the task, you write nothing at all. On the other hand, when Andrzej Grzegorczyk raised the problem of Jewish attitudes toward communism,[2] he in large part repeated the conventional wisdom mentioned above; and though he lacked neither courage nor goodwill, he lacked familiarity with the subject.

Every taboo concerning recent history is bad. The situation is sad when the only author to raise the question of "Jews and communism" publicly is Ryszard Filipski,* who does so with a passion clearly kindled by hatred. Yet this question not only provides a background for the current excitement about the "excessive number of Jews" in the opposition, which is an unimportant issue, but is also worth raising for purely intellectual reasons. Former communists, particularly Jewish communists and their children, who like myself are not personally responsible for anything but are aware of their parents' past, are particularly qualified to discuss this question.

Jews: The Group and the Individual

First, there is a certain difficulty that always crops up when there is talk of Jews. This is due to the imprecision of criteria for defining who is Jewish and the exceptional vagueness of the notion of "the Jew." What do we mean when we say "The Jews did something?" Do we mean a Yiddish-speaking, religious Jew, or a person who practices Judaism whose native tongue is Polish, or a nonreligious person who feels Jewish, or a person who no longer feels Jewish, or a Polish Catholic with Jewish ancestors, or someone whose Jewish ancestry has been unexpectedly revealed by anti-Semites? Were we to start from such considerations, there would probably not be much space left for any-thing else. Let us then skip it and adopt a very imprecise and barely satisfactory definition that makes all those mentioned above Jewish. According to this criterion, based on origin and religion, everyone who belongs to the Jewish community★ or has a significant number of Jewish ancestors, in particular members of the Jewish community, is a Jew. You can count your ancestors to, say, the third or fourth genera-tion, this way falling under the provisions of the Nuremberg Laws.★ I do not think we can avoid this (after all, even German scholars did not invent anything better). Converts to Judaism belong to the Jewish reli-gious community. All the same, it seems that in sociological thought, in particular when we discuss the connection with communism, the criterion of origin seems to be most suitable. After all, that was what those who warned against "Jewish-communism"★ believed when they blamed Jews for the imposition of communism and the like, and what the friend I cited at the beginning of the essay also had in mind.

Although such a broad definition of "Jewishness" simplifies my task, it might lead a less careful reader to interpret my text incorrectly. The point is that a Jew defined in this fashion can be a Pole and a Christian and feel no connection with Jewry. Such categories as "a Pole of Jew-ish origin" (who feels exclusively Polish) or "a Jewish Pole" (who feels both Polish and Jewish) are much more accurate with regard to many people, including the communists themselves. When I write about the postwar period, I will sometimes be deliberately inconsistent by add-ing a more precise description to the term "Jew."

There Is No Jewish Conspiracy

Having adopted the definition above, we must recognize that Jews form a heterogeneous group, not only socially but also from the point of view of their individual "Jewishness." This gives rise to a form of stratification that is less precise than that of other minority groups (be they religious, ethnic or . . .—actually there is no good term for them because there is no comparable group!). There is no structure that would encompass Jews in general, all the more so because there is no leadership all Jews would recognize, and no spiritual leadership recog-nized even by all those who affirm their link to Judaism. If one wanted to see the leader of all Jews in existing institutions such as the World

Jewish Congress, the Chief Rabbinate of Israel, or the Israeli government, he would have to exclude all the Jews who are not Zionists, or
all the nonreligious Jews, or those opposed to the current policy of
Israel (one must not forget that there also are anti-Israeli Jews, for example, among the passionately pro-Palestinian Trotskyites, and among
the ultraorthodox residents of Jerusalem's old Jewish quarter). This
means that one would have to adopt a hopelessly narrow definition of
who is a Jew, whereas our subject requires, as we already said, a broad
definition. To put it briefly—in all conflicts, Jews have taken different
sides, even in conflicts with anti-Semites.

The erroneous content of the "Jewish-communism" stereotype
causes many misunderstandings. Usually when one says "Jews created
communism" or "Jews were in power," one assumes that Jews acted in
a coordinated fashion, as a group. This assumption goes together with
the belief that Jews act together against the *goyim*,* Christians, Poles,
or somebody else. This worldview includes the theory of a Jewish conspiracy, the classical example of which is *The Protocols of the Elders of
Zion*, a notorious forgery by the Russian secret police at the end of the
last century. According to the *Protocols*, an imaginary central Jewish
leadership bent on conquering the world directs Jews to all major institutions such as banks, the press, parties, subversive movements, and so
on. I think it is important to mention this fantasy, because the theory
of a Jewish conspiracy continues to be attractive to some people. The
theory is based on the undeniable fact that one can indeed meet many
Jews in many institutions that have a decisive influence on the shape of
our world. Thus there is talk that they are everywhere, occupying important positions, and therefore are bent on dominating and exploiting
others. The point is that actually there is no reason for any "thus."·
Jews are everywhere, but this does not mean that they act together in
order to achieve common goals. Their ubiquity does not mean that
they act in a common interest, because they may not have one.

Let us take an example: people wearing glasses are everywhere; they
occupy the majority of eminent positions, and elsewhere there are
others who put on their glasses furtively at home, or who do not need
glasses at all but pull them out to pull the wool over the world's eyes.
Therefore we conclude: those who wear glasses support one another,
rule over everybody else, and benefit from this. Ernest van den Haag,
who quotes this example from Feuchtwanger, observes that group personification of evil was used in similar ways, for example, by Marxists

(the bourgeoisie) and C. Wright Mills ("the power elite"). Van den
Haag describes such an approach as a modern version of the belief in
demons.³ Regardless of the aptness of his examples, one has to admit
that he is right when he says that at the foundation of a belief in conspiracy theories lie deep psychological motives. The same holds for
anti-Semitism.

On Group Characteristics

It is therefore inappropriate to consider the question of "Jews and communism" in terms of group rivalry, as if Jews as a group used communism as a tool against groups of non-Jews. Yet there is no doubt that
particular individuals compete with one another, and only individuals
joined the communist movement. This fact, as well as the absurdity of
the theory of Jewish conspiracy, led certain people (leftists in particular) to the other extreme, namely, to repudiate the notion of group
characteristics, or at least to the repudiation of using them when discussing the role of Jews in the communist movement. This is wrong.
This too is a mistake or a failure to face up to unpleasant facts dishon-
estly justified by a fear of falling into nationalism or racism.

There are two kinds of group characteristics. First, there are certain
common traits that individuals share. We say that Swedes are taller
than Italians, although no doubt there are many short Swedes and tall
Italians. Nevertheless, the average Swede is taller. Second, there are
group characteristics that are not individual traits, such as the environment, predominant lifestyle, and traditions of a given group, as well as
its collective memory. To some extent, these affect even the children
of the people who have distanced themselves from the group. For example, parents who were shaped by their environment, in turn, affect
their children's sensibilities.

Obviously people are shaped by various factors. Therefore, individual members of a particular group may differ from the group norm,
whereas people from outside a group may share many of that group's
attributes (for example, a Swede with an "Italian" temperament). By
forgetting about this, one can easily become paranoid and see, for instance, attributes that are somehow Jewish in all Jews, and only in
Jews. For example, Leśmian's* poetry does not have any significant
characteristics that could be described as Jewish, whereas Gombrowicz's* works do!⁴ Not to remain a slave to stereotypes (even when

statistically justified), one should remember that as a rule it is never clear whether a given individual is typical of a group, not very typical, or completely atypical. One should also remember that everyone has more than one group affiliation.

I will examine the relationship between Jewish and communist characteristics. I understand communism loosely, without defining it, set against the broader background of such notions as socialism, the Left, and progress. My purpose is to discover facts concealed behind the stereotype of "Jewish-communism" and to explain the disproportionately large participation of Jews in the communist movement, especially in Poland, both before and after the war. Nobody denies the large role of Jews in communism. Some people say, however, "This had its causes, but it is of no consequence because Jewish communists did not differ from other communists," whereas others say, "This is important and demonstrates the fundamental Jewishness of communism." (It should be observed here that similar questions were raised about the so-called commandos★ at Warsaw University in the 1960s.) Both the former and the latter groups often spoke a priori, merely expressing their respective bias—that is, the conviction that "Jewishness" is either impossible or inevitable. One cannot say in advance, however, that the large number of Jews was of no significance even if Jewish communists did not really differ from other communists. Neither can one say in advance that the Jewish character of a given group results solely from a relatively high percentage of Jews. One must explain what this "Jewishness" is, and this can be done only by studying the traditions and the situation of the Jews, including those who have abandoned the Jewish community. The latter figure prominently in this discussion. It is not only that as a rule they preserved certain Jewish attributes, passing them on to their children, but beyond that their common uprootedness and the community's animosity toward them— turned them into "non-Jewish Jews." Among them, there was an even narrower group, Jewish communists.

Did Jews Create Communism?

According to the popular stereotype, they did. They allegedly did so in their own interest, in order to control the world. This stereotype, as false as it is naive, is nurtured by certain facts. These facts are the large Jewish membership of leftist movements, defense of the Jews by these movements, and also a certain similarity between some elements of Jewish tradition and socialist ideology. Although a closer examination of these and other facts does not prove that the idea of communism was a Jewish creation, it still does not disprove the thesis that there are certain connections between Jews and communism. Many Jews placed their hopes on liberal and progressive movements, on slogans of equality and human rights that promised Jewish emancipation. Even religious Jews could watch with hope the growing influence of the Left on governments, believing that this would reduce anti-Semitism. Active engagement in the socialist movement, however, was possible only for those who abandoned Judaism, at least in its traditional form. With the ongoing processes of secularization and emancipation, the ranks of Jewish socialists and nonreligious Jews grew. There were many instances where in the same family the father could be a pious Hasid, and the son a revolutionary poet; or the father a factory owner, and the son a communist strike-organizer.[5]

The whole picture, though, is much more complicated.

Jewish Organizations against Communists, and Vice Versa

Jews as a self-governing group (this wording assumes a narrower definition of Jewishness) did not create communism; on the contrary, they rejected it. In prewar Poland, communists neither enjoyed much popularity among the Jewish masses nor had any real influence on the Jewish community's leadership. Jewish national parties were anticommunist (the only exception being Poalei Zion–Left Wing). Even the socialist Bund (who did not differ very much from communists on social issues), because they demanded Jewish autonomy, were firmly opposed to the communists, who in fact worked for the disappearance of Jewish distinctiveness. Although the Bund and other socialist-oriented parties, both Jewish and national, were dominant among the Jewish population of certain towns, leftist ideology did not predominate in the Jewish community as a whole. The majority of Jews were conservative. Religion was the cement that bound the Jewish masses together. Rabbis were their highest authority, and religious circles opposed both the socialists and the communists. On the other hand, the Jews who abandoned religion, and such Jews were numerous among the intelligentsia, had choices other than supporting the Left. Zionists, who were (with only a few exceptions) decidedly anticommunist and looked at the Soviet Union with horror, were increasingly popular among the nonreligious. Although, with time, socialist (but not communist) ideology became an important element of the Zionist movement, the view of the founder of Zionism, Theodor Herzl, put forward in 1899, still carried weight: "In principle we fight, above all, with the revolutionaries. We lure Jewish academic youth and blue-collar workers away from socialism and anarchism by winning them over to the true national idea."[6]

Speaking about communism as a tool of Jewish domination is therefore groundless, because Jews—like everybody—had such differing attitudes toward it, and because so many Jewish organizations opposed it. That is why a vision of communism as a secret Jewish weapon can make sense only if it is based on a conspiracy theory. Only a world-view based on categories of struggle between the Jews and the *goyim*, or Christians, can lead many authors to express such opinions as "It is well known that Bolshevism is a Jewish product, that Bolsheviks are Jews, and that Bolshevik rule is Jewish rule. History does not know the kinds of cruelties inflicted by Bolshevik rule on the Christian population."[7]

The vision of harmony between Jews and communism is contradicted by yet another phenomenon. Despite the high level of Jewish participation in the modern socialist movement, there were clearly discernible anti-Jewish elements in it. In principle, although socialists defended Jews and struggled for their emancipation, this was often linked to a tendency directed at erasing traditional Jewish differences. Although this was based on general plans to do away with all religions and national differences, the socialists were particularly prejudiced toward the Jews (that is, Jews other than their own Jewish revolutionary colleagues). The well-known remarks made by Marx in *On the Jewish Question* can be reduced to a critique of a certain abstract construction of the Jew as the spirit of the market economy. In this construction, the Jew becomes a symbol of alienated market and money mechanisms and the opposite of mythic natural social relations. Movements of both the extreme Left as well as the extreme Right tried by revolutionary means to re-create the naturalness for which probably everyone living in modern mass civilization longed. Anti-Semitism masquerading as anticapitalism attracted not only fools (Bebel*: "Anti-Semitism is the fools' socialism") but distinguished thinkers and fathers of socialism as well. Proudhon saw Jews as both parasites and enemies of the human race and considered plans to expel the Jews from France.[8] National Socialism went even further. It replaced the abstract construction of the Jew[9] with the real Jew and treated genocide as a mere technical operation.

The (very) young Marx, who loathed his (or rather his parents'), background and who proclaimed the necessity of eradicating the distinct Jewish character, became the prototype of many Marxists. They fervently fought Zionism—that is, the idea of finding a national solution to the Jewish question, on the basis of Jews' right to self-determination. When at the beginning of this century Jaurès wanted to make socialist Zionists members of the Second International, the majority (including, needless to say, many Jewish delegates) opposed him.[10] Apparently, they considered Jews a relic of the past that simply did not represent a nation, religion, race, or any other group for whom one could demand the right to independence and self-determination. Later, in interwar Poland, the communists took an ambiguous position on the Jewish question. For example, the author of a pamphlet published in 1924 wrote that while in prison he tried to poll his communist colleagues, asking them questions like "Would you agree to Yiddish-language public schools?" (as demanded by Jewish parties). Unlike other questionnaires, this one produced hardly any response at all. His fellow prisoners explained that this was a "sensitive issue."[11]

Communism and Religion

Rejecting any discussion of communism as a Jewish conspiracy, I shall consider the merits of the question of whether Jews created communism from a different perspective, in the same sense as when we say that Christianity is a Jewish product. As a matter of fact, Christianity owes incomparably more to the Jews than communism does. After all, Jesus, Saint Paul, the disciples, and all the early Christians were Jewish. What is more, Christianity is based on the Old Testament and on the rabbinical tradition of the time, which are the foundation of Judaism. Pope Pius XI said, "Spiritually, we are Semites."[12]

Of course, socialism (unlike Christianity) never was a Jewish sect. Among its founders and adherents there have always been both Jews and non-Jews. Searching for the Jewish provenance of socialism, one

can quote Moses Hess, who, educated in the spirit of Jewish orthodoxy, started his own ontological pursuits from the concept of socialism as the achieving of harmony between man and God.[13] Hess was a
precursor of Zionism. However, other people—no less important to
the history of socialism—had nothing in common with Jewry. On the
other hand, one can find the "Jewishness" of socialism in the character
of its main ideas. Marxism is the foundation of "scientific" socialism. It
has often been observed that it can be treated as a secularized version of
Jewish messianism, as the secular development of the biblical concept
that history moves toward the fulfillment of an ultimate goal, which is
earthly paradise. The messiah here is the proletariat. Besides, the fascination with the prospect of revolution could be seen as a reflection of
the motive in Jewish theology, in which the coming of the messianic
kingdom must be preceded by apocalyptic convulsions.

Generally speaking, socialism is, as Sergei Bulgakov put it, "a religion founded on atheism."[14] One can draw quite a detailed parallel between socialism and religion. Abraham Kaplan presents it as follows:
"The communist myth of human history begins with the Eden of what
they call primitive communism; later, man is then cursed with class
differences and the class struggle, he moves through the trials of a
feudal and bourgeois period, enters the purgatory of socialism, and is
redeemed at last in the heaven of communism. Production takes the
place of Providence, ownership is a sin, revolution is redemption."[15]
Of course, to identify communism with religion is not the point. The
most significant difference is surely Marxism's inclination to see the
subject in classes, not in individuals, and its vision of salvation in
group terms rather than individual terms. Marxism is an "idolatry of
the collective."

No matter how accurate the comparison between communism and
religion, it is clear that one can point to communism's similarity to
Christianity just as easily as one can point to its similarity to Judaism.
The comparison with Christianity is even closer. The apocalyptic vision of history, characteristic of revolutionaries (revolution is the goal;
afterward all will be well) haunted radical Christian sects more than
Jewish sects. Medieval chiliastic and millennial movements developed
among Christians. They dreamt of utopias that were, in a certain
sense, communist. Pre-Renaissance and Renaissance philosophical utopias were a continuation of that dream. Attempts to put them into
practice failed (Taborites, Anabaptists, and so forth). The history of

one important and specifically Jewish messianic movement was similar. The movement took root in the mid-seventeenth century, around the false messiah Shabbatai Zevi.[16] In principle, the Jewish tradition is realistic, and instead of planning utopias it establishes an ethic that is adapted to life. Still, the messianic tension inherent in this tradition propels it toward utopia.[17]

Although the concept of linear historical development is derived from the Bible—and, according to Gershom Scholem, the notion of linear progress has its roots in the sixteenth-century Lurianic Cabala,★[18] —it had already during the Enlightenment become a part of the general European heritage and even a predominant vision of history, to which Europe has since adhered (suffice it to mention Hegelianism). Also, communism is much less "spiritually Semitic" than Christianity. Communism has its forerunners both in Plato's *Republic* and in the states of ancient Egypt and China. Igor Szafarevich maintains that socialist aspirations—namely, the program of abolition of private property, of family, and of spiritual autonomy (emphasis on material well-being alone)—have been accompanying civilization since its dawn.[19] Even if Szafarevich exaggerates, the examples quoted here, in any case, demonstrate that we should not treat communism as analogous to Judaism and that we cannot possibly consider (in contrast to messianism, for example) communism as a product exclusively of the "Jewish spirit," even in a very narrow sense. Erich Fromm puts it better when he says: "Marxist and other forms of socialism are the heirs of prophetic Messianism, Christian Chiliastic sectarianism, thirteenth-century Thomism, Renaissance Utopianism, and eighteenth-century enlightenment."[20]

About Communism's Appeal for Jews

Communism and Jewish Tradition

There are "structural" similarities between Marxism and Judaism. I have already mentioned the messianic vision. In the opinion of some people, the messianic longings aroused but never satisfied by Shabbatai Zevi were handed down from generation to generation[21] and perhaps prompted independent-thinking Jews to join revolutionary movements.

Rationalism and moralism are also elements common to both communism and Judaism. Marxism subscribed to the rationalist current and, like the Left as a whole, was heir to the Enlightenment and its admiration for science. Respect for science is an important part of Jewish diaspora traditions, in which the Talmud (the Hebrew word for "science") played a significant role. This tradition of learning is rooted in faith, not in the sense of reason isolated from the sphere of revealed truths. Thus it could seem that secular communism at this point stands in opposition to this tradition. Contrary to the formulas of "scientific communism," Marxism springs from the affirmation of moral values that precede reasoning. And these are not sinister values, but those of the Ten Commandments, universalized and spread by Christianity. Leszek Kołakowski, in comprehensively discussing the ethical sources of Marxism, points out that communism was to put an end to the "dehumanization of man."[22] Economic and historical reflections were subordinated to criticism of a society where justice, freedom, and equality were conspicuously missing, where egoism prevailed, where war was always imminent, and where human rights and dignity were violated. Society was evil bečause it did not attain those supreme values, the thirst for which guided Marx and led many others to turn to Marxism. The Jewish heritage was conducive to such conversion because in Judaism moral principles always ranked high. Judaism is a "moral monotheism"; it emphasizes the rights of the person (created in the image of God), and the Jewish God demands justice and obedience to the law. Social justice is the fundamental motive of the Jewish tradition.

To speak about the moral motives of Marxists might seem questionable. It is difficult to believe that the moral values of the Old and New Testaments were affirmed by people who proved to be ready to participate in the establishment of a system of mass enslavement, which ruthlessly violated the rights of individuals and of nations. It seems that the secret of that horrible path from lofty ideals to crimes against them could be exposed as the path of hubris. In their pride the communists (and their fellow travelers) wanted to become masters of the highest values. They identified good and truth with themselves, with their ideology and their organization—hence the fanaticism with which they set about ensuring the "true" freedom they had invented to replace the freedom of that time, which their harsh logic or rather dialectics proved to be partial and therefore false, and thus illusory and nonexistent. The path to crime was opened when they accepted that the ends were justified by all means. Their aim was to create a paradise on earth, and they saw themselves as the messiah who would open the gates of heaven. This path of hubris is the path of degenerated messianism. This degeneration stemmed from the rejection of the transcendent values and from self-deification or the rebellion against God. Such rebellion leads to a fall just as it led to the fall of the rebellious angels. The path of hubris is Lucifer's path. Communist godlessness is not atheism, but antitheism and "theophobia."[23]

Hatred of God can go hand in hand with the religious impulses springing from the primitive layers of the soul. Outside observers noted a certain tension of a religious nature in communism, in ritual collective elation, on communists' hope for redemption as a result of the apocalypse, and a readiness for martyrdom for their beliefs. Similarly, former communists spoke about having been spellbound and about having lost their faith, about having experienced "the God that failed." As early as the mid-nineteenth century, Hawthorne wrote that "the saints of the revolution" became priests of their idol, the Revolution, and thought it fit to sacrifice what was most precious to them.[24]

The communist party acted like a religious sect and somewhat like a gang—it accepted no heterodoxy or any questioning of orders from superiors. This raises the question of whether such communist traits as doctrinarianism, sectarianism, and dogmatism had any equivalents in the Jewish tradition. Such traits were not uncommon in contemporary Jewish society and could from there penetrate into communist circles attracting at the same time—and certainly not repelling—new followers among Jews. Aleksander Wat draws an analogy between the communists and Hasidic communities in talking about the sect psychology prevalent among Polish communists before the war.[25] He even compares one of their leaders, Adolf Warski, to a tzaddik.* This is not a compliment, considering that in the nineteenth century the petrified cult of tzaddikim gradually gained at the expense of the initial religious dynamism of Hasidism. However, we should not take Wat too literally. The hierarchical structures of communist parties are very far from the tradition and practice of Judaism. They seem to be closer to the Catholic church and some monastic orders. No tzaddik could be dismissed by an order from the central authorities or removed as a result of factional strife. Sectarianism or dogmatism are no closer to Jews than to non-Jews. Judaism is not a dogmatic religion, although sometimes it verges on being one.

In communist practice, the traits that were presumably most Jewish in nature were the reverential attitude toward works by Marx and other "classics," belief in the profound truths contained in them, and the belief that one could arrive at these truths through patient exegesis. The holy books were seen as a treasure trove of hidden truth about the world. Marxists believed that so-called scientific, objective, iron "laws of social development" revealed the whole secret of history and of the world's goals. They adopted this particular gnostic or, if you prefer, exactly cabalistic stance in its Enlightenment-rationalized, materialistically vulgarized version.

Neal Kozodoy presents yet another similarity between socialist ideology and the Jewish tradition. He maintains that "rationalized charity" was the essence of the social doctrine of socialism and that "rationalized charity" was one of the oldest and deepest principles observed by Jewish communities.[26] It has to be added here, however, that unlike the radical version of socialism Judaism does not condemn the free market, economic enterprise, or trade. The Jewish tradition taken as a whole, not selectively, is inconsistent with many socialist theses. A contemporary American theologian, Seymour Siegel, claims that Judaism assumes the preservation of group differences and is cautious toward reform, because of respect for the limited character of society. Judaism emphasizes the value of the family, law, and tradition in general; it is suspicious of utopias, of far-reaching changes, and of excessive concentration of power; and it advocates equal justice for all (namely, it opposes preferential quotas).[27]

In the final analysis, the considerations above do not make a convincing case. This is so for yet one more reason—to search for similarities between communism and the Jewish tradition should not blind us to the links with non-Jewish tradition. Analogies to Judaism are counterpoised, for example, by opinions such as Berdyayev's, that communism suits the Russian soul perfectly, or Proudhon's, that Jacobinism was a disease "specific to the French temperament."[28] Also, thanks to Christianity, messianism was no longer the sole property of the Jews (recall the messianic vision of Polish romantics); rationalism is also characteristic of the Hellenic heritage; communist designs were also pursued by pagans and by Christian heretics (especially by the latter, as noted above); doctrinaire scholasticism existed within the church; exegesis and charity are also strong Christian traditions; and sectarianism is characteristic of Protestantism, as is the primacy of ethics (for example, categories of obligation and guilt). In reply to a malicious polemicist who looks for Jewish influence everywhere, one could cite Christianity's origin in Judaism, and Protestantism's particular origin in a return to the Bible, which was written by Jews. One could even refer to Calvin, who while criticizing the Anabaptists' belief in the possibility of searching for "the kingdom of Christ in a worldly environment" called that belief "a silly Jewish phantasy."[29] However, such arguments do not prove anything, save, perhaps, the "Judaization" of Europe—that is, the Jewish provenance of a number of ideas prevalent in European civilization. Yet this does not distinguish Jews from Christians, or vice versa. Thus we see that the attributes of communism mentioned to this point could make it decisively attractive to people brought up in the Jewish tradition, but these same attributes would have been equally attractive, for example, to Protestants (in Protestant countries, however, communism never gained much influence). Communism's attractiveness to Jews also had other sources, which primarily had to do with their social situation.

Consequences of the Social Position of Jews

One should not forget that the majority of Jews, like the majority of people in general, did not like communism. This was primarily because it is normal for anyone who has something to lose to reject extremism that could result in turmoil. Another reason was the religiousness and the attachment to tradition in the Jewish community, which was often stronger than in other communities. One can also trace some specific Jewish motives for a dislike of communism. For example, the deeply rooted sense of menace in the psyche of European Jews, a fear that any social disturbance (to say nothing of a revolution!) could end in a pogrom. Such consciousness does not dispose anyone favorably to revolutionary programs. This disinclination can be overcome only by a faith that this is "the last fight they will face," and it will end the menace. Finally, when a sense of menace becomes unendurable, the vision of a revolution could no longer be terrifying; instead it can become attractive as a last resort.

Jews had one more reason to feel hostile to communism, and this was purely symbolic—they were associated with the market economy, which the communists wanted to eliminate. Therefore, the petite bourgeoisie, the shopkeepers, craftsmen, brokers, and profiteers who made up a considerable part of East European Jewry, who were supposed to "wither away," had reasons to be afraid. On the other hand, the same fact could have just the opposite effect. It could lead those who felt ashamed of being Jewish shopkeepers, those who hated their roots, to favor communism. This shame felt by assimilated intellectuals came from their adoption of the landed gentry's dislike of the bourgeoisie, and also from the adoption of the landed gentry's patronizing attitude toward Jews.

Jews were molded by a history that had not spared them the experience of oppression and discrimination. The recollection of persecution was a central facet of the traditional teaching of Jewish history and part of religious ritual (Passover, Purim). Therefore it was only natural that an ideology that held the struggle for the emancipation of the oppressed as its main purpose could seem attractive to them. It was easy for Jews to sympathize with victims of discrimination and injustice because they could easily see themselves as victims. This also was true of rich and powerful Jews whose position was (seemingly) secure. It is the same way today. How else can one explain the active participation of American Jews in the civil rights movement? This too is one source of the persistence with which American Jews (meaning a clear majority of them) vote for Democrats and, in general, for politicians further to the Left. Even Jewish residents of the most affluent areas do, despite the rightist leanings of their neighbors.[30] Earlier, the policy of the Left (liberals in the United States) was in the interest of Jews who were usually poor and wanted equal rights and upward social mobility. Today their situation is different. Despite the growing influence of neo-conservatism, the following statement by Eugene B. Borowitz is quite typical, "Messianic liberalism has died, but practical and Jewish reasons keep me and many Jews from going conservative."[31]

If someone already had radical leanings, solidarity with the oppressed as an impulse led to Marxism or anarchism. Radicalism is a desire to break with the continuity of social institutions, and it is a result of disbelief in their reformability. It requires distance from the existing social system. It was easy for Jews to develop this distance because they had occupied the social position of pariah for a long time. The age-old sense of expulsion (*galut*), of not feeling comfortable, made it easier still. However, that sense was rather difficult to discern, particularly among those who chose communism, and thus antitraditional assimilation.

In the interwar period, radicalism grew. It was a time of change, agitation, and crises that increased political polarization and made extreme ideologies more attractive. Disillusionment with democracy was quite common, and the parliamentary system with all its weaknesses and inefficiency became the favorite whipping boy of even leading Polish politicians, like Piłsudski and Dmowski.* What choice did a Jew, even if totally assimilated but perceived by others as a Jew, who came to the conclusion that the future belonged either to communism or to fascism, have? The choice was almost unavoidable, considering that the extremism of the right was tightly linked with anti-Semitism. Only a few people of Jewish ancestry wanted to "redeem [themselves] by national work" and to submit themselves to the "judgment of Polish nationalism,"[32] as Stanisław Piasecki, the editor of *Prosto z mostu* [In plain words] and an active anti-Semite, did. Only the Jews who wanted a separate national life for their people, namely, Zionists, had freedom of choice. Zionists represented all possible shades of political opinion, including fascism. Extreme right positions were—as everywhere else—a mixture of social radicalism and the elevation of the national idea to an absolute. Liberals and socialists opposed these ideas, whereas communists held class divisions absolute. The communists were nihilistic concerning both the nation and the state, at least until they seized power.

The most striking convergence between communism and the position of Jews was the ease with which they were able to see things in a perspective wider than that of the state—their so-called cosmopolitan bent. Their supranational contacts are well known—examples include international bankers, like the Rothschilds, and international revolutionaries, like Rosa Luxemburg. They were products of the Diaspora, repeated migrations of entire groups, and of long-standing trade contacts. In modern Europe, only the international connections of the aristocracy could be compared to those of Jews. To be sure, national minorities were always there. However, Jews constituted the only significant minority without their own national territory—Palestine (Jerusalem) was only a historical homeland and a symbolic spiritual center. The Zionists wanted to transform it into an actual homeland, in order to put Jews on a par with other nationalities. The majority rejected this solution (although with time religious Zionists who affirmed the Jews' "chosen" nature also appeared), just as they rejected the other extreme—the negation of nations and states in general. However, in times of sharpening social unrest it could seem that eventually every Jew would have to choose one of the radical proposals for the solution of the Jewish question. In 1920 Winston Churchill described this situation in his article "Zionism and Bolshevism, the Struggle for the Soul of the Jewish People."[33]

Communism and "Non-Jewish" Jews

In modern times, mass societies composed of individual citizens emerged. At the same time, old communities declined, uprooting people and causing insecurity. Tradition alone no longer satisfied people who thirsted for new experiences. This applied not only to Jews, but also, for example, to migrants in the large cities. Emancipated Jews, discarding the ghetto perspective, were fully aware of the challenge posed by the new era. Among Jews, professionals were particularly aware of that challenge, and Jews assimilating themselves into majority culture were even more acutely aware of it. The professionals sought an antidote to demoralizing insecurity and found it in Marxism, anarchism, Zionism, or other variants of redemptive ideology aimed at creating a new world in which they could sink new roots. Isaac Singer, who was distrustful of all new "isms," described the universality of such attitudes among the Jewish intelligentsia: "All my colleagues tell me that I live in the past."[34] All!

"Refugees from the Jewish caste"[35] suffered from rootlessness even more than those who did not assimilate. This was the product of a double rejection. They were already rejected by "Jewish" Jews, but not yet accepted by non-Jewish society. This "yet" more often than not embraced their children as well. Remember that the national-radical press and the national-democratic press declared that Leśmian and Tuwim★ were not Polish poets. Assimilation turned out to be a source of long-term spiritual illness, identity crisis, and neurotic hypersensitivity. That lack of acceptance was not total (baptism in particular could overcome many barriers); nevertheless, it was sufficiently widespread that it could be encountered at any time. Only in a few circles could the assimilated feel completely secure. They felt safest among "the reds." After all, the communists rejected considerations such as origin or nationality. The only thing that mattered was loyalty to the cause and the party. It was even possible for Jews to assimilate through communism. In this way they got a chance to be active on a national and even a world scale and to discard their Jewish heritage with all its limitations. By an irony of fate, however, those who dedicated themselves to this activity were largely surrounded by people similar to themselves. In the eyes of their adversaries, that meant that they remained within Jewish circles. (I think that their fate makes up not only a part of the history of communism, but also a certain chapter in the history of the Jews.)

Surely there were more politically active, polonized Jews in the moderate parties (in the Polish Socialist Party and among the followers of Piłsudski), but Jews also belonged to some extent to other existing parties. It is clear that in the face of social rejection and difficulty in making a career, the prospect of revolution as a remedy for anti-Semitism could be appealing.

The dual rejection described above marginalized these people. This had a powerful influence on individual behavior and on the behavior of the entire group. Their marginalization made them see things in a new light; it sharpened their analysis of the established order to which they already belonged yet had not belonged since time immemorial. It was conducive to revolutionism not only in the area of politics, but in the area of thought as well (for example, Marx or Freud). The readiness with which they had broken with their former lives in an isolated community that had been tied together by tradition only intensified their iconoclastic potential. J. L. Talmon explained that "nothing that existed could any longer be treated as a matter of course."

The notions of uprootedness and of marginalization are general enough to apply to different groups and allow useful comparisons. Aleksander Hertz writes that in the United States, "communist influence on the black masses is insignificant. At the same time, however, the high percentage of black professionals in the communist party leadership is striking."[36] This same example shows that even if marginalization explains political radicalism it does not explain the remarkable number of Jewish innovators in science and the arts. To point to various aspects of Jewish tradition (respect for education, books, analysis, critical reflection, or the art of interpretation) helps, but nevertheless some people believe (in keeping with Jewish tradition) that one should speak rather of a special Jewish separateness (vocation, the notion of "the chosen people"). According to Gombrowicz, "Even an average Jew is born to be great just by being born a Jew." After all, because marginalization is inescapable, Jews are "sentenced to a desperate and suicidal struggle with their own form."[37] This resembles modern art; a

conscious attitude toward form, its continuous questioning and renewal, was the point of departure for the artistic avant-garde.

Rootlessness and identity crises have become quite common in the
last few decades. The popularity of existentialism is an indication of
this. With regard to the Jews, that sense of uprootedness could more
easily occur and be stronger. "Jews are just like anybody else, only
more so," the anonymous saying goes.

This digression on the artistic avant-garde leaves us to face the question of what led artists and intellectuals to communism. It was a kind
of nihilism. It began with the mockery of authority, the ridicule of
every taboo, and the exploration of extremes on the basis of the principle that "everything is allowed." They rejected not only God, but all
restrictions as well. They found themselves in a void, without foundations, as they had managed to undermine all of them. Yet they could
not bear that void, and the anarchy and emptiness that ensued. It was
then that they made the jump from the realm of freedom to that of
necessity, accepting rigor, authority, and total sense. The futurists
were a glaring example. In Italy they chose fascism; in Poland they
accepted the "scientific worldview"—Marxism. They were attracted to
extreme ideologies because they were furthest from the establishment,
and thus least discredited in their eyes. As Wat remembers it, their
malady consisted of a "thirst for totality."[38] From where did this thirst
come? Why could they not bear the pressure of nothingness? Presumably because in the depths of their souls they longed for traditional
values, on which as we said before, Marxism (and also fascism) rested.
Here the Jewish heritage of moralism and of the messianic vision could
have played a role. Gombrowicz wrote about Jewish intellectuals:
"Those dangerous destroyers and revolutionaries were usually as
good-natured as children; it was enough to scratch them a bit to uncover a dreamy disposition, full of practically mystical faith."[39]

It was much easier and more natural for intellectuals of Jewish origin
(and among them were, for example, the majority of Polish futurists)
to choose a leftist, rather than a rightist, totality. One could add to the
reasons already mentioned (first and foremost the anti-Semitism of the
extreme Right), the antireligious and anticlerical stance of the Left. On
the other hand, fascist movements (with the exception of Nazism,
which was a specific case) tended to cooperate with the church or
rather to use the Catholic tradition as an agent to cement national
unity. The Jews who abandoned Judaism usually rejected the Holy

Covenant concluded thousands of years ago, the source of Jewish Life, as nonsense. They often denied God and, even more, all religions and churches. In struggling against the obscurantism of the clergy, they easily fell into the "antireligious obscurantism of the Left."[40] This shows how difficult it is to achieve tolerance between worldviews, not to mention in other areas of life. For example, the disintegration of the Second International in the face of World War I demonstrates how difficult it was to maintain a universalistic position. In fighting nationalism, the communists slid into positions just as far from universalism. They were loyal to Soviet Russia as their second homeland and thus became even more alienated.

Were the children of assimilated Jews prone to be attracted to communism? After all, their roots were deeper. They went to the same schools, and they celebrated the same holidays as others. But their roots might not have been deep enough to protect them against the psychic harm of anti-Semitism, which pushed them to the margins. Besides, characteristics typical of Jewish heritage could have also been passed on to children through the family atmosphere (that is, a messianic philosophy of history, the primacy of ethics, respect for intellect, "dialectic" mentality, a sense of solidarity with the oppressed, the cosmopolitan perspective, and the sense of threat). This is most likely in the case of feelings of external threat. Anti-Semitism had a fundamental influence on the frame of mind of even very "un-Jewish" Jews because it also turned against them—and in some of its versions, against them in particular. Therefore, the children dared not stray too far from their parents. Communism was alluring to them too.

Did Jews Rule the Polish People's Republic?

The large number of Jews in Poland's power elite directly after the war should not surprise anyone, considering that the communists took power and that there were many Jewish communists and fellow travelers in prewar Poland. As a result of the war, the situation in Poland and the world at large drastically changed, especially for Jews. New forces emerged that attracted those who had escaped extermination to communism. In Poland, communism ceased to be a pure idea and became a reality of power. And something new emerged—Jews became attractive to communists and to Moscow.

War and Its Results

The situation of the Jews changed radically, first and foremost because nearly all of them within German reach had been exterminated. This is well known. But very little is known about the consequences of the Soviet occupation of eastern Poland from 1939 to 1941. From the beginning the Polish underground press reported that Jews were friendly toward the occupiers. This had a considerable impact on future attitudes. It is hard to tell how widespread this was, how truthful such descriptions were, and how much in them was a product of bias. Even today the period has not been adequately described by either witnesses or historians. In any case, these charges are supported by facts. The statement by Israeli historian Yehuda Bauer "about a positive or even very cordial attitude of the majority of the Jewish population toward the Soviet invader," before "they got bitterly disillusioned," bears this out.[41] Communist promises won over many Jews who remembered their inequality, difficulties in obtaining civil service jobs in prewar Poland, the boycott of Jewish shops, or the plans of members of parliament from the Camp of National Unity* [OZN] to limit the civil rights of Jews. Even those who were repulsed by communist ideology were impressed that the new authorities gave everyone who agreed to be loyal the opportunity to advance socially. Absolute loyalty, however, was a must. The leaders of the Bund, Wiktor Alter and Henryk Erlich, who protested against the Soviet occupation, were arrested and executed. The threat to Jews who tried to resist or only asserted their independence was not one iota less. The Soviet authorities did not give Jews any special consideration. Those Jews who were German citizens were handed over to Germany, and mass deportations to the east affected Jews just like non-Jews. Little wonder that at the beginning of the war there were Jews who thought it would be better to live under German rather than under Soviet occupation. They were not exceptional in spite of the Jews' reputation for loving the Soviets. Juliusz Górski writes that "in 1940, about 100,000 Jews, who had arrived in Lwów in flight from German occupation, demanded from a relevant German commission the right to return to the occupied zone."[42] The fate of those willing to return was usually a locked railway car taking them, for example, to Kazakhstan, which they had boarded convinced that in accordance with their wishes they were heading for Warsaw or Kraków.

Relations between the Jews and the Bolsheviks were thus far from idyllic, with Jews present on all sides—among those executed at Katyń,* among the soldiers of Anders's Army,* and among the activists of the Union of Polish Patriots* [ZPP], which was formed in 1943 under the Kremlin's protection. The point is that after the war only the Jews in the ZPP were conspicuous because it created the new power elite in Poland.

In a twist of fate, Soviet deportations turned out to give Jews the best chance of survival. After the war there were more Jews repatriated from the east than Jews who somehow managed to survive in Poland. Although their experiences differed, the Holocaust hovered over them in the same way. With each step they confronted graves and the sharp absence of Jewish life. This caused the majority of them to emigrate to the West and to Israel (soon to be established with the blessing of the United States, the USSR, and the United Nations). There was, however, one other reason that they left—a sense of insecurity. As studies by Irena Nowakowska reveal, the reason for leaving most frequently mentioned, beside the impossibility of living "in a graveyard," was precisely the threat of anti-Semitism.[43]

At the end of and for some time after the war, extreme rightist groups sometimes physically threatened Jews and Poles of Jewish origin. One hero of one of Czesław Miłosz's novels recorded this dangerous fact of Jewish life: the National Armed Forces* [NSZ] professed sublime ideas; "In practice, however, the operations of their squads boiled down to purging the country of Jews and communists, which to them, as you know, were the same."[44] Needless to say, after the war Jews were not the only victims of assault and robbery, but Jews were treated particularly cruelly—as if people "got used to Jews being killed."[45] Even more common and widespread was the sense of threat resulting from a lack of acceptance, from the lack of a place for Jews in Poland. Henryk Grynberg captures in literary form the situation of Jews from small towns who managed to survive. Upon their return, they saw surprise in the eyes of their neighbors, because after all, they should have died. Not that anyone wished them death, but that was the law of Nazi rule. To return was a faux pas, because everybody had already come to terms with—and, what is more, taken advantage of—their death, because after the Jews departed "so much space in the village had opened up."[46] Such Jews easily fell into the arms of the communists because they needed the support of an authority that would defend them.

In towns the situation was different. In addition to all the threats of the time there was the threat of anti-Semitism symbolized by the "Kielce pogrom."* According to Stefan Otwinowski, despite all the spontaneous solidarity with and campaigns to help Jews, the occupation did not end Polish anti-Semitism, and in certain areas it brought "even a rise in hatred and a program based on prejudice."[47] The end of the war only intensified the proclivity toward anti-Semitism as a surrogate for anti-Sovietism. The struggle against the Soviets was obviously hopeless, but one against Jews, perhaps not so hopeless. Under the influence of the Kielce pogrom, Julian Przyboś wrote passionately that "in Poland, among all the countries of Europe still only in Poland, the attitude toward the Jewish citizen is a test of humanity."[48] To Jews and to the world at large, the Kielce pogrom became a symbol of Polish anti-Semitism. The stereotype of Polish anti-Semitism contains an unjust generalization. However, this stereotype was a fundamental determinant of Jewish self-consciousness in occupied Poland and directly afterward. During the occupation, Jews in hiding were menaced on all sides—from all sides, because even if there was only one informer in the village, he could prey on a Jew at any time. Cities were even more dangerous, because there every stranger inspired fear, even if in reality only one stranger in a thousand was a blackmailer. In my opinion the memory of that constant wartime menace and of the pressure of the postwar period was enough to make Jewish emigrants sustain that unfair stereotype of Poles.

The situation described above affected even fully assimilated intellectuals of Jewish origin who were not subject to the drama of the "Jewish" Jews—namely, the impossibility of returning to their prewar collective existence. Jews attached to the prewar Jewish community found there was practically no choice between the new order and the desire to rebuild prewar Jewish life. The only choice they had was between the new order and emigration. The hero of Miłosz's book explains, "They can go on living only as non-Jews. Those who remain Jews will emigrate."[49] In Poland (although not only), Jews who felt drawn to the new regime or who were so assimilated that they did not miss prewar Jewish life too much stayed. The latter were usually members of the intelligentsia.

Thus the majority of the Jews who found themselves in Poland just after the war emigrated.[50] Of the several tens of thousands who remained, the majority had the opportunity to secure a good position in life. Of course, the prewar communists, precisely the members who had not joined the party for career reasons, were the first to make careers. Before the war, none of them could have seriously considered having power, except during the short period of the war against the Bolsheviks. Those "old" communists—irrespective obviously of their origin—had participated in a mystic phenomenon, the real mystique of martyrdom. I mean here the fact that when they were in exile in the USSR, as the majority of them were, they had witnessed the pervasive terror and often had experienced it themselves simply because they belonged to the Communist Party of Poland* [KPP], which had been dissolved and whose leaders had been put to death. Undeterred, they arrived in Poland at the side of the Red Army in order to build socialism. In their fanaticism they believed that civilized Poland could avoid what they called Soviet degeneration. Their prescription for putting out the fire was faithfulness to Stalin and his doctrines—that is, pouring gasoline on the fire.

What Did the Jews Want?

The majority of the Jews who remained in Poland after the war accepted "the building of socialism," whereas the majority of non-Jews did not. No matter how big the disproportion between the two groups was, it was primarily a result of a peculiarity of the Jewish community. There were no anticommunists; they had simply left the country.

Jewish organizations were loyal to the new authorities. This was partly out of the traditional loyalty of Jewish leaders to the powers that be, and partly from the emphasis that Jewish organizations placed on two kinds of activities, social relief and sponsoring emigration, first and foremost, to Palestine. For a time the communist authorities helped the Jews emigrate, just like the governments of the 1930s.

Jews who participated in ruling the country were usually (more or less) assimilated. They acted as individuals, not as a group, and as communists, not as Jews. All the same, their Jewishness was not an insignificant factor. The average Jew was more open to the influence of the new regime and less open to certain repulsive aspects of the regime.

The official communist policy of firm opposition to anti-Semitism appealed to Jews who felt threatened by it. It seems that in the early postwar years, Jews saw the so-called reactionary camp as the source of anti-Semitism. Communist propaganda tried hard to persuade the public that the reactionaries included all those who opposed the domination of the Polish Workers' Party* [PPR]. Such arguments seemed to carry weight with many Jews, especially since the political polarization of society undermined the importance of any differentiation other than the basic division between the procommunist and anticommunist camps. Besides, it seemed that profound social change would soon lead to the disappearance of anti-Semitism. This would mean the disappearance of Jewish distinctness as well, and as such only appealed unambiguously to those who were either already assimilated or ready to assimilate. Such Jews were relatively numerous, and many of them did not even tell their children about their ancestry. Attempts to conceal one's Jewish origin, common before the war, had a much better chance of success after the war. But in many cases these attempts brought disappointment and disillusionment. In 1956 and 1968 there were new waves of emigration. Sooner or later nearly all Jews for whom the cultivation and development of Judaism and Jewish culture were important emigrated. In Poland, where Jewish life had flourished for centuries, it ebbed even lower than in other Eastern European countries.

The widespread belief that the war was evidence of the bankruptcy of civilization based on parliamentary democracy, and that the old world would inevitably be replaced by the new one, was an important factor underlying support for systemic change. Comparisons with the decline of the Roman Empire became popular. Belief in a ruthless logic of history became for some an antidote to the shock of the war. For those who had gone through the horrible experience of the war, especially Jews, it was easier to identify with that new beginning and to abandon tradition. As for intellectuals of Jewish origin, this was perhaps easier because their way had already been paved. They themselves, or their parents, or maybe even grandparents, had already made a radical break with tradition.

The new authorities attracted leftist circles with their social reform program, plans to bring culture to the masses, a policy of mass social mobility, and a universal and anti-nationalist orientation. These advocates of progress were in for bitter disappointment. The practical implementation of reforms became sovietization, and the propaganda of universalism, became Russification. In Poles, this aroused both national and religious resistance. It seems that among Jews resistance was somewhat weaker. Assimilated Jews were less sensitive than Poles to the loss of national sovereignty and the threat to Polish national traditions. That was because they simply had not been brought up in the atmosphere of adulation for independence in which the average Pole was raised (although many assimilated and a considerable number of Polish Jews were raised in such an atmosphere).

Jewish religious life never revived in Poland to any great extent. The war turned Jews into atheists (not least through selection). Fifty-six percent of the Jews registered with the Central Committee of Jews in Poland in a poll described themselves as nonbelievers.[51] This was why the antireligious stand of the government evoked less repugnance among Jews than among Polish Christians, and why its policy of secularization did not provoke as much resistance from Jews as from the majority of Poles (but not all of them). It should be remembered that it was still many years before the Second Vatican Council, and the image of a rich church linked to the prewar authorities had not yet faded from people's memories. Many progressives only later understood that the postwar struggle against the church was in fact a struggle against freedom of conscience and for the totalization of life.[52] Meanwhile, even irreligious Jews had other reasons to distrust the Church. Judaism had been attacked from the pulpit for centuries. This had been one of the causes of anti-Semitism, even though members of the church hierarchy had often taken up the cause of the Jews when ordinary Christians had wanted to settle accounts with those whom they blamed for the Crucifixion.

Although there were both Jews and non-Jews among the communist activists, the communist bureaucracy as a whole acted in ways that could be seen as "Jewish." An example of this was the cult of dialectical materialism. Janusz Szpotański correctly observes that "at that time, only melamdim★ could bask in the glory of the Party."[53] Communists sought enlightenment in the classics of Marxism. They used to upstage each other in quoting from the prophets of communism and from the greatest masters of the doctrine. In this way the honored Talmudic method, which was used to justify every one of the authorities' policies and the all-encompassing terror, sank to the depths of degeneration.

The sensitive or outright oversensitive stand on anti-Semitism was another "Jewish" attribute of the top authorities. Michnik writes, "In postwar Poland, anti-Semitism was applied as a sort of a test of honor for everyone. . . . More often than not, one's position regarding anti-Semitism replaced one's attitude toward everything else."[54] For example, that "everything else" could be the Home Army★ [AK]. Jerzy Andrzejewski wrote in 1947 that one could not allow posters that read "Glory to the heroic defenders of the ghetto" and "Shame on the fascist lackeys from the AK" to be pasted next to each other.[55] From the point of view of Polish-Jewish relations, it was tragic that the monument to the heroes of the ghetto was unveiled in Warsaw in 1948 during a campaign of slander against the Polish underground and intensified persecution of AK soldiers by the police and courts. Even an outside observer, to say nothing of someone involved, had to treat the turn of events as a sign of a pro-Jewish and at the same time anti-Polish attitude, even if one agreed that the ghetto fighters deserved a monument.

It is quite possible that the authorities' ostentatious pro-Jewish sympathies were intended for the West, that they were meant to impress Jewish circles, as well as the public at large, who still remembered the Nazi extermination campaign. In the opinion of some researchers the communist authorities treated anti-Semitism instrumentally, which was nearly criminal. Analysis by the Polish Independence Compact★ [PPN] shows that "the NKVD★ and the UB★ organized the so-called Kielce pogrom, a mass murder of Jews, to show the world that Poles were a nation of racists incapable of self-government."[56] The propaganda of the PPR and its allies was quick to accuse their political opponents of organizing the pogrom. In this way they somehow managed to divert attention from the falsified results of the referendum★ held only four days earlier. All the same, no matter how important the element of provocation was, the breeding ground for provocation was there. Everything began with a rumor that Jews had killed a Christian child to make matzoh.

Regardless of how large and noticeable Jewish participation in the power elite was, their role should not be demonized. First and foremost, every institution abounded with non-Jews who held positions as influential as or more influential than those of Jews. Furthermore, Poland's fate had been essentially determined by the international balance of power. The agreements reached at Teheran and Yalta meant that the West accepted the Soviet sphere of influence and, in fact, as it would soon turn out, the "Stalinization" of all the "people's democracies." Poland succumbed to Stalinism too, although here its intensity was perhaps somewhat less because of specifically Polish conditions (the church). It is true that individuals of Jewish origin played an important role in that process. The same cannot be said, however, about the Jewish community or Jewish organizations. The latter did not fare better than any other institution that was not an agency of the party-state authorities. The Central Committee of Jews in Poland, which had included the majority of Jewish secular activists and had from the very beginning declared its loyalty to the new regime, was disbanded at the end of the 1940s. Also at that time, all Jewish parties, private schools, and so forth, were dissolved. Since then all Jewish institutions have been entirely dependent on the communists.

Whatever the reasons for why communism attracted Jews, each individual is morally responsible for his or her choice. Some of them certainly should be brought before a court on an equal footing, needless to say, with the non-Jews guilty of similar crimes. One can speak, however, only about the guilt and responsibility of individuals, not of Jews as a group.

Why Jews Were Attractive for the Authorities

The symbol of the role Jews played in the first decade of the Polish People's Republic in the public's consciousness is the Jewish secret policeman. Jews or people of Jewish origin did indeed occupy a large number of managerial positions in Bierut's* Ministry of Public Security [MBP]. This fact, little known in the West and only reluctantly recalled by Jews in Poland, cannot be overlooked. Westerners as well as Jews in Poland prefer to speak about Stalin's anti-Semitism (the "Doctors' Plot,"* and so forth). The terror apparatus in Poland worked just as it did in other communist countries in Europe and beyond. It is necessary to explain why Jews or Poles of Jewish origin worked there, rather than try to prove that Jews organized the horrific rule of terror. The simplest explanation is that in a sensitive part of the system, in the political police, trustworthy people were needed and thus the preference was for prewar communists, among whom were many Jews and people of Jewish origin. However, that was not all. Since there were not so many old and trusted comrades, everyone from whom the authorities could expect 100 percent loyalty was good enough. This could include someone who was alone in the world, without the support of family or neighbors, or someone attracted by socialism and ready to make the party his circle of reference. Many Jews, but by no means Jews alone, satisfied such requirements. Władysław Bartoszewski once spoke about a group of young repatriates from France who immediately upon their arrival in Poland had been incorporated into the UB. They were as isolated as the Jewish repatriates, and it was easy to make them dependent on the regime.

Jews also had a specific reason to be loyal to the authorities—their fear of anti-Semitism. In his novel, Grynberg writes about two simple small-town Jews who were secretly given party cards without asking for them. They dared not refuse, even more so because the argument made by the party secretary rang true: "Remember that if someone threatens you no one will come to your defense—only us, our authorities and our Party!" The year was 1945 and in the houses of the small-town Jews who had managed to survive and return home were quartered Soviet officers who, according to the narrator, "felt much better in Jewish homes, and we too, although cramped for room, felt better with them than alone."[57] At that time Jews had a reason for fear. Their behavior, nevertheless, only confirmed the convictions of anti-Semites in organized groups that their struggle against Jews was just and convinced an unknown number of others. This, in turn, made Jews even more dependent on the communists because of expectations of loyalty. A similar sort of tragic feedback mechanism worked on both educated and uneducated Jews who were given jobs in the power apparatus.

Let us then once again name all the reasons Jews and Poles of Jewish origin were attractive to the communists: loneliness, lack of community support, fewer misgivings about the new regime because of fewer contact with people ill-disposed toward the new regime (it has to be remembered that the Jews who were ill-disposed toward communism had usually emigrated), and, as a rule, less contact with the church and the tradition of the struggle for independence.

Thus I repeat that there was no Jewish conspiracy after the war. The situation, however, seemed to have been that the Jews who were attracted by the prospect of "newness" were made welcome. They did not hesitate to take advantage of their connections, a normal thing for people looking for work. Because of the large number of Jewish officials or, rather, communists of Jewish origin, Jews received swift promotions.

The leadership did take the large Jewish membership, particularly among activists, into account. It was probably no coincidence that the leading positions were given to non-Jews, whereas the highest position reserved for Jews was that of deputy. An anecdote that circulated among old communists was indicative of another, more significant side of the problem. According to that story, the profiles of "old" comrades who reported after the war were examined by Zofia Gomułka*, who then decided whether the poor fellow could be given a job "among the people," changing his name if need be, or whether he was to stay in the background in a position not requiring contacts with the wider public. This is another reason why there were relatively more Jews in the "discreet" MBP than in other ministries. This explanation seems more convincing to me than another theory often advanced, that Jews were sent to the terror apparatus on purpose because there was a conscious policy of "divide and conquer" in which the dirtiest jobs were reserved for a minority group who could become a scapegoat for a terrorized population if anything went wrong. Who, however, was to manipulate people in this way? Gomułka* and his wife, Bierut, Berman,* or Kliszko*? Or was it to be Soviet advisers? Yet how could the Soviets choose without consulting the Poles? This explanation seems to be another conspiracy theory, this time of an anti-Jewish conspiracy.

It is worth remembering that the security apparatus did not spare Jews and was not free of its own brand of anti-Semitism. Aniela Steinsbergowa maintains that "prisoners of Jewish origin were, because of their Jewishness, treated even worse than gentiles, suffering more insults and humiliation."[58] The situation in Russia was similar to that in Poland. Wat mentions that "a Jewish 'enemy of the people' was treated even worse than a non-Jew, even though there were a lot of Jews in the Cheka.*"[59] The seed of this attitude toward all those who did not want to obey the new regime can probably be traced to communist orthodoxy. Singer says that his resistance to revolutionary ideologies prompted his colleagues to threaten that he would be "severely punished once they came to power."[60] They thought it natural for the locomotive of history to crush the recalcitrant. Sometimes, in the case of Jewish officials, a certain psychological mechanism could also have been at work. At heart they might have felt like traitors to their heritage and therefore felt even greater hatred toward those who remained faithful to the Jewish tradition. Also, by treating Jews worse than others they could prevent charges of partiality.

The review above indicates that in postwar Poland new reasons for the rise in anti-Semitism existed. Alongside the traditional arguments (for example, the belief that if it was not for Jews, Poland would be thriving), this created a situation that helped those who orchestrated the memorable anti-Jewish campaign of 1968. Those new reasons for antipathy toward Jews are encapsulated in the comments a rabbi made to one of the torturers interrogating him in the Office of Security: "Because of people like you, there will be pogroms in Poland."[61]

It goes without saying that nothing can justify pogroms. Nevertheless, we should remember that Polish-Jewish relations were affected by such factors as Jewish relations with the Bolsheviks and then with the Soviet army; the presence of the Jews in the power elite and in the terror apparatus; the "rule of melamdim"; the uneven assessments of the Warsaw Ghetto and the Warsaw Uprisings; the processes of atheization and Russification (associated with Jews who had fewer misgivings about such campaigns); and last but not least, the struggle against the rightist-nationalist deviation (in which Jews also played a part). Later, the activities of revisionists within the party would also become a question. These last two issues require a more thorough discussion.

Jewish Communists and Party Factions

A battle against "rightist-nationalist deviation" was waged in the party beginning in 1948, and soon thereafter Gomułka and his associates were toppled from power. Gomułka's refusal to condemn Tito was the direct reason for his removal. To some extent the intraparty conflict of the time was fought between the members of the wartime PPR and the communists who had come from Russia, usually in the ranks of the First Polish Army.* (This division is not, of course, hard and fast as "internationalists" like Bierut, Jóźwiak,* or Mijal* spent the war in Poland.) In any case, the majority of communist activists of Jewish descent had come from Russia. Furthermore, it was rather difficult to accuse Jews of "rightist-nationalist" deviations. There was, therefore, a certain correlation between ancestry and being accused.

In every communist party there was a struggle with an internal enemy. However, it was different in every party. Those condemned in the Slansky trial in Czechoslovakia (a majority were Jews) were charged with Zionism. Thus not all the Stalinist purges were persecutions of "national" communists by the "international" ones, including Jews. After all, the division into factions is quite imprecise. One should not be too eager to project onto the past the divisions of 1968.[62]

The last years of Bierut's rule were the time of the thaw* and growing revisionism within the party. The party conservatives of the so-
called Natolin group glared at the partisans of the "Polish October."*
The Natolin group were doing their best to curb the reforms, so that
control did not slip from their hands and, God forbid, so that Poland
did not adopt an anti-Soviet line. Among activists in the Polish United
Workers' Party* [PZPR] there seemed to be a correlation between
Jewish descent and a proclivity toward revisionism.* At least this was
the case in the party's upper circles. Witold Jedlicki captured this in the
title of his pamphlet *Żydy i chamy** [Kikes and boors].[63] Why did the
communists of Jewish descent so often switch from orthodox Stalinism to enthusiastic support for liberalization and to resistance to Moscow? Why were there relatively few Jews among the proponents of a
continued hard line? Although the answers given below seem worthy
of quoting, none of them seems to be fully satisfactory.

The argument most often put forward maintains that a division
within the party ran "between the intellectual and plebeian elements,
and that the party intelligentsia was largely represented by Jews,
which, after all, only continued the disposition of forces in the prewar
KPP."[64] As intellectuals are naturally prone to liberalism, the softer line
suited them better. This explanation is correct, but only in part. It does
not explain either the zeal with which some of them pursued de-Staln-
ization, or why only a few years earlier the same people had supported
the hardest Stalinist line. The "natural liberalism" of intellectuals manifested itself earlier in a nuanced fashion—for example, in the conviction that a prewar philosophy professor should not go to jail but
should be allowed to translate philosophical works (which actually
happened in several cases). Following Lenin and Stalin (and later the
Western followers of Mao), communist intellectuals as a rule, however, suppressed their liberal sympathies and were fascinated by the
ruthlessness and totality of the revolution. Wat recollected, "Coarseness appealed to us." So did cruelty and blood, "which had purifying
power."[65] This fascination changed only after the death of Stalin.

Jedlicki explains the liberal faction's enthusiasm in a different fashion. He presents it as a conscious maneuver of party activists who,
aware of the rising wave of change, wanted to place themselves at the
wave's head, and thus hold on to their own and the party's power.[66] To
this it is possible to add that Jewish communists flowed with the tide
in pursuit of their interests, afraid to act otherwise or for other motives. Although this reasoning can explain the change in their position

and their fervor to expose "errors and deviations," it certainly does not completely explain the evolution of many activists later during the Polish October of 1956. Their revisionism led many Jews into conflict with Gomułka and then to open opposition to the regime, which provoked [anti-Jewish] harassment from the authorities. For revisionists, ideology was not an instrument but the proper arena of struggle with others and with themselves.

I can furnish two other explanations for why revisionism appealed to so many party-affiliated Jews. One explanation bears on the Jewish question directly. At the end of his rule, Stalin began to show his vehement anti-Semitism, which found adherents in both the Russian bureaucracy and others. That must have come as a cold shower to many Jews who had consciously or unconsciously seen communism—and not just its ideal, but existing Soviet communism—as their defense against anti-Semitism and a guarantee of its disappearance. This disillusionment could have led Jews to question the regime and to desire to correct it by returning to its sources. Surely this led down the road to revisionism, but Jews, just like gentiles, were most affected by the general ferment, by the successive changes in Moscow, by "Khrushchev's revelations," and last but not least, by the events in Poznań* and by the invasion of Hungary.

I also think there is another explanation at the heart of the question. To be sure, it applies to all communist intellectuals, irrespective of their descent, but this one, like the hypothesis on the "natural liberalism" of intellectuals, assumes that a relatively large number of Jewish party activists came to communism intellectually.

Understanding communism in an intellectual, idealistic (and perhaps religious) manner meant a life in the world of abstractions, among beloved myths, in the atmosphere of a doctrine through which one pondered reality. But when reality forced its way into that world of words and ideas, it shook it and its inhabitants profoundly. They realized they had traveled a road that began with an ideal and led to crimes. They did not necessarily see it as hubris, but they felt so tormented inside that in order to save their sense of the world they set out to patch up the enfeebled doctrine. Years later, some of them rejected all forms of communism when they became convinced of the weaknesses of communism's foundations. Meanwhile, they sought a basis for the renewal of the doctrine in those foundations and fought fiercely against comrades who turned out to be fully impervious to reality and who, by their refusal to revise the Stalinist dogmas, became one of the groups opposed to the thaw. Another, probably much larger, group consisted of party activists who came to communism in a more "plebeian" fashion—that is, in a narrower but first and foremost more realistic fashion; they were not so much drawn to communism by their vision of the classless paradise as driven to it by their class grievances and resentments. For them, the drama played out not so much in the ideological arena as in the realm of strength and power. It was clear to them that their rule and privileges depended on the continuation of that status quo which the Soviet Union guaranteed. They trusted society less than the revisionists, but knew it better. The revisionists, for their part, knowing society less well and being idealists, believed in the purity of the party and in popular support for socialism and for their faction, which, in party terminology, was engaged in party conflict

The opposition sketched out between idealistic and pragmatic communists allows one to see the evolution of revisionists as a drama of "the captive mind." It explains both the violence of their transformation and the anti-Stalinist fury of the ex-Stalinists, their readiness to confront the authorities, and finally their painful withdrawal from the party. But why had their minds desired captivity earlier? Why had they put themselves in the bonds that they later broke with such a strain?

May 1980

Epilogue 1983

1. After three years, the only part of my original text requiring any additions is the introduction. One might expect that a national revival involving millions of people would consign the issue of "Jews and communism" to the appropriate sphere of historical research, that it would cease to be a burning contemporary issue. It has turned out once again, however, that in Poland the events of the past forty or even one hundred years are still a live issue, something that affects contemporary attitudes and disputes. It is a shame that the situation today delayed the publication of my essay to, as it has turned out, quite another epoch. But I must state that, in the interval, I doubted

whether painstaking investigation of all Jewish motives for participation in communism, and for an objective and detailed analysis of the role of Jews in that regime, would ever strike home. Such a primitive picture still continues to hold sway, so that it is possible to fear that the whole complex truth about Jews and communism in all its subtleties will be lost on quite a large group of the population, who will grasp only the handful of facts that reinforces their prejudice. This prejudice persists despite new evidence. After all, an otherwise respectable, well-known Solidarity activist did not hesitate to lay the blame for the government's machinations on Jews who allegedly sat in the government. [This is a reference to a speech made by Marian Jurczyk, the leader of Solidarity in Szczecin, in Trzebiatów in late autumn 1981.] He said this several years after the top party and government apparatus had been almost totally purged of Jews, or rather, Poles of Jewish descent! On the contrary, his statement was not representative of Solidarity as a whole. For instance, Solidarity in Kielce made a declaration worth mentioning on the thirty-fifth anniversary of the Kielce pogrom. This declaration broke the conspiracy of silence. The underground press had done this even earlier. *Biuletyn Dolnośląski** [Lower Silesian bulletin], edited by a future member of Solidarity's National Commission, had already published materials on the pogrom (no. 11 [1980]). Krystyna Kersten presented an exacting description of the pogrom and its consequences in an article published in *Tygodnik Solidarność* (4 December 1981).

The freedom of speech and assembly of the Solidarity period was bound to bring diverse results. The anti-Semitism of the Grunwald Patriotic Association outdid Filipski. Those Polish nationalist communists, following the Soviet lead, rehashed slogans from 1968 (and earlier) blaming the Jews for the Stalinist terror and other deviations from socialism. To all those who treat such slogans seriously, one should cite the remark Leopold Unger made in an interesting article about the 1968 emigration (*Kultura* 7/8 [1979]): "Were there too many Jews? All the same, once the PZPR rid itself of Jews, it did not become any more popular or authentic! Gierek's rule ended in the total defeat of the party and its ideology."

For a long time Grunwald was led by Zdzisław Ciesiołkiewicz, the author of the maniacal book, *Inwazja upiorów* [Invasion of the ghosts], which fancifully applies the theory of a Jewish conspiracy to the history of the Polish People's Republic (and not to it alone; the Prague Spring is described as "counterrevolution with a Zionist face"). That

activist's particular achievement was an extraordinary interview he
gave to a Swedish newspaper in which he argued that all of Poland's
economic problems had been caused by Jews in the Polish government who ran up an excessive debt to Western Jews in order to ruin
Poland.

This is worth mentioning for two reasons. First, Grunwald has close
links with some sections of the party apparatus as well as with the
police and the army. Its activities were not suspended during martial
law, although they were toned down. Second, in the atmosphere of
freedom in 1981 Grunwald did not seem serious, and it was obvious
that it represented small numbers of hard-line extremists. That element, however, although small on a national scale, was quite important within the party. The majority of the press, not only that related
to Solidarity, simply made fun of Grunwald. This is optimistic, but
not the whole story. Anti-Semitism proved to be marginal within Solidarity, but it was not completely absent. In the second half of 1981 the
so-called true Poles* used a certain version of the "Jewish-communist"
myth in internal struggles with activists connected with the Workers'
Defense Committee* [KOR], the Solidarity Agency,* and so forth.
Those charges were made anonymously in a poster campaign that attacked such activists as Karol Modzelewski* or Bronisław Geremek*
for Stalinist activity and for their alleged or real Jewish origin. It is
painful to write that at a meeting of Solidarity's Mazowsze* branch a
charge was made that the logo of Solidarity's congress suggested the
Star of David. Only someone with a sick imagination could level such
a charge. Maybe after the experience of 13 December 1981 Poles will at
long last become wiser!

But will they? Honestly speaking, I am not so sure whether, in the
eyes of some people, the notoriety of Urban* will not overshadow all
the others and that people will come to the conclusion, contrary to
reality, that the Military Council for National Salvation* [WRON] is
so dreadful because Jews are predominant in it. This, of course, will
not shake the security police from the conviction that underground
Solidarity is a Jewish creation. Maybe I will even find a colleague more
patient than I who will begin to research "Jews and the New Trade
Unions." I must therefore state from the outset that this is paranoia!
Jewish factors are completely irrelevant here.

2. In recent weeks we have seen the authorities pursue a peculiar policy. In order to improve its reputation in the West, the junta has been

playing the role of great protector of the Jews. It has been boasting of its concern, for example, for the restoration of a synagogue in Warsaw. When, however, after many years of repair, the synagogue is finally restored, the hard currency contributions that were and continue to be made will probably exceed the cost of the project. There would be nothing wrong with this, if not for the hypocrisy and untruthfulness.

A solemn and sorrowful anniversary is approaching: the fortieth anniversary of the Warsaw Ghetto Uprising. This will be an occasion to pay homage to the six million Jews murdered by the Nazis. However, the anniversary "campaign" in the press is offensive because of its ostentatious character and the absence in the mass media of any mention of other anniversaries and matters. Freedom (sham freedom, when all is said and done) for Jews only is a parody of freedom.

Marek Edelman★ has been fighting a lone struggle against this hypocrisy. He refused to take part in the official commemoration, although as one of the leaders of the Ghetto Uprising he was the best person to do this. Edelman has become a symbol—he was a well-known Solidarity activist in Łódź and a delegate to Solidarity's national congress.

3. In recent years several texts on the same subject as my essay have come out. One such publication is Stanisław Jerzmanowski's account of the early postwar years (*Zeszyty Literackie* 54 [1980]). It is a story of a young AK-man whom fate—or rather the Soviet policy of deporting deep into Russia AK-soldiers who reported to the People's Army—placed in a partisan unit where he fought the new occupation and, against his will, found himself fighting shoulder to shoulder with comrades who were murdering Jews. Łukasz Socha★ described the wider context of the events of this time in an article based on original sources (*Krytyka*, no. 13/14 [1983]), which show that the UB and the People's Militia★ [MO] had infiltrated underground groups and bands of robbers. In his fascinating lecture on the Jewish question, read to a meeting at Warsaw University to commemorate the anniversary of the March 1968 events, Jan Józef Lipski mentioned the physical danger to which Jews who came out into the open had been exposed. When discussing the large number of Jews within the UB, Lipski compared it to the large presence of Poles in the Cheka after the October revolution. Its causes were similar: in Russia, Poles were a national minority who did not have their own land and who were discriminated against.

In opposition to attempts to blame the Jewish people for the role of Jews in the UB, Lipski argued that the torturers of the UB (or Cheka) had stood outside the bounds of their own people (Dusza or Kaskiewicz, outside the Polish people; Fejgin or Różański, outside the Jewish people).

4. An interesting book by Artur Sandauer, *O sytuacji pisarza polskiego pochodzenia żydowskiego w XX wieku* [The situation of the Polish writers of Jewish ancestry in the twentieth century] (Warsaw, 1982) is full of precise analyses of the situation of the Jewish-Polish intellectuals in the interwar period. Commenting on particular writers he says Leśmian "had a Polish subconsciousness"; that Tuwim's strength was his autodemonization, which stemmed from his convictions on Jewish uniqueness, which was based on his own demonological experience; and that Szenwald* and Peiper* longed to be connected with the people.

However, his tendentiousness in the description of the postwar situation is striking. Clearly Sandauer becomes more critical of writers the closer they are to the democratic opposition. It seems that the only reason Sandauer continues to criticize Andrzejewski (although Andrzejewski, being a gentile, should not be discussed in the book at all) as he did in an earlier book is that Andrzejewski was a member of KOR. Why does he praise Świrszczyńska* and Szymborska* for their works on the Holocaust and not mention Ficowski's* poem "Letter to Marc Chagall" or his *Odczytanie popiołów* [Interpretation of the ashes] collection? It seems to me that the only reason for Sandauer's omission was the poet's membership in KOR and the publication of the collection by NOW-a.* To find fault with Miłosz for an apt description of poetry lovers within the ranks of the UB is a pinprick. This nitpicking reaches a crescendo in his chapter on Julian Stryjkowski,* a longtime opponent of the regime. It is senseless to charge Stryjkowski with incompetence.[67]

The Jewish life and the language of Stryjkowski's heroes are indeed exotic and not to everybody's liking, but why is that all Sandauer has to say about Stryjkowski's works?

Sandauer makes no secret of who is preordained to be the victim of his critical scalpel: the underground writers, who have gone over to "Western patrons" after they found themselves at odds, "nobody knows why" [sic], with the state sponsors. Artur Sandauer "does not

know why," but he certainly knows why during martial law he appeared on television eating soup from the soldier's kettle. I do not
know to whom he will be able to explain this.

It is worthwhile to study the history of and the reasons for association of Jews with communism. Some of the speculations presented
here should be checked against precise factual data. It is time to do
that, especially since the period of close association of Jews with communism is over. But that is yet another subject.

Notes

1. A. Michnik, *Kościół, lewica, dialog* (Paris, 1976).
2. Andrzej Grzegorczyk, *Spotkania* 7 (1979).
3. E. van den Haag, *The Jewish Mystique* (New York, 1977), 90.
4. For Witold Gombrowicz's own remarks on this, see *Wspomnienia polskie* (Paris, 1977), 159.
5. Literature describes situations that led Jews toward communism. See, for example, works by I. B. Singer or by I. J. Singer (*The Brothers Ashkenazi*) and by those writing in Poland, such as J. Stryjkowski (*Czarna róża*, and recently *Wielki strach*) or A. Sandauer (*Zapiski z martwego miasta*).
6. See Herzl's letter to Berta von Sutter, cited in F. Kupfer, "O genezie syjonizmu," *Biuletyn ŻIH* 2, no. 4 (1952): 77.
7. Father J. Kruszyński, *Talmud—co zawiera i co naucza* (Lublin, 1925), 56. There were many publications similar to this one.
8. P. J. Proudhon, *Wybór Pism* (Warsaw, 1974), 1:46.
9. G. L. Mosse, *Kryzys ideologii niemieckiej* (Warsaw, 1977), especially chap. 7.
10. Cited in A. Kriegel, *Les Juifs et le monde moderne* (Paris, 1977), 191.
11. *Głos w kwestii żydowskiej* (Warsaw, 1924).
12. Pius's statement of 1938, condemning anti-Semitism as repugnant to Christianity, was cited in a very interesting article on Christian-Jewish relations in the quarterly *Spotkania* 1 (1977).
13. Moses Hess, *Pisma filozoficzne, 1841–1850* (Warsaw, 1963).
14. Quoted in I. Szafarewicz, *Le phénomène socialiste* (Paris, 1977), 267.
15. A. Kaplan, *The New World of Philosophy* (New York, 1961), 173.
16. G. Scholem, *The Messianic Idea in Judaism* (New York, 1971).
17. According to M. Lasky (*Utopia and Revolution* [London, 1977], 32), in utopias one hears a prophetic, Hebrew voice that translates ideals into reality and a bewitching, Athenian voice that expresses the abstract contemplation of the good.
18. Scholem, *Messianic Idea*, 37.
19. Szafarewicz, *Le phénomène socialiste*.
20. Cited in Lasky, *Utopia and Revolution*, 66. There is one more probably unusual exam-
ple illustrating Jews' intimate association with communism. It seems that Jews have been the only ones to attempt to realize a certain version of communism understood in the original sense of the word (community). I do not mean postrevolutionary communism in one coun-

try, but voluntary communism on a local level, involving several dozen or several hundred people. I mean the Israeli kibbutzes, which have been operating for decades without having yet degenerated. What is more, unlike other prosperous communes, they have nothing to do with isolated religious sects, do not shun modern life, and do not isolate themselves from the rest of society.

21. Scholem, *Messianic Idea*.

22. L. Kołakowski, *Główne nurty marksizmu* (Paris, 1976). Before him, Nikolai Berdyayev penetratingly substantiated this thesis in *Marksizm a religia* (Russian edition, 1929).

23. A term coined by Szafarewicz; see his *Messianic Idea*.

24. Cited in Lasky, *Utopia and Revolution*, 73.

25. A. Wat, *Mój wiek* (London, 1976), 132.

26. Neal Kozody, *Commentary*, January 1980, 51.

27. Ibid., 72.

28. Cited by Lasky, *Utopia and Revolution*, 78.

29. Ibid., 231.

30. A lot on this subject can be found in the January 1980 issue of *Commentary*.

31. Ibid., 23.

32. From S. Piasecki, *Prosto z mostu* 14 (1937); cited in K. Koźniewski, *Historia co tydzień* (Warsaw, 1976), 249.

33. Kriegel, *Les Juifs*.

34. Isaac Bashevis Singer, interviewed by J. Święcicki, *Zapis* 12 (1979): 67.

35. A. Hertz, *Żydzi w kulturze polskiej* (Paris, 1961).

36. Ibid., 205.

37. W. Gombrowicz, *Dziennik*.

38. Wat, *Mój wiek*, 79. Earlier, C. Miłosz raised a similar point in *The Captive Mind* (1953).

39. Gombrowicz, *Wspomnienia polskie*, 160.

40. This expression comes from Michnik's *Kościół, lewica, dialog*.

41. Cited in an article by the PPN (Polish Independence Compact) Problem Group, in *Głos* 7, no. 19 (1979): 48. The authors refer to theses put forward in *The Holocaust in Historical Perspective* (Washington, D.C., 1978).

42. J. Górecki, *Najgorsi* (Warsaw, 1947), 66. Even if the figure he reports is exaggerated, it nevertheless reflects the extent of the phenomenon.

43. I. Nowakowska, "Analiza więzi społecznej ludności żydowskiej w Polsce powojennej" (Ph.D. diss. [later published as *A Social Analysis of Postwar Jewry* (Jerusalem, 1986).])

44. C. Miłosz, *Zdobycie władzy* (Paris, 1953), 20.

45. H. Grynberg, *Zwycięstwo* (Paris, 1969), 61. *Zdobycie władzy* by Miłosz and Grynberg's *Zwycięstwo* are the only two honest and profound books to discuss the period immediately after the war and the situation of Jews in particular.

46. Grynberg, *Zwycięstwo*, 45.

47. S. Otwinowski, "Sąsiedzi," in *Martwa fala* (Warsaw, 1947), 53.

48. J. Przyboś, "Hańba antysemityzmu," in *Martwa fala*, 61.

49. Miłosz, *Zdobycie władzy*, 94.

50. The list of Jews in Poland, supplied by the Central Jewish Committee in Poland, confirms my thesis. In June 1946, there were 240,489 Jews (+/− 10–15%). See the brochure *Zarys działalności CKŻwP za okres 1 I—30 VI 1946*, 23. In 1947 only 88,257 Jews remained. See Nowakowska, "Analiza."

51. Michnik discusses this extensively in *Kościół, lewica, dialog*.

52. Nowakowska, "Analiza."

53. J. Szpotański, "Towarzysz Szmaciak," in *Utwory wybrane* (Warsaw, 1979), 77.

54. A. Michnik, "Intelektualiści i komunizm w Polsce po roku 1945," *Puls* 4–5 (1978/79): 25. The statement by Przyboś quoted above was characteristic of this attitude.

55. J. Andrzejewski, "Zagadnienie polskiego antysemityzmu," in *Martwa fala*. In this interesting essay Andrzejewski traced the causes of Polish anti-Semitism to a mixture of feelings of superiority and inferiority toward Jews.

56. PPN Problem Group, "Polacy—Żydzi," no. 32 (April 1979): 5.

57. Grynberg, *Zwycięstwo*, 33, 27.

58. A. Steinsbergowa, *Widziane z ławy obrończej* (Paris, 1977), 38.

59. Wat, *Mój wiek*, 55.

60. Singer, interview with Święcicki, 67.

61. Steinsbergowa, *Widziane*, 38.

62. See F. Płaskowicki, "O genezie PRL—polemicznie," *Biuletyn informacyjny* 19/20 (1978).

63. W. Jedlicki, *Klub Krzywego Koła* (Paris, 1969).

64. PPN, "Polacy—Żydzi," 4.

65. Wat, *Mój wiek*, 80, 83. Also see G. Watson, "Czy intelektualiści dali się nabrać?" *Aneks* 19 (1978).

66. Jedlicki, *Klub Krzywego Koła*.

67. You do not need ten adult Jews to say a prayer; only certain parts of the liturgy, including the Kaddish, require a minyan. "Taiku" means what Sandauer says it does, but, after all the coming of the prophet Elijah heralds the advent of the Messiah. On the other hand, the remark that Stryjkowski only "discovered" Jewish subject matter in 1955 is untrue. Stryjkowski wrote his *Głosy w ciemności* [Voices in the dark] in the 1940s.

Glossary

Michael Bernhard and Henryk Szlajfer

"Active strikes": A tactic proposed by Zbigniew M. Kowalewsk:, one of the leaders of Łódź Solidarity, in response to the extreme shortage of goods and raw materials that developed in late 1981. Rather than halt production, Solidarity was to strike by not turning the goods produced over to factory management. The output prc-duced during the strikes would be disposed of as the representatives of the workforce (for example, self-management and Solidarity bodies) saw fit.

"Advanced School for Social Sciences" (*Wyższa Szkoła Nauk Społecznych*): An institution of higher learning run by the Central Committee of the PZPR to train party, military, and government intellectuals in the social sciences. Later renamed the Academy cf Social Sciences, it was dissolved in 1990.

All-Poland Trade Union Alliance (*Ogólnopolskie Porozumienie Związków Zawodowych*, or OPZZ): Solidarity's main competitor in postcommunist Poland. With the birth of Solidarity, the old trade-union central, the Central Council of Trade Unions (CRZZ), went into decline and was eventually dissolved. Activists from the CRZZ continued to be active in residual union structures that survived in individual branches of industry. After union activity was suspended in 1981 and Solidarity was outlawed in 1982, these unions became the focus of the regime's strategy toward organized labor. In 1984 they were reorganized into a new national organization, the OPZZ. The OPZZ remains active in postcommunist Poland and effectively competes with Solidarity for membership. It is represented in parliament in the Alliance of the Democratic Left (*Sojusz Lewicy Demc-kratycznej*) and supports the Pawlak government coalition.

Anders's Army: The remnants of the defeated Polish army reorganized on Soviet soil in late 1941 and early 1942 and put under the command of General Władysław Anders. The army was later evacuated through the Middle East in 1942 to the Western Front, where it distinguished itself in several theaters, most notably in Italy, where it took Monte Cassino and opened the way to Rome.

Asnyk, Adam (1838–97): One of a handful of well-respected Polish poets to write in the latter half of the nineteenth century.

Associations of enterprises: Bureaucratic organizations controlling, on behalf of economic ministries, all the vital activities of enterprises in a given industry. The dismantling of these organizations was one of the demands of Solidarity and of the self-management movement in 1981.

Auszra (Dawn): Lithuanian dissident group named after a late-nineteenth-century journal of the same name that was important in the Lithuanian national revival.

Balcerowicz, Leszek (b. 1947): Economist and longtime faculty member at the Main School of Planning and Statistics (SGPiS). In the 1970s he also lectured at the PZPR party school. He became active in Solidarity in 1980–81 and worked with the opposition throughout the 1980s. From September 1989 until December 1991 he served as deputy prime minister and minister of finance.

Bartoszcze, Roman (b. 1946): Peasant activist and politician. Bartoszcze's family was highly active in Rural Solidarity. His father was one of the activists beaten up by security agents during the Bydgoszcz crisis of March 1981. His brother, Piotr, also a Rural Solidarity activist, perished in mysterious circumstances in 1984. Bartoszcze led the month-long peasant strike in the Bydgoszcz region following the events there in March 1981 and was a member of the Rural Solidarity's presidium in 1981. After internment during martial law, he was one of Rural Solidarity's underground leaders and played an important role in its rebirth following the Roundtable Agreement of April 1989. He was elected to the Sejm on the Solidarity ticket in June 1989. In November 1989 he was elected to the leadership of the PSL (Polish Peasant Party—built on the organizational structures of the United Peasant Party, the PZPR's ally in the countryside from 1949 to 1989). In his bid for the presidency he was supported by most peasant and agrarian parties and organizations. In 1991 he lost the leadership of the party to Waldemar Pawlak, the present prime minister, and resigned.

Bebel, August (1840–1913): One of the founders of the Social-Democratic Workers' Party (1869) and the Socialist Workers' Party of Germany (1875). He was one of the most influential and respected leaders of the Second International.

Besançon, Alain: French publicist known for critical studies of the Soviet Union, such as *The Soviet Syndrome* and *The Intellectual Origins of Leninism*.

Beck, Józef (1894–1944): Colonel and politician, associated with the last years of Piłsudski's authoritarian rule and the so-called Colonels' Regime that followed Piłsudski's death in 1935. Beck was well known among the colonels because he served as Polish foreign minister from 1932 to 1939. He went into exile in Romania in 1939 and died there during the war.

Belvedere: The palace in Warsaw that was the official seat of the Polish president.

"Belvedere Camp": A popular description of the political current in interwar Poland connected with Marshal Józef Piłsudski. Piłsudski moved into the Belvedere Palace after his May 1926 coup d'état.

Bereza: internment camp established in 1934 at Bereza Kartuska where Piłsudski and his successors confined left, right, and nationalist opponents to the dictatorship.

Berman, Jakub (1901–84): prominent Polish Stalinist. He was a member of Bierut's inner circle, with responsibility for ideological and security matters. He was expelled from the PZPR in 1957.

Białołęka: a notorious Polish prison located on the outskirts of Warsaw.

Bierut, Bolesław (1892–1956): activist in the Communist Party of Poland and the Comintern in the interwar era. He spent the early part of the war in the USSR and German-occupied Belarus until he was infiltrated into Warsaw in 1943. In 1948, his faction of staunchly pro-Moscow communists removed Gomułka, the leader of the Polish Workers' Party (PPR) since 1942. As Poland's leading Stalinist, he led the Polish United Workers' Party (q.v.) until he died in 1956 while attending the Twentieth Congress of the Communist Party of the Soviet Union in Moscow.

Biuletyn Dolnośląski (Lower Silesian bulletin): an underground informational monthly founded by oppositionists in the Wrocław area in the late 1970s.

Bobrzyński, Michał (1849–1935): a renowned representative of the

partition-era historians known as the "Kraków School." He wrote
the classic, *Dzieje Polski w zarysie* (An outline of the history of Poland), published in 1879.

Borderlands (*kresy*): the eastern limit of Polish settlement. These areas
were ethnically and religiously mixed and underdeveloped. Today
they constitute the western areas of Ukraine and Belarus, as well as
parts of Lithuania.

Börne, Ludwig (1786–1837): German-Jewish writer, publisher, and
critic.

Borusewicz, Bogdan (b. 1949): historian, member of KOR, founding member of Gdańsk-based Founding Committee for Free Trade
Unions of the Coast in 1978; member of the editorial board of *Robotnik* (The worker) and *Robotnik wybrzeża* (Coastal worker). Borusewicz was a crucial activist in the formulation of the "Twenty-one
Demands" during the strike of August 1980. Until the dissolution of
the Sejm in June 1993, he was an MP in the "Solidarity" caucus. At
present he is an MP in the Union of Freedom caucus.

Branch-line ministries: economic ministries concerned with a single
sector of the economy, such as the ministries of mining, energy,
light industry, food processing, metallurgy, and construction.

Bratkowski, Stefan (b. 1934): journalist and sociologist associated
with the reformist wing of the party. In 1956–57 he was a member of the editorial board of *Po prostu*, the leading journal of the Polish October. In the late 1970s he was one of the moving forces
behind the critical discussion society "Experience and the Future."
His outspoken criticism of hard-line solutions to Poland's problems
led to his dismissal as the editor of the weekly supplement of the
newspaper *Życie Warszawy* (Warsaw life). During the Solidarity
period he was elected chairman of the Journalists' Association and
resumed his duties at *Życie Warszawy*. Bratkowski was expelled
from the PZPR in September 1981 because of outspoken reformist
views. With the declaration of martial law he once again lost his job.
In the 1980s he was active in the opposition and reemerged in 1989
to once again lead the Polish Journalists' Association. Since then, he
worked as a freelance journalist, contributing frequently to *Gazeta
wyborcza*.

Broch, Hermann (1886–1951): Austrian novelist and literary critic
noted for his innovative novels, including *The Sleepwalkers*, *The Se-
ducer*, and *The Death of Virgil*. Broch was a political prisoner for a

short time in Nazi Germany and in 1940 emigrated to the United States.

Broniewski, Władysław (1897–1962): considered by some to be the most important Marxist poet of interwar Poland. Before turning to Marxism, he was an officer in Piłsudski's legions (under the name Captain "Orlik") and fought bravely against the Bolsheviks in the war of 1920. He is noted for his incorporation of Polish romantic themes in his revolutionary poems. Broniewski had a decidedly political view of poetry, considering his poems a weapon in the class struggle. He was arrested by the NKVD in Lwów in 1940 for writing several poems critical of Stalinism.

Brześć: a political prison in interwar Poland. In 1930 Piłsudski had the leaders of combined center-left opposition (Centrolew) to his rule arrested after they issued a manifesto calling for the restoration of democracy. In 1933 several of them were sentenced to three years' imprisonment, and while confined in Brześć prison were brutally mistreated. Other important party leaders had earlier been effectively sent into exile by being allowed to escape.

Bujak, Zbigniew (b. 1954): worker at the "Ursus" tractor factory outside of Warsaw; collaborated with *Robotnik* (The worker); in 1980–81 chair of the Warsaw chapter of "Solidarity"; and member of Solidarity's National Commission (KK). After 13 December 1981 he became the de facto leader of underground Solidarity. At present he is an MP and deputy chairman of the Union of Labor (UP).

Bydgoszcz crisis: see "Warsaw Agreement of March 1981."

Cabala: medieval Jewish mysticism, in this case referring to influential cabalist Isaac Luria, who brought the Cabala to the Holy Land when he settled in Safed in 1569.

Camp of National Unity (OZN, commonly referred to as "Ozon"): a movement created by the "colonels'" regime that ruled Poland after the death of Piłsudski. Founded in 1937, it was a more nationalistic and conservative version of the BBWR (the Nonparty Bloc for Cooperation with the Government), which supported the Piłsudski regime. Its purpose was to provide support for the government by "uniting" the nation through a program of Polish nationalism, and respect for traditional values and institutions such as the church and the army.

CBOS, or *Centrum Badań Opinii Społecznej* (Research center for social opinion): one of the leading public opinion polling concerns in Poland.

Celiński, Andrzej (b. 1950): sociologist, member of KOR and coordinator of the Society for Academic Courses (TKN, the so-called Flying University). In 1980–81 he served as secretary to Solidarity's National Coordinating Commission. Until the dissolution of the national assembly in June 1993, he was a senator affiliated with the Democratic Union (UD) caucus and deputy chair of the UD. At present he is an MP with the Union of Freedom caucus.

Central Council of Trade Unions (CRZZ): the official trade union central in Poland up to 1980, when it was dissolved in the face of competition from Solidarity. The CRZZ was eventually replaced by the All-Poland Trade Union Alliance (OPZZ).

Cheka: a Russian acronym that stands for the Extraordinary Commission to Combat Counterrevolution and Sabotage. It was the first Soviet secret police organization. Created on 7 December 1917, it was headed by Feliks Dzherzhinsky, a Bolshevik of Polish gentry background. The Cheka served as the Bolshevik terror apparatus during the civil war and was replaced in 1922 by the State Political Administration (GPU).

Cimoszewicz, Włodzimierz (b. 1950): lawyer, lecturer at Warsaw University, farmer (he owns a modern farm in Białystok province), and communist party activist (1971–90). In 1990–91 he was chairman of the postcommunist Parliamentary Club of the Democratic Left. His bid for the presidency was supported by postcommunist parties and organizations. In 1993 he became a deputy prime minister and minister of justice in the Pawlak government (a coalition of the Polish Peasant Party and the postcommunist Alliance of the Democratic Left).

Club of the Seekers of Contradictions: a discussion club organized in 1963 by Adam Michnik that brought together students from several elite high schools in Warsaw. Members went on to play important roles in student politics in 1968, the democratic opposition of the 1970s, and in Solidarity.

Clubs of the Catholic Intelligentsia (KIK): a discussion society of Catholic intellectuals, both pro-regime and independent, in Warsaw. During the Polish October of 1956, a number of discussion societies were created in Poland. Although most of the discussion societies were closed after 1956, KIK was allowed to exist in five cities (Warsaw, Kraków, Poznań, Torun, and Wrocław). The Clubs were a source of independent thought throughout the period of communist rule. In the Solidarity era many of its prominent members served as Solidarity advisers.

COCOM (Coordinating Commission): an economic council established by the United States and its allies in 1950 to oversee trade with the Soviet Union and its allies. COCOM formalized U.S. restrictions on the export of strategic goods to the Eastern bloc, a condition for Marshall Plan assistance.

Commandos: what the leaders of oppositional student movement at Warsaw University in 1967–68 were called by communist activists. Some of the commandos were of Jewish origin.

Committee for the National Liberation of Russia (*Komitet osvobozhdenia narodov Rossii*): a movement recruited from among Soviet prisoners of war held by the Germans. Led by captured General Andrei Vlasov, the committee and the associated Russian Liberation Army did not get very far because of Hitler's hostility toward Russians in general. Reduced to a German propaganda ploy, the committee published a fairly democratic manifesto, which was purportedly based on the demands of the Kronstadt uprising of 1921 and which promised to free Russia from communism.

Communist Party of Poland (KPP): the original Third International Party in Poland. It was created in 1918 by activists to the left of the Polish Socialist Party (PPS). The party was declared illegal in 1919 and took a strong position against Polish independence. During the interwar era it remained on the margins of Polish politics and never attracted a large membership. However, it did have some influence in intellectual circles, particularly after the rise of fascism in Europe. The party was hard hit by the Great Purge in the Soviet Union (1936), where many of the leading activists lived. Stalin had the KPP dissolved in 1938 for allegedly being riddled with Trotskyites, fascists, and Polish Intelligence agents. It was replaced during the war by the Polish Workers' Party (PPR).

Confederation for an Independent Poland (KPN): a nationalistic opposition group founded in the late 1970s. Throughout its existence it has been led by the flamboyant and outspoken Leszek Moczulski. Since the collapse of the communist regime in Poland, it has become an important political party. The KPN parliamentary caucus has twenty-three MPs and two senators.

"Constitutional amendments of 1975": a number of changes to the Polish constitution proposed by the party leadership under Gierek that brought an outcry from the church and Polish intellectuals. These measures would have constitutionally enshrined the leading role of the party and the alliance with the Soviet Union, and would have made fundamental rights dependent on fulfilling obligations to the state. After a protest campaign the first two proposed changes were watered down and the third was dropped.

Daniel, Yulii (1925–88): Russian writer and dissident. Daniel and Andrei Sinyavsky were arrested and imprisoned in 1965–66 on charges of "anti-Soviet agitation and propaganda" for publishing their writings under pseudonyms in the West. Daniel's was Nikolai Arzhak. The protests that followed were a watershed in the development of the Soviet dissident movement.

December events: major strikes in Gdańsk, Gdynia, Elbląg, and Szczecin protesting the Gomułka regime's December 1970 price "reform," which included a steep rise in the price of food. Confrontations with the police resulted in the death of several dozen workers. These events led to Gomułka's fall from power.

Delegate: the head of the mission (*delegatura*) the Polish government-in-exile maintained in Poland during World War II. The mission oversaw the work of the underground state. During the course of the war, the government named four delegates, who held a range of plenipotentiary powers.

Democratic Party (*Stronnictwo Demokratyczne*, or SD): the prewar party of the radical intelligentsia. It split into pro-Moscow and pro-London factions during World War II. The party was resurrected by the pro-Moscow faction in postwar Poland and was allied with the PZPR until 1989. The SD received ten seats during the quasi-contested elections of 1989. Although it is still politically active, it currently has no seats in parliament.

Déry, Tibor (1894–1977): Hungarian socialist writer, political prisoner under the Stalinist regime, active in the revolution of 1956. After the revolution he faced renewed imprisonment and persecution.

"The destruction of reason": *Die Zerstörung der Vernunft* (Berlin, 1955), an essay by Georg Lukács.

Dmowski, Roman (1864–1939): the leading politician and theoretician of modern Polish nationalism. In 1895 he founded the journal *Przegląd wszechpolski* (The all-Polish review), around which he began to organize the most important Polish nationalist movement,

the National Democrats (known as the "Endecja" from the movement's initials—ND). Under Dmowski, the Endecja pursued a line
that favored the Russian occupiers over the two Germanic occupiers
(Germany and Austria) and was intransigently hostile toward Jews
and Ukrainians, who were seen as pro-German. Dmowski led the
Polish national delegation in the Russian Duma after the revolution
of 1905. His best-known book is *Myśli nowoczesnego Polaka* (The
thoughts of a contemporary Pole), in which he criticized the weakness of his countrymen and called for the elevation of the idea of
nationhood to the level of religion. During World War I, Dmowski
resided in the West and pursued diplomatic support for Polish independence as head of the Polish National Committee based in Paris
and then represented Poland at the peace conference. Dmowski was
Piłsudski's primary and lifelong political rival. Although the Endecja
was often the strongest political party in interwar Poland, it never
commanded a parliamentary majority and never held power. After
Piłsudski's coup d'état in 1926, it met with periodic repression. Late
in the 1930s the movement began to disintegrate as some members
drifted into fascism and others gravitated toward the ruling camp
(Ozon) as it became more reactionary in policy and tone.

"Doctors' Plot": the last campaign of Stalin's policy of terror. Several
Soviet doctors, mostly of Jewish origin, were arrested in December
1952 and accused of plotting to kill high-ranking Soviet officials.
The charges against them were exposed as a fraud after Stalin's
death. The Doctors' Plot probably heralded a new round of arrests
and purges, including a campaign against Soviet Jews. Because of
Stalin's timely death, this never occurred.

Dogmatism: an error in the lexicon of communist politics. Dogmatists, according to Jakub Karpiński, are "activists, who insufficiently
adapt their decidedly Marxist ideological convictions to reality."
Hard-liners were usually accused of this ideological sin when they
tried to attack the party leadership for being insufficiently Marxist.
In the Polish People's Republic dogmatists were usually treated less
harshly than their ideological enemies—revisionists. Gomułka, in
the late 1950s, put this into words comparing dogmatism to a
"cold," which could not be cured by revisionist "influenza."

Duda-Gwiazda, Joanna (b. 1939): engineer; founding member of the
Gdańsk-based Founding Committee for Free Trade Unions of the
Coast in 1978; coeditor of *Robotnik wybrzeża* (Coastal worker),

member of the Interfactory Strike Committee (MKS) in Gdańsk in August 1980. At present Duda-Gwiazda is in opposition to Lech Wałęsa and the government and coedits the journal *Poza Układem* (Outside the system).

Dziady (Forefathers' eve): see "March 1968."

Edelman, Marek (b. 1921): Cardiologist and the only surviving member of the leadership of the Warsaw Ghetto Uprising of 1943 to remain in Poland after World War II (as of 1994 he is the sole survivor). Edelman became one of the leaders of Solidarity in Łódź in 1980–81. In 1983 he made headlines by refusing to participate in the commemoration of the fortieth anniversary of the Ghetto Uprising staged by the Polish authorities because he considered the record of the Jaruzelski regime to be at odds with the ideals for which the Ghetto defenders fought. Today, he continues to be politically active as a member of the Union of Freedom (UW).

Endecja: see "National Democrats."

"Enfranchisement of the nomenklatura": in 1988–89 many communist functionaries acted to preserve and privatize their power by purchasing state property at artificially low prices.

The February Agreement: an accord reached in Rzeszów on 18 February 1981 by the government and striking peasants. It ended widespread peasant strikes and the occupation of buildings in Ustrzyki Dolne and in Rzeszów (January–February 1981). The agreement settled issues concerning the private ownership of land and its sale, and opened the way to the official recognition of peasant trade unions (this matter was finally settled by the Warsaw Agreement, which led to the registration of "Rural Solidarity" under Jan Kułaj in May 1981).

Ficowski, Jerzy (b. 1924): poet, essayist, translator, and cultural ethnographer. Ficowski has been instrumental in preserving and publicizing the writings of the great Polish-Jewish writer Bruno Szulc. A member of KOR, he was an important figure in Polish oppositional politics in the 1970s.

Filipski, Ryszard (b. 1934): theater actor and director. One of the leading figures of the Grunwald Patriotic Association, a shadowy hard-line and anti-Semitic organization that emerged in 1981. In 1968 Filipski came to public attention for his anti-Semitic and anti-German performances.

First Polish Army: Polish armed forces organized by the communist-led Union of Polish Patriots in the USSR in 1943–44. After 1944, in conjunction with the Security Office (UB), it constituted the backbone of local communist power.

"Free Trade Unions": the Founding Committee for Free Trade Unions of the Coast (KZWZZW or WZZ), an organization founded in 1978 and devoted to the creation of trade unions and other worker initiatives free of the control of the party-state. The initiative in Gdańsk published its own underground paper, *Robotnik wybrzeża* (Coastal worker), and organized the strike in the Lenin Shipyard in Gdańsk in August 1980. It also played the essential role in bringing together the Interfactory Strike Committee that negotiated the Gdańsk agreement with the authorities. Similar but less successful committees were also founded in the Szczecin and Katowice areas.

General-Gouvernement: Nazi zone of occupation encompassing a large part of Poland. Hitler did not try to create a quisling state in Poland, probably because of his overwhelming hatred of the Poles. His former lawyer Hans Frank was installed as governor-general of the territory. The form of government might best be described as the direct rule of the Gestapo. Any resistance to German rule was punished by summary execution, confinement in a concentration camp, or death in an extermination camp.

Genoa Conference: an unsuccessful international conference held in April–May 1922 to solve postwar economic difficulties, including reparations payments.

Geremek, Bronisław (b. 1932): medieval historian. Until 1968 he was a member of the PZPR. At that time he resigned in protest of the Warsaw Pact invasion of Czechoslovakia. Geremek was a member of the Society for Academic Courses (TKN), the so-called Flying University. In August 1980 he served as an expert to the Interfactory Strike Committee (MKS) in Gdańsk. He was an important opposition leader in the 1980s. At present, he is an MP from the Union of Freedom (UW) and chair of the Sejm Foreign Affairs Commission.

Gierek, Edward (b. 1913): leader of Poland and the Polish United Workers' Party from December 1970 to the summer of 1980. His reign was marked by several crises. He assumed power during the strikes of 1970–71 and immediately faced the challenge of restoring social peace. This was followed by another wave of strikes in June 1976 and then the unrest of the summer of 1980, which led to his removal from power. His ruling team was notorious for its corruption.

Glemp, Józef (b. 1929): cardinal and primate of the Catholic church in Poland since 1981.

Gojawiczyńska, Pola (1896–1963): novelist noted for her realistic treatment of social issues in interwar Poland.

Gombrowicz, Witold (1904–69): the outstanding figure of Polish literary modernism. He lived in exile from 1939 to his death. His work constitutes a powerful and far-reaching critique of Polish cultural tradition. The significance of his work is comparable to that of James Joyce in English.

Gomułka, Władysław (1905–82): the leader of the communist underground in Poland during World War II. Gomułka went on to lead the Polish Workers' Party (PPR), the successor to the Communist Party of Poland, and the Polish United Workers' Party (created by the merger of the PPR and Polish Socialist Party). Gomułka was removed as party chief in 1948 but staged a political comeback in 1956 and ruled Poland until 1970 when strikes on the Baltic coast led to his second fall from power.

Gomułka, Zofia: the wife of Władysław Gomułka and a noted hardline communist activist. She was of Jewish origin.

Goyim (Yiddish): non-Jews.

Grottger, Artur (1837–67): Polish painter trained at the Vienna Academy. He is famous for his paintings of the January Insurrection of 1863 against Russian rule. He worked largely in the classical style and painted patriotic themes.

Gwiazda, Andrzej (b. 1935): engineer, founding member of the Gdańsk-based Founding Committee for Free Trade Unions of the Coast in 1978, coeditor of *Robotnik wybrzeża* (Coastal worker), and member of the presidium of the Interfactory Strike Committee (MKS) in Gdańsk in August 1980. Until September 1981 Gwiazda was the deputy chair of Solidarity. At present he is in opposition to Lech Wałęsa and the government.

"Hatchet": a reference to Lech Wałęsa's statement from his 1990 presidential campaign that he would create a new order in Poland, if need be, with the help of a hatchet (that is, by destroying the remnants of old, communist structures and their influence).

Herling-Grudziński, Gustaw (b. 1919): Polish writer, who has lived in exile in the West since World War II. He and his friends organized

an early anti-Nazi organization in Warsaw where he was a student.
In 1940 he fled to Soviet-occupied Poland and was imprisoned in a
labor camp. After his release from the camps in 1942, he joined the
Anders's Army and was evacuated from the USSR. He fought with
the Polish army in the West and was decorated for his bravery. He
was one of the moving forces behind and remains a regular contributor to Paris *Kultura*. He is well known in Poland for his *Diary*
[*Dziennik*] and short stories, and widely recognized in the West for
his memoir of life in the Soviet Gulag, *A World Apart*, considered by
some to be the best account of life therein.

Holzer, Jerzy (b. 1930): contemporary Polish historian and political
scientist. The book referred to here is *"Solidarność" 1980–1981. Geneza i historia* (Solidarity 1980–1981, genesis and history). The book
was first published underground in Poland in the *Krytyka* library.

Home Army (AK): the partisan forces of the Polish underground
state loyal to the government-in-exile in London. The AK carried
out extensive operations in both urban areas and the countryside.

Horizontal structures movement: a movement that emerged within
the party soon after the formation of Solidarity in 1980. Horizonta-
ists favored the weakening of party centralism and its replacement
with horizontal links between local party groups and generally favored extensive political and economic reform. The movement's activists were eventually isolated within the party and politically defeated at the Extraordinary Ninth Party Congress in the summer of
1981.

Husák, Gustav (1913–90): a Slovak communist leader who was persecuted under Stalinism and then staged a political comeback during
the Prague Spring as a supposed "moderate." In April 1969, he replaced Alexander Dubček, the reformist first secretary of the Czechoslovak Communist Party. Husák's "normalization" policies combined harsh repression of intellectuals and the cultural sphere with a
consumer orientation in the economy. This bought temporary social
peace at the price of long-term investment in the economy. By the
time of the Velvet Revolution of 1989 Husák had already retired as
party general secretary. He continued to hold the office of president
(which he assumed in 1975) until he was replaced by Václav Havel.

Interfactory Strike Committee (MKS): the representatives sent to
the Lenin Shipyard by the factories of Gdańsk and surrounding areas
to express their grievances against the authorities. The MKS in

Gdańsk presented the "Twenty-One Demands," which formed the basis of the Gdańsk Agreement legalizing independent trade unions and strikes. A number of other interfactory strike committees were formed in August–September 1980; other influential committees emerged in Szczecin and Silesia.

Internment: the policy after the declaration of martial law in 1981 under which the police and Security Service held large numbers of potential opponents in detention camps without formally charging them.

Irzykowski, Karol (1863–1944): literary critic and novelist associated with the Young Poland (*Młoda Polska*) movement in the arts. Like other turn-of-the-century literary and artistic movements, Young Poland was known for its modernism, symbolism, decadence, and neoromanticism. Irzykowski's novel *Pałuba* (Pudgy), published in 1901, is considered one of the earliest examples of this tendency. He is also well known for his pioneering book on film theory *Dziesiąta muza* (The tenth muse, 1924).

Jakimowicz, Mieczysław (1881–1917): graphic artist and painter known primarily for his miniatures in a symbolist/art nouveau style.

January Insurrection: simultaneous attacks were made on many garrisons in Russian-occupied Poland in January 1863. Guerrilla warfare against the Russians organized by an underground conspiratorial Polish state continued into 1864. The Russians eventually restored control and ushered in an era marked by harsh rule, deportations to Siberia, and Russification.

Jastrzębie Agreement: After the strikes of the summer of 1980, the Polish government signed an agreement not only with the Interfactory Strike Committee in Gdańsk, but with similar bodies in Szczecin and in Jastrzębie Coal Basin in Silesia.

Jaworski, Seweryn (b. 1931): skilled worker in the "Warszawa" steel plant. In 1980–81 he was deputy chair of the Mazowsze (Warsaw and environs) chapter of Solidarity. At present Jaworski is in opposition to the government as a leader of a small trade union.

"Jewish-communism": an expression (*Żydokomuna*) used by ultranationalists, fascists, and anti-Semites in Poland to identify communism as a Jewish plot against Poland.

Jewish community: In Poland, this notion has a stronger connotation than in the United States. During the late medieval–early modern period, Polish Jews had their own autonomous niche within the estate system and their own organs of autonomous self-government.

Jóźwiak, Franciszek (1895–1966): originally a member of the Polish Socialist Party who had fought in Piłsudski's legions. Soon thereafter he joined the illegal Communist Party of Poland. He was infiltrated into Poland in 1942, where he served as chief of staff of the communist-controlled partisan forces, the People's Guard (GL), and the People's Army (AL). After the war he commanded the People's Militia (police) and finally, as a hard-line Stalinist, was retired from politics in 1956.

June 1956: the most important event leading up to the Polish October. Workers in the city of Poznań struck, demonstrated, and took control of the city for several days before the authorities regained control in pitched street battles.

Katyń: After Germany and the Soviet Union partitioned Poland in September 1939, several thousand Polish officers detained by the Red Army were put to death in 1940 by the Soviet secret police in the Katyń woods and at other camps in the area.

The Kielce pogrom: the killing by a mob of forty-two Jews in this city on 4 July 1946. Recent historical research suggests that it was not a spontaneous attack, but that elements of Soviet and/or Polish security provoked the attacks by planting rumors.

Kisielewski, Stefan (1911–91): Polish journalist, writer, composer, satirist, and politician. Kisielewski was strongly associated with the liberal Catholic milieu of *Tygodnik Powszechny* based in Kraków and the Znak group, which he represented in parliament (1957–65). In February 1968, during a meeting of the Union of Polish Writers (*Związek Literatów Polskich*) Kisielewski attacked the regime, calling it a "dictatorship of dimwits" (*dyktatura ciemniaków*). Afterward in a notorious incident, he was beaten by "unidentified persons." Although Kisielewski was always very supportive of Solidarity, he maintained his personal independence. Many of his writings in Poland appeared under the pseudonym "Kisiel." He has also lived outside Poland and contributed to Paris *Kultura* (also under pseudonyms) and published a number of books in the West as "Tomasz Staliński." He was best known for his short satirical essays. Despite the strong criticism explicitly leveled against the state of affairs in communist Poland, Kisielewski managed to have most of his work published there.

Kliszko, Zenon (1908–89): an important Polish communist closely linked to Gomułka. He fell from power with Gomułka in 1949. He later held a number of important positions after Gomułka's comeback in 1956 and was removed from power after his boss fell again in 1970.

Kołakowski, Leszek (b. 1927): Polish philosopher and Poland's most important revisionist Marxist in the 1960s. When Gomułka cracked down on revisionist intellectuals in 1968, Kołakowski went into exile in the West. He is probably best known for his three-volume *Main Currents of Marxism* but has written widely on politics and philosophy. His non-Marxist political writings of the 1970s were very influential among Polish intellectuals. Kołakowski was very active in organizing material assistance and public support from the West for the Polish opposition of the 1970s and for Solidarity. At present he is a professor of philosophy in the United States and England.

Kołodziej, Andrzej (b. 1959): skilled worker and activist in the Gdańsk-based Founding Committee for Free Trade Unions of the Coast, who after being dismissed from the Lenin Shipyards found work in the "Paris Commune" Shipyard in Gdynia in the summer of 1980. He became the leader of the strike committee in his new shipyard in August 1980 and became a deputy chairman of the Interfactory Strike Committee in Gdańsk. Kołodziej became a member of Solidarity's National Commission in 1981 and was active in the Solidarity underground after 13 December 1981. At present he is in strong opposition to Lech Wałęsa and the government as an activist in the politically marginal "Freedom" Party.

Kołodziejski, Jerzy: a professor who in 1980 and 1981 served as the provincial governor in Gdańsk. He was instrumental in arranging the dialogue with the Interfactory Strike Committee in 1980. Kołodziejski was removed as governor after the declaration of martial law in 1981. He served as a minister without portfolio in the government of Tadeusz Mazowiecki.

Konwicki, Tadeusz (b. 1926): prolific contemporary Polish novelist and film director. A large number of his novels have been translated into English, including *A Dreambook of Our Times*, *The Polish Complex*, *A Minor Apocalypse*, *The Anthropos-Spectre Beast*, and *Moonrise, Moonset*. In the 1970s Konwicki had increasing difficulty publishing his work officially in Poland and began to publish illegally, notably in the underground review *Zapis* (The record).

Kościuszko, Tadeusz (1746–1817): leader of the anti-Russian insurrection in 1794 that attempted to resist the partitioning of Poland and sought to enfranchise the Polish peasantry. Kościuszko is well known in the United States for his service in the Continental army from 1775 to 1783.

Kosmowski, Patrycjusz: leader of Solidarity in Bielsko Biała. During the Solidarity Congress he strongly opposed any dialogue or compromise with the government. He emigrated after 1981.

Kossak, Juliusz (1824–99): popular Polish painter noted for his realistic depictions of nature, horses, and battles.

Kossak, Wojciech (1857–1942): son of Juliusz Kossak, who followed his father as a painter and is also noted for his military themes.

Koźniewski, Kazimierz (b. 1919): novelist and journalist connected with the weekly *Polityka* (Politics). After the declaration of martial law he was a strong supporter of military rule.

Kraepelinian school: a school of psychiatry based on the work of the German psychiatrist Emil Kraepelin (1856–1926).

Kultura (Culture): an influential postwar Polish monthly published in Paris. It was commonly smuggled into Poland. *Kultura* published the works of many of the most talented writers, poets, historians, critics, and political commentators living in exile, as well as critical works and documents smuggled out of Poland.

Kuś, Bogdan: miner, deputy chairman of the Jastrzębie-based Interfactory Workers' Committee (MKR) and its representative on Solidarity's National Coordinating Committee.

Łabędzki, Jan (b. 1943): worker and first secretary of the PZPR in the Gdańsk Shipyard in 1981. During the Solidarity era he was elected to the politburo and supported dialogue with the union and radical reform. After 1981 he lost his positions.

Lange, Oskar (1904–65): Polish socialist economist who, unlike Hayek and von Mises of the Austrian School, argued that a socialist economic system could be just as efficient and rational as a capitalist economy. Lange, along with Abba Lerner, argued that planners could simulate the market mechanism through managing inventory levels through adjustment of prices. He was politically active during October 1956, pressing for economic reform.

Lasota, Eligiusz (b. 1929): journalist. Lasota edited *Po prostu* from 1953 until its demise in 1957. Since then he has served as a member of parliament (1957–61) and held a number of editorial jobs. At present he works for the Center for International Studies of the Polish Senate.

"Law of the faster development of department I": not so much a law of economic development as a statement of priorities and a guiding principle of Stalinist development. Planners concentrated investment and thus stimulated rapid growth in department I (heavy industry) at the expense of department II (production geared toward final consumption).

Legions: During World War I, the Habsburg authorities allowed Józef Piłsudski to organize all-Polish units to fight in the Austro-Hungarian army. With the collapse of the Habsburg, tsarist, and German empires at the end of the war, these "legions" became the core of the new Polish national army.

Leśmian, Bolesław (1877?–1937): born Lesman, an important Polish poet of the early twentieth century. Born in Warsaw to a polonized Jewish middle-class family, Leśmian created a unique poetic style in the 1920s and 1930s, which incorporated elements from Polish folk culture. He is considered by many critics to be the best poet of the "Young Poland" movement.

Lewa wolna (Make way on the left): a reference to the military command that directs a column on the march to move to the right side of the road to allow vehicles, convoys, and the like to pass on the left. Mackiewicz used this as a title symbolically.

Liberum veto: a device by which any member of the Sejm of the noble democracy of the Polish-Lithuanian Republic (1569–1795) could delay its proceedings by withholding his consent, because then the Sejm required a consensus before it could act. Up until the seventeenth century the *liberum veto* allowed the nobility to limit the power of the crown. However, in the late seventeenth and eighteenth centuries, the practice allowed minority factions to block important legislation. The abuse of the *liberum veto* was one of the factors leading to the decline and demise of the Polish state in the late eighteenth century.

Lis, Bogdan (b. 1952): skilled worker in Gdańsk "Elmor" enterprise; activist in the Gdańsk-based Founding Committee for Free Trade Unions of the Coast. Until early 1981 he was a member of the Polish United Workers' Party (PZPR). Lis was also a deputy chairman of the Interfactory Strike Committee during the August 1980 strike. In 1980–81 he served as deputy chairman of Solidarity. He was active in underground Solidarity and served as a Solidarity senator in 1989–91.

"Little stabilization" (*mała stabilizacja*): popular description of

Gomułka's policy of normalization after 1956. It involved a withdrawal from the more revolutionary and far-reaching proposals for change that emerged in 1956, and a reconsolidation of the system without the excesses of Stalinism.

Lukács, Georg (1885–1971): Hungarian Marxist philosopher and politician. Lukács was active in the Hungarian revolutions of 1919 and 1956. He stayed out of politics after 1956 and pursued an academic career.

Lwów: present-day Lviv, a major city in western Ukraine. Lwów was a major Polish cultural center from medieval times. It was also known as Lemberg and served as the capital of the Habsburg province of Galicia until Polish independence. It was an important center of culture, administration, and commerce in interwar Poland. In 1939, it was annexed by the USSR and incorporated into Ukraine. After the war it was retained by the Soviet Union (during this period it was most often referred to as Lvov), and most of its Polish inhabitants were resettled in western Poland in areas that had formerly been German or mixed German and Polish.

March 1968: a nationwide political and social upheaval in Poland. In January 1968, the authorities closed a production of the play *Forefathers' Eve* (*Dziady*) by Adam Mickiewicz because audiences reacted enthusiastically to anti-tsarist references in the script. This led to unrest at Warsaw University and the expulsion of two politically active students, Adam Michnik and Henryk Szlajfer. The expulsions precipitated a demonstration at Warsaw University on 8 March, during which students also protested against censorship and their living conditions. The authorities responded by sending in units of the Voluntary Reserve of the People's Militia (ORMO), who restored order and arrested students. Demonstrations followed in a number of other Polish university towns. During this period a party faction around Mieczysław Moczar (the "Partisans") began to attack "Zionists" (read Jews) in Poland. In the aftermath many of Poland's remaining Jews emigrated, and Gomułka used the opportunity to destroy the remnants of the revisionist faction in the party.

"Marking of the apartment doors of militia and Security officers": an example of the junta's use of provocation to instill a fear of Solidarity among its own supporters. By marking their doors, the junta gave the impression that Solidarity was singling them out for harassment or injury.

Matejko, Jan (1838–93): the most popular and influential Polish

painter of the nineteenth century. His large realistic canvases roman-
tically celebrated the achievements of the Polish past.

Mazowiecki, Tadeusz (b. 1927): Catholic activist, politician, and editor. After World War II, Mazowiecki worked with PAX, but was
expelled in 1955. He later founded (1958) and edited the respected
Catholic monthly *Więź* and served (beginning in 1961) in the Sejm
as a member of the Znak delegation. When he protested the actions
of the authorities in March 1968, his parliamentary career came to a
quick end. Mazowiecki was active in the 1970s in the Warsaw Club
of Catholic Intelligentsia (KIK) and the Society for Academic
Courses (TKN). In August 1980, he and Bronisław Geremek delivered a letter of support for the Interfactory Strike Committee in
Gdańsk from sixty-four Warsaw intellectuals. He became an adviser
to the Interfactory Strike Committee and then to Solidarity. Mazowiecki was the original editor of *Tygodnik Solidarność* [*Solidarity
weekly*] and active in the Solidarity underground. When Solidarity
formed a coalition government in 1989, he became prime minister
and then ran against Lech Wałęsa for president in 1991, losing in the
first round due to the unexpected strength of Stan Tymiński. He is
at present the head of the Union of Freedom (UW) party and is a
member of its parliamentary delegation.

Mazowsze: one of Solidarity's regional organizations. It included
Warsaw and the surrounding area.

Melamdim: plural of *melamed*, a teacher, particularly of younger children. With time it took on the derogatory connotation of a teacher
of low quality.

Message to the Workers of Eastern Europe: a statement issued by
the delegates at the Solidarity Congress of September 1981, addressed to workers of Albania, Bulgaria, Hungary, Romania, Czechoslovakia, East Germany, and all the nations of the Soviet Union that
expressed support for those who were fighting for free trade unions
and expressed the hope that they would soon "meet in order to exchange our experiences as trade unionists." This message was received as "a provocation" by party politicians both in Poland and the
other Soviet bloc states.

Mijal, Kazimierz (b. 1910): communist leader in Kraków and Warsaw during World War II. After the war, as a trusted Stalinist, he
headed the Cabinet Office (1952–56) and held other important positions. In 1966 he fled Poland and led the tiny underground pro-

Chinese Communist Party of Poland from Albania. In 1984 he returned to Poland.

Military Council for National Salvation (WRON): the official name of the junta led by General Jaruzelski that declared martial law on 13 December 1981.

Minc, Hilary (1905–74): economist and politician. From the 1920s he was an activist in the Polish communist party. During World War II he played an important role in reorganizing the communist movement on Soviet soil and returned to Poland in 1944 as one of its leading members. After the war he held a number of central economic positions—minister of industry, head of the Planning Commission, and deputy prime minister. He was also a member of the politburo of both the PPR and PZPR from 1944 to 1956. Minc was one of the leading figures of Polish Stalinism and oversaw the construction of a Soviet-type economy in Poland. With de-Stalinization in 1956, he was forced into retirement.

The Miners' Charter: a package of special benefits for miners in Poland. It includes an earlier retirement age, special bonuses (in kind and in money), and medals for years of service. There were (and still are) "charters" of this type in Poland, for example, for teachers, but the miners' was the most generous.

"Miracle on the Vistula": how Poles commonly refer to the Battle of Warsaw (1920), the final decisive battle of the Polish-Soviet War of 1919–20. Heavily outnumbered Polish forces stopped the westward advance of the Red Army along the line of the Vistula river. The Treaty of Riga (1921) later settled the question of the border between Poland and the Soviet Union.

Moczar, Mieczysław (1913–86): interwar communist and commander of communist partisans (AL) in World War II. Moczar held a number of important positions in the postwar era, including minister of internal affairs, central committee secretary, politburo member, member of the Council of State, and chairman of the Supreme Chamber of Control. Moczar had a strong hard-line and nationalistic following and challenged both Gomułka and Gierek for power. As minister of internal affairs he had a strong hand in staging the "anti-Zionist" campaign of 1967–68.

Moczulski, Leszek (b. 1930): historian, journalist, and politician. Moczulski is an expert on Polish-German relations during World War II. His early work received awards and praise from the Ministry of Defense. He worked, beginning in 1960, for the magazine *Stolica* (The capital), which in 1968 was associated with the hard-line Moczar faction of the party. During this period Moczulski wrote articles attacking students and intellectuals. In 1972 he fell out of favor with the publication of a book, *The Polish War*, which contained unflattering descriptions of the Soviet army during World War II. In 1977 Moczulski was one of the founding members of the Movement for the Defense of Human and Civil Rights (ROPCiO), an opposition movement that was more socially conservative and outspokenly nationalist than KOR. When ROPCiO split into competing factions in 1978–79 he founded his own movement, the Confederation for an Independent Poland (KPN). Moczulski was imprisoned for much of the 1980s. KPN continues as a significant political party today and is still led by Moczulski, who is a member of parliament.

Modzelewski, Karol (b. 1937): professor of medieval history, Polish Academy of Sciences. In 1964, together with Jacek Kuroń, he wrote the famous, critical Marxist "Open Letter to the Party," which resulted in 1965 in a prison sentence of three and a half years. Released on bail in mid-1967, he was rearrested in March 1968 and sentenced, together with Kuroń, to another three and a half years in prison for playing a role in the "March events." Modzelewski was one of the co-organizers of independent trade unions in Wrocław in August–September 1980. He is reported to have coined the name "Solidarity." Until April 1981 he served as Solidarity's press spokesperson and was elected to serve on the union's national board at the Solidarity Congress in September 1981. He continued to be active in the underground in the 1980s and was arrested in this period as well. He represented Solidarity in the Senate from 1989 to 1991. At present he is associated with the Union of Labor (UP) as its honorary chairman.

Moraczewski, Jędrzej (1870–1944): Polish socialist politician, follower of Józef Piłsudski. In 1918 he was premier of the short-lived government of People's Poland. At Piłsudski's demand, he withdrew from this government.

Mrożek, Sławomir (b. 1930): Polish dramatist and writer. He is noted for his plays (among them, *Tango*, *The Striptease*, *Vatzlav*) and short stories, which are marked by black comedy, absurdism, surreal situations, and deep satire. He left Poland for the West and since 1968 has lived in Paris and Mexico City.

Nagy, Imre (1895–1958): Hungarian reformer, communist politician, and the leader of the Hungarian Revolution of 1956. Nagy was executed in 1958 for his role in the revolution.

Narożniak, Jan: a volunteer in the office of Solidarity in Mazowsze, arrested by the office of the procurator general in November 1980 for possessing a document from their office, "On the Present Methods of Prosecuting of Illegal Antisocialist Activity." Both Narożniak and Piotr Sapeło, the clerk in the procurator's office who had passed him the document, were eventually released when the workers of Warsaw began a citywide general strike. Mazowsze chair Zbigniew Bujak subsequently had trouble getting some factories to demobilize. The Narożniak affair was significant because it hinted at how little the apparatus of repression had changed and pointed to the periodic difficulties the Solidarity leadership would have in controlling mobilized workers.

Narutowicz, Gabriel (1865–1922): the first elected president of Poland (1922). Shortly after his election he was assassinated by Eligiusz Niewiadomski. See Chapter 18.

National Armed Forces (NSZ): an ultra-right-wing partisan formation established in 1942. In 1944, part of the NSZ subordinated itself to the command of the AK and to the Polish government-in-exile in London. Another part refused to join the AK, collaborated with the Germans at the end of the war and withdrew with the German army. The NSZ was dominated by falangists and ultranationalists. They fought both the Germans and the Soviets. They also executed Poles with whom they did not agree politically, as well as members of national minority groups, including Jews returning from Nazi camps.

National Coordinating Commission: Solidarity's executive organ.

National Democrats (*Endecja*): the largest party of the right in interwar Poland. Led by Roman Dmowski (q.v.), the party was noted for its ardent nationalism, social conservatism, and chauvinist attitude toward national minorities.

National List (*lista krajowa*): during the 1989 parliamentary elections thirty-five seats were to be filled by candidates from a "national list." This list was composed of the most prominent leaders of the communist party and its allies (the "coalition"). The Solidarity leadership was offered places on the list but declined to participate. In order to be elected, a candidate on the national list had to receive valid votes on at least 50 percent of the ballots cast nationwide. Only

two of the thirty-five candidates on the list received the required
votes.

"Newspeak" (or *nowomowa*): the special propaganda language developed by the leadership of "Oceania" in George Orwell's *1984*. Poles
used the term to describe the communist regime's propaganda.

NKVD: the People's Commissariat for Internal Affairs (Soviet
Union). It was a forerunner of the KGB.

Nomenklatura: a reference both to the procedures that the communist system used to staff key positions and to the elite that filled
those positions. The central committee secretariat maintained lists of
key positions of national importance and files on the personnel who
filled them. Appointment to such positions required the approval of
the secretariat. The personnel who filled the top positions controlled
by the nomenklatura system constituted the elite of the communist
system and were themselves referred to as the "nomenklatura."

November Night: 29 November 1830, the start of the anti–Russian
insurrection in Warsaw.

Novotný, Antonín (1894–1975): first secretary of the Czechoslovak
Communist Party from 1953 to 1968 and president of Czechoslovakia from 1957 to 1968. After paying lip service to the idea of reform
early in his tenure in power he continued many of the Stalinist policies of his predecessor, Klement Gottwald, until his removal.

NOW-a: an acronym standing for "independent publishing house,"
one of the first underground publishing concerns established in Poland in the late 1970s. Its first director was Mirosław Chojecki.

Nowa Huta (New steelworks): a city built adjacent to Kraków by
Poland's new, communist rulers after World War II. The city's centerpiece was the Lenin Steel Mill, one of the largest plants of its kind
in the world. Nowa Huta was trumpeted as a new planned, socialist
city.

Nowak-Jeziorański, Jan (b. 1913): one of the couriers sent by the
Polish Underground State to report to the government-in-exile during World War II. His experiences are chronicled in the memoir
Courier from Warsaw. After the war he remained in the West, where
he headed the Polish section of Radio Free Europe from its inception
to 1976.

The Nuremburg Laws: one of the most significant legal acts taken
by the Nazis against the Jews. The laws defined who was Jewish and
isolated Jews from the population at large. Promulgated in 1935, the
Nuremburg Laws deprived Germany's Jews of their rights as citi-

zens and banned sexual contact and marriage between Jews and non-Jews.

OBOP, or *Ośrodek Badania Opinii Publicznej*: (Public opinion research center) a leading public opinion polling concern in Poland associated with Polish Radio and TV.

Olszewski, Jan (b. 1930): lawyer and politician; associated with the "revisionist" weekly *Po prostu* (Simply speaking) in 1955–57; member of the independent *Klub Krzywego Koła* (Club of the crooked circle) until its dissolution in 1963. From 1959 Olszewski was active as a lawyer in defending political prisoners and was associated with KOR in this capacity from its inception. In 1980 he served as a legal adviser to Solidarity. In 1991 Olszewski was elected to parliament from the Center Alliance (PC) list, and became prime minister. On 4 June 1992 he was recalled from this post by the parliament in conflict over his government's way of handling (and manipulating) the contents of secret police files from the period of communist rule. At present Olszewski is in strong opposition to the government and Lech Wałęsa.

Osmańczyk, Edmund Jan (1913–89): journalist. During the interwar period he was an activist among the Polish minority in Germany. After the war he worked as a foreign correspondent and diplomatic reporter. In 1989 he was elected to the Senate on the Solidarity ticket.

Otwock: a town near Warsaw where on 7 May 1981 an enraged crowd, demanding the release of two local men who had been detained for drunkenness, attacked and set fire to a local police station. Adam Michnik and Zbigniew Romaszewski, acting on behalf of Warsaw Solidarity, convinced the crowd that their action would be harmful to Solidarity and rescued the surrounded policemen.

Palka, Grzegorz (b. 1950): a member of the Solidarity leadership in Łódź and after the Solidarity Congress in September 1981 a member of the presidium of Solidarity's National Commission. He led Solidarity's radical wing and was a strong supporter of self-management in state enterprises. Until July 1994 he was the president of Łódź, supported mainly by the Christian National Union (ZChN), one of the more important conservative parties from the Solidarity camp.

Paris and Vienna Agreements of 1981: agreements reached in the second half of 1981 on the rescheduling of the Polish debt with both private and state creditors.

"Parliamentary elections of 1989": semifree elections to the Polish parliament held in June 1989 as a result of the Roundtable Agreement of April. Elections to a newly created upper chamber, the Senate, were fully contested. Elections to the Sejm, now a lower chamber, reserved 65 percent of the seats for the communists and their allies. The other 35 percent were fully contested.

Patriotic Movement for National Revival (*Patriotyczny Ruch Odrodzenia Narodowego*, or PRON): a pro-regime national front organization created in 1982 after the declaration of martial law. It replaced the National Unity Front. Composed largely of members of the PZPR, its allied parties, and pro-regime Catholic groups, its purpose was to try to act as a broader social support movement for the Jaruzelski regime.

PAX: an organization of pro-regime Catholics. Officially founded in 1952, many of the association's members were active in procommunist Catholic circles directly after the war. Bolesław Piasecki, a falangist politician of the interwar and wartime eras who had been arrested by the NKVD in 1945, led PAX until his death in 1979. PAX was one of a number of such organizations the regime used to co-opt Catholics and pressure the church. Among such organizations, PAX was known for its hard-line stance and substantial private wealth. Under a different name, PAX is at present a part of Jan Olszewski's electoral bloc and its daily *Słowo* (The word) is one of the leading Christian-national newspapers in Poland.

Peiper, Tadeusz (1891–1969): a leftist poet of the interwar period. Peiper, a leading figure of the Kraków avant-garde, founded the poetry review *Zwrotnica* (The switch) in the 1920s. It was the main journal of the Kraków avant-garde, publishing socially conscious, futurist, and constructivist poetry. Peiper was better known for his critical essays than his poetry. Although never a party member, he worked with the communists both before and after World War II.

People's Councils (*Rady Narodowe*): local organs of political "representation" under the communist system, abolished in 1990.

People's Militia (MO): the official name of the police under the communist system in Poland.

Piasecki, Bolesław: see "PAX."

Pieńkowska, Alina (b. 1952): nurse and member of the Founding Committee for Free Trade Unions of the Coast. Pieńkowska was an important organizer of the strike of August 1980 at the Lenin Shipyard and was elected a member of the presidium of the Interfactory

Strike Committee. During Solidarity she served as the chair of Solidarity's National Coordinating Committee for Health Services and sat on the board of the Gdańsk region. Until the dissolution of parliament in June 1993 she was a senator with the Solidarity caucus.

Polish Catholic Social Union (PZKS): a Catholic organization created in January 1981 by the members of Neo-Znak. PZKS was an attempt to create an organization combining pro-regime and independent Catholics. It was at first led by Neo-Znak's former leader Janusz Zabłocki until it was suspended during martial law. Allowed to resume activity in 1984, Zabłocki and other figures of greater independence left or were forced from executive and responsible positions. PZKS eventually joined the Patriotic Movement for National Revival (q.v.).

Polish Catholic Union (PZK): a short-lived group formed by opponents of Zabłocki's PZKS after the declaration of martial law.

Polish Independence Compact (PPN): a group that beginning in the mid-1970s, published anonymous reports on important issues, present and past. A number of prominent contemporary politicians, including Zdzisław Najder and Jan Olszewski, took part in drawing up the reports.

The Polish October: a reference to a political crisis in October 1956. With popular pressure building, reformist and hard-line factions in the PZPR became deadlocked. The situation was resolved when Gomułka emerged as a compromise candidate and reassumed power after a tense standoff with the Soviet leadership under Khrushchev.

Polish Peasant Party (*Polskie Stronnictwo Ludowe*, or PSL): a party organized in 1945 by politicians from the interwar Peasant Party (SL) and other rural activists who did not wish to join the SL resurrected in 1944 by procommunist politicians. This party was the bulwark of opposition to the communist-led coalition that ruled postwar Poland. It was led by Stanisław Mikołajczyk, the former head of the London government-in-exile, who was allowed to return to the country through the intervention of the Western allies. The PSL was decimated by the Soviet and Polish security services in the period 1945–49 and was forcibly merged with the SL to form the United Peasant Party (ZSL). The present-day Polish Peasant Party was created out of the United Peasant Party.

"Polish realism" (*polrealizm*): in Mackiewicz's vocabulary a derogative used to describe all compromise and adaptation to the reality of the communist system. It equates anything short of armed resistance to the de facto acceptance of communism.

Polish Socialist Party (PPS): the socialist party of the Second International in Poland. The PPS stressed both national independence and social justice and expressed an unbroken commitment to parliamentary democracy. Founded in 1892, the party played an important role in Polish lands in the Russian revolution of 1905 and the Polish struggle for independence. Józef Piłsudski was among its first leaders. It was the major political actor of the democratic left in Poland in the interwar period and supported the London government-in-exile during World War II. After the war it came increasingly under the control of pro-Soviet activists and was forcibly merged with the Polish Workers' Party to form the Polish United Workers' Party (PZPR) in 1948. The party was reestablished in 1988 under the leadership of Jan Józef Lipski. It only has a small electoral following. Its present leader Piotr Ikonowicz has led the party toward an electoral alliance with the postcommunist Alliance of the Democratic Left (SLD).

Polish–Soviet War of 1919–20: the war fought between the Red Army and Polish forces, commanded by Józef Piłsudski, which determined the border of the newly independent Polish Republic and the Soviet Union.

Polish United Workers' Party (PZPR): the former ruling communist party of Poland. In December 1948, the successor to the Communist Party of Poland, the Polish Workers' Party (PPR) forced the Polish Socialist Party into a merger. This new party, the PZPR, remained under the control of the communist leadership. The party disbanded itself in early 1990.

Polish Workers' Party (PPR): the party into which Polish communists were reorganized at the end of 1941, after the Comintern dissolved the Communist Party of Poland in 1938 because it was "infiltrated by Piłsudski's provocateurs."

Pomian, Krzysztof (b. 1934): philosopher. Pomian was a student leader in 1956 and worked with *Po prostu*. In 1966, he and Leszek Kołakowski were expelled from the party for their commemoration of the tenth anniversary of October 1956. Pomian was dismissed from his position at the University of Warsaw in 1968. Since 1973 he has lived in Paris and worked as a professor at CNRS where he continues to write extensively in Polish and French on Polish and East European affairs, as well as the history of ideas.

Po prostu (Simply speaking): a weekly for students and young intellectuals which developed in the mid-1950s into the voice of the young Polish critical intelligentsia. It became an outspoken advocate of reform both before and after the Polish October. Gomułka stopped its publication in 1957, which led to student demonstrations in Warsaw.

Poznań: the Polish city where, in June 1956, workers went on strike to protest their living conditions and to demand greater democracy. The attempts by the authorities to restore order by force led to pitched street battles between workers and the armed forces.

"Previously suspended magazines and journals": With the imposition of martial law the publication of almost all magazines and newspapers was suspended until control could be imposed over their staffs and editorial lines.

Program for a Self-Managing Republic: the program adopted by Solidarity at its first congress in the fall of 1981. This document stressed forms of economic and social organization that would bypass and exist side by side with the party-state without overthrowing or replacing it.

Provisional Coordinating Commission (*Tymczasowa Komisja Koordynacyjna NSZZ "Solidarność,"* or TKK): a coordinating body created by underground Solidarity leaders from Gdańsk, Warsaw, Lower Silesia, and Kraków in April 1982. The TKK functioned as Solidarity's temporary national leadership and coordination center for much of the period of underground struggle in the 1980s. In October 1987 it was replaced by a National Executive Commission.

Prus, Bolesław (1847–1912): born Aleksander Głowacki. The greatest of the Polish realist novelists, known for works such as *The Pharaoh* and *The Doll*. Prus was also an important journalist as well as one of the key figures of Polish Positivism, a national movement that eschewed romantic rebellion after the crushing of the January Insurrection (1863–64). Positivism stressed "organic work"—the building of the economic, cultural, and educational institutions under conditions of occupation in order to prepare for future national independence.

Prystor, Aleksander (1871–1941): a close political collaborator of Józef Piłsudski dating from the time of the latter's organization of "Fighting Squads" for the Polish Socialist Party. He served as prime minister from 1931 to 1933 and speaker of the Senate from 1935 to 1938. He was executed by the NKVD.

Puławy: see *Żydy i chamy*.

Rákosi, Mátyás (1892–1971): Stalinist dictator of Hungary. He fell from power in 1956 and went into exile in the USSR.

Rakowski, Mieczysław (b. 1926): Polish communist politician. Rakowski came to national prominence when he became the editor in chief of the weekly *Polityka* (Politics) in 1958. In the 1970s the weekly was seen in some circles as a centerpiece of the liberal-pragmatic wing of the PZPR. Rakowski stepped down as editor in 1981. In 1981 he became a deputy premier. With the declaration of martial law in 1981, Rakowski continued in this capacity. In the 1980s he became the most important civilian figure in the Jaruzelski regime, eventually elevated to premier in 1988 and first secretary of the PZPR in 1989. He has retired from politics.

Rapacki Plan: named for Adam Rapacki, Gomułka's foreign minister. The Rapacki Plan (1957) proposed the creation of a nuclear-free zone in Central Europe, including both Germanies, Czechoslovakia, and Poland. The plan received the support of the Soviet Union, but was rejected by the United States and went no further because of U.S. fears concerning the imbalance of conventional forces in Central Europe at the time.

Reduta Ordona (Ordon's redoubt): a famous poem by Adam Mickiewicz about the defense of a stronghold under the command of Julian K. Ordon in Warsaw during the November uprising (1830–31) against the Russians.

Referendum: the referendum organized by the communist-led government and held on 30 June 1946 to divert attention from their disregard of the provisions of the Yalta Agreement for "free and unfettered" elections in Poland. Three questions were put to the public, whether to abolish the upper chamber of the national assembly (*Senat*), whether to preserve the results of land reform and the nationalization of key industries, and whether Poland's new western borders were acceptable. The opposition Polish Peasant Party (PSL), led by Stanisław Mikołajczyk, although agreeing with all three provisions, called on the population to vote "no" on abolition of the *Senat*, the least significant of the questions, to demonstrate popular resistance to communist domination of the government. The communists called for three "yes" votes. At the time, the official count gave the communists overwhelming support. It is now widely acknowledged that the results reported were fraudulent.

Restoration of order: a reference to Milan Simecka's book *The Restoration of Order*, an account of the harsh normalization policies that followed the Prague Spring of 1968. Verso (London) published the English translation in 1984.

Revisionism: a grievous sin in the lexicon of orthodox Soviet Marxism. It was applied very imprecisely to various forms of reform communism, including the Polish October, Imre Nagy's policies in Hungary, and the Prague Spring. In Poland after 1956, Gomułka treated "revisionism" as a more serious "illness" than "dogmatism."

Revisionists: adherents of "revisionism" (q.v.).

Robotnicy (Workers): a documentary film, made by Andrzej Chodakowski and Andrzej Zajączkowski, of the strike at the Lenin Shipyard (25–31 August 1980). Initially the government blocked its distribution. It was finally released on 31 January 1981 after a string of protests.

Robotnik (The worker): bimonthly newspaper founded by a group of younger KOR activists in late 1977. *Robotnik* was a cooperative effort which came to include a large number of working-class activists in most major Polish cities. It had the highest circulation of any underground publication prior to the foundation of Solidarity and possessed an extensive distribution network which encompassed a large number of major factories across the country.

Robotnik wybrzeża (Coastal worker): underground newspaper for workers in Gdańsk produced by the Founding Committee for Free Trade Unions of the Coast in the period 1979–80.

Roitshvantz, Laz: the hero of Russian writer Ilya Ehrenburg's famous novel *The Stormy Life of Laz Roitshvantz*. The novel captures both the comic and tragic features of Jewish life in Russia. It was quite popular in Poland in the 1960s.

Rota: a famous Polish patriotic song with anti-German connotations. The lyrics were written in 1908 by the poet Maria Konopnicka.

Rozpłochowski, Andrzej (b. 1950): mechanic. In 1980 he was elected chair of the Strike Committee of the Katowice Steel Mill. He was an important and sometimes controversial Solidarity leader from Silesia during 1980–81. He later emigrated to the United States.

Russian Liberation Army (*Russkaia osvoboditel'naia armiia*, or RLA): armed forces associated with the German-sponsored Committee for the National Liberation of Russia. The RLA was composed of captured Soviet soldiers (approx. 50,000). It never developed into a serious military force because of its low priority for supplies and equipment. The Nazis only allowed it to go into action late in the war. Most of the RLA's soldiers surrendered to U.S. forces in Czechoslovakia and were then turned over to the Soviets, who imprisoned or executed them.

Samizdat: a modern Russian coinage meaning "self-publishing." It refers to the newspapers, magazines, bulletins, and books published illegally by oppositionists and dissidents in the Soviet bloc. The Poles more commonly refer to samizdat as *bibuła* (tissue paper), which in Poland has a history that goes back to the nineteenth century.

Sanacja (1926–39): one of the policies pursued by Piłsudski after the coup d'état of 1926. It refers to a so-called moral cleansing of public life. It has come to be the name by which Piłsudski's dictatorship and that of his successors is known.

Schaff, Adam (b. 1913): Polish Marxist philosopher. His work was orthodox until 1956. In the early 1960s he tried to reconcile aspects of Marxism and existentialism. In the 1970s he was supportive of Eurocommunism. Schaff was a strong supporter of martial law.

"Sienkiewicz affair": Jarosław Sienkiewicz was an economist in the "Borynia" mine in Jastrzębie who emerged as an outspoken leader in the miners' strikes of August–September 1980. He was elected chairman of the Interfactory Workers' Committee in Jastrzębie. It was later discovered that he was a plant of the Security Forces in Silesia and the hard-line PZPR leadership there. He effectively paralyzed the work of Solidarity in the Jastrzębie Coal Basin for more than half a year.

Sienkiewicz, Henryk (1846–1916): Polish novelist and Nobel Prize winner. Outside of Poland his best-known work is *Quo Vadis*. Within Poland both his *Teutonic Knights* and *Trilogy* are also very popular. *Trilogy*'s first volume, *By Fire and Sword* (1884), is set during the seventeenth-century wars between Poland and the Ukrainian Cossacks. The second volume, *The Deluge* (1886), is set during that century's Polish-Swedish wars. The last volume, *Pan Wołodyjowski* (1887–88), contains a romantic adventure story in which Sienkiewicz does not dwell on historical problems as extensively as in the first two volumes. Some critics on the Left were very critical of Sienkiewicz for his celebration of the gentry and the tradition of romantic nationalism.

Sikorski, Władysław (1881–1943): Polish general and statesman.

Sikorski went in retirement in 1928 following Piłsudski's ccup d'état. He was appointed prime minister of the Polish government-in-exile in France in 1939 and continued to head it in England until 1943 when he died in a plane crash near Gibraltar. After Hitler attacked the Soviet Union in 1941, Sikorski entered into negotiations with Stalin leading to recognition of the Polish government-in-exile by the Soviets, release of Polish military personnel detained by the Soviets since 1939, and the organization of Polish armed forces on Soviet soil.

Siła-Nowicki, Władysław (1913–93): lawyer and longtime political activist. Siła-Nowicki fought in the Polish Campaign of 1939 and later in the Home Army. After the war, as a leader of the Labor party in Lublin, he continued his underground conspiratorial activity. Sentenced to death in 1947, he received commutation to life imprisonment. Siła-Nowicki was released from prison in 1956 and readmitted to the bar in 1959. He was well known as a defense lawyer because of his role in a number of highly publicized political trials in the 1960s and 1970s. Siła-Nowicki became a Solidarity legal adviser during the strikes of August 1980 and coauthored the union's legal charter in 1980. He participated in the Roundtable Negotiations at the invitation of the PZPR. In 1989 he mounted an independent campaign for the Sejm, running unsuccessfully against Jacek Kuroń.

Silesian Uprisings: the three uprisings in Upper Silesia against German rule in August 1919, August 1920, and May–June 1921. As a result of the third uprising, Poland obtained territory in Upper Silesia, inhabited by substantial populations of Poles and Polish-Silesians.

Sinyavsky, Andrei (b. 1925): Russian writer and literary critic, key figure in the thaw and the origins of the dissident movement in the USSR. He was arrested and imprisoned, along with Yulii Daniel, in 1965–66 on charges of "Anti-Soviet Agitation and Propaganda" for publishing their writings under pseudonyms in the West (Sinyavsky's was Abram Tertz). Protests on their behalf were a watershed event in the development of the Soviet dissident movement. Since his release from prison in 1971, Sinyavsky has continued writing from exile in Paris.

Skrzypczak, Edward: first secretary of the PZPR in Poznań until early 1982. Skrzypczak supported the reform-oriented wing of the party and had good relations with Poznań Solidarity.

Słowacki, Juliusz (1809–49): poet and dramatist, considered one of the great figures of nineteenth-century Polish romanticism, along with Mickiewicz and the composer Chopin.

Socha, Łukasz: the pseudonym of Maria Turlejska (b. 1918), a historian who has written extensively on the occupation, Polish communism, and postwar Poland, mainly in *Krytyka*.

Society for Academic Courses (TKN): also known as the "Flying University." Founded in 1978, TKN organized uncensored lectures and small specialized seminars in private apartments and supported students and professors persecuted for their work or beliefs.

Solidarity Agency (AS): established in early 1981 during a meeting organized by the Solidarity periodicals *Independence* and *NTO*, and Solidarity activists from the Katowice Steel Mill. They published a bulletin titled *AS*. Many of the journalists and activists employed there had worked with KOR in the late 1970s.

Stasi: the state security service (*Staatssicherheit*) in the former German Democratic Republic.

Steinsbergowa, Aniela (1907–88): prewar activist of the Polish Socialist Party and lawyer. Beginning in the 1950s she acted as the defense attorney in a number of important political trials. She was also a founding member of both the Workers' Defense Committee and the Polish Helsinki Commission.

Stomma, Stanisław (b. 1908): lawyer, Catholic politician, and leader of the Znak delegation in parliament from 1957 to 1976. Stomma was the only member of the Sejm not to vote yes (he abstained) on the Constitutional Amendments of 1975. This action cost him his seat and led to the abolition of Znak and its replacement by a new organization that took its name and property. In the 1980s Stomma served on advisory councils to the primate of Poland and to Lech Wałęsa and continued to write for *Tygodnik Powszechny*, *Res Publica*, and *Znak*. In 1989 he was elected to the Senate on the Solidarity ticket representing Płock. He has since retired.

Stroba, Jerzy: archbishop of Poznań, member of the Church-State Commission in the 1980s.

"Strong and ready": a veiled reference to the assessment of Polish combat readiness made by Marshal Edward Rydź-Śmigły, the commander-in-chief of the Polish army, on the eve of World War II.

Stroński, Stanisław (1882–1955): politician, journalist, and historian of literature, who was active in the *Endecja*.

Stryjkowski, Julian (b. 1905): Polish novelist connected with the communist movement from the interwar period to the late 1950s. Many of his novels and short stories are drawn from his Jewish background.

Student Solidarity Committee (SKS): independent student organization founded in Kraków in 1977 after the murder of KOR activist and student Stanisław Pyjas. Other Student Solidarity Committees were founded in Warsaw, Gdańsk, Wrocław, Poznań, and Szczecin. Many of its activists went on to become important figures in Solidarity, the Independent Student Association, and other oppositional organizations of the 1980s.

"Sugar crop of 10 million tons": Under the slogan of "10 million zafra" (*zafra* means the cutting of sugar cane in Cuban Spanish) in 1969–70, Castro mobilized all human and material resources of the country. In order to reach a harvest of ten million tons of sugar, he sent industrial workers, clerks, university teachers, and so forth, to the fields. The result was anarchy and disorganization. The goal was not achieved, and on 26 July 1970, Castro delivered a "self-critical" speech.

Sulejówek: Piłsudski's family home located twenty kilometers east of Warsaw. The estate was given to him by his followers in the early 1920s. This is where Piłsudski began his march during the coup of May 1926.

Świrszczyńska, Anna (b. 1909): poet born into an artistic family in Warsaw. Her earliest poems were published before World War II. In the postwar period she wrote powerfully about the experience of the Warsaw Uprising. Czesław Miłosz has described her mature poetry as "violently feministic . . . brutally erotic . . . [and] fierce, lucid, ecstatic, and terrifying."

Szczecin: an important port in northwest Poland. Formerly the city of Stettin in Germany, it was ceded to Poland after World War II.

Szczepański, Jan (b. 1913): sociologist and member of parliament under the communist regime. During his political career Szczepański was also vice president of the Polish Academy of Sciences, deputy chairman of the National Unity Front, chairman of the Main Council on Science, and a member of the Council of State. He was a strong supporter of martial law in December 1981.

Szczepański, Jan Józef (b. 1919): Polish writer. He was president of the Union of Polish Writers from 1980 to 1983, when the union was dissolved by the Jaruzelski regime.

Szenwald, Lucjan (1909–44): leftist poet of the interwar era. He published his poems in the journal *Kwadryga* (Quadriga), which was known for socially committed poetry. He was a member of the Communist Party of Poland. During World War II he served in the Soviet army and the communist-led Polish army from its inception in 1943 as a political officer. He died in a car accident in Lublin in 1944.

Szumowski, Maciej (b. 1939): editor of the PZPR newspaper *Gazeta Krakowska* (The Kraków gazette) during the Solidarity period. During this time the paper was known for its accurate and balanced coverage of events and its open advocacy of reform. Szumowski was subsequently fired during martial law. At present, he is a freelance journalist working in television.

Szymborska, Wisława (b. 1923): one of the best contemporary poets in Poland. She is well known for reflective and philosophic poetry.

Targowica, Confederation of: in popular usage a term synonymous with treason. On 27 April 1792 a number of prominent Polish noblemen signed a pact usurping the power of the Polish Sejm. They then assembled an army in the Polish Ukraine and with the assistance of Russian forces attempted to take control of the country. This precipitated the Russo-Polish War of 1792–93, which led to the Second Partition of Poland.

Tenth Pavilion: the part of the Warsaw Citadel where political prisoners were incarcerated in tsarist times.

"Thaw": the period immediately after Stalin's death. Terror diminished and censorship was loosened in much of the Soviet bloc. The feelings of that time were captured in a book of the same title by Ilya Ehrenburg.

"Thick line": a reference to Mazowiecki's statement that his government wanted to draw a thick line to separate the past from the present (namely, forget, if not forgive, the communists' wrongdoings).

Torańska, Teresa (b. 1946): Polish journalist noted for the book *Oni* (Them), a series of interviews conducted in the early 1980s with surviving Stalinist leaders in Poland.

"True Poles" (*prawdziwi Polacy*): Solidarity activists who combined a strong xenophobic nationalism with working-class grievances. They first appeared among the members of the board of Warsaw Solidarity in mid-1981.

Trust: an imaginary anti-Soviet, right-wing underground organization created by the Soviet secret police (OPGU) in the mid-1920s. Vasily Shulgin, an important émigré politician, announced the existence of an extensive anti-Soviet Russian underground, following an "illegal" visit to the USSR supposedly organized by Trust. The OPGU quickly disclosed that Trust was a fabrication, leading to general political demoralization among Russian émigrés.

Turowicz, Jerzy (b. 1913): a member of the Catholic political groups Rebirth (*Odrodzenie*) and Pax Romana in the interwar period. From 1945 to 1953 he was the editor-in-chief of *Głos Narodu* (The voice of the nation) and since 1956 of *Tygodnik Powszechny* (q.v.). In 1989, Turowicz was a member of the opposition delegation to the Roundtable Negotiations.

Tuwim, Julian (1894–1953): like Leśmian, a member of the group of distinguished interwar poets associated with the Warsaw-based literary journal, *Skamander*. The connection between Tuwim and Leśmian is one made most readily by anti-Semites, because both men were of Jewish origin, not because of similar poetic styles. Tuwim was fiercely attacked by nationalist writers in the interwar period. While in exile during the war he wrote the famous essay, *My, Żydzi Polscy* (We, Polish Jews), following the Warsaw Ghetto Uprising, and the poem "Kwiaty Polskie" (Polish flowers).

Twentieth Congress of the Communist Party of the Soviet Union: the party congress at which Khrushchev made his famous "Secret Speech" denouncing Stalin in 1956.

Tygodnik Mazowsze (Mazovia weekly): a regional newspaper based in Warsaw that made its debut in early 1982. Edited by Helena Łuczywo, it became one of the most influential sources of information of the post–martial law underground press and reportedly had the largest print run and circulation of any such publication during the period. In 1989 its staff went on to become the backbone of the influential daily *Gazeta wyborcza* (Electoral gazette).

Tygodnik powszechny (Universal weekly): This newspaper, founded in 1945 and based in Kraków, was taken away from its original group of liberal, Catholic journalists, writers, and editors and given to the pro-regime Catholic PAX group in the early 1950s. It was returned to its founding group in 1956 and has since been edited by Jerzy Turowicz. Under Turowicz's editorship the weekly attained its great popularity and constantly tested the bounds of censorship. Many of Poland's ablest writers and journalists have been regular contributors.

Tzaddik (Hebrew): a "righteous man." It refers to rabbis whom Hasids consider so pious that they should be accorded the respect paid to the prophets. The Hasids seek out tzaddikim for their wisdom, advice, and miraculous abilities.

UB: the Office of Security, the Polish secret police during the Stalinist period. It was later replaced by the Security Service (SB).

Ukrainian Insurrection Army: the military arm of the Organization of Ukrainian Nationalists (OUN). Established in 1943, it fought the Germans, the Soviets, Jews, and both communist and noncommunist Poles. It continued to operate in southeastern Poland until 1948.

Union of Democratic Youth: a short-lived youth organization of the Democratic Party (SD), one of the political parties allied with the PZPR.

Union of Polish Patriots (ZPP): formed in 1943 in the USSR by Polish communists and military officers sympathetic to the Soviet cause. It played a major role in the raising of the First Polish Army (1943–44) that fought with the Soviet army and in the establishment of a pro-Soviet provisional government in Lublin in 1944.

Union of Polish Youth (ZMP): a communist youth organization formed in 1948 by the forced merger of youth movements associated with the communists, the agrarian parties, and the Democratic Party. It fell apart and was formally abolished in 1956.

Union of Socialist Youth (ZMS): the successor organization to the Union of Polish Youth, formed in 1957. In 1976 it was merged with two other small official youth movements to form the Union of Polish Socialist Youth.

United Peasant Party (*Zjednoczone Stronnictwo Ludowe*, or ZSL): formed in 1949 by the merger of the Peasant Party (SL) and the Polish Peasant Party (PSL). Under the communist system in Poland it served for many years as a loyal ally of the PZPR, so much so that many considered it little more than the PZPR's rural branch. When attempts by the PZPR to form a government came to naught in 1989, the ZSL broke ranks and became a junior partner in the Solidarity-led government of Tadeusz Mazowiecki. Soon thereafter the party renamed itself the Polish Peasant Party (PSL). The renamed party came in second in the parliamentary elections of 1993 and its leader, Waldemar Pawlak, is the prime minister of the present coalition government.

Urban, Jerzy (b. 1933): journalist associated with the weeklies *Po prostu* and *Polityka*. Under Jaruzelski he became the government press spokesman. His weekly press conferences became something of an event. His combative style and dogged defense of the regime's policies made him a focus of much antipathy. Urban's Jewish background made him a convenient target for those with anti-Semitic feelings. Today he is editor of the popular and irreverent anti-Solidarity and anti-church weekly *Nie* (No).

Ustrzyki Dolne: see "February Agreement."

Vlasov, Andrei (1900–46?): the commander of the Russian Liberation Army and leading figure in the German-sponsored Committee for the National Liberation of Russia during World War II. Lieutenant General Vlasov, a member of the Communist Party of the Soviet Union from 1930, distinguished himself during the defense of Moscow in 1941, but was captured in July 1942. While in captivity, he was persuaded to cooperate by the Germans. Vlasov was considered a threat by Stalin, because when he toured occupied Russia (behind Hitler's back), he met with an enthusiastic response from local inhabitants. Vlasov never won Hitler's support and thus his army and movement never developed any real strength. Vlasov was captured by U.S. forces in 1945, turned over to the Soviet army, tried in the USSR, and executed.

Voivodship: the highest level of subnational administration. Poland has forty-nine voivodships.

Walentynowicz, Anna (b. 1929): crane operator at the Lenin Shipyard in Gdańsk and member of the Founding Committee for Free Trade Unions of the Coast. Her dismissal in August 1980 was one of the grievances that sparked the strike in the Lenin Shipyard. After her release she was elected a member of the Interfactory Strike Committee. She held a number of different positions in the Gdańsk regional leadership of Solidarity, but lost a number of them in local political struggles. At present she is in strong opposition to Lech Wałęsa and the government.

Wałęsówka: a special pay increase for all employees negotiated and agreed to in the framework of the "Twenty-one Demands" issued by the Interfactory Strike Committee located in the Lenin Shipyard in Gdańsk in August 1980.

Walter scouts (*Walterowcy*): an informal movement organized within the official Polish Scout Union (ZHP). It emerged in the mid-1950s under the tutelage of reform-oriented scoutmasters like Jacek Kuroń,

Stefan Garwacki, Aleksander Musiał, and Stanisław Czubaty. The movement was influential among senior scouts in Warsaw and disappeared by the mid-1960s. The name of this informal grouping comes from the nom de guerre (Walter) of General Karol Świerczewski, a communist who fought in the Spanish Civil War (the inspiration for the character of General Goltz in Hemingway's *For Whom the Bell Tolls*). A number of revisionists of the 1960s and Solidarity-era oppositionists were active in the Walter scouts.

"War at the top": the spring 1990 conflict between the supporters of Solidarity leader Lech Wałęsa and the head of the Solidarity-led government, Tadeusz Mazowiecki, over a number of issues, including aspects of Mazowiecki's program and Wałęsa's desire to replace Wojciech Jaruzelski as president. This led to a heated and controversial campaign for the presidency in which Wałęsa periodically resorted to anti-Semitic innuendo (something from which he later distanced himself). The need for a "war at the top" was one of the slogans that Wałęsa coined at the time to justify his part in this dispute, which destroyed the political unity of Solidarity, leading to the creation of several new political parties.

Warsaw Agreement of March 1981: an agreement concerning a number of difficult issues between the government and Solidarity. These issues included the question of free Saturdays, the recognition of Rural Solidarity, the union's promised access to the mass media, and continued police harassment of union activists, including the brutal beating of several union activists in the city of Bydgoszcz (including the leader of Bydgoszcz Solidarity—Jan Rulewski). Solidarity threatened to stage a general strike, but this was averted by a last-minute agreement, into which Lech Wałęsa entered without consulting Solidarity's National Coordinating Committee, an omission that later became a source of serious friction in Solidarity's leadership. This series of events came to be known as the "Bydgoszcz crisis."

Wielowieyski, Andrzej (b. 1927): economist and lawyer, soldier in the Home Army. Wielowieyski was active in the Club of the Crooked Circle and the Clubs of Catholic Intelligentsia, and wrote extensively for the Catholic press. He was also active in the "Experience and the Future" discussion circle in the late 1970s. He served as an expert to the Interfactory Strike Committee in Gdańsk and continued to serve Solidarity in a number of advisory capacities. In the early 1980s he served on the primate's Social Council and in 1989 was elected to the Senate from the Solidarity camp. At present he is an MP associated with the Union of Freedom.

Wierzbicki, Piotr (b. 1935): writer and publicist, renowned for his sharp sarcasm, black humor, and uncompromising nature. Wierzbicki wrote extensively for the underground press of the 1970s and 1980s and for the Solidarity press. He is perhaps best known for the essay "A Treatise on Ticks" (1979), which mercilessly lampoons Polish intellectuals for their accommodation with the powers that be. From 1989 to 1991 he was an ardent supporter of Lech Wałęsa, whose presidential bid he strongly endorsed in a regular column he wrote for *Tygodnik Solidarność* (*Solidarity weekly*). Since then he has fallen out with Wałęsa and currently publishes the journal *Gazeta Polska* (Polish gazette), which is stridently nationalist with anti-Semitic overtones.

Więź (The link): monthly magazine established in 1958 as the journal of the Clubs of the Catholic Intelligentsia (KIK). Its editor from its inception until 1981 was Tadeusz Mazowiecki, who continues to head its editorial board.

Wilno: present-day Vilnius, the capital of Lithuania. This city was a major center of Polish culture until World War II. During the period 1939–41, the city was first given to Lithuania when Stalin and Hitler partitioned Poland in 1939. Soon thereafter Lithuania was incorporated into the Soviet Union. In this period the Soviet secret police, NKVD, repressed the inhabitants, deporting a large number to Kazakhstan. During the latter stages of the war, the AK in Wilno staged an uprising which helped to liberate the city from the Germans just as the Red Army was advancing. A large proportion of the Polish inhabitants of the region were subsequently deported after the war to the areas Germany ceded to Poland in the west.

Witos, Wincenty (1874–1945): the most important agrarian politician of the interwar era and leader of the Piast Peasant Party. He served as prime minister in 1920–21, 1923, and 1926. Witos led a number of center-right coalition governments in the period before Piłsudski's coup in 1926. Just before the coup Witos was preparing to form his third government in a three-year period. He was arrested and imprisoned in Brześć in 1930 where he was brutally treated. He went into exile in 1933.

Wojciechowski, Stanisław (1869–1953): Polish socialist politician who was elected president after Narutowicz was assassinated. He opposed Piłsudski's coup d'état in 1926 although the two were old comrades.

Workers' Defense Committee (KOR): formed in 1976 to protest the treatment of workers after the June strikes. KOR was the important center of opposition in Poland prior to the foundation of Solidarity. The committee disbanded itself in September 1981.

Wrocław: a large city in western Poland. Formerly the city of Breslau in Germany, it was ceded to Poland after World War II.

Wronki: a well-known Polish jail.

Wujec, Henryk (b. 1941): physicist. Wujec was an activist of the Workers' Defense Committee from its inception and one of the founders of *Robotnik*. He was a member of the board of Warsaw Solidarity and organized educational activities for workers. He was active in the Solidarity underground, and as secretary of Solidarity's Citizens' Committees he managed the electoral victory of 1989. Wujec was elected to the Sejm in 1989 and continues as an MP from the Union of Freedom (UW).

"Wujek": a coal mine practically in the center of the city of Katowice. A strike started there in response to the declaration of martial law on 13 December 1981 and involved approximately three thousand miners. On 16 December, as a result of a ZOMO attack supported by army tanks and armored personnel carriers, nine miners were killed and twenty-five seriously wounded.

Wyspiański, Stanisław (1869–1907): the quintessential representative of the "Young Poland" movement in the arts, which was part of the wave of modernism that swept through Europe in the late nineteenth to early twentieth century. Wyspiański was a important painter, poet, and playwright. However, his most important work was probably his play *Wesele* (The wedding), which addressed the major dilemmas confronting Poland, its culture, and society at the turn of the century in a powerful, linguistically provocative, and mystical fashion.

Wyszyński, Józef (1901–81): cardinal and primate of the church in Poland from 1948 to his death. Wyszyński is seen by many to be Poland's great postwar spiritual leader and also, perhaps, its most adept political figure. His policies from the period of Stalinism to the Solidarity period allowed the Catholic church in Poland to maintain its spiritual and organizational independence from the party-state.

Załuski, Zbigniew (1926–78): colonel in the Polish army, associated with the "Partisan" faction of Mieczysław Moczar. In the early 1960s he wrote a pamphlet, *Siedem polskich grzechów głównych* (The seven Polish deadly sins), which attacked writers and filmmakers who espoused a critical view of Polish nineteenth- and twentieth-century history (for example, Andrzej Wajda). Its publication led to a polemical debate within high party circles. Like other Moczarites, he mixed hard-line communism with national chauvinism.

Znak (Sign): a circle of Catholic deputies that was permitted to serve in the Polish Sejm (parliament) beginning in 1957 (originally composed of five deputies). Znak sought to collaborate on initiatives that would serve to expand human rights in Poland and the sovereignty of the Polish state. When changes came in the Soviet Union, Znak believed that it would be in a position to help lead Poland to independence. After the March Events of 1968, Znak filed a sharp interpellation with Premier Józef Cyrankiewicz asking for an explanation of the harsh treatment of protesting students. The party in turn unleashed a harsh press campaign against Znak and in subsequent elections manipulated its list of nominations to assure more servile deputies in the Sejm. The original supporters of Znak eventually disassociated themselves from the parliamentary club, which they then labeled Neo-Znak (PZKS). Znak was active in the field of publishing. It published a monthly, also called *Znak*, which although subject to censorship was far less dogmatic than official government publications. It also ran a publishing house that published many worthwhile books the state publishing houses had overlooked.

ZOMO (Zmotoryzowane Odwody Milicji Obywatelskiej): an acronym meaning Motorized Reserves of the Citizens' Militia. These units were specially trained and outfitted for breaking up demonstrations and strikes. They were known for their brutality.

Żydy i chamy (Kikes and boors): An essay by Witold Jedlicki first published in Paris in 1962. His choice of title is not derogatory. The factions referred to each other by these epithets in private. This divide roughly corresponds to the split between the "Puławy" (kikes) reform-oriented and "Natolin" (boors) hard-line factions in the party in 1956. These names refer to the places where the two groups met (Puławska Street and the Natolin Palace).

About the Authors

MICHAEL BERNHARD is an associate professor of political science at The Pennsylvania State University. He is the author of *The Origins of Democratization in Poland: Workers, Intellectuals, and Oppositional Politics, 1976–1980*. His work on Polish and East-Central European politics has also appeared in *East European Politics and Societies*, *Studies in Comparative Communism*, *Political Science Quarterly*, and *Krytyka*.

MAREK BEYLIN is a journalist and historian. He was an activist associated with the Workers' Defense Committee in the 1970s and has been a member of *Krytyka*'s editorial board since 1978. He is a researcher at the Institute of Political Studies, Polish Academy of Sciences.

RYSZARD BUGAJ is an economist who was active in the student movement of the 1960s and the opposition. He worked with KOR in the 1970s and in Solidarity as an economic adviser and a delegate to the union's first congress in 1981. He was a member of the opposition delegation to the Roundtable Negotiations of 1988–89 and served as an MP for the Solidarity caucus in parliament (1989–91). Since then he has headed the Union of Labor (UP) party and continues as an MP in their delegation.

ANNA BOJARSKA is a writer, known for her historical novels and as a leading representative of the new "novel of manners." She has been published both officially and in the underground. Her *Pięć śmierci* (Five death sentences) was published by the *Krytyka* Library.

MARIA CHMIELEWSKA-SZLAJFER was trained in English philology at Warsaw University and is a translator of English and American literature into Polish. At present she translates into English the *Polish News Bulletin of the British and American Embassies* in Warsaw.

KRZYSZTOF JASIEWICZ is a professor of sociology at Washington and Lee University in Virginia, and a researcher at the Institute of Political

Studies of the Polish Academy of Sciences in Warsaw. He has written extensively on values and attitudes in Poland in the *Poles* series (*Polacy '80, '81, '84, '88, '90*). Recently, he has begun writing on elections and voting behavior in Poland and Eastern Europe. His work on this subject has appeared in English in *Journal of Democracy, European Journal of Political Research*, and *Communist and Postcommunist Studies*. He is a member of *Krytyka*'s editorial board.

JAN KOFMAN, professor of history and political science at Warsaw University and the Institute of Political Studies of the Polish Academy of Sciences, is editor-in-chief of *Krytyka*. Active in the opposition since the student movement of the 1960s, he was a member of the Solidarity delegation that negotiated the Roundtable Agreement of 1989. He is the author of many books and articles on the economic history of Poland and Eastern Europe in the interwar period. At present, he is the editor-in-chief and deputy director of Polish Scientific Publishers (PWN), the largest academic publishing house in Poland.

STANISŁAW KRAJEWSKI, a longtime opposition activist, was one of a small number of younger Jews who in the last two decades have begun to modernize and revivify Jewish life in Poland. He is a member of President Lech Wałęsa's Council on Polish-Jewish Relations and the author of many articles on Polish-Jewish topics.

MARCIN KULA, a sociologist and historian, is a professor at the Institute of History, Warsaw University. He has written a number of books on Brazilian history, the process of nation-building, and diplomatic history.

JACEK KUROŃ is an educator. He coauthored the famous revisionist "Open Letter to the Party" (with Karol Modzelewski) in 1964. On this occasion he was sentenced to three of the nine years he has spent in prison. In 1976 he was a founding member of the Workers' Defense Committee. In 1980 he began to serve as an adviser to Solidarity. In 1988–89 he was a leading member of the Solidarity delegation to the Roundtable Negotiations. In 1989 he was elected to parliament on the Solidarity ticket. Since then he has served twice as minister of labor (1989–90, 1992–93). He is the author of a large number of books and articles. At present he is an MP in the Union of Freedom (UW) caucus.

JOANNA KURCZEWSKA is a sociologist specializing in the study of elites and the history of political ideas. She is an associate professor at the Institute of Philosophy and Sociology, Polish Academy of Sciences.

ADAM MICHNIK, historian, was expelled from Warsaw University in 1968 for his role as a student activist there, and subsequently sentenced to three years in prison. A member of the Workers' Defense Committee and a Solidarity adviser, he is one of the cofounders of *Krytyka* and a member of its editorial board. He was detained and interned on a number of occasions in the 1980s with other Solidarity leaders and intellectuals. Michnik was a member of the Solidarity delegation at the Roundtable Negotiations and an MP from 1989 to 1991. He is the author of several books on the Polish intellectual tradition, history, politics, and current affairs, and a frequent contributor to the *New York Review of Books* and *Der Spiegel*. He is at present editor-in-chief of *Gazeta wyborcza*, the best-selling daily in Poland.

EDMUND MOKRZYCKI is a professor of sociology at the Institute of Philosophy and Sociology of the Polish Academy of Sciences, and at the Central European University in Budapest and Prague.

PIOTR OGRODZIŃSKI is a political philosopher and coordinator of the East European Research Group, a team of independent Polish researchers. He is also a researcher at the Institute of Political Studies of the Polish Academy of Sciences. In 1980–81 Ogrodziński was coeditor of *NTO* (Science-Technology-Education), the bulletin of Mazowsze region of Solidarity. During martial law he was active in the Solidarity underground in Warsaw. Since August 1993 he has served as deputy director of the Department of Strategic Research-PISM, Ministry of Foreign Affairs.

JERZY OSIATYŃSKI, economist, was an adviser to Solidarity. In 1989–90 he was minister of planning in the government of Tadeusz Mazowiecki and in 1992–93 minister of finance in the government of Hanna Suchocka. He is the author of several books on modern economic theory and the editor of the works of Michał Kalecki. He is an MP from the Union of Freedom.

JERZY SURDYKOWSKI is a journalist and writer and was active in the opposition of the 1980s. Since 1990, he has been the consul general of the Polish Republic in New York.

HENRYK SZLAJFER, economist and sociologist, was expelled from Warsaw University in March 1968 for his part in student opposition there. Subsequently, he was sentenced to two years in prison. In 1980–81 he was an adviser and activist of the self-management movement in Solidarity. In the 1980s he was active with the Solidarity underground and the underground press. In 1989–90 he served as a Solidarity expert for the Parliamentary Commission on Privatization. A researcher at the Institute of Political Studies of the Polish Academy of Sciences and the author of a number of books and articles on comparative economic history, from 1993 to 1994 he was the director of the Department of Strategic Research-PISM, the Ministry of Foreign Affairs. At present he is a professor at the G. C. Marshall European Center for Security Studies in Germany.

ANDRZEJ WERNER is a writer and a literature and film critic who has long been associated with *Krytyka*. He works at the Institute for Literary Research of the Polish Academy of Sciences and is the author of many books and articles on modern Polish literature.

WŁODZIMIERZ WESOŁOWSKI is a professor of sociology at the Polish Academy of Sciences, internationally known for his work in the field of social stratification. After a period in the Central Committee in the 1970s, he left the party in December 1981 and joined the opposition.

JAN WINIECKI, professor of economics, was an adviser to Solidarity. He is the author of a number of books and articles on communist economic systems. He served as Poland's representative to the European Bank for Reconstruction and Development in London until October 1993.

KRZYSZTOF WOLICKI is a journalist and translator who was active in the opposition of the 1980s. A long-standing contributor to *Krytyka*, he is a political activist with the Union of Labor.

JÓZEF ŻYCIŃSKI is a philosopher at the Papal Theological Academy in Kraków. He is the author of many books including *Język i metoda* (Language and method) and *Listy do Nikodema* (Letters to Nicodemus). Since 1990 he has been the bishop of Tarnów.

Index

Page numbers in bold indicate glossary entries.